Herbal Renaissance

GROWING, USING & UNDERSTANDING
HERBS IN THE MODERN WORLD

Herbal Renaissance

by Steven Foster

GIBBS·SMITH
➜P
PUBLISHER

SALT LAKE CITY

Photo page ii; Monarda citriodora, Lemon Bergamot.
Photo page iii; Teucrium marum, Cat Thyme, Cologne,
    Germany
Photo page vi; Hamamelis vernalis, Vernal Witch Hazel.
Photo contents page; Liquidambar styraciflua, Sweet
    Gum Leaf.

97 96 95   10 9 8 7 6 5 4 3 2
Published by Gibbs Smith, Publisher
Peregrine Smith Books
P.O. Box 667, Layton Utah 84041

Printed in Hong Kong
Cover and interior design by DD Dowden.
Lynda Sessions, Editor
Dawn Valentine Hadlock, Editorial Assistant

Library of Congress Cataloging in-Publication-Data
Foster, Steven, 1957 —
    Herbal renaissance / Steven Foster
    p. cm.
    Rev. ed. of Herbal bounty! 1st ed. 1984
    Includes bibliographical references (p.   ) and index.
    ISBN 0-87905-523-5 (pb)
    1. Herbs. 2. Herb gardening. 3. Herbs—Utilization.
4. Herbs—Therapeutic use.
I. Foster, Steven, 1957— Herbal bounty!
II. Title
SB351. H5F627 1993
635' .7—ddc20   93-2197
                    CIP

Dedication

for Jude

CONTENTS

PREFACE

As a professional botanist who has spent forty-five years studying the medicinal plants of China (primarily in two ancient languages, Chinese and Latin), I found Steven Foster's book on herb cultivation a most welcome reference.

This work has been prepared for the layman by a self-made and practical botanist. The author reminds me of two eminent American botanists who enticed me to Harvard: They were Merritt L. Fernald, author of the eighth edition of *Gray's Manual of Botany*, and Elmer D. Merrill, who was honored as the American Linnaeus during his lifetime. I used to think it remarkable that these two professors (both from the state of Maine) could be self-taught botanists, yet outstanding in their field, because at the beginning of the twentieth century, botany was relatively young in America. I was surprised, indeed, to meet a third person from Maine, Steven Foster, who achieved the same distinction near the close of the century.

I met Steven Foster at the Sabbathday Lake Shaker Community. At the time, Professor Walter Judd, University of Florida at Gainesville, was working on his *Monograph of Lyonia, Ericaceae.*[1] We shared adjacent research benches on the third floor of the Harvard University Herbaria, and the excitement of our findings. One Monday, after a refreshing weekend in the Shaker Community in Maine, he said, "You must visit the Shakers at Sabbathday Lake. It is a beautiful and restful place, a simple and friendly society, and it has a very good herb garden." I did. There, a farm boy was assigned to take me to the field and building devoted to the drying and distribution of herbs. Our conversation reminded me of something that Confucius said two thousand years ago, "In any company of three persons, there must be one who can be my teacher." In the company of half a dozen persons who chose a lifestyle of simple living and honest dealing, I found in Steven Foster a teacher who could share a profound knowledge of economic botany (the study of useful plants), particularly in the cultivation and uses of herbs.

Steven Foster's botanical knowledge is not limited to herbs. He knows the native flora of Maine intimately, and has an extensive association with botanists and herbalists throughout the United States. He first showed me where to find wild American ginseng in New England. When I knew him better, I said, "Your botanical knowledge is as broad and sound as that of some of my friends who hold a college degree. Have you ever thought of registering in a university and working towards a degree?" In answer, he showed me his library and said, "I have taken the money which I should have used for a college education and invested it in these books. To me, practical work and extensive reading constitute a more economical way for obtaining botanical knowledge." Indeed, his library has an extensive collection of old herbals as well as modern textbooks, manuals, floras, and current botanical and horticultural publications. He has not only read them all, he knows exactly where and how to locate needed information in them. An excellent photographer, he has recorded his field observations in numerous slides and pictures. Readers of his book will soon find that this work crystallizes the author's philosophy of education and his practical approach to pursuing botanical knowledge.

In the first part of this book, after explaining the reasons for preparing the book, the author shares his knowledge of Latin botanical names, his ideas about designing herb gardens, and his experiences in propagation, harvesting, and drying of various herbs. Part two characterizes and identifies individual herbs, their folklores, phytochemistry, and usages. This portion of the first book contains eighty common herbs (ninety-three in *Herbal Renaissance*) useful in American homes and recommended for the herb-trade market, arranged alphabetically by their common names. Sixty (sixty-nine in *Herbal Renaissance*) of the entries represent one species. The remaining twenty entries (twenty-four in *Herbal Renaissance*) contain two or more species, making a total of one hundred and twenty-four plant species or hybrids covered by the work.

The material is illustrated with forty-five line-drawings and eight color-plates covering twenty species and/or hybrids prepared by a professional botanical illustrator, and forty-three color photographs and twenty black and white photographs. A glossary is provided for users unfamiliar with some of the descriptive terms. Those desiring more information about herbs may peruse the bibliography. A classified resources list is given for those who want to buy seeds or plants. Each section and entry contain useful information for users, growers, and dealers alike.

Shiu Ying Hu, Botanist (Emerita),
Arnold Arboretum, Harvard University

Reprinted from *Herbal Bounty,* 1984.

Matricaria recutita, German chamomile flowers

1. Published in *Journal of Arnold Arboretum* 62: (1981): 63-128-209, 315-436

FOREWORD

The recent upsurge of interest in the culinary use of herbs and spices has led to an interest on the part of the general public in the plants themselves. Thousands of gardeners are interested in growing many of the source plants, and herb gardens are common, especially in cities where space for many of the ornamental horticulturals is limited.

The last two or three decades have seen many books on the source plants, their lore, history, and role in human affairs. Most of these books have been written in a popular vein. Some have been well prepared. Others have not. And almost nothing comprehensive exists on the cultivation of herbs.

Steven Foster has produced such a book, and, in doing so, has contributed significantly to our total knowledge concerning herbs and their uses. A very appealing aspect is Foster's first-hand acquaintance with herb cultivation. But, while stressing the growing of these plants, he has presented a well-rounded discussion: brief descriptions of the plants in nontechnical terms, notes on the chemistry of the species, their value in folk-medicine, occasional folklore, and other relevant points of interest to devotees of herb use.

The beautiful illustrations by DD Dowden add immeasurably to the artistry and utility of the book.

Here is a volume which will easily find a place in the hearts of many who yearn to grow their own herbs and reap enjoyment from a hobby which brings us one step closer to the timeless rhythms of Nature in our hurried, harried world.

Asclepias tuberosa, Pleurisy Root

Richard Evans Schultes,
Jeffery Professor of Biology &
Director, Botanical Museum (Emeritus),
Harvard University

Reprinted from *Herbal Bounty*, 1984.

ACKNOWLEDGMENTS

*D*uring twenty years of herbal pursuits, I have been the fortunate recipient of inspiration, help, and support from many people who ultimately influenced this book. Special appreciation goes to the Sabbathday Lake Shaker Community, for endless encouragement, particularly the late Sister Mildred Barker, Sister Frances Carr, and the late Brother Theodore Johnson. Les Eastman taught me appreciation for plants in their native habitats; Dr. Shiu Ying Hu has continually broadened my view of life. Paul Lee has added a laugh to every situation; Thanks to Billy Joe Tatum, for a constant flow of inspiration; Bill Coperthwaite, for showing me how to look at every moment in a fresh way; Genevieve Paulson, for pointing me in the right direction; my grandmother, Lena Foster, for teaching me artistic appreciation; and my parents, Herb and Hope Foster, for allowing me to do what I felt was best. And thanks to Frank Lloyd Wright for saying, "The truth is more important than the facts."

I would also like to express deep gratitude to persons who helped at various stages of the book's preparation consciously or vicariously. Mark Blumenthal inspired me with the right attitude; Wesley Wong of Harvard University's Botanical Museum Library, Rebecca Perry of the Lloyd Library and Museum, and Dr. Reinhard Liersch of the Literaturabteilung, Madaus AG, helped locate many obscure and important references; Jeanmarie Morelli shared her work on Angelica; Louis and Virginia Saso welcomed me to their gardens; Kent Taylor shared experience and knowledge; Lon Johnson and the folks at Trout Lake Farm put theory into practice; Loren Israelsen sparked my interest in the European scene; Gibbs Smith for taking me seriously enough to publish my first book; the good doctors Dennis Awang, Rudolf Bauer, Lyle Craker, Jim Duke, Norman Farnsworth, Al Leung, Jim Simon, E. John Staba, Art Tucker, and Varro Tyler, thank you for overflowing file cabinets full of useful information. Thanks to Donna Farar for patience and persistence in typing the manuscript of the first edition. I am thankful for the fastidious work of Mary Pat Boian who typed the revision and labored over improvement. Lynda Sessions, thanks for careful editing and for keeping this project on track; Dawn Valentine Hadlock for your unseen behind-the-scenes assistance; and Barbara Bannon for your attention to detail in capital letters (and lowercase). I am happily indebted to DD Dowden for your special eye and creativity in the book's design, plus artwork of lasting beauty. Jude Farar, you lit the light of the midnight oil (on both ends) to see this project through—thank you. A special thanks to Ella Alford for conducive oblations, stimulating my writing habit for more than a decade. I am grateful to you, Hannah Bradford, for your feedback and friendship. The mistakes are mine.

Calendula officinalis, Calendula

HERBS
IN A MODERN WORLD

Any plant used for culinary, fragrant, or medicinal purposes is an herb. Botanically, an herb is any plant that does not possess a persistent woody stem and dies back to the root each year, even though woody plants having medicinal or culinary uses are herbs according to the first definition. Botanists estimate that there are between 200,000 and 800,000 members of the plant kingdom. How many can be considered herbs by our first definition?

It is impossible to say; but the following story, related by a friend returning from a trip to India, illustrates the plant kingdom's herbal potential. In India, my friend met an apprentice of an herbal healer who had recently finished his indenture. As a final test, the student's master directed him to go to the hills and gather plants without medicinal qualities. After several days of roaming the surrounding hills, the apprentice returned with his head hung low.

"Master," he lamented. "I was unable to fulfill the task. I found no plants without medicinal uses." The teacher threw back his head in laughter and announced, "You have passed the test."

Hundreds of plant species, "herbs" if you will, serve as important sources of medicine used in modern and traditional healthcare systems around the world. At least eighty thousand plant species can be documented as folk medicines worldwide. About one-third of the more than

a quarter million known species of flowering plants have been used as herbs at least in a historic context.

According to Dr. O. Akerele, recent past director of the World Health Organization's (WHO) Traditional Medicine Programme, interest in medicinal plant use worldwide has continued to grow over the past two decades. WHO estimates that as much as 80 percent of the world's population relies on various forms of traditional medicine (rather than modern, Western-style medicine). Herbal medicine is foremost among traditional medicine systems around the globe (Akerele 1988). The most well-known example is traditional Chinese medicine, which depends heavily on herbal treatments along with acupuncture. It serves as much as 60 percent of China's rural populations—not as folk medicine—but as primary healthcare. Over five hundred different plants are "official drugs" according to the 1985 Pharmacopeia of the People's Republic of China. Over five thousand medicinal plants are recognized in China (Foster 1991m).

The use of herbs as medicine is not limited to developing countries. The herbal medicine, or "phytotherapy," market in Europe has $2.2 billion in annual sales. Seventy percent of the market is in Germany alone. Dutch consumers are the highest per capita users of herbal products in Europe. In Japan, over 80 percent of physicians have had experience in the use of Chinese herbal medicines. In Australia, herbalists serve as primary healthcare providers, and herb products are required to have premarket clearance and must carry therapeutic indications (Steinhoff 1992). The Australians are the highest per capita users of herbal medicine in the English-speaking world. Herbal medicine can no longer be regarded as bush medicine. It is an integral part of primary healthcare in much of the modern world.

When the forerunner of this book, *Herbal Bounty*, appeared in 1984, sales of herb products through health and natural-food retail outlets were estimated to be about $150 million per year. Now, according to a survey published in the March 1992 issue of *Health Foods Business*, 1991 herb sales in the 7,300 health and natural-food store outlets in the United States represented 16.8 percent of retail sales in this market segment, up from 12.4 percent the previous year, an increase of 35 percent. Overall, herb products represented retail sales of $653.2 million, a 39.8 percent increase over 1990's $467.3 million in estimated retail sales. Over six hundred botanical commodities are sold as bulk or finished goods in health and natural-food markets in North America. An excellent source of information about the majority of herbs in this market segment is the American Herbal Product Association's Herbs in Commerce list.

Culinary herbs are gaining in popularity, too. The spice trade has well over a billion dollars in annual retail sales. The American Spice Trade Association reports that since 1960 in the United States, consumption of spices has continued to grow faster than the population rate. When I finished writing *Herbal Bounty* in 1982, the United States imported a record 162,292 metric tons of spices, valued at $221 million. In 1991, imported herbs and spices represented a record 242,719 metric tons, valued at $394,895 million.

When *Herbal Bounty* was completed in 1982, we were in the beginning phase of an herb renaissance that was about twelve years old at that point. It is clear from the figures above that interest in herbs in the United States has continued to increase. Now, ten years later, an emphasis on things herbal has mushroomed into a worldwide phenomena. This growth encompasses the entire herbal spectrum—the use of culinary herbs has become increasingly popular, not only dried herbs, but fresh herbs, and herb gardening as well. Literally hundreds of herb farms and other small herb businesses have sprung up across North America. Ten years ago fresh cilantro was found only in ethnic markets in larger cities. Now I can even buy cilantro at the grocery store in Eureka Springs, Arkansas. Today fresh culinary herbs are a common produce item throughout the country. Fragrant and decorative herb use has followed suit. Potpourri became posh in the 1980s, creating an entirely new commercial category for bulk herb suppliers. Aromatherapy, which utilizes essential oils of herbs for health, or at least to create pleasant olfactory sensations, has become a household word. Well, almost. Ten years ago one could only buy a few dozen different types of herb plants and seeds. Now several hundred species are available for American gardens.

Interest in the medicinal use of herbs, not only among consumers, but healthcare providers as well, has also blossomed. Underlying the entire herb renaissance is an explosion of information resources, including popular books on all aspects of herb cookery, health aspects, and herb gardening. This literary output has been spawned by a dramatic increase in professional research interest, on the part of the horticultural, agronomic, genetic, botanical, pharmacological, chemical, and clinical disciplines, which are now delving into the endless, infinite, and ongoing questions that need to be answered about those plants we call "herbs." The herbal information explosion and its array of practical applications is not a passing fad in the United States. It is permanent.

In the herb cultivation and production realm, research programs at the University of Massachusetts, Amherst, Purdue University's Department of Horticulture, and the Department of Agriculture and Natural Resources at Delaware State College have played an important role in developing data on the horticultural and agronomic aspects of herbs. Dr. Lyle Craker at the University of Massachusetts began publishing the *Herb, Spice and Medicinal Plant Digest* ten years ago, which serves as a primary source of information on horticultural developments. Dr. Craker also edits the new periodical, *Journal of Herbs, Spices and Medicinal Plants*, providing a multidisciplinary international forum for production data on medicinal and aromatic plants. His former student, Dr. James E. Simon, now an associate professor at Purdue University, is producing detailed and definitive studies on commercial cultivation of medicinal and aromatic plants. The Department of Horticulture at Purdue has emerged as the primary research group in the country on herb production. Dr. Arthur O. Tucker of Delaware State College has done much to sort out the taxonomic problems associated with complex plant groups such as the oreganos, mints, lavenders, and others. Tom

DeBaggio of Earthworks Herb Nursery in Arlington, Virginia, has worked alongside the academic community to produce and select new cultivars of lavender, rosemary and other plant groups. In addition, collaboration with international research groups through the Medicinal and Aromatic Plant Section of the International Society of Horticultural Science has produced multidisciplinary research efforts for further exploring worldwide medicinal and aromatic plant production and conservation.

In the popular herb-use realm, especially for cultivation, fragrance, decorative and culinary uses, two consumer-oriented magazines have played an important role in bringing herbs to a wider public. Both *The Herb Companion* and *The Herb Quarterly* provide detailed and timely informa-

tion for the herb-consuming public.

Herb businesses, large and small, are now served by two trade organizations. The International Herb Growers and Marketers Association (Mundelein, Illinois) serves as an information and business resource for hundreds of small and large, mostly family-owned herb businesses. Since 1986, in conjunction with Purdue University's Jim Simon, the IHGMA has sponsored annual international herb conferences that have brought together individuals and interests representing the entire spectrum of the herb business and research pursuits. The proceedings of these conferences have contributed a tremendous amount of detailed information for *Herbal Renaissance*. The American Herbal Products Association (Austin, Texas), primarily serving as a trade group for manufacturers and suppliers of herb products sold to the health and natural-foods industries, has sponsored research and an integrated, cooperative approach in working with regulatory agencies. In addition, the emergence of the *Business of Herbs*, a bimonthly periodical serving herb businesses for over a decade, has facilitated a steady flow of information for small and large herb businesses alike.

Great strides have been made in the scientific understanding of medicinal herb use in North America. That development has been spearheaded by a number of organizations, notably the American Botanical Council (Austin, Texas) and the Herb Research Foundation (Boulder, Colorado). These organizations jointly publish *HerbalGram*, a quarterly publication with international distribution that serves as a bridge between scientific research and popular understanding of medicinal herb use. The visibility of this publication has catapulted medicinal herb use from blind advocacy to critical scientific assessment. The American Botanical Council, under the direction of Mark Blumenthal, has worked to bring accurate herb information to scientists, consumers, regulators, and journalists. The Herb Research Foundation, headed by Rob McCaleb, has produced exhaustive dossiers on herb safety for regulatory agencies, and served as a clearinghouse for

Echinacea purpurea, Common Purple Coneflower

scientific data on medicinal herbs. In addition, other groups such as the American Herb Association (Nevada City, California), directed by Kathi Keville, and Christopher Hobbs's Institute of Natural Products Research have brought detailed information to the professional herb community.

Researchers, such as USDA's Dr. James A. Duke, the most prolific herbal author of the twentieth century, have kept down-to-earth information on herbs before both scientific and herb-consuming audiences. Jim Duke's *CRC Handbook of Medicinal Herbs*, and his dozen or more other books, have served as primary resources for hundreds of professionals in a variety of academic disciplines. Dr. Varro Tyler of the Department of Pharmacy and Pharmacognosy at Purdue University, author of *The New Honest Herbal*, has brought sometimes controversial attention to herb safety and rational medicinal applications. Dr. Tyler has received an undeserving "bum rap" from some segments of the herb community which view his approach to medicinal herb use as overly conservative. However, if his works, such as *The New Honest Herbal*, are approached with an objective rather than an emotionally biased viewpoint, one will find an accurate reflection of what the scientific literature really has to say about the safety and efficacy of herbs. The Natural Products Section of Health and Welfare Canada, headed by Dr. Dennis Awang, has brought new meaning to a sensible approach to regulatory affairs as they relate to herbs.

These are just a few of the important players in the development of herbs as medicinal, aromatic, flavoring, and crop plants in North America over the past decade. The addresses of most of these organizations and periodicals are available in the resource section at the end of this book.

I recently attended a conference in New York and during a social event, I introduced Dr. Awang to a Washington food and drug lawyer as "North America's most rational natural-products regulatory official." The lawyer laughed. "That's an oxymoron if I've ever heard one," he quipped.

Herb products sold for health purposes in the United States sit in what might be described as "regulatory purgatory." They are primarily labeled "dietary supplements." These products are "foods" rather than "drugs." Labels generally do not include information on the intended medicinal or health uses of the products. Herb product regulation in the United States is mired in bureaucratic interpretations of what constitutes a food and what constitutes a drug, with lines more clearly drawn by the label contents than by the consumer's intended use of the product.

At the time of this writing, there are a number of legislative and legal efforts pending that seek to develop regulatory structures that will allow herb products to be predictable in quality and labeled for their intended use. The outcome of these efforts will have a profound effect on

Digitalis purpurea, Foxglove, Cascades, Oregon

the future of the American herb industry, be it negative or positive. It is important for herb consumers to keep up with these developments, and to take appropriate action, including writing or calling legislators. Bill Clinton has just been elected president of the United States. I hope that President Clinton will exhibit some herb savvy when new legislation reaches his desk. During the campaign when he lost his voice, he was reported to be drinking "herbal tea" to soothe his sore throat. The Little Rock Unit of the Herb Society of America has maintained an herb garden at the governor's mansion throughout Clinton's reign as Arkansas governor. I had the pleasure of meeting Hillary Clinton at the dedication of the Heritage Herb Garden at the Ozark Folk Center State Park in Mountain View, Arkansas. Bill was there, too. May the Clintons not forget their roots (nor leaves, seeds, and bark) when it comes to considering the potential role of herbs in national healthcare. To keep abreast of regulatory developments, subscribe to *HerbalGram* (see American Botanical Council in the resource section).

What do we need in the future? We need a regulatory mechanism that will assure proper identification of herbs used in products, allow proper labeling including health claims, and require that herb products meet certain standards of quality and purity. At a 1989 lecture, by invitation of the Health Protection Branch of Health and Welfare Canada, Dr. Varro Tyler of Purdue University presented a rational approach to herb product regulation. In his lecture, "The Herbal Regulatory Dilemma: A Proposed Solution," in essence Dr. Tyler proposed: 1) that a Botanical Codex or similar compendium be prepared to establish standards of identity, purity, and quality for all crude vegetable drugs; 2) that all herbs sold be properly identified by their Latin binomial, and that a method of determining compliance with appropriate standards be implemented; 3) that the safety of all herbs sold to consumers be established; and 4) that herbs should be allowed to be sold with approved traditional claims of efficacy, provided all the other requirements have been met. Indeed, an approach such as that outlined by Dr. Tyler would, in my opinion, be a boon for consumers and the herb industry alike.

To some extent, a positive regulatory situation for herb products already exists in Canada, Germany and other Western countries, and their regulations could serve as models for the United States. In Canada, herbal product manufacturers can apply for a drug identification number (DIN), a Canadian regulatory category equivalent to the over-the-counter (OTC) drug category in the United States. If safety and efficacy can be established through literature reviews, current clinical trials, and other data supplied by the manufacturer, a DIN can be awarded, and specific medicinal claims can be placed on the product label. For example, Health and Welfare Canada has recently issued a DIN to a feverfew product.

Germany is a place of contrast and continuity. On the east side of the Rhine, on the stretch from Frankfurt to Bonn, is an endless array of thousand-year-old castles, with vineyards stretching up hillsides the way a ski lift tames a steep mountain. The train tracks run along the west side of the river, peppered by small towns, most rebuilt after the Second World War. Their air of newness blends with the ancient sentinels of Germanic culture across the river, serving as constant reminders of continuity in an endless loop of change.

And so it is with herbal medicine. The past is part of the here and now. One gets a sense that the past merges with the present, as if time were nonexistent. Germans are as likely to use herbal medicines today as they were a thousand years ago. According to Tyler (1986), 76 percent of German women interviewed used herbal teas for health benefits, and more than half used herbal remedies, at least at the beginning stages of a disease. In Germany, the regulatory system allows a relatively large number of companies—from small firms to large conglomerates—to competitively bring a rather large number of medicinal herb products—called phytomedicines—to the marketplace. The German equivalent to the FDA, the BGA has a special therapeutic-ingredient section for phytomedicines. This allows manufacturers to work within a reasonable set of guidelines, covering details such as labeling, quality control, and safety, to make a large number of generally well-defined, properly identified, quality-assured, and properly labeled medicinal herb products available to the German public. According to Dr. Tyler, a reasonable certainty of safety and efficacy is assumed based on the historical record of the plant coupled with modern scientific documentation. Quality and identity of products must be assured through approved analytical methods. Medicinal herb products registered for sale must include a package inset providing the consumer with information on constituents, indications, side effects, contraindications, dosage, etc.

Through its "Commission E," the BGA has developed a unique and extensive system of "Therapeutic Monographs on Medicinal Products for Human Use." There are nearly three hundred such monographs, which are periodically updated as new information on any aspect of a plant product, its intended medicinal use, or safety becomes available. The monographs include details on the name of the drug, its constituents, indications (including those for the crude drug or any preparations), contraindications (if any), side effects (if known), interactions with other drugs or agents (if known), details on dosage of the crude drug or preparations, the method of administration, and the general properties or therapeutic value of the herb or herb product. The German monograph system is the best government-sponsored information source on medicinal plant usage to be produced by a Western industrialized nation.

All German medical students are now required to pass an examination dealing with clinical use of phytomedicines. Ethical herbal medicine is part of mainstream public healthcare in Germany. While many herb products in the United States are sold in health-food stores, in Germany they are sold through pharmacies.

As it prepares to merge its markets in the 1990s, the European economic community is looking to the well-developed German phytomedicine system as the primary model for phytomedicine regulation in Europe. It is essential that European community member states harmonize phytotherapy regulations. ESCOP (European Scientific Cooperative for Phytotherapy), a fifteen hundred-member scientific organization, has been formed to help direct the harmonization of medicinal plant regulations throughout Europe. ESCOP is issuing proposed monographs to the entire European community for consideration as standards for regulating herb products throughout much of Europe. The German BGA Commission E phytomedicine monographs are serving as the basis for those being developed by ESCOP. The outcome of the European community's phytomedicine regulations will have a profound impact on the American herb market, both in the development of new regulations for product labeling, as well as the sourcing of plant materials from North America.

The future of herbs lies not only in their regulation, but also in assuring consistent supplies of properly identified plant materials. These concepts have been recognized and codified by the World Health Organization (WHO) and international scientific consensus. Conservation of herb resources is an important issue for the future. Rather than relying on wild harvested supplies of some medicinal plants, the world will have to learn to cultivate them in the future.

In 1977, the WHO initiated an ambitious goal of providing healthcare to all by the year 2000. Recognizing that medicinal plant therapies form a major aspect of traditional medicine systems worldwide, the WHO called for a comprehensive approach to the understanding and use of medicinal plants in 1978. In 1987, the fortieth World Health Assembly reaffirmed previous WHO resolutions on traditional medicine and instituted new mandates for future action, including: 1. "to initiate comprehensive programmes for the identification, evaluation, preparation, cultivation and conservation of medicinal plants used in traditional medicine"; and 2. "to ensure quality control of drugs derived from traditional plant remedies by using modern techniques and applying suitable standards and good manufacturing practices" (Akerele 1992).

In issuing these mandates, the WHO furthered its role in traditional medicine. In response to its mandate to initiate comprehensive programs for conservation of medicinal plants, in March of 1988 the WHO cosponsored an International Consultation on the Conservation of Medicinal Plants in Chiang Mai, Thailand. A result of the consultation was the Chiang Mai Declaration: "Saving Lives by Saving Plants," which recognized "the urgent need for international cooperation and coordination to establish programmes for conservation of medicinal plants to ensure that adequate quantities are available for future generations" (Akerele, Heywood, and Synge 1991).

The recent past head of the WHO's Traditional Medicine Programme, Dr. O. Akerele, has recently authored a position paper that addresses quality control, good manufacturing practices, evaluation, and preparation of herbal medicines. This is the landmark document, "WHO Guidelines for the Assessment of Herbal Medicine" (Akerele 1992). These guidelines address several major areas and include: 1) pharmaceutical assessments which suggest ways to document authentication and quality control of crude plant material, and plant preparations to control finished products and to guarantee product stability; 2) recommendations for safety assessment, which emphasize the significance of toxicological studies and the value of documentation of safety based on experience; and 3) suggestions for the assessment of efficacy and intended use, documentation of pharmacological activity, and evidence required to support medicinal use of herbs.

As I see it, one of the major points in the WHO guidelines deals with the vouchered identity of plant materials used in herbal medicines. "The botanical definition, including genus, species and authority, should be given to ensure correct identity of a plant. A definition and description of the plant from which the medicine is made (e. g., leaf, flower, root) has to be provided as well as an indication as to whether fresh, dried or traditionally processed material is used. The active and characteristic constituents should be specified, and if possible, content limits defined. Foreign matter, impurities and microbial content should be defined or limited. Voucher specimens, representing each lot of plant material processed, should be authenticated by qualified botanists and should be stored for at least a ten-year period. A lot number should be assigned and this should appear on the product label" (Akerele 1992, 107).

There are several major points to consider here. First of all, the general public of the United States has the right to choose herbal medicine as a modality of healthcare, just like consumers in the rest of the civilized world do. Herb products must be safe. They must carry therapeutic claims. They must contain properly identified and labeled ingredients, backed by standards of identity, including botanical voucher specimens. The source plants must be produced or harvested in a sustainable manner. If they must be harvested from the wild, that process should be completed in a manner that doesn't reduce their numbers. The best way to achieve this is through commercial cultivation.

The wild harvest of herbs throughout the world causes concern about the loss of information encoded in their genetic databanks. In the United States, plant-conservation efforts focus on rare, threatened and endangered taxa. Of the seventy indigenous medicinal plant species commercially harvested in the United States, there is no data to support how much of any of them can be harvested on a sustainable-yield basis, that is without reducing existing populations. Basic research on population dynamics, demographics, and reproductive biology of the involved species has yet to be conducted.

Factors affecting the reduction of medicinal-plant supplies and subsequent genetic erosion of medicinal-plant source species are not confined to the United States. Habitat

Stachys byzantina, Lamb's Ear in Rose Yarrow

destruction heads the list, including loss due to urbanization, agricultural development, housing development, and expansion of industry into wild lands. Over-collection of wild species, including rare or threatened taxa, has also reduced medicinal-plant natural resources and reduced their genetic diversity. The ultimate solution is cultivation.

If there's one constant factor characteristic of all plants, it is endless variation. Many of the plants we know as "herbs" cannot be lumped into a single neat category in terms of their flavor, fragrance, or medicinal qualities. It is now known, for example, that the chemistry of a plant such as feverfew cannot be defined simply by lumping it under the taxonomic entity of *Tanacetum parthenium*. There are at least three different chemotypes in which the essential oil reflects different chemical profiles. Only one, the chemotype containing parthenolide as the major constituent, is suitable for medicinal plant development. The same holds true for virtually all of the plants treated in this book. Therefore, for commercial development, specific cultivated varieties or chemotypes with the desired profile of chemical constituents (if known) should be selected for cultivation. Development of this simple, but multifaceted and complex, theory is now the focus of research groups throughout the world.

In the herb accounts to follow, you will learn more about the diversity, identification, cultivation (both for the home garden and on a commercial basis, culinary uses, traditional medicinal use, modern research (often vindicating historical use), the chemistry, and safety considerations of well-known, and not-so-well-known herbs. One of the best ways to get to know herbs is to grow your own. You will generally find your home-grown herbs to have superior flavor and fragrance, which will further help you to gain greater appreciation for herbs and their endless diversity.

Many of the plants familiar to the herb garden—parsley, sage, rosemary, and thyme—are Eurasian natives which over the centuries have found use as condiments and medicine. It is taken for granted that such plants deserve a place in herb gardens. There are in addition many native North American plants that are equally useful, easy to cultivate, and deserving of appreciation. Some of the species included in this book are appearing in an herb gardening book for the first time; they are indigenous to this continent and have a long history of use. The list includes wildflowers, woodland herbs, prairie plants, trees, and shrubs. In addition to indigenous American herbs and a strong complement of familiar herb-garden inhabitants, I have included several Eurasian

novelties and an African herb which I feel herb gardeners will find interesting and enjoyable. Additional plants included grow in the United States on their own, although they were originally native to other regions.

The United States has dozens of climatic ranges, making it difficult to produce any horticultural book with national appeal. A Maine gardener invariably experiences different conditions than those existing in Southern California gardens. But if any one category of plants lends itself to a great variety of climates, soil types, rainfall figures, and sun exposure, it is herbs. Many herb species including bearberry, bee balms, cat thyme, echinaceas, sweet goldenrod, horehound, lady's mantle, lavenders, wormwoods, sages, oreganos, and santolinas are exceedingly drought resistant. I have had equal success growing many of the herb species described in this book in the harsh cold of Maine, the cool coastal mists of the central California coast, and the sandy, acid soil of an arid, south-facing slope at my present Ozark home in northwest Arkansas. In August 1983, we had fourteen days in a row with temperatures over 100° F with

Rosmarinus officinalis, Rosemary

no rain for over a month. While most of my neighbors' vegetable gardens shriveled away, my herb garden remained lush. Most of the herbs in this book will do as well in New England as they will in arid Utah or the wet world of the coastal Pacific Northwest. Herbs are incredibly adaptable. As a general rule, an herb garden requires much less attention than a vegetable garden.

The potential for herb use in cooking is infinite. Many people don't use herbs simply because they don't know where to begin. If you shy away from herbs because you think they are reserved for French chefs, put away your fears and start stroking herbs to become familiar with their fragrance. Nibble a leaf. Imagine the dishes you prepare which may be enhanced by that herb. Experiment and enjoy!

Most books on herb gardening ignore medicinal aspects even though the history of plant use is preserved in pharmaceutical history right up into the twentieth century. It is only in the past fifty to eighty years that American culture has lost touch with the local flora as a source of medicine. Perhaps industrialization of Western culture and the attendant corruption of traditional folk wisdom have caused the loss. The promotion and acceptance of synthetic medicines in treating disease, beginning with the accelerated development of modern chemistry and its resultant application to pharmacology, have also contributed to the decline of herbal medicine. Certainly it is reassuring to have the expertise of the doctor and the pharmacist when you are dealing with potent—and potentially lethal—medicines. Still, expertise in the medicinal use of herbs is hardly beyond the grasp of most people, though herbal medicines must be approached with intelligence, respect, and caution.

An estimated 50 percent of prescription drugs are derived from natural sources. About 25 percent come from higher (flowering) plants. Worldwide, more people are treated with herbs than with Western orthodox medicine. Many age-old cures have a rational, scientific basis. Where scientific research vindicates folk use, I have tried to supply the information. I have used terms such as diaphoretic, stimulant, carminative, etc., to describe a plant's traditional or modern use. These terms are not necessarily specific. For example, tonic points to a general effect on a particular organ or body system. A diaphoretic, for example, brings on sweating. Many herbs will produce diaphoresis, as does a bowl of hot chicken soup.

The medicinal uses for herbs included in this book are intended as reference information, not medical advice. Some of these plants can produce toxic reactions, or may adversely affect individuals suffering from certain conditions. Please take reasonable precautions in harvesting, preparing, using, or administering all plant medicines. Remember, any substance, synthetic or natural, may produce undesirable effects. Medical reports exist of people dying from an overdose of water! I strongly recommend seeking the advice of a qualified medical practitioner and following his or her guidance rather than relying on self-diagnosis, which, all too often, is improper, inadequate, or incorrect. Qualified medical diagnosis is essential. The author and publisher hereby disclaim any and all legal responsibility connected with the use of the traditional and scientific medical information reported in this book.

The descriptions of plants I've included are derived from my interpretation of technical botanical descriptions and my own observations. I've tried to keep terms simple in favor of giving the reader a visual picture of the plant. DD Dowden's sensitive illustrations capture the visual spirit of the plants, and, in some small way, the descriptions enhance her work. Propagation and cultivation information to a large extent is based upon my experience and that of herb gardeners in various parts of the country who have shared their experiences. Projections for potential yields per acre are provided for those who contemplate growing and drying herbs for sale. The figures are in large part based on the work of USDA researchers D.M. Crooks and A.F. Sievers, 1941, 1942; W.W. Stockberger, 1935; recent compilations by USDA's Jim Duke; and my own experience.

Information has also been provided for purposes of general interest and comparison. It is no coincidence when a person smells sweet goldenrod for the first time and thinks of tarragon. Both plants contain estragole—the substance in their respective essential oils responsible for their flavor and fragrance.

In essence, I have attempted to write the book I needed when I began herb gardening, plus providing new, useful information to the experienced herbalist. But nature's school is one in which we are all—and always will be—students.

2

THE COMMON
LANGUAGE OF BOTANY

*"That botany is a useful study is plain; because it
is in vain that we know betony is good for headaches,
or self-heal for wounds unless we can distinguish
betony and self-heal from one another."*
—John Hill, *The Family Herbal*, 1812

Names are reference points, symbols—vehicles for communicating and distinguishing one thing from another. The nature of a person, place, or plant does not change because of its name. As Juliet reminds us, "What's in a name? That which we call a rose by any other name would smell as sweet."

Although the plant doesn't care what you call it, people do. Confusion inevitably arises if simultaneously more than one name is applied to a person, place, or plant. Similarly, if the same name is given to several plants or persons over a period of time, ambiguity may result.

With a name like Steven Foster, I lived with quips about "my" songs, taking such comments with a smile and my standard response, "I haven't written any songs for a hundred years." What do I say if someone asks if I'm the "real" Steven Foster? Yes, I'm real. But so was the other one.

As I sit here writing, I am brewing tea in a pot made by my ex-sister-in-law's ex-sister-in-law, that is to say, my brother's wife's brother's wife. Obviously, it is much easier to say that the teapot's maker is Ann Gordon.

Before Linnaeus introduced the Latin binomial system into general use, scientific plant names were long and cumbersome. Overlap and confusion threatened the sanity of scientific minds. In the early 1600s, when the gardener to Charles I, John Tradescant, introduced spiderworts (*Tradescantia* species) to England from North America, they were known as *Phalangum Ephenerum Virginianum Johannis Tradescanti*. The need for concise, well-defined, and unambiguous names soon becomes evident. Despite any inherent deficiencies, such names are indispensable.

At workshops when I mention the need to use Latin binomials instead of relying on common plant names, about half the audience yawns, slumps down, and tunes out. Many people think Latin binomials are archaic, difficult to pronounce, hard to remember, and, as it was once put to me, a reflection of the patriarchal structure of our society. Most people, though, can pronounce and remember sassafras, coleus, rhododendron, geranium, asparagus, and petunia. These are all generic as well as common plant names.

In today's herb market, the name *ginseng* has been applied to numerous plants and products. In product labeling, ginseng has referred to several species of *Panax* (*Panax ginseng, P. quinquefolius, P. pseudo-ginseng*); Siberian ginseng (*Eleutherococcus senticosis*), a shrubby member of the ginseng family native to parts of China and Russia; canigre or desert dock, *Rumex hymenosepalous*, a member of the buckwheat family native to the Southwest; and even Vitamin C. Several of these represent obvious marketing hoaxes, notably canigre. In most cases, I believe using the name ginseng with plants or substances other than species of Panax is a marketing strategy designed to make consumers buy a product on the reputation of a name.

In another example, sage generally refers to *Salvia officinalis*, an herb familiar to the fragrant garden and spice shelves; but it might also refer to certain species of the genus *Artemisia* (sagebrush) or to any number of more than seven hundred species in the mint family's genus, *Salvia*. Equally confusing is the fact that *Aralia spinosa*, the largest North American member of the ginseng family, and *Zanthol-*

xylum clava-herculis, a member of the rue family, both share the common names "Hercules's club, prickly ash, toothache tree, and tear blanket."

Dried French lavender sold in herb shops is not the same French lavender sold by herb nurseries. The French lavender of the herb shop is usually English lavender, *Lavandula augustifolia*, grown in France and sold on the American market under the name French lavender. "French" in this case denotes country of origin rather than the plant itself. The French lavender available from most herb plant sellers is *Lavandula dentata*, a plant not known for the quality of its dried flowers. *Lavandula stoechas*, described mainly as Spanish lavender, is also sometimes sold as French lavender. The potential for confusion is obvious. Common names do not distinguish between different plants.

You don't have to be a botanist to appreciate and use Latin binomials.

Not only do they clarify and distinguish one plant from another, they may also give us some insights as to the appearance, habits, uses, and history of a plant. The Latin binomial *Panax quinquefolius* clearly identifies American ginseng as a distinct entity. The generic term *Panax* is derived from the Greek *pan*, meaning "all," and *akos*, meaning "cure," signifying cure-all or panacea. The name quinquefolius means "five leaves." American ginseng's binomial thus tells us something of the plant's uses and leaf structure.

Some plants may have a hundred or more names in several languages. On the other hand, only one Latin binomial can validly apply to a plant. These names are precise and internationally recognized.

The naming of plants is governed by the rules and regulations of the *International Code of Botanical Nomenclature*. Every few years botanists the world over convene at an International Botanical Congress where certain rules are established or revised. The results are published as the *International Code of Botanical Nomenclature*, a standard botanists voluntarily follow to make plant names universal and unambiguous.

Every living organism has certain definite characteristics. Some features differ greatly,

Lavandula angustifolia, English Lavender

such as those that distinguish between a rattlesnake and an eagle. Other items, like peppermint and spearmint, have very similar features. These characteristics are used to classify organisms into taxonomic groups. Taxonomy, as the late Arthur Cronquist defined it, is "a study aimed at producing a system of classification of organisms which best reflects the totality of their similarities and differences" (Cronquist 1968, 3).

Botanists have estimated there are between 200,000 and 800,000 species in the plant kingdom. To conveniently study such a great number of organisms, the kingdom is divided into smaller groups based on natural relationships. Major taxonomic groups of the plant kingdom include divisions, classes, orders, families, genera, species, and several groups below the rank of species. The family, genus, species, and subgroups of species serve as the most useful reference points for herb gardeners.

The family can be likened to a broad group of motorized vehicles known as automobiles. There are several genera in the family automobile, including Chevrolets, Fords, Cadillacs, and Toyotas. In the genus Toyota, indigenous to Japan and naturalized throughout North America, is the species *Corolla.* Thus, for a specific organism in our hypothetical automobile family, we have the binomial, *Toyota corolla.*

The plant family is composed of one or more genera (genus) that resemble one another in general appearance and structural characteristics. Family names end in *aceae* with only eight exceptions. These eight genera include some of the more important families of interest to the herb grower: the *Labiatae*— the mint family (*Lamiaceae*), *Umbelliferae*— carrot family (*Apiaceae*), *Leguminosae*—pea family (*Fabaceae*), Compositae—aster family (Astericeae), and the *Cruciferae*—mustard family (*Brassicaceae*). For tradition's sake and the convenience of cross-referencing with other herb books, I will use the old family names not ending in *aceae* as the primary family names, though to help the reader become more familiar with the new names, they follow the traditional family name in parentheses under each species entry.

The mint family is perhaps the most important plant family to herbalists, with about 180 genera and over 3,500 species. In fact, while the family's members represent only 1–1.5 percent of the world's flowering plants, over one-fourth of those plants commonly called herbs belong to this family. Members include sage, rosemary, thyme, pennyroyal, peppermint, savory, and dozens of others.

The first word of the Latin binomial is the generic term (genus), the second word is the specific epithet. The genus name is a noun, always capitalized, and may stand alone. The species name is an adjective, possessive, is not capitalized, and may not be used alone.

Binomials may be followed by the name or abbreviation of the name of one or more persons. In *Panax quinquefolius* L., the "L" stands for Carl Linnaeus, who "authored" the name for American ginseng. In 1793, Linnaeus regularized the Latin binomial system through the publication of his *Species Planatarum* (The Species of Plants), which included

Herb Drying Attic; Sister's Shop, Sabbathday Lake, Maine

the descriptions and names of 5,900 plants. He named many of the herbs included in this book. Under the botanical code, the author of a Latin binomial is the first person who validly publishes a plant name and description.

Sometimes you will find two or more names of authorities written after a Latin binomial with the first name in parentheses. This double citation means the plant has gone through a change in taxonomic position or classification. The first name in parenthesis is the person who originally named the plant; the second is the person who reclassified it. Authority citations have a number of other variations which we need not explore here. Suffice it to say that the authority citation is an abbreviated bibliographical reference, a useful tool for those who name plants. The citation is not considered an essential part of the botanical name.

The appearance of a multiplication sign in the binomial means the plant is a hybrid produced by sexual crossing. *Mentha* x *piperita*, peppermint, is considered a cross between *Mentha spicata*, spearmint, and *Mentha aquatica*, watermint.

Several ranks of classifications are recognized below the species level, including subspecies, varieties, and forms. If one of these ranks is used, the term or an abbreviation for that term (variety; e.g., var.) must be included in the name of the plant.

One botanical name illustrating a double citation, subspecific rank, and hybrid is that for orris root, *Iris* x *germanica* var. *florentina* (L.) Dykes. Orris root is a hybrid of two species, *Iris germanica* and *Iris florentina*, that was first named *Iris florentina* by Linnaeus, then reclassified by William R. Dykes, producing the above name. But scrap all of that. It has been reclassified once again. Tucker and Lawrence (1987) note that the characteristics that have been used to identify the plant as a distinct variety are not constant. Therefore, the name for this taxon is expressed as a cultivar, *Iris* x *germanica* 'Florentina'.

The cultivars, cultivated plants distinguished by certain characteristics which are retained by asexual and sexual reproduction, are the most important subspecies rank of classification relevant to cultivated plants. Cultivar names begin with capital letters and are preceded by the abbreviation cv., or more often are placed in single quotation marks. Those of you who are still prejudiced against Latin plant names will be happy to know that since 1 January 1959, the International Code of Nomenclature for Cultivated Plants allows cultivar names only from modern languages. Latin

names may not be used. However, many Latin cultivar names were adopted prior to 1959 and are still in use.

Sometimes Latin names are changed. These changes tend to be annoying and reduce the efficiency of the nomenclature system. The botanical codes try to keep such changes to a minimum, but nevertheless it is sometimes necessary to change the rank or classification of a plant based on solid new information. This means a change in name as well. The nomenclature system is by no means perfect, but it is the best and most generally adopted system we have for relating to plant names.

There are no set rules for pronouncing binomials. Latin binomials may be pronounced differently by people from various regions or countries. In various parts of the United States, I've heard the generic name for mayapple, *Podophyllum*, pronounced three distinct ways by professional botanists. People tend to pronounce binomials as they pronounce words in their own language. It is only important that you be understood by the person with whom you are talking.

In this book, the Latin binomials and author citations generally follow those given in the various reviews of herb taxonomy expert Arthur O. Tucker of Delaware State College (see Tucker 1986, Tucker and Lawrence 1987, and Tucker, Duke, and Foster 1989). In *Herbal Bounty*, we relied upon *Hortus Third*, but that work is sufficiently outdated so that new sources were required. The American Herbal Products Association has also produced an *Herbs of Commerce* list of current botanical names of herbs, as well as suggested single common names to use in the herb trade. To help make the binomial more familiar to the reader, I have included a pronunciation guide for the genus and main species described in each entry. Rolling the names over on your tongue a few times offers just another taste treat!

References for further reading:

Bailey, Liberty Hyde. 1963. *How Plants Get Their Names.* New York: Dover Books.

Foster, S. 1979. *Latin Binomials: Learning to Live with the System.* Well-Being 48 (Dec.): 41–42.

Foster, S., ed. 1992. *Herbs of Commerce.* Austin, Texas: American Herbal Products Association.

Jeffrey, Charles. 1977. *Biological Nomenclature.* New York: Crane, Russack and Co.

Tippo, O., and W. L. Stern. 1977. *Humanistic Botany.* New York: W.W. Norton and Co., Inc.

3

DESIGNING
HERB GARDENS

Cultivating herbs means more than planting seeds, watering, fertilizing, and weeding. Cultivating is nurturing, refining, and encouraging. As the cultivator, you must establish a relationship with another living being—the plant. An herb garden will repay equally for you the energy you contribute to its growth.

The Shakers started the first medicinal herb gardens in North America; by the mid-1800s, they had over two hundred acres of herbs under cultivation. These herbs were dried and used for manufacturing high-quality herbal extracts sold the world over. One of the gentle, glowing leaders of the Shaker movement, Elder Frederick Evans, said in 1867, "A tree has its wants and wishes, and a person should study them as a teacher watches a child to see what he can do. If you love the plant and take heed of what it likes, you will be well paid by it" (Dixon 1867, 301). I think this is the key to a successful and vibrant garden—the mystery of the green thumb.

Chinese philosophy assumes that the universe is in a constant process of change—rhythms of life and death, growth and antithesis, waxing and waning, yin and yang. The cycles are never static. The garden is in constant metamorphosis with the rhythms of the seasons and ever-changing forces of weather and soil. Garden design must conform to natural impulses and not become stagnant under a gardener's management.

Romans practiced topiary gardening, clipping and trimming plants into the shapes of birds, animals, or geometric forms. Sculpted boxwoods, myrtles, and bays mimicked a myriad of shapes, often reflecting architectural style. In Francis Bacon's 1625 essay "Of Gardens," he disapproves of "images cut out of juniper and other garden stuff," saying, "topiary work is for children." In Bacon's day, though, cutting yews and rosemary into green gargoyles was common in the gardens of the rich. W. Robinson writes in his *English Flower Garden*, "What right have we to deform things so lovely in form? No cramming of Chinese feet into impossible shoes is half so foolish as the willful and brutal distortion of the beautiful forms of trees" (Robinson 1882, 337).

I believe foliage and flowers should not be clipped and tamed to satisfy the whims of a person's time and taste. If you want a six-foot hedge, plant a shrub that grows to six feet, rather than chopping off a shrub that normally grows to twice that height. To me, the ultimate achievement of the gardener is to be shaped by the forces within the garden, rather than to shape the garden by force.

A garden is a place for growth. A quiet mind can become one with nature's cycles. Respecting other life forms by cooperating with their natural needs fosters the growth of both the plants and the gardeners. Life's greatest treasures are often silent and unseen; the gentle gardener will find more in the garden than useful and

Leonotis leonurus, Lion's Tail

observe what surrounds it. Existing architectural lines, pathways, driveways, trees, fences, native plants, building materials, present use, projected use, even the view from the neighbor's yard should be taken into consideration.

Before working out a design on paper, go to the garden spot, become quiet, and imagine yourself expanding into the soil, nearby plants, a tree, and the surrounding area in general. Imagine that you are your favorite herb plant. What does it feel like to be in that spot? Keep a piece of paper and pencil handy to write down any impressions you have. Visualize how you would like the garden to appear. I know this may sound airy-fairy, but you may be amazed at the ideas that pop into your head.

Before diving into a grandiose plan, consider how much time you have for gardening. Is the garden going to be a weekend hobby, or a passionate career? Start small and expand as feasible. Other considerations include how and when the sun hits the site, soil type and conditions, water availability, and the herbs best suited to your climate. If you have several sites to choose from, you may wish to create a variety of habitats most favorable for your desired herbs.

Once you've chosen a site, test the soil, using any of the kits available to gardeners. County extension offices offer basic soil analysis at minimal costs. Tell the agent that you want recommendations for organic amendments; otherwise you'll receive a list of chemical amenders.

Herbs produce the most potent essential oils, responsible for most of the flavors and fragrances, when they receive at least six to eight hours of sunlight each day. In the mint family, oil glands can be seen with a low-power hand lens.

Most herbs do best in sun except for those indigenous to the deciduous forests, plus angelica, sweet cicely, woodruff, Corsican mint, and *Salvia divinorum.* As a general rule, herbs prefer a slightly alkaline situation. If you have an acid

beautiful plants for healthful and aesthetic consumption.

Most artistic endeavors are based upon control of the medium. The gardener, on the other hand, is more like the brush of the painter, the words of a writer, or the instrument of the musician. The gardener is dependent upon the variables of sun, climate, weather, season, insects, soil life, planetary and lunar influences, and the unseen architects of the natural world. The gardener is steward rather than creator in the truest sense, though designing a garden necessitates recognizing all influences affecting plant life and creating a harmonious balance of growth factors for individual plants and the garden as a whole.

When designing an herb garden, you must have a starting point. Walk around your potential garden site and

soil, the pH can be balanced with the addition of lime or wood ashes. Good drainage is essential. Poorly drained soils can be improved by deep cultivation or by adding sand or compost. Herbs require less water than most vegetables. Many herbs originate in the dry, gravelly soils of the Mediterranean region; therefore, watering will be required only in times of drought. Some herbs, such as mints, angelica, lovage, and basil, grow best in a fairly moist soil. Most soils will accommodate herbs. These are general guidelines, but each herb's specific requirements are listed in the plant-by-plant entries which follow.

Now put your design on paper. Graph paper is wonderful for designing. Another good idea is to take an eight-by-ten black-and-white photograph of your house, yard, or plot; then on a piece of tracing paper placed over the photo, sketch in general outline the garden's appearance, discovering how it contrasts and blends with architectural lines.

A garden design is a personal thing. Indeed, there are as many ways to garden as there are gardeners. The garden should reflect the lifestyle and inspiration of the gardener rather than reproduce a classical design—unless, of course, the garden is designed for preservation or restoration purposes.

To a great extent, herb gardens have become stylized and stagnant over the past fifty years. They echo gardens of old with little new creative input. The same ol' plants are often situated in the same ol' settings. However, elements of historical garden design cannot be discounted as major influences in creating new herb gardens. They are a source of ideas. If you have the opportunity, visit historical display gardens at museums. The herb gardens at Mount Vernon and the Williamsburg restoration in Virginia; Old Sturbridge in Sturbridge, Massachusetts; the William Penn Museum in Harrisburg, Pennsylvania; the National Herb Garden in Washington, D.C.; the Strybing Arboretum in San Francisco, and other museums and botanical gardens can be a source of inspiration for your herb-garden design.

When considering garden possibilities, it is fun to borrow ideas from several traditional horticultural themes

Monarda fistulosa, Purple Beebalm

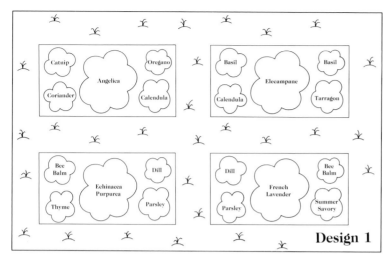

Design 1

such as the intricacies of the formal English knot garden, the peace of the medieval *Hortus Inclusus*, or the reverence for stone and flowing lines in a Japanese garden. Elements from these traditions can be blended with contemporary practices such as double-dug beds from biodynamic/French intensive methods, the permaculture principles of centering agricultural design around perennial plantings, biodynamic ideas on companion planting, and the inclusion of native plants in landscaping.

The following designs are presented to generate new ideas rather than to be copied. They blend elements from traditional and contemporary horticultural themes. They are meant to complement one another. The designs should be considered collectively and separately. Use the ideas to help you conceptualize the best herb-garden design for you and the plants under your care.

DESIGN ONE

A backyard is a retreat for quiet and relaxation—a place to enjoy family and friends. Paul Lee, friend of herbs, has turned his backyard into a setting to enjoy those friends.

As a student of Paul Tillich at Harvard, Paul Lee became fascinated with *thymos*—an old Greek word for courage and vitality—"the courage to be." Discovering that the names for thyme and the thymus gland were both derived from thymos, he set out to learn as much as he could about both. Paul opened a restaurant in Santa Cruz, California, called The Wild Thyme, featuring sweetbreads or *ris de veau* (calves' thymus glands) as the house specialty. He also put herb beds in his backyard and started collecting varieties of

thyme. Today, in a peaceful residential neighborhood in Santa Cruz, Paul's entire backyard is a checkerboard of herb beds, perpetuating Paul's love of thyme and the biodynamic/French intensive techniques of Alan Chadwick.

While a professor at UC Santa Cruz, Paul met Alan Chadwick and invited him to start a garden on the UC campus. A Shakespearean actor and horticultural genius, the British-born Chadwick was once a student of George Bernard Shaw and Rudolf Steiner. He had served as gardener to the state of South Africa and was a musician and artist. At the UC campus, he turned a hillside covered with rock and poison oak into a brilliant paradise, abounding with lush vegetables, flowers, fruits, and herbs. Over the next decade, Chadwick gardens graced a number of California sites, inspiring all who experienced their magic. Since Chadwick's death in 1980, his teachings are carried on through his apprentices. These apprentice programs are listed in the resource section of this book.

Chadwick's methods combine techniques from biodynamic agriculture, begun in 1924 with a series of eight lectures delivered by the Austrian philosopher and spiritual scientist, Rudolf Steiner, plus French intensive horticulture, begun in the 1890s outside Paris. Steiner's lectures on agriculture responded to farmers' questions about the formative forces of nature, the "etheric" nature of plants, and the decline of crop quality and productivity on a given piece of land. Steiner taught that the farm itself is an organism. Soil is a living entity rather than just a chemical mix. Soil health, the basis of a healthy farm organism, is achieved by using compost treated with preparations from fermented plant and animal materials, intended to support microbial soil life and enhance plants' utilization of light. The effects of soil depletion and crop improvement are kept in balance through crop rotation. Companion plantings make use of the subtle interrelationships between plants. The life of the soil, atmospheric influences, and lunar influence are considered along with the effect of the human spiritual nature on the farm organism. Over the past sixty years, the biodynamic approach has proven successful in practice by farmers and gardeners the world over. Like the Chinese concept of the universe, the biodynamic farm organism never remains static.

In French intensive gardens, vegetables were grown in eighteen-inch-deep beds, heavily fertilized with horse manure. Plants were grown closer together so that their mature leaves would touch, creating green mulch that reduced weed growth and helped to retain soil moisture. During winter months, bell-glass jars were placed over seedlings to help them get an early start.

One of the basic tenets of biodynamic/French intensive gardening is the preparation of the raised bed. The beds are usually three to six feet across and as long as desired. The soil is double-dug to a depth of two feet, allowing roots to breathe and encouraging the microbial life of the soil.

This technique is an old gardening practice. In 1821, William Cobbett writes of double-digging, or trenching as he calls it, in his *American Gardener.*

"As to the experience of this preparatory operation, a man that knows how to use a spade, will trench four rods [sixty-six feet of two-foot-wide beds] in a day.... Supposing the garden to contain an *acre*, and the labourer to earn a dollar a day, the cost of this operation will, of course, be *forty dollars. . . .* Poor ground deeply moved is preferable, in many cases, to rich ground with shallow tillage; as when the ground has been deeply moved *once*, it feels the benefit for ever after. A garden is made to last for ages. . . . It is well known to all who have had experience on the subject, that of two plants of almost any kind that stand for the space of three months in top soil of the same quality, one being on deeply moved ground, and the other on ground moved no deeper than is usual, the former will exceed the latter one half in bulk. And, as to trees of all description from the pear-tree down to the currant bush, the difference is so great, that there is no room for comparison" (chapter one, paragraph 21).

You may find it best to start with one hundred- or two hundred-square-foot beds, which can be dug in a day or two, rather than spending forty days trenching an acre, but you'll find the toil necessary for initial preparation worth the effort in higher yields and healthier crops. The beds should be three to six feet wide so you can comfortably reach the

center of the bed without stepping on it. In wide beds, I place a stone or two on which to step or lean at strategic points so as to prevent soil compaction. The soil should be moderately moist before digging. It is too dry if you cannot squeeze it into a ball in the palm of your hand, and too wet if it clings to your shovel. If the soil is dry, water it for two hours a couple of days before digging. Add a one-to-four-inch layer of compost on top of the bed before digging, as well as any other desired soil amendments—lime, wood ashes, rock phosphate, or well-seasoned manure.

To double-dig a bed, start at either end, and with a garden spade dig a trench about one foot wide across the breadth of the bed. Pile this soil at the other end of the bed, or put it directly into a wheelbarrow. You'll need it to fill the last trench. Once the first trench is dug, take a spading fork and loosen the soil at the bottom of the trench to a depth of one foot. If the soil is hard, pry the bottom with a fork and break large clods into smaller pieces as you come to them. Repeat the procedure down the entire length of the bed, piling the soil dug from each trench into the previously dug trench, and forking about a foot deeper. Once you reach the

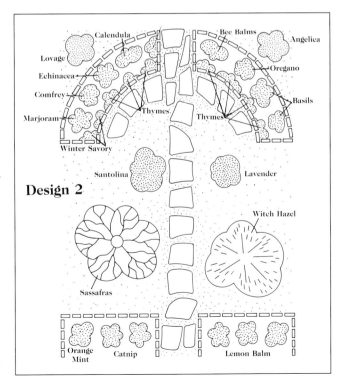

Design 2

Teucrium marum, Cat Thyme, with feline

end, the soil from the first trench can be transferred into the last trench, using either a wheelbarrow or shovel. During the digging process, stand on a piece of plywood placed across the bed so as to minimize soil compaction. For more detailed information on double-digging and biodynamic/French intensive gardening, see John Jeavon's *How to Grow More Vegetables,* listed in the bibliography.

The double-dug bed forms the skeletal structure of the herb-garden designs to follow. Paul Lee's backyard herb garden consists of about forty beds, many of which are three feet by three feet and separated by eighteen-inch sections of grass. His collection includes over one hundred and fifty herb varieties.

Using your own design inspired by the Lee garden, you can plant perennials in some of the beds, reserving others for annual herb crops. In intensive annual beds, plantings can be close together, creating a "green" mulch. Design One is simple and elastic. It can be stretched along existing walkways and borders, or placed in the middle of a lawn. The shapes can be round, oval, square, or rectangular. You can put in one bed or thirty beds—it depends on the size of your lot and your inclination.

DESIGN TWO

The herb garden is often considered independently from the vegetable garden or the overall landscaping scheme. Herbs, however, can serve as primary elements in landscape design. They can be used as borders, as ground covers, and for shade. The warm orange-yellow blossoms of calendula can brighten a border, lavenders planted against a foundation offer a fragrant contrast to a dark-colored house, camomile and creeping thymes can be used as ground covers in a sunny situation, and woodruff and Corsican mint are useful ground covers for shaded areas. Sweet gum, sassafras, and slippery elm trees provide good summer shade. Witch hazel offers shade and brilliant fall foliage, culminating with a display of delicate blossoms after the leaves have dropped.

Double-digging methods can be used in preparing a spot for one tree or, over a period of time, preparing the soil for the entire garden. It takes about five minutes to prepare and double-dig each square foot of surface area. The 288 square feet of surface area in this design would take a total of twenty-four hours to dig by hand.

In this design, Roman camomile, either the petalless variety or the flowerless cultivar 'Treanague', is used as a ground cover along with creeping thyme or the gray-colored creeping woolly thyme. I once had a six-foot by twenty-foot bed of creeping woolly thyme which was started from ten seedlings. Over a period of three years, they spread to fill in the entire one hundred and twenty-square-foot area. Maintenance was minimal. Occasionally we watered it. The plant stands less than one-half-inch tall so it never needed mowing. We walked on it, sat on it, lay on it, even drove tractors over it with little sign of wear or injury. The soft, fuzzy, gray-green foliage satisfied the senses of smell, vision, and touch. Roman camomile doesn't mind some traffic, either, as long as it's random. Stepping stones can be worked into the design to save wear on heavily traveled paths.

Start out with a four-foot by four-foot plot the first year, then increase the size of the ground cover each year for a three-year period until the entire area is planted. By the fourth year, the herbal ground cover will be ready for full use and enjoyment. It's a great summer project for bored high-school or college students. If they start working on it their freshman year, it will be completed by graduation time—the growth and expansion of the garden symbolizing the progress of the student. Ecology Action sells a booklet entitled *Self-Fertilizing Herbal Lawn,* listed in the resource section, offering excellent information on establishing herbal ground covers (see chapter four of Jeavons, Griffin, and Leler 1983).

The raised bed at the rear of the lot can be planted with a mix of annuals and perennials for kitchen use. Tall angelica and lovage can flank either side of the walkways at the bed's ends. Plantings of thymes, prostrate rosemary, or winter savory can spill over the sides of the stones bordering the bed. Calendula and echinacea can be added for color. Just off the walkway in the middle of the herbal ground cover are miniature island beds of lavenders or grey santolina. Their foliage produces a striking and harmonious contrast with the ground cover.

The foundation plantings can be in groups—three or more plants of the same species. In this design, the beds

Asclepias tuberosa, Pleurisy Root

against the house are planted with lemon balm or catnip, both of which will do well in the partial shade of the sassafras tree, and witch hazel is planted near the entryway. Orange mint can be planted under a dripping faucet for use in fresh, iced mint tea.

DESIGN THREE

The Japanese feel that nature is mysterious and incomprehensible. Early inhabitants of Japan viewed their beautiful landscape as the home of numerous nature spirits called *kami*. Kami inhabit mountains, rivers, trees, stones, or any natural objects unusual in shape and form. Stones are thought to be hollow, and as the kami dwelling inside grow, so do the stones. The kami have personalities that can be soothed and persuaded into cooperating with the garden.

This garden design is for those who live in a spot where gardening might be perceived as impossible—among large rocks. It is inspired by the reverence for stone in the Japanese garden, and an appreciation for the weathered limestone bluffs of the Ozarks. Here the twisted forms of the native Ashe's juniper, *Juniperus Ashei*, bow from rocky crags, reminding me of conifers in a Han-dynasty jade carving. This must be the home of the kami.

The design is dictated by the lay of the land. Paths are quietly laid between immovable rocks. Next to the path, spaces between rocks are dammed with small stones to hold soil. Balance and harmony are achieved by striking a casual order in the seemingly random disorder of the eroding bluff.

In a hundred-yard radius, nature provides all of the material for the garden: soil, stones for paths and bed walls, even some plants. Growing of its own accord near the garden entrance, sweet goldenrod, *Solidago odora*, is absorbed into the design. Calamint, *Satureja arkansana*, a local mint, is transferred from its nearby habitat to a garden bed. If this was California, native yerba buena (*Satureja Douglasii*) or mugwort (*Artemisia Douglasiana*)

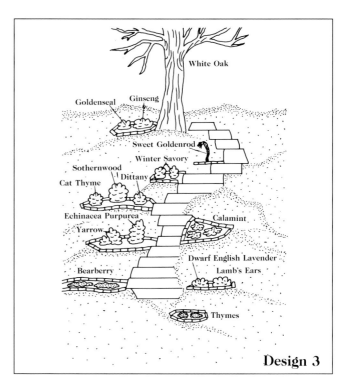

Design 3

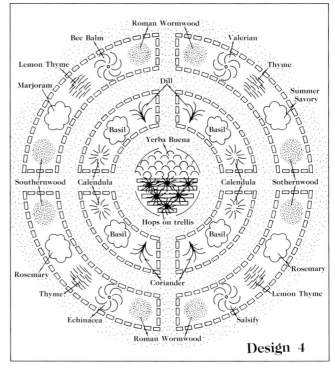

Design 4

might become part of the garden. The garden gently eases into the natural surroundings.

In a one hundred and fifty-square-foot area, we create nine individual beds—all at different levels, and ranging in size from one to six square feet. Half the garden gets full sun, the other half is under the shade of a white oak—the bark of which is a powerful herbal astringent. This makes a unique combination of herb species in a limited space. Wild ginger, goldenseal, and the shade-loving *Echinacea purpurea* grow in the oak's shadow. Thymes and germander are used as evergreens. At the south end of the garden, thymes drape themselves over stones. Native calamint decorates one bed with sprays of delicate foliage and lavender blooms. Can kami possibly take refuge in the tortured shrubbery and cement-entombed earth of the average suburban yard? Perhaps kami delight in sensitive human integration rather than the usual destructive dominance (Mitchell and Wayembergh 1981).

DESIGN FOUR

A place of solitude created within an enclosed garden space dates to Roman times. The *Hortus Inclusus* of medieval times was a garden within a garden, enclosed by hedges or fencing. Planted entirely in turf, it made a quiet space for contemplation and meditation. Such a space, placed in the center or rear of a modern herb garden, provides quiet escape from garden toil and household tasks. An enveloping buffer of hops or passionflowers can filter out environmental noise and create a pleasing shaded habitat just right for relaxing. Lattice sides make a good home for climbing herbs, and provide shade and valuable screening. Sides can be rustic wood posts latticed with thin half-inch-diameter branches of willow, sassafras, oak, or any pliable native wood. If hops or passionflowers are trained up the sides of the structure, they will die back in autumn. Using short, flexible wood sticks as lath, you can create a pleasing design for winter scenery. The top can be covered, left open for a view of the sky, or protected by an overhanging tree branch. Simplicity of design, materials, and execution make the modern *Hortus Inclusus* quick and easy to build, serene, and private.

A bench can be arranged among a floor of yerba buena, Corsican mint, woodruff, or other shade-loving ground covers. The seat can be a slab of oak supported by a stone foundation, flat rocks laid in appropriate positions to provide a reasonably comfortable seat, a simple wooden bench, or metal garden furniture. The enclosed space can be closet sized or as large as desired.

In Design Four, the *Hortus Inclusus* is the garden's focal point. The enclosed area can face the garden, providing a place to reflect upon the garden's design, or it may be placed back-to, enhancing the feeling of seclusion. All paths—those for feet and the flowing visual lines—lead to the space of quietude.

Herbal borders leading to the peaceful space can be in waves of soft textures and subtle coloration. Low-growing *Artemisias*, producing a silver-gray foliage, can blend with springtime sprays of spiderwort and calamint blooms. Rose or golden yarrows spark the colors of late spring and early summer. A background of tansy or St. Johnswort provides late-summer yellow hues.

Over thirty-six million Americans have home gardens. A rapidly growing number of Americans—two million to date—are involved in community-garden programs. One herb garden designed as the focal point of a community-garden site with a *Hortus Inclusus* in the center can provide herbs for fifty gardeners or more, and a relaxing retreat for resting between work spurts. Design Four is inspired by an herb garden designed by David Lansford and volunteers for a community-garden site in Santa Cruz, California; it was a vacant lot that fell victim to development—now a parking lot.

Thymus spp., Thyme

4

PROPAGATING HERBS

In his 1790 *Metamorphosis of Plants*, Goethe observes that plant growth is a rhythm of contractions and expansions; and in its growth progression, the metamorphosis of one plant organ into the next is simply a modification of the previous organ. Thus, flower parts are modified rhythms of leaf growth. According to Goethe's theory, the formative forces of a plant are most highly concentrated in the seed. With the germination of the seed comes the first unfolding expansion in the leaves. At this point, the form concentrated in the seed spatially expands in the leaves. In the flower's calyx, the forces again contract, this time around the central axis. The corolla (a flower's petals) produces the second expansion. The stamens and pistils are produced by the next contraction, the fruit by the third and last expansion, and in the seed, the final concentration of the forces of plant life lie hidden and dormant until its rhythms are again activated by suitable environmental conditions.

As an herb grower, you are the catalyst to set an herb's latent life forces in motion, perpetuating a species for use and enjoyment. Herb gardeners should consider themselves herb propagators. By mastering the simple techniques of propagating annuals, biennials, and perennials, you will find that the potential for expanding garden design, size of plantings, ability to save money on plant purchases, and opportunities for increasing stock for sale or trade is limited only by the amount of time you can

devote to generating new plants.

"Propagating herbs is simple. Anyone can do it," says Kent Taylor. And Kent should know. He operates North America's largest herb nursery, Taylor's Herb Gardens, in Vista, California. Chances are, if you buy herb plants at a commercial greenhouse, natural-food store, or from many small herb plant sellers, the original stock came from the Taylors.

The Taylor nursery is nestled on a peaceful twenty-five acre spread only minutes away from the suburban sprawl bordering San Diego. Herbs thrive in Vista's Mediterraneanlike climate through much of the year. Most of Taylor's seedlings are grown outdoors to produce a heartier stock more likely to endure shipping and display.

A two-acre shade house dominates a visitor's view of the nursery. Here shade-loving herbs such as yerba buena, gota kola, Corsican mint, woodruff, and chervil are matured. Ivy, *Hedera helix*, is also grown in the shade house as a supplemental cash crop. This familiar evergreen perennial is not well known as a medicinal plant; but in both the European and Chinese traditions, a decoction or poultice of the leaves was used to treat skin eruptions and itching.

Each year the Taylors sell over one million herb plants. In one day, as many as fifty thousand plants of one species may be shipped to a broker. Rows of tens of thousands of potted herb seedlings fill an acre-and-a-half near the nursery's entrance. Some of these plants are being started from seed, though most are ready for sale. In this section of the nursery, annual and biennial herbs are started from seed. Hundreds of dill, marjoram, summer savory, caraway, coriander, anise, and fennel plants are at various stages of growth, from tiny emerging leaves to eight-inch-high seedlings ready for sale.

At Taylor's Herb Gardens, seed-grown herbs are sown directly into the pots a consumer will purchase, but you can sow seed for annual and biennial herbs directly in your herb garden as soon as danger of frost has passed. To get a jump on the growing season, start them in flats indoors about eight weeks before the last spring frost. As a general rule of thumb, it is best to start most annual and biennial herbs from seeds.

When you sow seeds outdoors, prepare the seedbed well. Level the soil with a rake, removing any rocks larger than an inch in diameter. Make shallow furrows with a rake or the edge of a hoe as a guide to planting. Seeds should be covered by two to four times their diameter with soil. Tiny seeds, like German camomile, can be mixed with fine sand to help insure even distribution. Fine seed can also be sown on the surface of a well-prepared seedbed, then tamped down to bring the seed into contact with moisture-holding soil particles. At the Taylor nursery, fine seeds start in flats under shade to prevent them from drying out. After you plant the seeds, keep the soil moist but not soggy. The germinating seeds should never be allowed to completely dry out.

Young seedlings can be thinned or transplanted after the first two true leaves appear. What look like first leaves are not actually leaves, but the food-storing tissue of the seeds, known as cotyledons. The true leaves, which have the general appearance of the plant's mature leaves, emerge after the cotyledons. Seed-sown plants at the Taylor nursery take about six to eight weeks to reach a salable size. Most herb seeds germinate in seven to fourteen days, though parsley takes patience. It may need six weeks or more to germinate.

Seeds can be started indoors in almost any type of container. If commercial nursery flats are unavailable, take an empty gallon milk jug and cut it down with scissors or a knife to make a two-inch-deep tray. Cut slits in the bottom for drainage. My favorite seedling medium is a mixture of one part sterile potting soil, one part fine sand,

and one part peat moss. Commercially prepared seed-starting mixes are also available.

Fill the containers with soil mix to about half an inch from the top. Firm the soil down with your hand; then with a pencil, ruler, or finger, mark out rows at two-inch spacings. Sow seed evenly in rows and cover with soil. Make sure the seeds are not planted too close together, as crowded seedlings tend to be weak, leggy, and difficult to transplant.

Spray with a mister to keep the soil moist, or place the container in a larger pan with an inch or two of water so moisture can soak up into the mix through capillary action. Remove from the pan as soon as the soil surface becomes visibly moist. Repeat as necessary. Avoid letting the seeds dry out, but keep the mix from becoming too moist.

The flat can be placed in a window and maintained at a temperature between 65° and 75°F. Seedlings may also be placed under a grow light. Sill-grown seedlings will have to be turned every couple of days because they will bend toward the light.

Poor circulation and excess moisture in a warm situation may cause damping off. Damping off is a fungus disease that appears as a greenish mold on the soil's surface. The primary culprits are the fungi *Pythium ultimum* and *Rhizotonia solani*. Damping off may cause rotting before germination, stem rot near the surface of the medium, or girdling of the stem, which stunts growth and eventually kills the plant. It can be controlled by proper environmental conditions for seedling development or by starting out with sterilized soil containers.

Once seedlings have developed two true leaves, they can be transplanted into larger containers or planted in their garden location if danger of frost has passed. Before planting in the garden, seedlings must be "hardened off" or acclimated to the outdoors by placing them in a shaded area outside and gradually exposing them to full sun over a week's time. Bring plants indoors if there is a danger of frost. Young seedlings should be transplanted on an overcast day or in the late afternoon, and watered well.

Seeds of some perennials, particularly woodland plants, go through a period of dormancy. This may be the result of impermeable seed coats. The seed coats can be softened to allow for faster water uptake and aeration using one of several presowing treatments. In some species, dormancy may also result from immature embryos that need to grow and develop before germinating, or the food-storage tissue and the embryo must undergo physiological changes before germinating. Seeds of such species need to be stratified to break the dormancy and hasten the germination process. Stratification is a long-term treatment (two or three months) under temperatures just above freezing. Successful stratification has three basic requirements: a source of moisture for the seed; low, near-freezing temperatures (35° to 45° F); and aeration—seeds need to breathe, too. Seeds can be stratified in moist sand, peat moss, sphagnum moss, vermiculite, or weathered sawdust. Usually I'll place seeds in a jar of moist sand in the refrigerator for the winter months. I punch holes in the top of the jar for aeration as for a captured butterfly. The stratification medium must be kept moist but not wet. After about three months, plant the seeds in a well-prepared seedbed. Ginseng, goldenseal, sweet gum, spice bush, and witch hazel are among the species whose seed will need to be stratified.

One section of the Taylor nursery is devoted to preparing and maturing seedlings from cuttings or slips. Nearly all of the perennials at Taylor's Herb Gardens are regenerated by this method. Dozens of flats of herb cuttings line tables in checkered patterns as they develop roots and mature into seedlings. Kent feels propagating herbs from cuttings is one of the easiest and most economical ways of increasing his stock.

"We can produce ready-for-sale plants faster from cuttings than by seed. They take four to six weeks to develop roots. Then we pot them and they are ready to sell," Kent explains. "To make a cutting, take pruning shears, scissors, or a knife and cut the desired stem two to five inches long, leaving two leaf nodes or joints. Select cuttings from the vigorous growth of the spring and summer months. Fall cuttings take longer to root. New tip growth is most desirable. With woody-stemmed herbs such as rosemary and lavender, we choose the tender wood."

"After making the cutting, carefully remove the leaves from the lower inch of the stem and stick this section into your rooting medium. Our rooting medium is clean, coarse sand or sponge rock. It should be kept moist until the cuttings develop roots. After several weeks, you can test a cutting to see if it has grown roots simply by tugging gently on the stem. If it firmly resists, it is ready for transplanting."

A half-acre planting of fully matured herbs serves as a specimen garden for visitors and as propagating stock for herbs started from cuttings. Here, beds of English camomile and thymes reach their full potential, lavender blooms entice honeybees, and stately rosemary shrubs grow to splendor. Experimental crops not listed in Taylor's catalog grow in this garden as well. Some of these herbs are propagated in the spring or fall by root divisions others are increased by layering.

Many perennial herbs such as catnip, thymes, the mints, wormwood, bee balm, and tarragon can be propagated by root division. Simply dig the plant in the spring or fall and cut the root into several pieces with a shovel, or pull the roots apart with your hands. Plant in the desired location and water well. The only expenditure with this technique is time.

Layering can be used successfully with lavenders, thymes, rosemary, and other perennials. This method produces new plants while they are still attached to the parent plant. Select a healthy, flexible stem that is growing close to the soil or can be easily bent toward the ground. Dig a small hole with a trowel, place a portion of the stem into the hole, and cover it, leaving three to eight inches of the stem's terminal end above ground. If necessary, pin it down with a tent peg or a hooked stick. It is helpful to remove the leaves and scrape the underside of the stem to be placed in contact with the soil. Within a few weeks, this stem will develop roots and can be clipped from the parent plant for transplanting. The process can be hastened with frequent watering. This is a good way to increase stock in a small garden.

For Kent Taylor, propagating herbs is a livelihood. For you, the herb gardener, it is a way to increase the enjoyment of the garden and the size of your stock at little or no cost. You need only master the skills required to effectively propagate individual plants. It may seem like magic to unleash the concentrated life forces of a seed or coax a stem into producing roots, but you needn't be a wizard to perform the magic. Just follow the simple instructions in this book for each species, and you will gain confidence in your ability to create the best herb garden for your needs.

HARVESTING
& DRYING HERBS

The Algonquin tribes of the northeastern United States, and many other peoples with a close tie to nature, regard plants as real beings, alive and vital as humans are. In many Indian cultures, medicinal herbs are gathered with respect and with attention toward maintaining the goodwill of the plants. When plant lives are to be sacrificed for human benefit, their gifts of food, fragrance, and healing should be respected. Herbs often receive grateful thought and prayers before they are harvested. Usually an offering is made, frequently of tobacco (Algonquin practice) or cornmeal (Hopi practice). If too many plants are pulled or injured, an herb gatherer will replant roots and even offer a prayer for the plant's reincarnation, if the species is rare. If the colony of plants is small, care is taken not to eliminate the population or show disregard for family relationships. Goethe called the relationship of one plant to another the real science of botany, though little information (beyond observations of plant ecologists) exists on the subject. The gatherer's motivations are gratitude, hope for the continuation of the species, and respect for dependence on nature. Ingratitude and wastefulness are considered sins against the forces that created the universe.

Herbs can be considered allies of humans. Dozens of plants counteract human ills. If you are growing herbs for health purposes, you are seeking the goodwill of the plant. Harvesting herbs requires sensitivity. Although it is difficult to measure the efficacy of herbs harvested with care compared to plants that are mined, I believe the attitude and methods of the harvester have a substantial effect on the herb's quality.

I'm not really advocating that you don headdress and beads and recite incantations, dancing circles around your basil bed. What I am advocating is due respect for another life form. If the very existence of the ecology movement has taught us one thing, it is that Western industrialized society has lost respect for the earth and her myriad life forms. A fear of nuclear desecration shadows the world like a vulture. The attitude that produced this ultimate monstrosity of industrialized society continues to breed disregard and disrespect for all life on the planet. I feel it's time civilized men and women start relating to nature with a greater degree of civility. What better place to start than in an herb garden?

Before harvesting, weeding, trimming, mowing, or injuring a plant in any way, let it know your intentions are. If you're concerned about other people's opinion of your sanity, look around to make sure no one is watching. Speak to the plant in a clear voice of appreciation and gratitude. The gentle genius George Washington Carver said, "How do I talk to a little flower? Through it I talk to the Infinite. And what is the Infinite? It is that silent small force. . . . When you look into the heart of a rose, there you experience it" (Clark 1939, 44–45).

Given this respectful and appreciative attitude of the herb gatherer, here are some specific practical points. If you plan to use fresh herbs from the garden, pick sparingly from the plant throughout the growing season. Pinch off flower buds as they develop to encourage a more vigorous and bushier leaf growth. To ensure a plentiful supply, water the plants frequently and sidedress with compost. For many culinary purposes, fresh herbs are superior to dried herbs. It's like the difference between the flavor of a store-bought tomato and one freshly plucked ripe from the backyard vine.

Herbs harvested for leaf material should be cut just as the plant comes into bloom. At this point, the essential oil content of most herbs peaks. This timing is best illustrated by the chemical changes in the essential oil of peppermint at various stages of growth. Premium-quality peppermint oil contains a high percentage of menthol. In the tissue of young peppermint plants, pulegone (the chief chemical component of pennyroyal oil) is the predominant aromatic chemical along with menthofuran. This substance produces a bitter flavor in mint. Before flowering, menthone is the chief constituent of peppermint oil. It possesses a harsher flavor than menthol. As the plant blooms, menthol becomes the oil's primary constituent, producing a clean, sharp peppermint flavor. When flowering ceases, menthol is replaced by methyl acetate, giving the herb a somewhat bitter, fruity flavor. Such studies indicate the importance of timing in harvesting peppermint. Because peppermint is such an important economic plant, many studies have been made on its chemical constituents. Unfortunately, clear information of this nature is not available for most herbs. Therefore, the experience of herb gatherers is your best information on harvest times.

The best hour to harvest is in the morning, just after the dew has dried off the leaves. Later in the day as the sun becomes more intense, chemical changes may occur in the essential oil, lessening its quality. Herbs should be harvested on a clear day; avoid overcast or rainy days as drops of moisture on newly harvested herbs can cause undesirable rust spots or browning.

Catnip, though, is an exception to the rule. At the Sabbathday Lake Shaker community, we had a patch of one hundred and thirty lush catnip plants, a real favorite with honeybees. On sunny days, the catnip bed hummed like an electrical transformer as the honeybees feverishly worked the blossoms. After a few stings on sunny days, we resorted to harvesting catnip on overcast days when the bees were

Calendula officinalis on drying rack
Sister's Shop SDL, Shaker Community

more subdued.

Many leaf herbs will provide several cuttings during the growing season. In one Maine summer, I got as many as seven cuttings off a quarter acre of comfrey. Alfalfa may produce three cuttings, and commercial mint fields are often harvested twice during the growing season. Annuals such as summer savory and basil will produce a second crop if you leave the lower three to six inches of the stem during the first harvest. The remaining stem will soon sprout new shoots, and in a few weeks another harvest can be expected.

Herb flowers such as camomile and calendula should be harvested just as the plant comes into bloom. Handpicking such crops can be slow and tedious work. I have found that a blueberry rake works well for harvesting camomile and calendula blossoms, as well as seeds of some members of the carrot family. The combing action of the blueberry rake allowed me to harvest four three hundred-foot-long rows of camomile in about ten minutes. If we had picked the same camomile by hand, it would've taken several hours.

For best performance in herb harvesting, blueberry rakes need a slight modification. On a blueberry rake, the base of the teeth is blunt edged, causing the rake to pull up the entire plant rather than simply cut off the flower heads. A thin strip of metal can be soldered at the base of the teeth to serve as a cutting edge. A length of piano wire strung across the base of the teeth can serve the same purpose. Drill holes in both sides of the rake near the base of the teeth. Stretch the piano wire across the teeth and fasten it through the holes with appropriately sized screws or nuts and bolts. This modification disassembles easily, allowing the rake to be converted to its original intended use.

An herb harvester needs the proper implements for the job. A good sharp knife is indispensable. A nurseryman's pruning knife is also a good herb-harvesting tool. The pruning knife has a curved blade useful for slicing off one bunch of herbs that can immediately be tied and hung to dry. A tea-pruning knife is another wonderful tool for harvesting herbs. Designed for pruning tea bushes, it has a hooked point and is great for cropping a comfrey patch. My favorite herb-harvesting tool is a banana knife. Banana-knife blades are four to six inches long and slightly curved at the end. A new banana knife is difficult to find; but on an average, one out of every four junk stores with a tool display will have one or two banana knives. A good pair of pruning shears works well for harvesting woody-stemmed herbs. A sturdy, well-sharpened garden spade is indispensable for harvesting root crops. For those who wish to harvest tree barks, a draw knife is the tool you need. See the resource section for these and other tools.

Roots are dug either in the spring before leaf growth commences, or in the fall after the leaves have died back. Spring-dug roots generally contain more moisture than fall-dug roots, and therefore take longer to dry. Roots need to be washed before drying. Calamus, and other plants with small, lateral rootlets, are washed with greater ease if the rootlets are cut off. Angelica has a tendency to entangle itself, forming pockets where dirt collects. Care should be taken to wash as much dirt as possible from these areas, but a stiff brush will whisk away what remains after drying.

Larger roots, such as those of elecampane, will need to be split lengthwise to expose a greater portion of the root to the air so they can dry without molding.

Biennial roots are best harvested in the fall of the first year's growth or in the following spring. As the plant flowers in the second year, the strength of the root is exhausted. At this time, the roots may become woody, pithy, and hollow.

Barks of trees and shrubs are time consuming but fun to harvest. If you must strip the bark from the main trunk because lower branches are too high to reach, take care to ensure that the tree survives. Never girdle the tree. Cut only from one side. The north side is the best place to gather bark as it tends to be more constricted and dense. The growth does not have the added catalyst of direct sunlight as it does on the south and west sides. Anyone who makes maple syrup hangs buckets on the south and west sides of trees where the sap flow is greatest.

Many barks can be gathered in the winter. The outer barks of many trees, including slippery elm, sassafras and wild cherry, are discarded. Only the inner bark is used.

Herb seeds should be gathered as they begin to ripen. Some seeds such as anise tend to ripen on the plant over a period of time so that immature and completely ripe seeds are found on the same seed head. If the seed is fully grown but not ripe, harvest the unripe seed along with the mature seed and cure it in your drying space.

Commercial anise growers harvest the seed while it is still green, tie the tops in bundles, and then stack them in conical piles until the seed has ripened. Early harvesting ensures that seeds do not shatter from the plants. The tips of anise, as they begin to turn a gray-green color, should be harvested. If left to the weather, seeds may turn an undesirable black color, lessening the quality.

Every herb gardener should let a small patch of each annual herb mature, then collect the ripe seed for planting the following spring. A few calendula or basil plants left to go to seed will produce more than enough for the next year. Some plants can be left to self-sow in the garden, and the resulting seedlings can be transplanted the following spring. If given the chance, coriander, dill, German camomile, and angelica will replant themselves.

You can grow the finest, lushest, most potent herbs; but if you dry them poorly, all your efforts will be for naught. Drying is simply a means of preserving herbs. By removing moisture, you prevent molding, enzyme activity, or chemical changes.

Unless you have a specialized drying structure where airflow and temperature can be monitored and controlled, you will deal with new circumstances each time you dry an herb. Herb drying is an art, and book knowledge is no substitute for practical experience.

Herbs should be dried in the shade. Direct sunlight will cause leaves to turn dark brown or black. The object in herb drying should be to retain as much of the fresh herb as possible.

Rapid evaporation of the essential oil or changes in its chemical constituents may occur if an herb is dried at temperatures exceeding 90° F. If heat is forced too quickly over the outer cells of a leaf, those cells may harden before they can be replaced by moisture from the leaf's inner tissue, thereby sealing moisture in the leaf and causing it to mold in storage. Air temperature should be kept relatively low at first (80° to 85° F), then increased when the plant material is almost dry. Temperature control and continuous airflow over plant material are the most important factors for efficient drying.

Herbs can be spread to dry on racks covered with muslin, newspaper, wood splint, or lath. About one pound of fresh leaf material can be dried in a square foot of space. Pile herbs loosely at first. Adequate air circulation is essential.

For small amounts of herbs, tying them in bunches and hanging them to dry work best. Bunches should be relatively small; a loose handful allows for good air circulation. Once I lost forty bunches of comfrey because in attempting to save space, I had made bunches that were too large and tight. The leaves on the inside of the bunches literally composted. For your own benefit, you might want to record fresh weight, dried weight, and the percentage of weight lost to moisture. Experience will show you the limitations.

As soon as the herbs are dry—when they feel crisp to the touch—they should be stored in airtight containers. If left to hang after drying, some herbs will reabsorb moisture from the air. On a humid day, wormwood may reabsorb 25 percent of its dried weight. Glass containers are best. Plastic and paper bags "breathe," allowing essential oils to evaporate.

Matricaria recutita, German Chamomile Harvest, Sabbathday Lake, Maine, Shaker Community, with blueberry rake.

CHAPTER

6

YOUR FRIENDLY NEIGHBORHOOD HERBS

ANGELICA

Angelica archangelica L., *A. atropurpurea* L.
(an-jell'-ik-a ark-an-jell'-ik-a; at-ro-pur-pur'-ee-a)
Umbelliferae (Apiaceae)—Carrot Family

The genus Angelica is represented by about fifty species in the Northern Hemisphere. *A. archangelica*, a European species, and *A. atropurpurea*, a North American species, are bold, stout biennials or short-lived perennials (lasting three to five years) which die after forming seed. These stately plants are useful as a focal point in an herb garden. Before producing flower stalks, the immature stems are about a foot high. After maturing, the stalks of *A. archangelica* are large, ribbed, smooth, hollow, and often have a light purple cast. *A. atropurpurea's* stalk is usually dark purple. When backlit, the leaves are a pleasing chartreuse color. Each leaf consists of numerous leaflets divided into two or three main groups, which are again divided into smaller groups. The edges are finely toothed. The leaf stalks flatten horizontally as they clasp the main stem. The flower head is a spherical umbel, often as large as a softball, with numerous tiny greenish-white flowers. The seeds are about one-fourth inch long, flattened on one side and convex on the other, with three ribs. They have thin, paperlike, winged sides. About twenty-five to thirty oil tubes (vittae) adhere to the seeds in each fruit. The taproots are short, thick, and

fleshy with numerous intertwining rootlets. The taste of the fresh leaves is warm and pungent, sweet at first, with a slightly bitter aftertaste. *A. atropurpurea* has a lovagelike odor, while the fragrance of *A. archangelica* is similar to musk. (Lovage is a close relative of angelica in the carrot family.)

Angelica is propagated from seeds or by dividing offshoots from old roots, possibly a better method since angelica seed has limited viability and generally only remains viable for about six months. The seed can also be refrigerated for planting the following spring, stored at about 41° F. Kent Taylor has frozen angelica seed and kept it viable for two years. It is best to plant seeds in late summer or early autumn soon after they have ripened. Be patient. Angelica may take a month or more to germinate. The seed needs some light for germination, so it should be tamped into the soil rather than buried. Occasionally, self-sown seedlings appear and can be transplanted to a permanent location in the spring. Sow seed in the fall or spring one-half inch deep in well-prepared seedbeds. Give the plants one to two feet of space in each direction.

Angelica enjoys a fairly rich, light, well-drained but moist loam. It loves partial shade and being close to running water, yet is adaptive to most garden soils. It likes a cool climate. It prefers a slightly acid soil with a pH of 5 to 7. If you dig the plant without disturbing the roots, angelica transplants with ease, and in hospitable habitats will grow eight feet high. When the seedlings reach a height of three to four inches, they can be transplanted at one-foot spacing in rows two to three feet apart, with about twenty thousand plants per acre (Hälvä 1990). An acre will produce eight to eleven pounds of seed and eight hundred to thirteen hundred pounds of dried root (twelve thousand pounds of fresh root per acre). Large roots may weigh up to three pounds. Planted as a companion with angelica, stinging nettles reportedly increase angelica's oil content by 80 percent. Angelica is subject to aphid attacks. Spray infested flower heads with a cup of water that has had six crushed cloves of garlic soaked in it.

All parts of the plant are useful. The leaves should be harvested carefully the first fall so that the main stem is not damaged. The root is harvested the first or second fall or in the spring of the second year. Two-year-old roots are most desirable. The globe-shaped umbels are harvested as the seeds ripen and dry in shade at 80° F. Roots should be carefully cleaned before drying, and larger roots should be sliced into smaller pieces. Dried angelica is subject to insect infestations and should be stored in sealed containers. The root must be harvested soon after the seeds ripen, as it will quickly rot in the ground after the plant has matured.

The young stalks of angelica can be peeled and eaten sparingly in salads or cooked in two waters as a vegetable. Honey added to the second boiling creates a delightful sweetmeat. The Laplanders preserve the main and flower stalks as seasoning for butter or milk, or to eat fresh. Cooked with milk and *Rumex* species, angelica was used to make a coagulated dish stored for winter use (Hälvä 1990). The dried leaves make a delicate tea substitute. Norwegians use the powdered root as a flour for baking bread. The Lapps preserve fish by wrapping them in angelica leaves. As vindication of this bit of folklore, researchers have found angelica-root oil to have antibacterial and antifungal properties.

Angelica species have diaphoretic, expectorant, nervine, carminative, stimulant, and emmenagogic qualities. In Europe, angelica is used for treating colds, coughs, bronchial troubles, urinary disorders, and indigestion.

In China, at least ten species of angelica are used, the most common being *A. sinensis* (Oliv.) Diels., generally called "dang-qui." It was listed in the earliest Chinese materia medica, *Shen-nong Ben Cao Jing* (ca. A.D. 200). "Dang-qui" means "proper order." Dr. Shiu Ying Hu states, "The root stock of Chinese angelica is by far the foremost drug consumed in China. It is used more frequently and in larger amounts than the generally recognized drugs in China: licorice and ginseng" (Morelli 1980, 12).

It is taken for menstrual irregularity, dysmenorrhea, rheumatism, boils, ulcers, anemia, and other ailments. Water extracts cause the smooth uterine muscles to contract and alcohol extracts cause them to relax. It tranquilizes the cerebral nerves and serves as a cardiotonic.

Both the seeds and roots contain about 1 percent of the essential oil. The root oil consists mainly of phellandrene, alpha-pinene, and limonene. The seed oil is similar to that of the root. The oils are rich in coumarins, including osthol, angelicin, umbelliferone, bergapten, and psoralene, which, if

Angelica

taken internally, can cause photodermatitis when skin is exposed to the sun. If ingesting large amounts of angelica, you should avoid direct sunlight. The seed oil contains imperatorin, a coumarin. Next to juniper berries, angelica is the main flavor in gin. It is also used in liqueurs such as Benedictine and Chartreuse.

ANISE
Pimpinella anisum L.
(pim-pi-nel'-a an-ize'-um)
Umbelliferae (Apiaceae)—Carrot Family

Of the one hundred and forty species in the genus *Pimpinella*, only anise, *P. anisum*, is familiar to gardeners. Anise, native to Europe, has been cultivated for at least two millennia, although its exact origins are unknown, perhaps in the Mediterranean from Greece to Egypt. Anise has sporadically escaped from cultivation in North America. It's an erect, though sometimes sprawling, annual which grows to twenty inches in height. The leaves are long stemmed, rounded, or three-lobed, and coarsely toothed at the base of the plant. As the plant matures, the leaves become more finely divided, producing feathery wisps toward the flower head. Delicate yellowish-white flowers are borne on large umbels. The greenish-gray fruits (generally called seeds) are pear shaped and about one-eighth inch long with ten prominent ribs and short hairs. Each fruit contains about thirty vittae (tubes containing essential oil).

Propagation is by seed. Because anise does not transplant well, it should be sown directly into the garden. Seed should be planted in the early spring, as anise takes one hundred and thirty to one hundred and forty days to mature. It needs a temperature of 70° F to germinate. Use fresh seed, as viability deteriorates rapidly after two years. Sow to a depth of one-fourth to one-half inch. Three-inch seedlings should be thinned to six-inch spacings. Folk wisdom holds that anise will germinate better if sown with coriander. Seedlings develop slowly and must be kept free of weeds. One ounce of seed should sow a row one hundred and fifty feet long; five pounds will plant an acre with rows every three feet.

Anise is the most persnickety of all herbs. It demands perfect weather and relatively uniform rainfall and temperatures during the growing season. Long wet or dry spells will not help this fastidious plant. Anise wilts under excessive heat and therefore is difficult to grow in the South. A light, well-drained, moderately rich sandy loam is preferable. Given a good supply of nitrogen, anise has been found to yield larger quantities of high-quality fruit. A beneficial, fine-textured, moisture-retentive soil can easily be created in a raised bed. Soil pH should be around 6 to 7.5. Anise needs full sun. An acre, grown under good conditions, may produce four hundred to six hundred pounds of seed.

The ripening fruits should be carefully monitored, as some seeds on the same umbel ripen quicker than others. As soon as the tip of the fruits turn gray, harvest. If left to the weather, seeds may turn an undesirable black color.

Anise's culinary potential far exceeds its traditional use in breads, cookies, cakes, candies, and liqueurs. Try a half to a whole teaspoon in four quarts of potato or lentil soups. Crush one-half teaspoon of seed with a mortar and pestle and add to salads. Use your imagination!

Anise is an aromatic stimulant, carminative, expectorant, stomachic, and galactogenic. It is one of the best herbal remedies for relieving gas in the digestive system. Used in laxative formulas, anise helps prevent cramping in the bowels. A strong tea will break up bronchial mucus and stimulate milk flow.

The oil of star anise, *Illicium verum*, is almost chemically identical to that of anise. They are used interchangeably in the distilling, confectionary, and perfume industries.

The seeds contain 1 to 4 percent of volatile oil by weight. The oil contains 75 to 90 percent trans-anethole, estragole, beta-caryophyllene, and anise ketone. Anethole is the main substance responsible for anise's so-called licorice flavor.

Anise

ANISE HYSSOP

Agastache foeniculum (Pursh) O. Kuntze, *A. rugosa*
(Fisch. & C. A. Mey.) O. Kuntze.
(a-gas-take'-ee fee-nik'-you-lum) (rue-go'sa)
Labiatae (Lamiaceae)—Mint Family

I often wonder where some common plant names
originated. Anise hyssop is a common name that could
confuse even a botanist. The plant does not resemble hyssop
or anise, though its flavor is aniselike. The thirty or so
members of this genus are collectively known as giant
hyssops. They are native to eastern Asia and North America
and are found in the north-central, central, and southwestern United States in dry thickets, plains, and barrens.

Agastache foeniculum is robust and attractive, an erect,
hardy perennial growing two to four feet high. Usually
when it reaches a foot, it begins to branch. The stems are
square and generally smooth between the internodes, while
the nodes and lowermost stems are slightly hairy. The leaves
are opposite, generally oval shaped, slightly heart shaped at
the base, tapering to an acute angle at the apex. They are
about three inches long and two inches wide. The margins
have sharp-edged teeth. Small, soft, gray hairs cover the
lower leaf, while the upper surface is hairless, but rough to
touch. Flowers are borne on dense, terminal, cylinder-
shaped spikes two to four inches long. The flower head has
large conspicuous bracts, often casting a slightly lighter hue
of purple than the flowers. The flowers are blue-purple,
about five-sixteenths of an inch long, and have two pairs of
stamens: the upper pair curve downward, the lower pair
curve upward, causing the pairs to cross. Anise hyssop's
showy violet display begins from June to August and lasts
well into autumn. It occurs in moist woodlands, particularly along lake shores and streams and sometimes in wet
ditches or prairies. It ranges from southern Ontario to
northern Iowa and northwestern Nebraska, through the
Dakotas, westward to Colorado and Saskatchewan.

Another common species in American gardens is often
sold as either Korean mint or anise hyssop, the Asian
native—*A. rugosa*. For the casual observer, the main points
that distinguish it from *A. foeniculum*, without getting
technical, are that its stems are usually white and hairy on
the upper part, and it tends to be more strongly branched
than its American counterpart. Korean mint blooms from
August through November. It is indigenous to East Asia,
occurring in Japan, much of the Chinese mainland, Korea,

eastern Siberia, and Taiwan. It grows in moist grassy places
in mountains, valleys, and along streams.

Other Agastache species found in American gardens
include mosquito plant (*A. cana*), Mexican giant hyssop
(*A. mexicana*), yellow giant hyssop (*A. nepetoides*), purple
giant hyssop (*A. scrophulariifolia*), and nettle-leaf giant
hyssop (*A. urticifolia*).

Propagation is by seed sown in the spring or fall,
cuttings, or root division. The seed germinates easily.
Self-sown volunteers often pop up under established
plants. Young seedlings are easily transplanted, and even
the mature plant transplants with ease at any point in its
growth cycle.

It thrives in a sandy but moist, well-drained loam, and
grows lush in a rich soil. Full sun is preferable, but it will
grow without stretching in light shade. Plants should be
given about eighteen-inch spacings. In China, *A. rugosa* is
grown commercially in Taiwan, Hainan, and Yunnan.

Anise hyssop makes a fine tea. I feel it is a classic example
of an herb tea with good economic potential. It is easy to

Anise Hyssop

grow, harvest, and dry; it produces well and it has a familiar, much-enjoyed flavor. Members of the genus have been grown for use as a beverage tea, spice in foods, honey plant, and in China, as a medicinal plant.

In China, the aerial parts of *A. rugosa* are harvested in late summer or autumn, when the plant is beginning to flower. The herb is dried in shade or after the stems are cut into slices. The dried herb (including stems) of the Asian *A. rugosa* is the Chinese herb "huo-xiang." It is used in prescriptions for heatstroke, headache, fever, and tightness in the chest, and to increase appetite, allay nausea, and treat diarrhea. The stems with leaves have also been used in prescriptions to treat angina pain. The leaves are applied as a poultice for sores of the hands and feet. In experiments the plant has been shown to stimulate gastric secretion, increase digestion and relax blood capillaries. It also has a strong antifungal effect.

Anise hyssop was used by northern Plains Indians as a beverage tea, and the infusion was also used as a sweetener. The flowers were often included in Cree medicine bundles. The Chippewa used the root for coughs and respiratory problems. The Cheyenne utilized an infusion of the herb for chest pain due to coughing, colds, fevers, and most importantly, to correct a dispirited heart, weak heart, or chest pain (Moerman 1986). The fact that both Asian populations and American Indian groups used two different Agastache species found on opposite sides of the world for the treatment of pains associated with heart conditions would seem to suggest an interesting research lead for the future.

A. rugosa has a volatile oil containing methylchavicol, anethole, anisaldehyde, and p-methoxycinnamaldehyde. Methyleugenol has also been identified as a major component (83.5 to 96.3 percent) in Japanese studies. *A. foeniculum* contains methylchavicol, limonene, caryophyllene, and germacrene B (up to 92 percent of the oil content), in addition to thirty-five other compounds (Nykänen, Holm, and Hiltunen 1989). In some germplasm, eugenol and methylchavicol have been found in equal amounts (43.7 percent). According to a recent study by Purdue University and USDA researchers, methylchavicol is the chief constituent of the essential oil in both species (ranging from 46.7 to 94.6 percent). High variations in the quality and quantity of the essential oil were observed in ten accessions of *A. foeniculum*. For example, the main constituent, methylchavicol, ranged from 6.27 to 94.6 percent of the oil!

The oil itself varied in content from 0.07 to 2.45 percent. The flowers in this species generally contained higher levels of essential oil, with lower values in *A. rugosa*. Other compounds found in both species, at levels above 1 percent, include beta-bourbonene, bornyl acetate, cadinene, alpha-cadinol, camphene, damascenone, ionone, isomenthone, linalool, myrcene, ocimene, pulegone, and spathulenol (Charles, Simon, and Widrlechner 1991). This study confirmed what could be predicted from reviewing the small amount of research on the chemistry of this plant—endless variation.

BASIL

Ocimum basilicum L., *O. kilimandscharicum* Guerbe, *O. sanctum* L., *O. gratissimum* L.
(oss'-i-mum ba-sil'-ik-um; kil-i-mand-shay'-ree-um; sank'-tum; gra-tis'-i-mum)
Labiatae (Lamiaceae)—Mint Family

If I had space for only one herb in my garden, it would be reserved for basil, *Ocimum basilicum*, or its varieties. Basil is probably the most widely cultivated herb in American gardens. The genus *Ocimum* is represented by over 160 species of annuals and short-lived perennials native to warm, temperate regions of Asia, Africa, and South and Central America. Despite the economic importance of basil, its taxonomy remains confused because of its endless variations under cultivation.

O. basilicum and its large-leafed 'Italian' and 'Lettuce leaf' varieties are extensively cultivated in the United States and account for most seeds sold as sweet basil. *O. basilicum* is an erect, branched annual and grows three feet high. The leaves are bright green, smooth, oval, and acutely pointed with entire (without teeth) or slightly toothed margins. Leaves of *O. basilicum* are about one-and-a-half to two inches long, though the leaves of the lettuce-leaf variety may reach four inches in length. Flowers are arranged on racemes. They are one-fourth to one-half inch long, in whorls (verticillasters) of six flowers, with two opposite groups of three flowers. The whorls may be compact or spaced some distance apart. Two tiny, leaflike bracts are arranged opposite one another below each whorl. The cuplike calyx has a broad, rounded upper lip, its margin curving upward. The lower lip has four sharp, pointed lobes, two on the sides and two at the lower edge. The flowers are white to purple in color, with broad, four-lobed upper lips and a narrow, four-lobed lower lip. The black seeds are about one-sixteenth of an inch in diameter and produce mucilage when soaked in water.

Bush basil, *O. basilicum* 'Minimum' (*O. minimum* L.), is a dwarf variety with tiny leaves, usually eight to twelve inches tall. The flowers may be in short terminal spikes with three to four whorls, or on the stems among the leaves. One form grows in a round mass or ball shape, another has purple leaves and flowers.

O. basilicum 'Purpurascens,' purple basil, has deep purple stems and leaves, sometimes mottled with green. The flowers are lilac toward the centers, becoming a paler white-lavender on the edges. The cultivar 'Dark Opal', developed in the 1950s at the University of Connecticut, is consistently purple with no mottling.

O. basilicum 'Citriodora,' lemon basil, has a pleasing citrus scent. It grows to be about a foot tall and has small leaves about five-eighths of an inch wide and one-and-a-half inches long. This tender annual hails from Southeast Asia and Australia.

O. kilimandscharicum, camphor basil, is a tender perennial native to tropical Africa, growing more than three feet high. The leaves have a strong camphor odor and are about one inch wide and three inches long. This is a good perennial for southern climates, but will not survive a freeze. Unlike sweet basil, the leaves of this species have tiny hairs, giving it a grayish cast. It is best propagated from cuttings. The racemes may be up to one foot long.

O. sanctum, holy basil, is a native of Malaysia and India. It grows from one to two feet tall and has many branches. In India, it is called "tulasi" and is venerated by the Hindus. Tulasi is used as an amulet to protect the body in life and death and is a "giver of children." An immortal plant of the gods, it is worshipped in hymns and embodies perfection itself—the mystery of the creator is contained in the mystery of tulasi. According to Helen H. Darrah, author of *The Cultivated Basils*, (1980) most seed sown in the United States as *O. sanctum* or "spice basil" is probably a hybrid of *O. canum* and *O. basilicum* var. True, *O. sanctum* is seldom seen in American gardens.

O. gratissimum L., East Indian or tree basil, may grow six feet tall in regions with no frost, and the hairy leaves may be as long as six inches with a width of three and one-half inches, though the plant seldom attains such size under cultivation in North America. Smaller forms grow from

two to three feet tall. It has a strong clover scent.

Basil is started from seed sown indoors in late March or early April, or directly in the garden as soon as the danger of frost has passed and the soil has warmed up. Seed germinates in five to fourteen days, blooming begins eight to ten weeks after planting, and full bloom takes twelve to fourteen weeks. Seeds may rot in a cold, damp soil, as happened to my basil planted in the spring of 1978. We had over twenty-five days of rain that June. The soil surface became crusty on the few sunny days we had, and the seed was sealed in the ground, rotting before it could germinate. Seed may also slip up to the soil's surface after a rain because of the slippery coat produced by the mucilage in the seed. Sow to a depth of one-fourth to one-half inch. Expected germination rates should be between 80 and 95 percent. The seed will remain viable for over a decade if refrigerated. About six pounds of seed will plant an acre.

Basil

Ocimum basilicum — Basil, Meadowbrook Herb Garden, Wyoming, Rhode Island

Basil is perhaps the most useful cooking herb with diverse culinary potential. It is excellent with tomato dishes, carrots, green beans, lentils, zucchini, chicken, red meats, and fish. Chop fresh leaves for soups and salads. Use the following recipe for a delicious pesto:

1 cup fresh basil leaves
1 cup fresh parsley leaves
1/2 cup olive oil
1/3 cup water
3 cloves fresh garlic
1 handful of chopped almonds

Mix ingredients in blender, starting out with the olive oil and about one-fourth of the basil and parsley. Slowly add the remaining ingredients. Serve cold on pasta or any of the foods mentioned above.

Make basil vinegar for salads by placing one plant's leaves in a pint of your favorite wine, rice, or cider vinegar.

Basil is high in vitamin A, vitamin C, calcium and iron. It contains about 14 percent protein and over 60 percent carbohydrates.

In his *The Family Herbal* (1812), John Hill states, "Basil is little used [medicinally], but it deserves to be much more. A tea made of the green plant is good against all obstructions. No simple is more effective for gently promoting the menses, and for removing the complaints which naturally attend their stoppage" (26). In old herbal literature, crushed leaves are recommended for the stings of bees and scorpions. Basil has been used for mild nervous disorders and rheumatic pains. A snuff of the dried leaves is used for nervous-tension headaches. In Central America, *O. basilicum* is put into the ears to cure deafness. The Chinese use basil to relieve stomach spasms and kidney ailments and to promote blood circulation before and after childbirth. Mexican-Americans use basil for menstrual and labor pains. For earache, the powdered leaves are steeped in olive oil.

Camphor basil, *O. kilimandscharicum*, is used in Nigeria for colds and children's stomachaches. The fresh leaves are chewed or the roots are boiled in water.

The leaves of *O. gratissimum* are used in India for chutneys and as a cooling agent for gonorrhea. Rheumatism and paralysis are treated with fumigations and baths made from the herb. A soothing decoction is made from the mucilaginous seeds. A decoction of the leaves or whole plant

O. basilicum and its varieties like a fairly rich, moist garden soil and full sun. If the soil is too rich, the plants will produce lush leaf growth with poor oil content. The soil should be well aerated; a double-dug bed is perfect for basil culture. The soil pH should fall between 5 and 8. Cultivate the plants when young, being careful not to damage the fast-growing root system. After the first crop is cut, the soil around the roots should not be disturbed. Pull weeds by hand. Give basil seedlings eighteen to twenty-four-inch spacings. Water basil at the base of the plant, as cold water may produce spotting on the leaves—especially if it's watered in the morning and exposed to intense sunlight. Basil is not drought tolerant and can be damaged by heat stress. Judicious irrigation with even moisture throughout the growing season, supplied by drip irrigation, will help ensure a good crop. An acre of basil may produce one to two tons of dried leaf. The basils are tender annuals, usually succumbing to the first frost.

Leaf harvesting may begin just before the plants bloom. At this time, the lower leaves begin to turn yellow. Cut three to six inches above the ground to ensure a good second growth. For fresh harvest, pinch off the flower buds as they develop, causing the plants to branch. Take leaves as needed. From the field to the drying area, basil must be handled with care. Bruising the leaves releases the essential oil and causes the leaves to turn black. Basil has a fairly succulent stem and takes longer to dry than other herbs.

(known as "agbo" in Nigeria) is used for the treatment of fevers, stomach ailments, constipation, and to expel worms. The oil has been shown to be antimicrobial. Several chemotypes have been identified. Eugenol and thymol have been considered major components of the plant's oil, but a recent study found one chemotype to be very high in geraniol (83.7 to 88.8 percent). Geraniol is widely used as a fragrance and flavor ingredient, and this chemotype of *O. gratissimum* could in the future serve as an important source (Charles and Simon 1992).

The sacred "tulasi" (Sanskrit) or "tulsi" (Hindu), *O. sanctum*, is an ingredient in rheumatic prescriptions, is an expectorant, and its root is boiled for fevers. Tulasi has been used to alleviate vomiting, expel intestinal worms, and remove cold and evil spirits. In the Philippines, a tea of the roots is given to women in childbirth, and the flowers are rubbed on the head as a perfume.

O. basilicum has stomachic, tonic, carminative, galactogenic, emmenagogic, and gastric-antispasmodic qualities. A recent study showed that both water and alcoholic extracts of the plant produce strong antiulcer activity. This effect may result from flavonoid glycosides augmenting the gastric mucosal barrier and decreasing gastric-acid output and peptic activity (Akhtar, Akhtar, and Khan 1992).

The essential oil of basil contains linalool and methylchavicol as the main components, with varying amounts of 1.8—cineole, alpha-pinene, beta-pinene, mycrene, ocimene, terpinolene, camphor, methyl cinnamate, eugenol, borneol, geraniol, anethole, safrole, camphor, and other components. Concentrations of these chemicals vary greatly depending upon the species, variety, time of harvest, soil, and weather conditions. Different qualities of basil essential oil are traded on commercial markets. The European type is characterized by higher levels of linalool and methylchavicol. Egyptian-type basil oil has higher concentrations of methylchavicol and lower levels of delta-linalool. The type known as Reunion or Comoro basil oil is virtually linalool-free, and contains high concentrations of methylchavicol, in addition to 1.8—cineole, borneol, camphor, and eugenol. It has a spicy, harsher odor (Simon, Quinn, and Murray 1990). Basils having a strong clove scent contain high amounts of eugenol—clove-bud oil contains up to 90 percent eugenol. Basil oil reportedly has worm-expelling qualities, plus antimicrobial, fungistatic, nematocidal, and insecticidal properties. The oil is used commercially for fragrance in perfumes, soaps, toothpastes, mouthwashes, and in flavoring liqueurs such as Chartreuse.

BAY TREE, SWEET BAY, BAY LAUREL
Laurus nobilis L.
(lor'-us no'-bil-iss)
Lauraceae—Laurel Family
Plate 9

The bay tree is a familiar spice; the flat, dried leaves are known as bay leaves commercially. It is an evergreen shrub or small tree, up to sixty feet in height in subtropical climates, but is usually seen in the United States as a small container-grown bush. The twigs are slender and smooth with narrowly oblong-lanceolate, glabrous, glandular-dotted, entire (without teeth), aromatic leaves two to four inches in length, and about three-fourths to one-and-one-half inches wide. The small ovoid fruit is black when ripe. The plant is native to the Mediterranean region and other places in Europe with favorable climates. In Europe, the leaves are both cultivated and harvested from the wild. Major production countries include Belgium, France, Greece, Portugal, Spain, and the Canary Islands. It is also grown in Turkey, Algeria, Guatemala, and to some extent in southern California.

Bay is propagated from seeds or cuttings. Seeds need to be fresh to remain viable and are difficult to obtain. Cuttings of young twigs taken in late summer can be heeled in sand, but they may take more than six months to produce roots. The easiest way to establish a plant is simply to buy one. It thrives best in a deep, rich soil, well supplied with moisture, and likes full sun. While the tree is subtropical, it will withstand a frost or two during the year, but in most of the United States, it will have to be grown as a tub plant and brought indoors for the winter. According to Hill and Barclay (1987), an established tree can endure a frost of 15° F. A mix of sand, loam, peat, and well-rotted manure in equal portions provides a good soil for a bay tree in a permanent container. It likes plenty of moisture, and provision for drainage should be made in the tub. The bay tree is a classic, formal container plant that is commonly seen in and outside of restaurants and hotels in much of Europe. It thrives on being trimmed into forms such as globes, cones, standards, hedges, or various topiary shapes.

The leaves are harvested by hand during early morning in late summer or autumn. To help retain a bright green color, they are spread to dry in thin layers in the shade, and toward the end of the process pressed with boards to keep them from curling. Drying the leaves in the sun causes them to turn brown or black. They take about two weeks to dry.

Bay leaves are a very common spice, even in American households where no other spices are used. They are primarily enjoyed as a flavoring for meat, poultry, stews, soups, and sauces and they are a popular pickling spice. In ancient times, the leaves and branches were placed as a garland upon the heads of heroes and statesmen as a symbol of victory. In fact, decorative use was the tree's major purpose until the middle ages, when the plant was used medicinally. The leaves have been traditionally considered to be astringent, aromatic, carminative, stimulant and stomachic. The leaf decoction has been used in diseases of the urinary organs, primarily as a diuretic.

In India, the dried berries have been imported as a medicinal herb. The fruits are seldom seen in the West. The berries have been used as an aromatic stimulant, once employed for amenorrhea and colic. The oil distilled from the fruits was once used as a liniment for sprains. It is sometimes used as a perfume ingredient. At one time, the oil was a more important item of commerce than the leaves.

The leaf oil contains cineole (up to 50 percent), eugenol, geraniol, pinenes, alpha-phellandrene, delta-linalool, and other components. This oil is reportedly antibacterial, antifungal, and in animal experiments depresses the heart rate, while lowering blood pressure. It is used in some cosmetics as an antidandruff ingredient (Leung 1980).

BEARBERRY, UVA-URSI

Arctostaphylos uva-ursi (L.) K. Spreng.
(ark-toe-staf´-il-os oo-va-er´ see)
Ericaceae—Heath Family

Bearberry, a prostrate evergreen shrub of northern climates, is creeping its way into herb gardens. There are about fifty species in the genus *Arctostaphylos*, most native to western North America. However, *A. uva-ursi*, a perennial four to six inches tall, hails from northern Europe, Asia, and North America. This circumpolar shrub likes cool surroundings. Its stems are generally short, trailing, and woody. The leathery, bright, glossy leaves are oval, entire (without teeth), one-fourth to one inch long, and the undersides are a lighter color than the upper surface. They turn a dull reddish-purple during winter

cold. The urn-shaped, waxy, white-rose blossoms are borne in clusters on terminal racemes, blooming from May to June. The shiny, bright red fruits have tough skins and contain five stonelike seeds. They persist on the plant through spring.

Bearberry is propagated from cuttings or layerings made in the early spring, summer, or fall. Cuttings take about twice as long to root as most herbs. The best cutting is a side branch from the middle of the plant. A two to six-inch long cutting can be placed in sand, with a bottom heat of 72° F. It should be misted and dipped in an appropriate rooting hormone. Bearberry can also be grown from seed, but the seeds have impermeable coats and dormant embryos. In the nursery business, the seeds may be scarified by acid treatment for three to six hours, followed by two to four months of warm, then two to three months cold, stratification (Dirr and Heuser 1987). Obviously, the seeds are difficult to germinate and are the realm of the specialist, rather than the home gardener.

For dense, vigorous growth, bearberry needs a very acid soil with a pH of 5 or less. It is happy in a poor, gravelly soil with full sun or light shade. Plants are slow to start and must be kept free of weeds until well established. Bearberry transplants with difficulty. Disturb the roots as little as possible, and give new plantings plenty of moisture to encourage root growth. This plant loves a coastal breeze and is well suited for steep slopes interspersed with rocks. It makes a good ground cover, controlling erosion in the cool regions of the Northwest, mountain areas, and the northeastern United States. It will stand a freeze of -50° F.

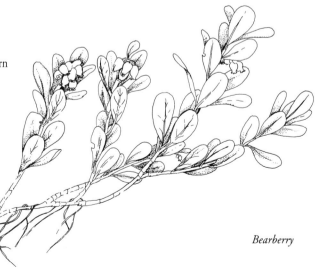

Bearberry

Kinnikinnick, as the leaves were known to groups of Pacific Northwest Indians, was smoked alone or mixed with tobacco. Apparently the smoke was swallowed and retained for a few seconds for an intoxicating or stupefying effect as is the custom with marijuana. However, those who have tried to smoke the leaves to test these reports say there is no stupefying effect. It is likely that this sensation was achieved by mixing other ingredients with the plant.

It is unclear whether the ancient Greeks had knowledge of the plant, though Galen may have written of it. The uncertainty lies in the difficulty of ascertaining the true identity of the plant about which Galen wrote. In assessing its history, Bigelow (1817) put things in perspective: "it is well known that the brief and imperfect descriptions of the ancients were productive of little else than uncertainty in botany" (70).

Modern use of the plant evolved in the mid-eighteenth century, according to Bigelow. His critical clinical observations on the plant, as well as the comments of his contemporaries, which he reviews, suggest its efficacy in various kidney-related conditions. "The late Professor Barton," Bigelow reveals, "found the plant of much service in his own case of nephritic paroxysms, alternating with gout in the feet" (Bigelow 1817, 72).

Medicinally, the dried leaves are used as a tea or tincture for their diuretic, strong-astringent, tonic, and urinary-antiseptic qualities. Bearberry has proven helpful in nephritis, bronchitis, gonorrhea, and with kidney and gallstones, with the primary use for chronic cystitis and urethritis. A tea is made by soaking the leaves in cold water for twenty-four hours or by simmering one-third ounce (10 g) of the dried herb in a quart of water to about half of its original volume. Peppermint leaves can be infused in the decoction to improve flavor. One to two-fluid-ounce doses are taken three to four times daily. This is an effective urinary disinfectant only if the urine is alkaline (pH 8). Sodium bicarbonate should be taken first if the urine is acidic. Use of the herb is contraindicated with other remedies which acidify the urine.

Bearberry leaves contain mostly arbutin. In the body, arbutin hydrolyzes to form hydroquinone glucuronides and hydroquinone sulphate esters, which give the plant its antibacterial qualities. The antibacterial activity of the plant reaches its height about three to four hours after ingesting. Methylarbutin, tannins, flavonoids, monotropein, allantoin, and organic acids are also found in the leaves. In large and frequent doses, hydroquinone can irritate the mucous lining

of the stomach and cause vomiting, ringing in the ears, diarrhea, delirium, and convulsions. Generally, bearberry should be avoided by patients with delicate stomachs and not given to children. Prolonged use is discouraged except under the direction of a qualified medical practitioner. In cystitis, when the urine decomposes in the bladder, it may turn a dark green color if the patient has drunk bearberry tea.

The tannins in the plant make it suitable for treating leathers. Given its abundance in northern Europe, it became economically important as a tanning agent. Bigelow (1817) wrote that "the leaves and stems of the Uva ursi Bearberry are used in Sweden and Russia for the purpose of tanning leather. According to Linnaeus, large quantities are annually collected for this use" (68).

BEE BALMS, HORSEMINT, BERGAMOT, OSWEGO TEA
Monarda bradburiana Beck, *M. citriodora* Cerv. ex Lag., *M. didyma* L., *M. fistulosa* L., *M. russeliana* Nutt., *M. punctata* L.
(mow-nar'-da brad-burr-ee'ay-na; sit-ree-oh'-door-a; did'-i-ma; fis-too-low'-sa; rus-el-ee'-ay-na; punk-tay'-ta)
Labiatae (Lamiaceae)—Mint Family
Plate 7

The genus *Monarda* has twelve species native to North America, occurring primarily in the east from Ontario to Mexico. Most are perennial, though some species are biennial or annual.

M. didyma is the best known of garden-grown bee balms. It reaches four feet tall, and has smooth, toothed, oval-shaped opposite leaves about three inches long with acutely pointed tips. The leaf stems (petioles) are about one-fourth inch long. Leaflike bracts blend the colors of the leaves and flowers. Flowers are borne on a single headlike whorl (verticillaster). The calyx is starshaped; individual sepals are sharplypointed. The curve-lipped corollas are about one and one-fourth inches long. Vividly scarlet, this bee balm blooms from July into September. Plants spread from root runners, creating colonies in open woods. *M. didyma* ranges from New England, south to Georgia and west to Tennessee. Numerous cultivars exist, including scarlet, pink, salmon, deep red, purple, and white-flowered varieties. A plant breeder is reputed to have produced a cultivar with almost black flowers. Red- or scarlet-flowered cultivars include

'Adam', 'Cambridge Scarlet', 'Kardinal', 'Mahogany', 'Mrs. Perry', and 'Scarlet Monarch'. Purple to violet cultivars include 'Blue Stocking', 'Prairie Night', 'Sunset' and 'Violet Queen'. Pink-flowered cultivars, such as 'Croftway Pink', are less common, as are white-flowered forms like 'Snow White' (Duke 1990b).

M. citriodora, as the name implies, is known as lemon bee balm. It is an annual or sometimes biennial, growing two to three feet in height, with leafy, branched stems. The leaves are lanceolate to elliptical, lance-shaped, and one-and-one-half to two-and-one-half inches long, with serrate margins. As in *M. punctata,* the flowers are on interrupted tiers, whorled around the stem. The flowers are whitish to pale lavender, though cultivars have been developed with beautiful lavender bracts beneath bright violet flowers. The plant occurs in rocky or sandy soils in pastures, prairies, and on gravelly hillsides from Missouri to Arkansas, Texas, southeastern New Mexico, and Kansas.

M. fistulosa is a variable species ranging from western New England to Georgia, west through the southern coastal states to east Texas and north to Minnesota, then westward to British Columbia. It is a hardy perennial which reaches four feet tall. The leaves are ovate to ovate-lanceolate, one-and-one-half to three inches long, and about one-half to one-and-one-half inches wide. The margins are coarsely serrated, or only slightly toothed. The typical bright, lavender flowers, about one-and-one-fourth inches long, are crowded on a flower head, about one-and-one-half inches in diameter, sitting singly atop the stalk. One type has white flowers.

M. russeliana has been confused with *M. bradburiana* in recent works. However, *M. bradburiana* flowers are wider (one to two inches wide), while those of *M. russeliana* are less than one-half to one inch in width. In *M. bradburiana,*the upper lip of the flower has a cottony beard, and is about as long as the corolla tube, while the corolla lip of *M. russeliana* is not bearded, and it is half the length of the corolla tube. Furthermore, in *M. bradburiana* the corolla is not exerted from the calyx, while in *M. russeliana,* it is greatly exerted (E. B. Smith 1988). Both grow to about two feet and bloom earlier than other species of *Monarda,* from April to mid-June. They are found in open rocky woods from Kentucky to Iowa, south to Arkansas and northeast Texas. The leaves are shiny above, dull green beneath and have widely spaced teeth. Bracts are pale purple. Mid ribs of the leaves occasionally have purple coloration. The flowers display a creamy

white throat speckled with purple. The first flowers come from the center of the head and, as they develop, blooming corollas progress from the center to the head's outer edge, crowning each plant with a wreath of blossoms.

M. punctata is an annual, biennial, or perennial and occurs in sandy soil. Its branching stems grow to three feet. The four-inch-long leaves are oblong or lance shaped, ending in a sharp point. The bracts are light yellow to purple. Purple spots dot the yellow corollas. The whorled flower clusters are stacked in tiers of two or more whorls. *M. punctat*a and its varieties grow on the eastern coastal plains, west to Minnesota, and south to northern Mexico.

Monardas can be grown in a variety of habitats. *M. didyma* likes a fairly rich, moist, slightly acid soil in full sun or partial shade. It should be protected with shade in the hot South. A fairly light, dry, limey soil and full sun are preferable for *M. fistulosa. M. russeliana* and *M. bradburiana* favor partial shade and dry, sandy, acidic soils. Essentially a lime-loving plant, *M. punctata* likes an alkaline, dry, sandy soil and full sun. All of the Monardas make good border plants—some under shade, others in full sun. At least one species should be grown in every herb garden.

The dried leaves of bee balms, especially *M. didyma, M. citriodora,* and *M. fistulosa,* make a good hot or cold tea. A few leaves can be added to lemonade to enhance the flavor.

M. didyma is also known as Oswego tea, after the Oswego Indians who are said to have used it. After the Boston Tea Party, *M. didyma* leaves were used by settlers as a tea substitute. The leaves of *M. citriodora* were used by the Hopi as a spice for flavoring cooked rabbits. Harvest *M. citriodora* leaves before blooming for a mild, minty tea. After blooming, the leaves are more pungent and bitter. Individual blossoms may be added as a colorful and spicy treat in salads.

M. punctata is an aromatic stimulant, diaphoretic, and carminative. It is useful for settling an upset stomach and treating colds accompanied by diarrhea. Hard-to-find horsemint oil has been used as a liniment ingredient for neuralgia and muscular rheumatism.

Monardas are sometimes called bergamot. Bergamot oil, readily available on the natural-food market, comes not from a Monarda, but from the rind of a citrus fruit closely related to oranges. The two should not be confused.

The Cherokees used the leaf and top tea of *M. didyma* and *M. fistulosa* for weak bowels and stomach complaints, colds, female obstructions, and as a carminative for colic and flatulence. The hot leaf tea is used to bring out measles pustules, to induce sweating to treat flu, and for heart trouble. Externally, a poultice of the leaves was used to treat headaches. The Meskwaki used the leaves of *M. fistulosa* in cold remedies. The Teton Dakota boiled the leaves and flowers together as a tea to relieve abdominal pains. The Tewa Indians used the leaves to flavor meat, and rubbed the dried or powdered leaves on the head to cure headaches. The Winnebagos applied a preparation of the boiled leaves to pimples and other skin eruptions.

Oil of *M. fistulosa* and *M. punctata* contains limonene, carvacrol, and cymene. *M. fistulosa*, which has been grown commercially in Italy, contains limonene, cymene' carvacrol, thymohydroquinone, pinene, and a number of other components. Carvacrol is the main constituent (at about 67 percent).

M. punctata's essential oil (up to 3 percent dry weight) contains limonene, cymene, thymol, thymohydroquinone, and acetaldehyde. *M. punctata* is a rich source of thymol (about 61 percent of its essential oil), a major ingredient in Listerine and other antiseptic preparations. *M. punctata* has been commercially cultivated as a source for thymol, though today it is produced in the laboratory. Thymol is strongly fungicidal and anthelmintic. Some chemotypes, however, have carvacrol as the main constituent.

M. citriodora essential oil contains carvacrol, thymol, thymohydroquinone, and citral.

BLACK COHOSH

Cimicifuga racemosa Elliot.
(sim-iss-if-you'-ga ray-see-mo'-sa)
Ranunculaceae—Buttercup Family
Plate 9

Black cohosh, *Cimicifuga racemosa*, is another plant suitable for woodland production beds. It is a large, bushy perennial, three feet tall without flowers, but growing to eight feet or more when flowering. It grows in rich woods, generally on hillsides in crowded colonies, from southern Ontario to Georgia, west to Arkansas, and north to Wisconsin. The leaves are three-divided. The terminal leaflet on each cluster is three-lobed, with the middle lobe the largest. The base of the leaves is heart shaped or triangular with sharply serrated teeth along the margins on the upper half of the leaves. The slender, long wands of delicate white flowers are conspicuous and showy. They can usually be seen from a distance. Typically the long flower stalk has one or

two branches, though the main flower raceme is the most elaborate. It blooms from late May in its southern range, to early September in its northern range.

The genus *Cimicifuga* includes about fifteen species, one of which is native to Europe, six to North America, and the remainder to northeast Asia. *Cimicifuga* is derived from cimex (a bug) and fugo (to drive away) in reference to insect-repelling claims for the plant. Some species are also known as bugwort or bugbane. In far-flung cultures from Siberia to India to Europe, bugbanes have been used for centuries to repel insects. Black cohosh was first described in 1705, and was cultivated by 1732 in Sherard's garden at Eltham. It was grown in the famous Chelsea Physick Garden in England as early as 1737. European and Asian species of the genus are also available in the American horticultural trade.

Black cohosh is relatively easy to grow, given a moderately rich, somewhat-moist, shady situation. Propagation is achieved by sowing seeds in a well-prepared seedbed as soon as ripe in autumn for germination the following spring, or by division of the roots in early spring or autumn, after the leaves begin to fade. Plants should be given two-foot spacings. Black Cohosh thrives under cultivation in lightly shaded conditions and is adaptable to relatively poor, acidic, rocky woodland soils. The plant does best, however, in a relatively rich, moist woodland soil. A number of cultivated varieties are sold in the nursery trade as ornamentals. It makes a good back border for a lightly shaded area in an herb garden. This is certainly a plant with potential as a commercial crop for the future.

The average weight of the matted roots is four to eight ounces. No information on yields is available, but if a planting scheme with about twelve thousand plants per acre is developed, a projected conservative yield of dried root might be about three thousand pounds per acre. J. U. and C. G. Lloyd (1884–1885) reported that they had seen exceptional roots, weighing as much as four pounds. The Lloyds also reported that *Cimicifuga* often occurs in sterile (non-flowering) populations along with *Actaea pachypoda*, a closely related plant that has been implicated as a possible poisonous species. They suggested that the root of the latter has entered commerce under the name of *Cimicifuga*.

Traditionally, the resinous root is used in tincture for menstrual irregularities, bronchitis, fevers, nervous disorders, lumbago, rheumatism, snakebite, menstrual cramps, and as an aid in childbirth. Science suggests the plant strengthens female reproductive organs in rats and has estrogenic, hypoglycemic, mild-sedative and anti-inflammatory effects. It is traditionally important in treating various menstrual-related conditions (Foster and Duke 1990).

The root contains glycosides, including actein, cimigoside, cimifugine, and racemoside, as well as isoferulic acid, a volatile oil, and tannins. Antiinflammatory, antispasmodic, central-nervous-system-depressant, and peripheral vasodilation activities have been experimentally established (Wren 1988). An isoflavone, formonetine, found in alcoholic extracts of the root, has been shown to have estrogenic impact. This and other compounds in the root are able to bind to estrogen receptors in the uterus (Jerry and Harnischfeger 1985). Recent studies have also shown that extracts of the root reduce symptoms associated with cessation of ovarian function during menopause, such as depression and hot flashes. A placebo-controlled clinical study involving 110 menopausal women demonstrated that a commercially available extract of black cohosh selectively suppresses luteinizing-hormone secretion, further confirming an estrogenic effect of the alcoholic fractions of the root. Occurrence and increase in hot flashes have been linked to luteinizing-hormone release, and serve as a parameter by which the endocrinological activity of black cohosh can be measured. This study provided evidence to confirm traditional use of the plant in the treatment of menopausal-related symptoms for women who refuse to undertake steroid hormone replacement or when such treatment is contraindicated (Düker et al. 1991). Weiss (1988) states that black cohosh is specifically indicated for conditions related to estrogen deficiency. Use of the herb is contraindicated during pregnancy.

BLUE COHOSH

Caulophyllum thalictroides (L.) Michx.
(call-o-file'-um thal-ik-troy'-dees)
Berberidaceae—Barberry Family

Blue cohosh, no relation to black cohosh, is supplied from the root of *Caulophyllum thalictroides*, a perennial growing to about two feet in height. The plant produces one large, thrice-compound leaf, with two to three leaflets, on a thick, blue-green, glaucous stalk. The name *Caulophyllum* describes the leaf habit. Kaulon (a stem) and phyllon (a leaf), refer to the fact that the stem seems to form a stalk for the single, compound leaf. The yellow-green to green-purplish flowers unfurl in terminal clusters from the middle of the leaves from April to June as the plant arises from the root. In

late summer, the plant produces globe-shaped, bluish-black fruits. Blue cohosh occurs in moist, rich woods from New Brunswick to South Carolina, west to Arkansas, and north to North Dakota and Manitoba. It is most abundant in the northern part of its range. The plant was introduced into English gardens by 1755.

The name "cohosh" is an Algonquin word, which was applied by whites to several plants, meaning "it is rough," yet the plants are actually smooth.

The genus *Caulophyllum* has two species, one an eastern North American native, the other an East Asian species, *C. robustum* Maxim. (*C. thalictroides* var. *robustum* [Maxim.] Regel) occurs from Sakhalin to Heilongjiang, Jilin, Liaoning, and forests in the mountains of Japan, through the mountains of Hubei and Sichuan to northern Yunnan. It is a Chinese folk medicine in the area of Omei-Shan in Sichuan. The root is soaked in rice wine for two weeks, then the wine is drunk for the treatment of mechanical injuries. It has also been used to treat menstrual disorders, stomach and digestive problems, injuries from fractures, and rheumatism. In short, the Asian species seems to have parallel purposes with its North American counterpart (S. Foster 1986, 1989f).

Blue cohosh can be propagated by seeds or root division. The seeds can be planted in midsummer as soon as the blueberrylike fruits ripen. Fall division of the root stocks is also a good means of propagation. Plants grown from seed will have to be in the ground for up to five years before the roots can be harvested.

This plant likes a humus-rich soil in deciduous forests with a pH of 4.5 to 7 (acid to neutral). It seems to like at least 75 percent shade, and can be grown in a similar habitat as ginseng and goldenseal. Under cultivation, at least in a garden situation, blue cohosh is not subject to pests and requires a minimum of care. With its interesting foliage and rich blue ornamental fruits it is a good plant for the back of a deep-shaded border as well as a good candidate for commercial cultivation.

An interesting historical note about the introduction of the plant into medicine is found in J. U. Lloyd and C. G. Lloyd (1886–87). "In the year 1813 Peter Smith issued an illiterate publication in the way of an advertisement, and among other substances, introduced blue cohosh under the name 'squaw root'. He asserted that the Indian women made use of a decoction of the root, taking it regularly for a period of two to three weeks before the time for parturition, and that to it they ascribed freedom from the difficulties common to whites. He also stated that it was a valuable emmenagogue. This statement of Smith's was accepted by botanics and the drug became a recognized remedy" (2:154).

Uncharacteristically, the Lloyds failed to cite the original reference. Instead they relied on its mention by Rafinesque (1828). The Lloyds had not seen the original reference, and erroneously refer to the plant as Peter Smith's "squaw root." In a note in their monograph on blue cohosh, they wrote, "In endeavoring to find a record of the history of this individual. . . it is a little curious that, in this city [Cincinnati], all trace has vanished of this man to whom Rafinesque referred to as authority. We are familiar

Caulophyllum thalictroides, Blue Cohosh

with many persons who should bear witness, but none remember him" (2:141).

John Uri Lloyd searched in vain for the book for over twenty-five years and finally gave up looking. Then, late in the summer of 1897, he spoke at the Toledo Club at Middle Bass Island, Lake Erie. There he met General J. Warren Keifer. Keifer, in a conversation with Lloyd on antiquarian books, incidentally remarked that he possessed Peter Smith's work. The lost book was found. Furthermore, Lloyd was able to develop a detailed biographical sketch of Peter Smith, for Smith had been General Keifer's maternal grandfather. In 1901, the Lloyd Library published a reprint of *The Indian Doctor's Dispensatory* by Peter Smith. It is here that we find the first reference to blue cohosh, not under "squaw root," as the Lloyds had stated in 1886–87, but under the "blue berry or sore throat root."

Peter Smith's first account of the medicinal use of the plant so closely proximates its modern use that it is worth reproducing here: "The blue berry root is said to be the great medicine that the squaws use at the birth of their children. Experience has however proved among white women, that its assistance is very special. It is to be made use of in the following manner—take a good handful of green or dry roots, make it into a tea (say half a pint), give the half of it and fill up with hot water; repeat the drinking every ten minutes or oftener, until it has its effect.

When a woman finds that she is taken in labor, let her drink as above, having her help at hand—if it is not her time, she will probably get easy and be well; but if it is her time, expect the delivery will be facilitated with much safety. It is to be noticed, that if the anguish attending the delivery is not moderated, the doses have not been strong enough; for they act on the same stimulant principles that opium does—and a suitable degree of indirect debility will moderate the great distress that must otherwise be experienced. The delivery is facilitated by it, so as seldom to be slow and lingering. But the great benefit is the state of safety and of speedy and sure recovery that the mother experiences afterwards.

The squaws, I have heard, drink a little of a tea of this root for two or three weeks before their expected time. I have given this tea in a case of inflammation of the uterus, and found it a speedy cure." (P. Smith 1813, 38–39)

Usage of the plant by settlers obviously came from the Indians. The Meskwaki (Fox) and Menominee used a decoction of the root to treat profuse menstruation. The Menominee considered it a very valuable female remedy (H. H. Smith 1928, 1932a). The Ojibwa found the root especially useful for stomach cramps due to painful menstruation (H. H. Smith 1932b). The Potawatomi utilized it to treat profuse menstruation and as an aid in childbirth (H. H. Smith 1933). The Omaha considered it their most effective fever medicine (Gilmore 1919). To what extent the plant was employed for gynecological purposes by native groups prior to its adoption by empirical practitioners in the early nineteenth century will never be known. The plant was primarily a remedy used by eclectic practitioners of the late-nineteenth and early twentieth centuries. In addition to gynecological applications, eclectics used it as an anti-spasmodic in bronchitis, pneumonia, and whooping cough.

The root extracts do have estrogenic activity and are antispasmodic and antiinflammatory. An alkaloid in the root, methylcytistine, acts similarly to nicotine, increasing blood pressure, stimulating the small intestine and respiration, and producing hyperglycemia, but this compound is only about one-fortieth as toxic as nicotine. Glycosides, including caulosaponin and caulophyllosaponin, are believed responsible for uterine-stimulant activity (Tyler 1987; Foster and Duke 1990). Plant extracts have also been shown to be antimicrobial and in low doses to inhibit ovulation, uterine changes, and the embedding of the embryo into the uterine mucosa, suggesting further research on contraceptive possibilities. Despite interesting research leads from studies conducted in the 1950s and 1970s, little follow-up work has been done on the plant.

The leaves and seeds contain the alkaloids anagyrine, baptifoline (lupine alkaloids), and magniflorine. Ether extracts from the aerial portions of the plant have demonstrated antiinflammatory effects in rat experiments (Leung 1980).

The powdered root can irritate mucous membranes. Given its uterine-stimulant action, it is contraindicated during pregnancy except under the direction of a qualified, experienced birth attendant.

BLOODROOT

Sanguinaria canadensis L.
(sayn-gwin-ay'ree-a kan-a-den-sis)
Papaveraceae—Poppy Family
Plate 9

The blooming of bloodroot is a sure sign that spring has arrived, for soon after the first flowers appear, deciduous trees begin to leaf out. This herbaceous perennial grows to about eight inches high. The leaves are distinctive, each with undulate, rounded lobes toward the top half of the leaf, which is usually broader than long. A single, waxy, white, twelve-petaled bloom, two to three inches in diameter, emerges before the leaves in spring, from the end of March in the south to June in the north. The leaves, stems, and especially the thickened, fingerlike rhizome exude a red latex

when broken, hence the name Sanguinaria, from the Latin sanguinarius, meaning "bloody." The plant occurs in cool, moist, rich, shaded deciduous woods from southern New York and New Jersey to northern Florida, west to east Texas, and north to Wisconsin and southern Canada.

There is much that needs to be learned about the biology of bloodroot. Attempts to germinate or stratify seeds for future planting usually result in failure. The seeds mature about a month after the early spring flowering period ends. The elongated seed capsule gives no outward sign of maturity, but immediately upon ripening, the seeds fall from the pod. About a month after flowering, the pods have to be monitored on a daily basis if one hopes to collect seeds. Then, for best results in germination, the seeds must be immediately sown before the aril dries. At this time, the seeds can be planted in a well-prepared woodland seedbed, high in organic matter, at a depth of about one-half inch. The seedbed should be kept moist throughout the growing season. The plant can also be propagated by planting rhizome cuttings in late summer or early fall as the leaves begin to wilt and die back to the ground. Each piece of root should have a bud or an eye (H. R. Phillips 1985). While this method is difficult, seeds are still considered the most reliable means of propagation. Detailed, controlled studies are needed to determine the best methods of propagating bloodroot, especially for commercial purposes.

The plant needs to grow in a shaded situation, protected from full sun, although it blooms in early spring before leaves appear in most deciduous forests, exposing the plants to nearly full sun at the beginning of its life cycle. It is adaptable to different soil types, but a soil rich in humus, with good drainage, and not excessively moist, is most suitable. Individual plants can be spaced from four to six inches apart. The plant is slow growing and likely to take three to four years before a crop is obtained. Based on the size and density of roots compared with other commodities, one thousand pounds per acre of dried root at six-inch spacings would be a reasonable estimate of yield.

As is the case with many perennial root crops, wisdom suggests that the root is best collected in autumn when moisture content is lower. The roots shrink considerably, losing about 70 percent of their weight upon drying. However, a recent study which surveyed over one hundred native populations of the plant found that the highest alkaloid yields occurred during the flowering and fruiting stages. Plants in the southern part of its range, especially in the southern Appalachians, had the highest alkaloid content. Levels of the alkaloid sanguinarine varied widely (from 0.6 to 6.3 percent). Soil pH and humus were also found to be significant factors in alkaloid content. High-yielding populations are found in mature, undisturbed deciduous forests dominated by tulip trees (*Liriodendron tulipifera*), maple (*Acer saccharum*), and beech (*Fagus grandifolia*) (Bennett, Bell, and Boulware 1990).

The plant seems to have been used extensively by native groups of the eastern deciduous forests. The Cherokees used tiny doses of the root in the treatment of lung inflammations, croup, and coughs, and externally as a wash for ulcers and sores (Hamel and Chiltoskey 1975). The Iroquois used the roots as an emetic, a cold remedy, for intestinal problems, and externally for sores and cuts. The Ojibwa squeezed a little of the fresh root juice onto a lump of maple sugar, letting it melt in the mouth, to treat sore throat (H. H. Smith 1932b). The Omaha-Ponca used the root as a decorative skin stain and boiled it to make a red dye. For general debility, the Delaware ate a pea-sized piece of the root each morning for a month. The root was also used as a face paint for the Delawares' Big House Ceremony (Tantaquidgeon 1942). As a love charm, a bachelor would rub the root on the palm of his hand, shake hands with the woman he desired to marry, and if the charm was successful, then she would be willing to marry him after five or six days (Gilmore 1919).

Bloodroot was so unique and biologically active (primarily due to its highly toxic compounds) that it was brought to the attention of white settlers at an early date. Under the direction of physicians, it was used for a wide variety of purposes. Few plants attracted as much attention from the early nineteenth-century medical community as bloodroot. Externally, the dried roots were used as a wash to treat "ill-conditioned ulcer." Bloodroot served as an expectorant ingredient in cough preparations. It was considered to be an emetic and cathartic. Even a small dose of the fresh root was well known to produce symptoms such as heartburn, nausea, faintness, vertigo, diminished vision, and vomiting.

Bloodroot is an obscure woodland botanical of the past that has experienced a dramatic increase in marketability in recent years, mainly for the production of an antiplaque agent for dental-care products. This has resulted in increased interest in the plant generally. Various benzophenanthridine alkaloids are found in the plant root, including sanguinarine (about 50 percent of the alkaloid fraction), chelerythrine, and others. Sanguinarine has been the subject of recent

research as a broad-spectrum antibacterial agent against gram-positive and gram-negative bacteria. Sanguinarine also has experimental antispasmodic and expectorant effects (Karlowsky 1991). As noted, it has been used as an antiplaque and antigingivitis agent in dental products, and its efficacy and safety have been both supported and questioned in the dental literature. One study, for example, found that small amounts of the alkaloid in a dentifrice and a mouthwash effectively killed bacteria considered important in the formation of plaque. However, another assessment found it to be no more effective than tap water. Bloodroot is also a well-known folk cancer remedy, and topical products containing the plant extracts have been used to treat cancer of the nose and ear (Olin, 1990).

The bottom line with bloodroot is that, while it serves as an attractive and historically interesting herb for the rich, deep-shaded herbary, it is certainly not a plant for which the herb gardener can find more than ornamental usage, given its toxicity. As for commercial production, it is unclear whether demand for the plant's alkaloids will continue into the future.

BORAGE
Borago officinalis L.
(bor-ray'-go of-iss-i-nay' lis)
Boraginaceae—Borage Family

The genus Borago is represented by three species native to the Mediterranean region. *B. officinalis* is the familiar species of the herb garden, occurring in dry soils, often in waste places in southern Europe. Long cultivated in herb gardens, it is now naturalized in much of Europe. This coarse annual usually grows one-and-one-half to two feet tall, although in a rich soil it may exceed five feet. The leaves are thick, covered with stiff, rough hairs, oval shaped, pointed at the ends, and alternate. They grow from three to six inches long. The stems are succulent, hollow, and hairy, like the leaves. The terminal flowers are star shaped, bright blue, and distinguished by prominent black anthers forming a conelike structure in the center of the blossom. The flower clusters nod downward. Each flower produces four brownish-black nutlets.

Borage grows well in an average garden soil, and will even tolerate poor, dry soils. Soil pH should fall between 5 and 8. Full sun or partial shade is suitable. It grows readily from seed and self-sows profusely. Plant on a back border or at a central focal point. Borage sprawls and should be given two-foot spacings. The seeds produce broad, large cotyledons similar in appearance to those of cucumbers. Borage develops a taproot, making it difficult to transplant. Plants take about eight weeks to mature. They will continue blooming until the first frost, when they wither to a black mass. One ounce of seeds will plant about a five-hundred-foot row. We had three 250-foot rows of borage at the Sabbathday Lake Shaker community gardens, from which we harvested the flowering tops for drying and packaging. The three rows produced about fifty pounds of dried material—more than enough to supply our limited demand for the dried herb.

This planting was literally humming with bees. Standing close to borage on a sunny day is like listening to the steady buzz of high-tension electric wires. And there is high tension for the gardener who tries to pick a drooping flower before checking to see if a bee is collecting nectar!

Harvest borage as it begins to flower. It can be harvested

Borage

two or three times during the growing season, or you can make a couple of successive plantings. Drying must be done with care. If you are drying small amounts, carefully remove the leaves from the succulent stem and, if time allows, peel the stems for a noon salad. Fast drying under moderate heat is preferable. Borage tends to turn brown or black without good air circulation. If you spread it to dry on an open-frame drying rack, make sure the leaves are not overlapping, potentially hampering airflow.

The fresh leaves and flowers of borage possess a delicate cucumberlike flavor. Young leaves are good chopped in salads. The leaves may also be boiled as a pot herb. However, beware as it is now believed that the leaves have subtle toxicity. The flowers are a colorful and tasty addition to salads. Gently grasp the flower stem behind the sepals, then pinch and pull the anthers, and the entire corolla will slip from its pedestal.

Medicinal uses are somewhat limited. Borage is diuretic, demulcent, emollient, and diaphoretic. It is used for kidney ailments, pulmonary troubles, and fevers. A poultice of the fresh leaves with the hairs scraped off is used for inflammations. A handful of fresh leaves steeped in a quart of water with a sprig or two of spearmint makes a cooling, soothing summer beverage.

During the last decade, new uses have evolved for the plant. The seed oil is the richest plant source of gamma-linolenic acid (GLA) which is a potentially valuable dietary supplement and treatment for essential fatty-acid deficiency (Awang 1990b). GLA is an intermediate chemical link in prostaglandin synthesis. The oil content ranges from 13 to 33 percent in the seeds, consisting of palmitic acid (12 percent), stearic acid (4.7 percent), oleic acid (18.6 percent), linoleic acid (38.9 percent), and up to 22 percent GLA. GLA deficiency has been reported to be involved in a variety of health problems. GLA supplementation has been linked to therapeutic promise in the treatment of atopic eczema, premenstrual syndrome, diabetes, alcoholism, and inflammations (Janick et al. 1989). The primary commercial source of GLA-rich oils has traditionally been evening-primrose seed.

The problem with producing oil from borage seed is that most of the seeds shatter and drop to the ground before they can be harvested. If harvesting is attempted with conventional machinery, the vibration of the machinery causes the seeds to drop to the ground before they can be gathered. The plants also mature at different times and different heights. In order to solve these and other problems associated with the commercial development of the seed oil, researchers at Purdue University's Department of Horticulture conducted intensive research on the plant's production in the 1980s. One solution was the invention of a prototype seed or plants harvested from the ground with a powerful vacuum. The researchers also worked on improving genetic selection, spacing regimes, and other factors to enhance seed production and harvesting. For the details, see Beaubaire and Simon (1987); Janick, Simon, and Whipkey (1987); Janick et al. (1989); Quinn et al. (1987); Quinn, Simon, and Janick (1989a, 1989b); and Whipkey, Simon, and Janick (1988).

Borage contains mucilage, calcium, and up to 3 percent of potassium nitrate. Because of the potassium nitrate, the dried herb emits explosive sparks when it is burned. The leaves contain tannins as well as various organic acids. The fresh plant is high in vitamin C. Recently, however, several pyrrolizidine alkaloids (PAs) have been identified in the dried leaves and stems of borage (see comfrey for more information on the toxicity of PAs). While the PA content of borage is much lower than that of comfrey (two to ten parts per million), the herb has been taken off the market in Germany. Thesinine, which is nontoxic, is the only PA that has been found in the flowers. Consumers can assume, at least for the time being, that the flowers are relatively safe to eat in small amounts.

CALAMINT

Satureja arkansana (Nutt.) Briq.
(sat-you-ree'-a ar-kan-say'-na)
Labiatae (Lamiaceae)—Mint Family

In the seldom-admired rocky glade where few plants bloom in splendor, a native American member of the mint family resides, flaunting a soft spray of lavender blooms in the transitory summer-weathered days of late spring. This plant begs for a place in herb gardens. Botanists have been confused by its plethora of names and ranks, including *S. glabra* (Nutt.) Fern., *S. glabella* (Michx.) Briq var. *angustifolia* (Torr.) Svenson, *Clinopodium glabrum* Ktze., *Calamintha nuttallii* (Gary), *Micromeria Nuttallii* (Torr.), *Micromeria glabella* var. *angustifolia* (Torr.), *Hedeoma glabra* (Nutt). (where it all started), and the name we used in *Herbal Bounty*—*S. arkansana*. Well since then, it has appeared under yet different names. Yatskievych and Turner (1990) use *Calamintha arkansana* (Nutt.) Shinn. for the plant,

while in the second edition of Gleason and Cronquist (1991), the designation is *S. glabella* var. *angustifolia* (Torr.) Svenson. Confused? I am. The persistent and continued taxonomic confusion leaves me with only one choice. As an Arkansawyer, I will arbitrarily continue to call this little plant *S. arkansana*.

Botanists do agree, however, on several points about this plant. Its leaves are glabrous or smooth and they are narrow (angustifolia). The plant was first described by naturalist Thomas Nuttall (1786–1859), who encountered this pennyroyal-like plant, "upon the banks of the St. Lawrence and the upper lakes," and on calcareous rocks at Niagara Falls. (Graustein 1967, 37).

Calamint, a perennial native to the eastern United States and south central Canada, occurs from Minnesota to Ontario, western New York, south to Arkansas and Texas and grows in limestone glades, on banks of streams, moist ledges of

Calamint

limestone bluffs, and escarpments. The plant stands only six to twelve inches tall. The leaves are smooth with upright branching flower stems. They are one-half inch long or less, oblong, linear, entire (no teeth), and peppered with oil glands. The gaping, almost inquisitive-looking, two-lipped flowers occur in clusters starting halfway up the stems. Flowers are bluish-lavender color about one-eighth to one-fourth inch long. Like European pennyroyal *Mentha pulegium,* calamint sends out root-runners after blooming.

Thickly growing calamint brushes the calves of bare legs like seedling grasses. Stroke the leaves and the surrounding air explodes with a sweet pennyroyal-like fragrance.

Propagate by dividing the runners in spring or late summer after the plant has finished blooming. Calamint likes a limey, gravelly soil with good drainage. It prefers full sun but will tolerate some shade. A group planting of calamint makes a soft-textured, mid-summer border.

The individual blossoms make a colorful and spicy addition to salads. A tea of the flowering herb has a pennyroyal flavor. It is diaphoretic and soothes an upset stomach. Its strong pennyroyal fragrance is undoubtedly due to a high pulegone content. Definitely a plant deserving of great study and certainly worth developing further as an herb garden plant.

CALAMUS, SWEET FLAG

Acorus calamus L.
(ayk'-or-us kal'-a-mus)
Araceae—Arum Family

Most people glancing at boggy areas harboring calamus might pass it by as a grass, sedge, or cattail. Trudging through the bog, though, you will notice a sweet musky fragrance and will soon discover this arum with grasslike leaves. Calamus is a semi-aquatic perennial inhabitant of marshy places in Europe, Asia, and North America. The smooth, slender leaves, one and one-half to six feet high, arise from horizontal rhizomes creeping in all directions just below the soil's surface. The sword-shaped leaves are a light green color, and have a prominent midrib. The minute flowers are borne on a fingerlike green spadix, protruding one-third to one-half way up the leaf stalk at a 45° angle. The tiny, yellowish-green flowers are arranged on the spadix in diamond patterns. Calamus inhabits the edges of slow-moving creeks, ponds, and marshes. Because its rhizomes spread, it grows in thick mats. The branching rhizomes are about as big around as a

finger. The undersides of the rhizomes are anchored by numerous stringy rootlets. The fresh rhizome has a spongy texture. A seldom-seen cultivar 'Variegatus' has yellow-striped leaves. The American material has been treated by botanists as synonymous with *A. calamus,* a separate species (*A. americanus*(Raf.) and a variety *A. calamus*var. *americanus* (Raf.) H. D. Wulff. A separate taxonomic designation is useful from the standpoint of reflecting the differences in the chemistry between Eurasian material and North American material, as we shall see later.

Another Asian species *A. gramineus* (Soland. ex Ait.), is a diminutive species with slender, grass-like leaves (less than one-fourth inch wide) and without a prominent mid-rib. It grows to about eighteen inches in height. It is indigenous to China, Southeast Asia and Japan. A number of cultivars have been developed, best known to aquatic gardeners and rock garden specialists. In China, both *A. gramineus* and *A. calamus* are used interchangeably as the same drug known as *chang-pu.*

Despite its propensity to grow in or at the edge of water in wild habitats, calamus may be grown in a fairly rich, moist, garden loam with a pH from 5 to 7.5. Calamus enjoys full sun but will do well under partial shade. Plants are easily propagated by rhizome divisions. Plant the growing leafy end with an inch or two of attached rhizome.

Commercial plantings of calamus have been made on upland soils which produce crops of corn or potatoes, yielding two thousand pounds of dried root per acre. The rhizome is harvested about a year after planting.

Harvesting is easy with a sharp garden spade. Roots should be dried between 85° and 90° F. The rhizome shrinks considerably when dried, losing seventy to seventy-five percent of its fresh weight. I've often dried it in the sun on the dashboard of the car. Before drying, cut off the rootlets on the underside of the rhizome or remove them by rubbing when dry.

It is not generally subject to attack by insect pests. In fact in India, the powdered rhizome is traditionally used as an insecticide to kill fleas, bedbugs, moth, lice and other vermin. The dried roots are stored with rice to kill insects. According to R. A. Locock (1987) components of the plant have shown an ability to sterilize certain insects—hampering the maturation of the ova in low concentrations, while in high concentrations, the oil impedes the copulation of several insect species (makes them dizzy I guess).

Calamus has many uses, including insecticidal, food,

medicinal, decorative, and ceremonial uses. Also known as sweet flag, The Sabbathday Lake Shakers made candied sweet flag root as a sales item, the manufacture of which was discontinued as recently as 1960. The young tender fresh leaves can be added to spring salads. The leaves, stalks, and rhizomes were used as (or in) foods by various American Indian groups. Use of the plant dates back at least two thousand years in Chinese traditions and in Western traditions back to the time of Moses. Medicinally, the rhizome has long been esteemed as an aromatic bitter to tone and settle the stomach and relieve indigestion, gas, and heartburn. Small bits of dried or candied calamus root are chewed for these purposes. The root is considered a stimulant, carminative, spasmolytic, tonic, bitter, and aromatic.

Tribes of the Great Plains used calamus for numerous purposes. Ethnologist Melvin Gilmore enumerated the position of the plant, "All tribes hold this plant in very high esteem. It was used as a carminative, a decoction was drunk for fever, and the rootstock was chewed as a cough and toothache remedy. For colic an infusion of the pounded rootstock was drunk. As a remedy for a cold the rootstock was chewed or a decoction was drunk, or it was used in the smoke treatment. In fact this part of the plant seems to have been regarded as a panacea" (Gilmore 1919, 70). Teton Dakota warriors chewed the root and applied the resulting paste to their foreheads and temples to help them be fearless in the face of enemies. Garlands of the leaves were worn around the neck by hunters when they arrived at places where the plant grew, and the garlands were used for ceremonial purposes. Kindscher (1992) notes that use of the herb is still a popular remedy at the Rosebud Sioux Reservation in South Dakota.

In his excellent books on the medicinal and edible plants of the prairies, botanist Kelly Kindscher, provides evidence that suggests the plant was consciously planted by native groups of the Plains, perhaps being maintained at frequented locations. Gilmore observed that the plant occurred in localities in the vicinity of old village sites or near camping places on old Indian trails, which led him to believe the patches may have originated from intentional planting by medicine men. The rhizomes were also conspicuously abundant among the remains of the Ozark Bluff-dwellers (Kindscher 1987, 1992). In an eighty-day, 690 mile trek across the prairie (from Kansas City to Denver) that Kindscher and a companion made in the spring of 1983, they observed calamus growing near his-torical trails or encampments and found that the rhizome helped assuage thirst.

During the depression, calamus was chewed as a tobacco substitute, and some people claim chewing the root will deter the desire to smoke. At least it's a good oral fixation (to which I can attest).

In American Indian, European, and East Indian traditions, the rhizome is considered useful for clearing the throat of phlegm. In India, calamus root is used for insecticide, worm expellant, and for diarrhea, dysentery, and bronchial trouble. Aphrodisiac properties are also attributed to the root.

Hoffer and Osmond (1967, 55–56) in *The Hallucinogens* report numerous uses of flag root, rat root, or sweet

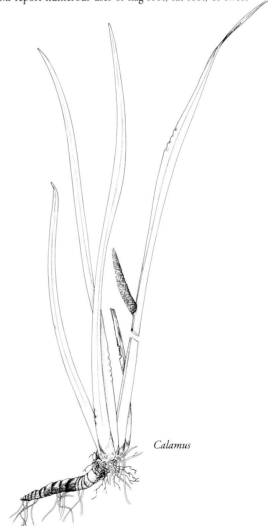

Calamus

calomel by the Cree of Northern Alberta. One Indian informant stated that calamus dispelled fatigue on long walks and made him feel as though he were walking with one foot off the ground. Hoffer and Osmond also report that large doses of calamus root in controlled experiments created an experience like that of LSD. Several tribes ascribed mystic powers to the plant, and Pawnee mystery ceremonies included songs about calamus. Whether the plant was used hallucinogenically by North American Indians, and whether, in fact, the plant is hallucinogenic remains a mystery to modern science. However, after chewing dried calamus root for several years, I've found that one or two inches ingested over an hour's time does leave me feeling vigorous. Nibbling on the root during long drives helps to keep me awake.

Calamus has at least five chemotypes with different geographic locations. For purposes of designation, let's refer to the American type as *A. calamus* var. *americanus*. It is a diploid with twenty-four chromosomes. The carcinogen beta-asarone and toxic phenylpropanoids are not found in this type. Major constituents of the American type include the sesquiterpenes shyobunone, and 6-ephishyobunone, plus acorones, including isoacorone (up to thirty-five percent) acorone (up to twenty-five percent), and acorenone. Other constituents include calamendiols in small amounts.

The second type is the indigenous European material, sometimes designated *A. calamus* var. *vulgaris* (or var. *calamus*). It contains only about five percent of the carcinogenic beta-asarone. The European variety is a triploid with thirty-six chromosomes. Over 184 volatile components have been identified in its oil alone. The tetraploid Asian varieties, including *A. calamus* var. *augustatus* and *A. calamus* var. *versus,* contain high amounts of beta-asarone (isoasarone) at up to ninety-six percent, or alpha-asarone (up to eighty-two percent). Asarone resembles mescaline in structure, though it has an opposite effect. Experiments with rats have shown Asian material containing high levels of beta-asarone to be carcinogenic. Because of this potential carcinogenicity, in 1968 the FDA forbade the use of calamus root, oil, and extracts in human foods. However, this blanket action covering all calamus products must be questioned as only the Indian variety *Jammu* was used in the testings. American, European, and East Indian calamus oils vary considerably in composition due to the polyploidism of the genus. The offending calamus, for example, contained high levels of beta-asarone, considered to be the primary

carcinogenic constituent. It is primarily found in the Asian tetraploids and to a lesser extent the European tetraploid. Again it is important to realize that the essential oil from the American strain is beta-asarone free.

Calamus oils also contain eugenol, azulene, pinene, cineole, camphor, elemene, caryophyllene, calmenese, cadalene, humulene and dozens of other components. Sesquiterpene ketones found in calamus varieties include acorone, calarene, calacone, shyobunone, etc. Acorones are also found in calamus, along with choline, acoric acid, acorin (a resin), tannins, mucilage, and calcium oxalate (Council of Industrial and Scientific Research 1985). In rats and cats the oil and extracts of calamus have exhibited hypotensive, anticonvulsant, and central nervous system-depressant activities. Recent studies have shown that water and alcoholic extracts of Indian calamus significantly prolonged the effects of barbiturates, indicating a central nervous system depressant effect, which was accompanied by a decreased spontaneous motor activity of laboratory animals. However, the extracts did not exhibit an anticonvulsant activity (Martis et al. 1991). The root oil is strongly antibacterial. Other studies have shown that calamus has demonstrated serum cholesterol, serum triglyceride, and blood fibrinogen lowering activity while increasing fibrinolytic activity. Experimentally, the American calamus has been found to have strong spasmolytic activity (Kindscher 1992).

Given the chemical and pharmacological differences of the Asian, European, and North American material, it would probably be useful to retain separate taxonomic designations for them. Various researchers have recommended that the beta-asarone free varieties of calamus should be used in herbal medicine, based on their good spasmolytic activity and safety (Locock 1987).

CALENDULA, POT MARIGOLD
Calendula officinalis L.
(kal-end'-you-la off-iss-i-nay'-lis)
Compositae (Asteraceae)—Aster Family
Plate 8

The common pot marigold has captured the appreciation of poet, gardener, and healer alike. Calendula is native to south central Europe and North Africa. The genus has about fifteen species. A venerable annual for borders or garden nucleus, the buoyant light-yellow-to-orange blossoms bring color and vitality to the lush shades of summer and the fading hues of autumn. With coarse surfaces and many branches, it reaches a height of two feet. The leaves are oblong, without teeth, or with small, inconspicuous teeth. Leaves are three to six inches long, and their stalks gently clasp the stem. The flower heads, one and one-half to three inches across, consist of several rows of ray florets and a central cluster of tubular flowers. Calendula blooms continually from the appearance of the first blossoms about six weeks after planting to the first light snows of late autumn. In Maine, my calendula beds continued blooming into November. The seeds (achenes) are curved and taper to a point at one end. The blossoms close at night and on overcast days but open with the sun. One cultivar, 'Chrysantha,' produces double blossoms that are a rich buttercup yellow. Kieft Seeds, a Dutch firm, lists thirty-four calendula cultivars in its catalog. Herbalists consider single-flowered varieties to be medicinal, however, this notion has not stood up to scientific scrutiny in other members of the aster family (see feverfew).

Calendula should not be confused with other marigolds—members of the genus *Tagetes*. This genus of familiar marigolds is represented by about thirty species and numerous cultivars. They are indigenous mainly to South and Central America, though several species are found as far north as Arizona and New Mexico. The genus name *Calendula* means that the plant will bloom nearly year around, or blooms on the "calends"—the new moon of each month. The species name *officinalis* denotes it was the "official" calendula of the apothecary's shop. Marigold is derived from the association of the plant in Catholic traditions with festivals held in honor of the Virgin Mary.

Sow seeds as soon as the ground can be worked in the spring. They germinate in ten days to two weeks. If allowed to go to seed, calendula self-sows freely, and the resulting seedlings can be transplanted the following spring. Thin to one-foot spacings.

They grow well in moderately rich, well-drained soil with a pH range of 5 to 8, and tolerate full sun or partial shade. In southern states, plantings do better under partial shade. Calendula is very easy to grow.

At the Sabbathday Lake Shaker Gardens we planted four three-hundred-foot rows of calendula from four ounces of seed. We harvested the flower crop three times. A week after each cutting the rows were again covered with blossoms. About twenty pounds of dried flower heads were gathered from this planting.

The plant's most useful part is the ray florets or petals, though the entire flower is usually harvested as a matter of economy. Try spending an afternoon plucking the individual flower petals from the central disk, and you'll soon realize why commercial growers choose to harvest the whole flower head. Gathering individual flowers is great for the home gardener, but unfeasible for the farmer. Petals stripped from the disks dry much faster than the whole flower head, but I find it easier to dry the entire flower, then remove the dried petals by hand as needed.

Calendula is referred to as "poor man's saffron" since the flavoring and coloring potential are similar to that of true saffron. Calendula adds a subtle saline flavor and a delicate yellow hue to food. It can be used for coloring rice and other grains. Calendula lends itself well to soups and chowders. In medieval Europe calendula blossoms were used as a base for soups and broths and could be found literally by the barrel in marketplaces. Use the fresh flower petals in salads.

A tea of calendula promotes sweating and is useful in treating ulcers, both internally and externally. Two centuries ago it was widely used as a home remedy for jaundice. Its primary traditional and modern use, besides for color and flavor in the kitchen, is in the form of a lotion, tincture, ointment, or a wash of the cooled tea, as an embrocation on sprains, bruises, cuts, minor infections, and burns. It has been reported to help promote the reconstruction of tissue, reduce swelling and discharges, and lessen scarring from burns, abscesses, or abrasions. It is generally agreed that the plant is without any known toxic side effects.

The first edition of the *United States Homeopathic Pharmacopoeia* (1878, 84) lists two methods for preparing calendula. One method expresses the juice of fresh calendula gathered in summer, then adds alcohol equal to the volume of the expressed juice. In the second method the plant is soaked in five parts alcohol for two weeks.

A ninety-year-old friend, who had been using a homemade calendula tincture for all his family's cuts, abrasions, burns, and scalds for close to seventy years, made a tincture by soaking the whole fresh plant in vodka for two weeks. He diluted the tincture with nine parts water with each use.

In recent years the main use of calendula has been as an ingredient in homeopathic preparations, primarily used in the treatment of minor burns, abrasions, cuts, infections, and related conditions. Homeopathy is the specialized branch of medicine based on the work of an eighteenth century controversial German medical scholar, Samuel Hahnemann.

The basic premise of homeopathy is that a substance that will produce a specific set of symptoms in a well person will cure those same symptoms in a diseased person. Important factors include the condition of the mind and the exact wording in which the patient expresses the symptoms. A wide variety of symptoms are taken in to account when the homeopathic physician decides upon a remedy, not just the acute symptoms of a particular ailment.

Infinitesimal doses are used in homeopathic medicine. The most highly "potentized" doses contain the smallest amount of the material, in concentrations so minute, they cannot be detected by modern chemical assay methods. Because of the lack of a physical fingerprint, modern science has long turned its nose up at any scientific basis for homeopathy, discounting most homeopathic remedies as nothing more than placebo.

At the end of June 1988, a controversial article was published in the British journal *Nature*, which attempted to prove a scientific basis for homeopathy. In the presence of certain reactors, an infinitesimal dose of pollen, so small as to be beyond detection by standard chemical methods, still caused immune system cells to react as if the pollen was available in detectable doses. Because the researchers themselves didn't believe the results, their experiments were conducted more than seventy different times in several laboratories around the world in an attempt to detect any flaws in the research method. In an interview conducted by Philip J. Hilts, deputy editor of *Nature,* Peter Nemark, commented that if the results were indeed true, " we will have to abandon two centuries of observation and rational thinking about biology, because this can't be explained by ordinary physical laws." (*Washington Post,* June 30, 1988.) The results of the study were later debunked in *Nature.* Perhaps the truth lies somewhere in between.

Dr. Hildebert Wagner, one of the world's leading medicinal plant researchers at the Institute of Pharmaceutical Biology, University of Munich, has pointed out that up until recent years, the purpose of medicinal plant research has been to discover a "magic bullet"—a strong acting chemical compound that affects a specific pathogen or disease condition, like the heart-affecting glycosides of digitalis (foxglove), or potent chemicals for use in chemotherapy against cancers. Now the research focus has shifted into discovering the mechanism and scientific basis for the use of substances that work in a more subtle level, often helping the body heal itself. One such class of plant remedies

is immune system stimulants or modulators. Science is beginning to move in an exciting new direction of vindicating or denying traditional medicinal uses of plants.

Calendula is one plant that has been researched for immune system activity. With the AIDS epidemic the phrase "immune system stimulant" automatically raises warning flags. Just because a substance may be alleged to enhance the immune system in some manner does not mean that it is a cure-all. Calendula, for example, has simply been shown to help activate the body's own cells, which gobble-up foreign debris or invaders at the sight of the infection then help to activate other defense mechanisms. Its effect is subtle and localized—nothing sensational or spectacular. Such

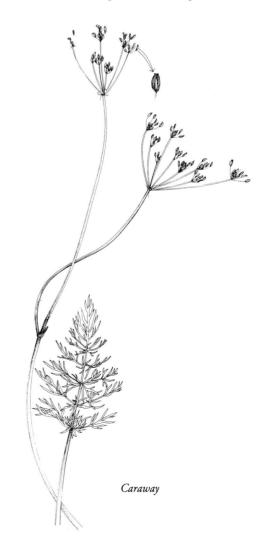

Caraway

research begins to provide a rational scientific basis for the long standing historical use of the herb.

The flowers have been used as an external folk cancer remedy, and water extracts of the plant have been shown in experiments to inhibit certain cancer forms, although any hope of this as a cancer cure would be a false hope at best. Over thirty chemical components have been identified from the plant. The fresh plant contains the analgesic (pain relieving) compound salicylic acid. The flowers contain a resin, a bitter compound, a saponin, an essential oil with carotene, calenduline, and lycopine. The plant contains a number of pentacylic alcohols including faradol, brein, arnidiol, and caldenduladiol. Rutin, quercitin, and isorhamnetin are among the flavonoids in the plant. Tocopherols, mucilage, and chlorogenic acids are also found in the plant. A scientific basis for anti-inflammatory, antiviral, and antibacterial activity has been suggested by various studies, and an ointment containing the flower extract has been shown to stimulate wound healing.

In modern Europe, internal use of the herb includes treatment for inflammatory lesions of the oral and throat mucosa and externally for patients with poor-healing wounds. The plant is apparently non-toxic. At least anecdotally, it is a good example of a medicinal plant with a long history of safe and efficacious use that should be further researched to discover the mechanism of action, followed by well-designed clinical studies that could, once and for all, confirm or deny its usefulness.

CARAWAY

Carum carvi L.
(kay'-rum kar'-vy)
Umbelliferae (Apiaceae)—Carrot Family

Caraway is a biennial (or perennial in tropics) herb native to Europe and western Asia, widely naturalized in North America. Of thirty species of Eurasian origin only *Carum carvi* is grown in American gardens. Caraway grows to a height of two and one-half feet. The leaves are finely divided, resembling those of carrots. White, sometimes pink flowers are borne on terminal or lateral compound umbels. The roots are thick and carrotlike. The seeds (fruits) are crescent-shaped and about three-sixteenths of an inch long. Each half of the fruit (mericap) contains one seed and six oil tubes (vittae). It flowers from May to August. Major producers of caraway seed include Egypt, the Netherlands, Spain, Turkey, India, Morocco, and the United States. It is also produced commercially in eastern Europe. Depending upon the production region and chemotype, there is a wide variation in the quality and quantity of the components of caraway's essential oil.

Caraway is easily grown from seed sown in early spring or autumn. Seed sown in September will flower and produce seed the following summer. In the first year an annual cover crop such as dill or coriander can be planted along with caraway. Caraway will grow rapidly after cover crops are harvested. Side dress with compost or seasoned manure in the fall or following spring to help seed growth. Sometimes caraway matures in the third summer of growth. Thin seedlings to stand at six-inch spacings. Four to eight pounds of seed will sow an acre.

Caraway likes full sun and will grow well in a variety of soils including dry, heavy clay soil containing a fair amount of humus. A humus-rich, well-drained sandy loam is preferable. Soil pH can range from 6 to 7.5. Cultivate plants when young to remove competing grasses. Caraway does not like competition from weeds and is sensitive to mechanical injury and frost (Simon et al. 1984). Yields of five hundred to two thousand pounds of seed per acre have been obtained from biennial plantings of the herb in the United States.

Harvest as soon as the fruits begin to ripen to minimize shattering, which causes caraway to self-sow and possibly become weedy. Seeds may ripen from June to August of the second year. Place harvested plants on a ground cloth to avoid seed loss.

The roots, leaves, and seeds are all useful. The roots, with a flavor suggesting a mix of parsnips and carrots, can be boiled as a vegetable. Use young shoots and leaves cooked with other vegetables or chopped in salads. The seeds, of course, are the familiar little flavor morsels scattered through a loaf of ryebread. They are good in sauerkraut, cheese, applesauce, soups, salad dressings, and apple pie. Caraway seeds contain small amounts of protein and B vitamins.

The seeds are diuretic, carminative, astringent, anthelmintic, and galactogenic. In India, a bath of the seeds is used to relieve swellings of the womb, as a poultice for hemorrhoids, and as an eyewash. Combined with laxative herbs, caraway seeds will help prevent griping. Rheumatic pains are lessened with an external wash made with the seeds. The seeds are chewed to relieve toothache, and a tea is used for pleurisy. Above all, caraway seeds are best known medicinally for a carminative effect. Phytotherapists in Europe consider the seeds to be one of the most reliable and effective carminatives. Seed preparations in Germany, especially caraway seed liqueurs known as kummel, may also aid in the digestion of fatty foods, as a result of its ability to reduce gastrointestinal foam.

The main constituents of the oil are carvone and limonene. Carvone is generally found at levels between forty to sixty percent. The components have recently been shown to have an experimental cancer chemopreventive effect. See dill and the cited reference (Zheng et al. 1992) for more details. Other components of the oil include carveol, dihydrocarvone, dihydrocarveol, pinene, thujone and other components. The essential oil, found at levels of three to six percent of the seed weight, is antibacterial, antifungal, larvicidal, antispasmodic, and antihistaminic. Carminative and antispasmodic activity are experimentally confirmed.

CATNIP

Nepeta cataria L.
(nep-ee'-ta ka-tare'-ee-a)
Labiatae (Lamiaceae)—Mint Family

N. cataria is the best known of the more than 250 species in its genus. Native to the dry, temperate regions of the Mediterranean, inland Europe, Asia, and Africa, catnip is a hardy perennial growing to four feet in height. It is widely naturalized in North America particularly in Virginia and North Carolina. The fuzzy, grayish leaves are somewhat oval in shape, acute at the tip, heart-shaped at the base, and toothed, and range from one to three inches in length. The flowers occur in tight terminal spikes. Individual flowers are about three-eighths of an inch long and are white with light purple spots. Flowering begins at the end of May in the South, lasting through late summer in northern climates. This Eurasian native has become naturalized worldwide. A lemon-scented cultivar, 'Citriodora', is available from some plant sources. It is a naturally occurring variety (*N. cataria* var. *citriodora*).

Another commonly encountered species in American herb gardens is *N. mussinii* K. Spreng ex. Henckel. This low-growing sprawling perennial reaches up to one foot in height. The gray-green leaves look similar to *N. cataria,* but are only an inch long. The flowers, borne on a loose raceme, are about three-eighths of an inch long and rich blue. This species has a peculiar pungent citrus-like fragrance and is the showier of the two species. It is often sold under the name

catmint and cats do enjoy it.

Catnip is easily propagated from seeds or root divisions. Seeds can be sown directly in the garden in spring or fall. Seeds germinate in two weeks. Low quality seed is prevalent in the trade, so a germination test should be conducted to make sure that the seeds are viable. Root divisions can also be done at either time. Young seedlings should be spaced eighteen to twenty-four inches apart. Established plants will self-sow.

Catnip thrives in a variety of habitats. It grows well in the poorest dry garden soils and in rich, deep-shaded woods. It enjoys full sun, but will tolerate partial shade. It will thrive in almost any garden soil and become weedy if given the opportunity. Soil pH can range between 5 and 7.5. The plants will become more fragrant when grown in a sandy soil in full sun than in a heavy loam under shade. Frequent shallow cultivation encourages vigorous growth.

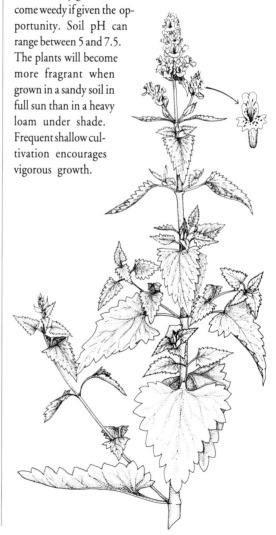

A field of catnip usually produces for about three years.

The flowering tops are the most desirable part of the plant. Catnip is by weight sixty to eighty percent stem material. Dried catnip available on the herb market is often of inferior quality, being mainly stem chards. However, commercial plantings can be expected to produce between fifteen hundred to two thousand pounds per acre. However, commercial fields in North Carolina, with plants spaced at nine to twelve inches in rows on thirty to thirty-eight inch centers have yielded between three thousand and five thousand pounds of dried herb per acre (Ferguson et al. 1988).

"If you sow it cats won't know it, if you set it cats will get it" is a bit of folk wisdom the herb gardener will find true more often than not. Plants sown from seeds seem to be left undisturbed by cats until harvested or transplanted. Bruised leaves release essential oils and attract cats. Once after harvesting catnip I visited a nearby farm to look at some machinery. I hadn't changed my clothes or washed and, to the discerning nose, I smelled like a catnip plant in human disguise—or so the twenty-three cats on this farm thought. I hadn't been out of the car for more than two minutes before more than a dozen cats surrounded me. When two of them clawed my pant leg, I decided on a quick retreat.

The effect the herb produces on cats is known as the "catnip response," and includes sniffing, licking and chewing with head shaking, chin and cheek rubbing, and head over-rolling and body rubbing. The domestic cat responds to other plants in a similar manner. Other members of the cat family including lion, tiger, leopard, and jaguar experience the catnip response. The effect usually lasts for fifteen minutes, but may last for up to an hour. The catnip response has been found to be inherited as an autosomal dominant gene. About one-third of domestic cats do not enjoy the pleasurable effects of catnip. The effects are not achieved by chewing the plant, rather they are induced by smelling the herb, and the plant must be crushed, bruised, or broken to release the chemicals responsible for the effect. (Tucker and Tucker 1988).

Though mainly thought of as a feline euphoric, catnip has a rich tradition of folk use. Catnip tea is used for headaches, stomachaches, colic, and sleeplessness in children. The fresh leaves can also be chewed for headache. It's an old home remedy for colds, nervous tension, fevers, and nightmare. It is diaphoretic and antispasmodic. Sister Mildred Barker of the Sabbathday Lake Shakers told me that catnip tea was the sole medication given her as a young child at the Alfred, Maine, Shaker Community. A seventy-year-old friend, native to Aroostock County, Maine, related that his grandmother would give him a tea of boneset, *Eupatorium perfoliatum,* turtle head, *Chelone glabra,* and catnip to remedy the symptoms of cold and flu. Herbalists use it to allay diarrhea and chronic bronchitis. Catnip has also been used for anemia, menstrual, and uterine disorders.

The essential oil contains carvacrol, beta-caryophyllene, nepetol, thymol, geraniol, citronella, nerol, valeric acid, and most important, nepetalactone. Nepetalactone and its isomers are the components responsible for the catnip effect. It is found at levels of from 0.1–30 percent of catnip's essential oil. Nepetalactone probably evolved in the plant to protect it against insects that might otherwise feed on it. The compound is related to repellent secretions identified from certain species of insects.

CAT THYME

Teucrium marum L.
(to'-kree-um may'-rum)
Labiatae (Lamiaceae)—Mint Family
Plate 5

If you think cats like catnip, you should see how they react to cat thyme. A cat's curiosity is tantalized by the tingling essential oil as they fuss, nibble, and caress this herb. The inquisitive herb gardener will be amazed at the explosive bite in the nose this herb's fragrance inflicts.

The genus *Teucrium* is represented by over 300 species, mainly originating from the Mediterranean region. *T. marum* is a subshrub native to southern Spain, southern France, Italy and Yugoslavia, including islands of the western Mediterranean and one island off the northwest Yugoslavian coast. It is a small perennial shrub reaching twelve to eighteen inches high, with slender stems, and linear-lanceolate to oval-shaped leaves three-eighths of an inch long. The leaves are entire (without teeth), though they occasionally develop small teeth. The margins of the leaves curve downward. Soft white fuzz covers the leaf's upper surface, while a gray pubescens is on the underside. The flowers, tightly packed on a cylinder-shaped head, are five-sixteenths to seven-sixteenths of an inch long, and of a soft rose-red to purplish color.

This relatively tender shrub prefers chalky, sandy loam with good drainage. It needs full sun and is best propagated from cuttings. It forms a dense low mass of pleasing color. Where temperatures dip below 20°F during winter months, bring this herb indoors. Where the temperature goes below freezing, mulch it well. If need be, protect it from cats. At Taylor's Herb Gardens, in Vista, California, cat thymes are caged in chicken wire.

Cat thyme's odor is strongly camphoraceous and its taste pungent and bitter. As a medicinal herb it is known as *herba mari veri*, or herb mastich. Tonic, stimulant, diaphoretic, diuretic, emmenagogue, and expectorant properties have been attributed to it. It is used in chronic bronchitis, leucorrhea, amenorrhea, gout, and stomach ailments. A snuff made from the powdered herb has been used for nasal polyps. It was once an ingredient of *pulvis asari compositus* - compound powder of asarabacca, sweet marjoram, Syrian herb mastich, and lavender flowers. The 1789 (557) *Edinburgh Dispensatory* listed this herbal snuff as a remedy for "cases of obstinate headache and of ophthalmias resisting other modes of cure." Its immediate effect was to induce frequent sneezing.

Cat thyme contains an essential oil, a saponin, tannins, and choline. While isolated compounds from the plant have not been tested on felines, its effect is well-known. Once again we have a member of the mint family with varying quality of its essential oil, depending upon where the plant evolved and the local growing conditions. Plants from Sardinia were found to contain about four percent dolicholactone C, and seventy-six percent of the oil was dolicholactone D. The former compound was found in trace amounts in the oil of plants from Corsica, and the latter lactone formed seventeen percent of the oil (Tucker and Tucker 1988).

CAYENNE

Capsicum annuum L. and *C. frutescens* L.
(kap'-si-kum an-you'-um; fru-tes'-enz)
Solanaceae—Nightshade Family.
Plate 10

At the time I am writing this, it is a few days after the 500th anniversary of the arrival of Columbus in the New World. Columbus departed the Canary Island with his three famous ships on September 6, 1492, with a primary goal of discovering a westward route to the "spice islands." He "discovered" America instead. In his log book entry of 4 November 1492, he noted that he ardently sought a source

of pepper—true pepper (*Piper nigrum*)—the premier spice imported from the East. But none was to be found among the Arawak, the first native group he encountered. When dining with the Arawak, however, Columbus did experience a familiar, but more pungent peppery flavoring. In the stews served to him by the Arawak, he became the first European to taste the New World peppers—members of the genus *Capsicum*.

While Columbus did not find the true pepper plant that he sought, he instead stumbled upon what has been the most important herb that the New World delivered to the Old. Whatever your opinion of the man's deeds, one neglected and perhaps vicarious accomplishment was the introduction of *Capsicum* to the Western palate.

Columbus called the new spice "red pepper." Eventually, "red peppers" spread throughout the world and are now an important part of the cuisine of Europeans, Asians, Africans, and Americans. Chili peppers are today the most widely consumed spice in the world.

Capsicum species are believed to have originated in an area of southern Brazil and Bolivia, from which they spread to various parts of South and Central America. In pre-Columbian Latin America, centuries before the arrival of Columbus, five species had already been domesticated. In addition to *Capsicum annuum* and *C. frutescens*, other domesticated species include *C. chinense* (which originated in the Amazon region not China), *C. pubescens*, and *C. baccatum*, or "aji," still the preferred chili species in the Andean region ranging from Ecuador, Peru, and Bolivia to Chile.

Recognizing that habitat loss, such as the destruction of the Amazon rain forest, was resulting in a loss of the *Capsicum* gene pool, a concerted effort among plant breeders and conservators in the Americas has produced a collection of more than 1,700 different pepper varieties, both wild and cultivated, since 1987. In addition, a new worldwide collection of *Capsicums* has been established in Taiwan. Despite 500 years of collective human experience with the "red peppers," scientists are only beginning to document and preserve the astounding genetic diversity of "red peppers."

There are about twenty species and hundreds of varieties in the genus *Capsicum*, indigenous to tropical America. In their native habitat, they are perennial and woody, growing to seven feet tall, though in American gardens they are grown as annuals, reaching a height of three feet. Two highly variable species of the genus provide New World peppers—

the red peppers. Bell peppers, pimento, paprika, chili, and cayenne peppers all belong to the species *Capsicum annuum.* The Tabasco peppers come from *Capsicum frutescens,* grown commercially in the Gulf states and New Mexico. Both species and their endless numbers of variety are cultivated in this country. These much-branded, smooth, shiny herbs have alternate leaves, oval to lance-shaped, one to five inches in length. *Capsicum annuum* flowers are solitary, arising from leaf axils. *Capsicum frutescens* may have flowers in pairs or several from each axil. The flowers on both species are white and star-shaped. Blooming begins in July to August; fruits mature by October. The familiar pods range from inch-long pea-sized fruits to banana-shaped fruits over a foot long. Their colors range from deep blues, cream yellow, green, orange, and scarlet.

Wild chilies also occur in the United States. *Capsicum annuum* var. *aviculare* is found in western and southern Texas and in only a handful of populations in Arizona. A conservation group, Native Seeds/ SEARCH has developed a cooperative effort with the U.S. Forest Service to preserve and study populations of the plant in Arizona, providing protection for the plant in its native habitat, rather than in a botanical garden. The tiny, super-hot peppers from this variety are known as chiltepin, which sell for as much as $72 per pound in retail markets in the Southwest. It is just one example of the many chili pepper varieties enjoyed in specific cuisines.

Peppers are grown from seed sown indoors in flats six to eight weeks before the spring's last frost. In southern states, cayenne can be sown directly in the garden after danger of frost has passed. Young seedlings are tender and easily destroyed by frost, though mature plants may survive an autumn frost or two. Give seedlings eight to twelve inch spacings.

A rich, sandy loam is good for pepper culture. Peppers like full sun, but will tolerate some shade. A light soil will usually produce a healthier crop than heavy clay soils. Peppers tolerate a pH ranging from 4.5 to 8. Irrigation may be necessary for young seedlings until the root system is well-established.

Just before a fall frost, harvest the ripened fruits and string them up to dry. Be careful not to break the stem at the top of the fruit, causing it to spoil before drying. The whole plant can be pulled and hung to dry. Peppers may take several weeks to dry, losing about 75 percent of their fresh weight.

The Vitamin C content nearly doubles as the pods turn red. Cayenne is high in Vitamin A, B vitamins, calcium, phosphorus, iron, and contains up to 15 percent protein.

Cayenne is a must for Mexican food. It will enhance the flavor of tomato dishes, egg salad, eggplant, and beans. In American herbalism, the use of cayenne as a stimulant was promoted by Samuel Thomson in the late 1700s and early

Cayenne

1800s (see lobelia). He used it as a follow-up to lobelia to "retain the internal vital heat of the system and cause free perspiration" (Thomson 1835, p. 80).

Cayenne has been used as a gargle for sore throats. Rheumatism and arthritis have been treated with a poultice or liniment made from powdered cayenne. A teaspoon of cayenne suspended in a tablespoon of olive oil has been given to relieve nausea at the first signs of seasickness. Small amounts in food increase saliva and help digestion. Taken internally, cayenne produces great warmth in the stomach, and to a lesser extent in the extremities. It opens capillaries and increases blood flow. In Oriental medicine, cayenne is considered a yin herb, bringing heat to the surface capillaries where it dissipates, and thus ultimately has a cooling effect.

Various cayenne products have reached mainstream medicine in recent years. Capsaicin is the most pungent of several components in the plant. Two pharmaceutical creams, Zostrix and Axsain, contain .025 percent and .075 percent capsaicin, respectively. Zostrix first appeared on the market in 1987 as a treatment for the pain of post-herpetic neuralgia, a complication of shingles (caused by the herpes zoster virus). The more potent Axsain is prescribed for chronic foot and leg pains in diabetes patients (McCourt 1991). Use of these products does not produce instant results. They require continuous application for two to four weeks before desired results are achieved (Gossel 1990). *Capsicum* preparations using the primary active component of the plant, capsaicin, in the form of a dilute solution or ointment, have been examined in a study of cluster headache sufferers. The solution, when applied to one nostril brought relief on the side of the head where the headache occurred, but when applied to the opposite nostril, produced no results. When the ointment was applied to the temples, patients did not experience pain on the days when the ointment was in use. The temple area normally experiences a heat loss during headache episodes, but as you might expect, the cayenne preparation kept the temples warm. The jury is still out on this experimental treatment. Check with your physician or pharmacist for specific health care needs involving pharmaceutical capsaicin-containing products. They must be used with proper caution since capsaicin, itself, can be extremely irritating especially to mucous membranes and the eyes.

Like other herbs, cayenne in excess can cause problems. It irritates the skin and mucosa. External application can cause dermatitis with blistering. Gastroenteritis and kidney lesions can result from excessive internal use.

Capsicum fruits contain a pungent component—capsaicin—and capsanthin—a cartenoid pigment. Capsaicin produces a strong alkaline reaction likened to lye, producing intense pain and burning (initially), dizziness, and high pulse. In producing an inflammatory response, histamine release is involved in early phases, while both histamine and "substance P" are involved in later phases of capsaicin-produced inflammation. Small amounts in appropriate delivery forms act by disrupting substance P, a protein that serves as a key neurotransmitter to relay pain messages from the brain nerve endings. Capsaicin initially causes a release in substance P, hence the pain and burning, though with repeated dosages of capsaicin, nerve endings somehow stop replenishing their substance P supplies, resulting in desensitization of the nerve endings (McCourt 1991). Scientists who work with the highly irritating purified substance must protect themselves from the dust by donning space-suit garb to protect themselves. Capsaicin is not water-soluble and cannot wash off. The effect is termed "Hunan Hand." If peppers are soaked in vinegar for several hours, capsaicin is neutralized. Capsaicin is currently the subject of clinical studies for a wide range of topical applications, including psoriasis, vitiligo, intractable pruritus, post mastectomy pain, phantom pain syndrome, postsurgical pain, sciatica and arthritis pain (Gossler 1990). Stay tuned.

CHAMOMILE

Matricaria recutita L., *Chamaemelum nobile* (L.) All.
(mat-ri-kay'- ree-a rek-you-tie'-ta;
kam-ee-mel-um no'-bil-ee)
Compositae (Asteraceae)—Aster Family
Plate 9

Chamomile is one of those ambiguous common names applied to a variety of closely related species. We will concern ourselves with two: Hungarian or German chamomile, *Matricaria recutita* (*M. chamomilla* or *Chamomilla recutita*), and Roman or English chamomile, *Chamaemelum nobile* (*Anthemis nobilis*).

German chamomile is an annual native of Europe and western Asia, growing from one to two feet high. It has a pale green, smooth, shiny stem with striations. The finely divided, linear leaf segments are borne on numerous branches. The many terminal flower heads make a comblike formation, and are about one-half to five-eighths of an inch in diameter. The disk flowers are yellow, surrounded by ten to twenty white ray flowers. The receptacle is smooth, conical, elongated, and hollow inside. The fruit is a slightly curved, pale gray, smooth achene. Good-quality German chamomile is about three times cheaper than Roman. Major suppliers to the world market include Argentina, Belgium, Bulgaria, Czecho-Slovakia, Egypt, Germany, Hungary, Poland, and Russia.

German chamomile is a plant of genetic diversity, producing several chemotypes. Appreciation of this fact led European researchers to entirely reassess chamomile production in the late 1970s and 1980s. Consequently, plant breeders, producers, and other scientists worked in concert to develop intensive improvement programs for the plant. According to Slovak chamomile specialist Ivan Salamon, four basic chemical types of German chamomile are now recognized (Salamon 1992a, 1992b, 1992c). Selection and breeding programs have resulted in better-quality chamomile with more stable, predictable, and higher levels of active components. Crop-improvement programs continue in earnest in both eastern and western Europe. In addition to genetic differences, quality and quantity of the essential oil depend upon variables such as environmental factors, cultivation practices, plant part, plant age, and postharvest handling. Articles relative to these subjects are cited by Mann and Staba (1986) and Simon, Chadwick, and Craker (1984).

English or Roman chamomile, a perennial native to western Europe, northward to Northern Ireland, is a low-growing herb with a creeping rhizome, reaching a foot in height. The stems are branching, slightly hairy, and usually prostrate or drooping, though sometimes erect. The downy, alternate, green-gray leaves are two to three, divided into linear segments which are flatter and thicker than those of German chamomile. The flower heads are about an inch across and sparse compared with German chamomile—a solitary head sits atop each flower stalk. The disk flowers are yellow; the ray flowers are white, though sometimes absent. The receptacle is conical and solid. One showy double-flowered variety has large white blossoms. Nearly all the yellow disk flowers become white ray flowers. A petalless flower form is available from some herb plant sellers. 'Treanague', a cultivar named after the estate where it originated, is flowerless. There are also double-flowered cultivars (well known by the sixteenth century). Commercial supplies come from England, France, Belgium, and

eastern Europe.

German chamomile is grown from seeds sown directly in their garden location. The plants will self-sow freely. Watch out. They can become weeds! The second year that I grew German chamomile, I found plants springing up along the driveway several hundred yards away! In Boulder, Colorado, you can find the plant naturalized along roadsides and in the cracks of sidewalks, where seeds have "escaped" from Celestial Seasonings. The seedbed should be well prepared as the seeds are very tiny—almost

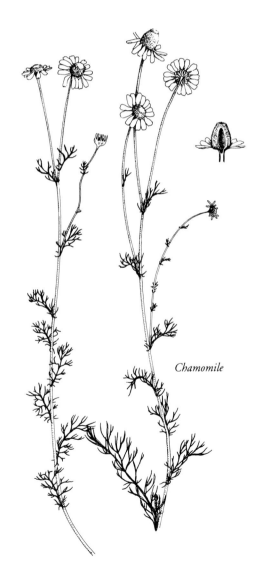

Chamomile

dustlike. They can be scattered on the soil's surface, then gently tamped down with the flat side of a hoe. Sow as early in the spring as possible because seedlings tend to become leggy and flower quickly under hot summer sun. You can plant chamomile about the same time you would plant peas. The young seedlings will withstand a mild frost. The seeds generally germinate in a week to ten days. Germination begins at temperatures of around 45° F. The plants grow slowly at first, and need to be well weeded. After four to five weeks, a growth spurt occurs, forming a rosette of leaves. Flowers soon follow. Young seedlings, about one to two inches tall, are easily transplanted. Older seedlings do not survive transplanting.

If planted around June 1 in the North, expect flowering in late July or early August. Blooms develop continuously. Here in the southern Ozarks, self-sown plants complete their life cycles by mid-June. When I was at the Sabbathday Lake, Maine, Shaker community back in the late 1970s, we planted double rows of German chamomile ten inches apart, and harvested the flowers with a blueberry rake. Once flowering commences, harvesting is possible every ten days to two weeks. Commercial growers in northern Europe get two to three cuttings of flowers during the plant's annual life cycle. An acre may produce three hundred to five hundred pounds of dried flowers.

German chamomile is an adaptable plant. It likes full sun and will tolerate almost any soil, though a light, sandy, somewhat-moist loam, high in nitrogen and potassium, will produce optimum growth. Typically, plants do best with about eighteen inches of rainfall during the growing season. Soil pH should fall between 6 and 8.5. In short, this plant is easy to grow, and loves a brief, cool season.

Roman chamomile likes full sun and a slightly acid-to-neutral garden soil with good drainage. It does not tolerate hot, dry weather. I have a very difficult time trying to grow it in the Ozarks. It is an excellent, but slow-growing, ground cover for cooler areas. English chamomile can be started from seeds, cuttings, or by root division. Seedlings should have a six-to-twelve-inch spacing. When cultivating with a hoe, cover exposed or loose roots with soil.

A rich soil will produce a lush leaf growth, but few English chamomile flowers. An acre may yield four hundred to six hundred pounds of the dried flowers. England produces most of them.

Most seeds purchased as chamomile, and dried chamomile for tea, are usually *M. recutita*. To determine whether dried chamomile flowers are German or English, carefully slice open the receptacle of the flower head. The German receptacle is hollow; the English is solid. Teabagged chamomile often contains seeds. Tear open a package, plant the contents, and see what happens.

In Europe, chamomile is highly esteemed as a medicinal herb. According to a recent article by Ivan Salamon (1992b), *M. recutita* is included in the pharmacopoeias of twenty-six countries. Writing on the plant in the June–August 1992 issue of the Australian journal *Focus on Herbs,* Salamon also noted that in Czecho-Slovakia, a common folk saying has it that "an individual should always bow before the curative powers of the chamomile plant."

"As a popular remedy, it may be thought of as the European counterpart of ginseng," writes Varro Tyler in *The New Honest Herbal* (1987, 66). Dr. Tyler tells us that the Germans describe it as *alles zutraut*—"capable of anything." He also notes that the Germans refer to *M. recutita* as the "genuine chamomile."

Speaking before the 1992 annual meeting of the American Chemical Society, Purdue University's Dr. Tyler called chamomile "perhaps the best example of the wide chasm separating medicinal practice in Western Europe and the United States." Tyler notes that in the U.S., chamomile is best known as a pleasant-tasting herbal beverage tea. In Europe, it is most familiar as a phytomedicine (herbal medicine), used for a wide range of ailments, including everything from spasms of the gastrointestinal tract to skin irritations. According to Dr. Tyler, in 1987 chamomile was designated as the medicinal plant of the year in Europe.

Medicinal herb use is much more popular in many parts of Europe than in the United States. Chamomile exemplifies that. With the expected merger of the European economic-community (EC) countries, in which free trade will become like interstate commerce in the U.S. as borders between countries practically evaporate, the twelve member countries will have to harmonize their drug laws. In other words, they will all have to operate under the same regulations. To make the transition smoother, a coalition of national phytomedicine (plant medicine) organizations, known as ESCOP (European Scientific Cooperative for Phytotherapy), is developing suggested regulatory texts or monographs. Among the first five issued was one for German chamomile.

How do the Europeans use chamomile? It takes a wide

variety of forms, and is included in dozens of products. Compresses, rinses, or gargles are used externally for the treatment of inflammations and irritations of the skin and mucosa, including the mouth and gums, respiratory tract, and for hemorrhoids. Chamomile can also be added to bathwater. The ESCOP monograph calls for about a quarter ounce of the dried flowers in a quart of water. Extrapolate that to a bathtub containing thirty gallons of water, and you're talking about a pound and a half of dried flowers. Alternately, alcohol extracts of the flowers are available in Europe. Pour the recommended amount in the tub and you have a more convenient way to take a chamomile bath.

Internally, a tea can be made from just two to three grams of the herb, or appropriate amounts of tinctures or proprietary preparations are also popular. The tea or tincture is taken to relieve spasms and inflammatory conditions of the gastrointestinal tract, as well as peptic ulcers. A mild tea also acts as a gentle sleep aid, particularly for children. All of the medicinal recommendations of the ESCOP monograph are backed not only by intensive recent research, but also by many centuries of common use.

Over the last decade, it has often been repeated in the popular press and even the medical literature in the United States that drinking chamomile tea may cause severe allergic reactions. Each ESCOP monograph, including the one on chamomile, addresses issues relative to potential side effects or adverse reactions. These include discussions on contraindications, side effects, use during pregnancy and lactation, special warnings, interactions, duration of administration, and overdose. Under contraindications, we find "none known." Use during pregnancy and lactation? "No adverse effects reported." Special warnings? "None required." Interactions? "None reported." Duration of administration? "No restriction." Overdose? "No intoxication symptoms reported."

What's all the fuss that has branded chamomile an allergenic substance in the U.S. been about? Under the side-effect heading in the ESCOP monograph, it says, "Extremely rare contact allergy." How much is rare? Dr. Tyler has already answered that question in *The New Honest Herbal.* Between the years 1887 and 1982, fifty allergies resulting from chamomile use were reported in the literature. Of these, only five were attributed to German chamomile. Chamomile seems to have a better safety record than some recent reports would indicate. However, if you experience allergic reactions to members of the aster family, you could be one of the rare individuals who may have trouble with chamomile.

Traditionally, chamomile is perhaps the best known of herbal teas besides peppermint. English chamomile tea has tonic, stomachic, diaphoretic, soporific, and antispasmodic qualities. German chamomile is tonic, sedative, carminative, emmenagogic, antiinflammatory, stomachic, antispasmodic, and diaphoretic. It has traditionally been used in treating colic, diarrhea, insomnia, indigestion, toothache, swollen gums, skin problems, gout, sciatica, and a host of other ailments. Both chamomiles have been used as folk cancer treatments.

As a good rinse for blonde hair, steep the dried flower heads in hot water, cool the infusion, then strain. Extracts of the two species are used in cosmetics such as hair dyes, shampoos, sunburn lotions, bath lotions, and other products. The oil is used as a fragrance in soap, detergent, perfumes, and lotions.

The oil of German chamomile contains chamazulene, farnesene, alpha-bisabolol, and other components. High-quality oil should be a deep blue color. The oil has antibacterial and fungicidal properties. The component chamazulene is anodyne, antispasmodic, antiinflammatory, and antiallergenic. The plant also contains flavonoids, coumarins, a polysaccharide, choline, and amino acids. Over 120 components have been identified in oil of chamomile. Chamazulene was once thought to be the primary active component. But now scientists believe that chamomile's pharmacological benefits are primarily the result of a component chemists call alpha-bisabolol (see Foster 1991e, 1993).

CHASTE TREE

Vitex agnus-castus L.
(veye'-tex ag'-nus-kass-tus)
Verbenaceae—Verbena Family.

The chaste tree is from the genus *Vitex,* which includes over 250 mostly tropical shrubs and trees. A few temperate-climate species are found in Asia, and *V. agnus-castus* is the sole species to occur in Europe. It is a shrub growing from nine to seventeen feet tall, and is common throughout much of Europe and West Asia. It is actually native to West Asia, but was introduced into European gardens in 1570, and has since become naturalized on much of the Continent. It has palmate leaves, usually with five to nine (rarely three) leaflets. The leaf stalks, up to three inches long, are densely hairy and resinous. The long, narrow leaflets are white hairy beneath. The leaflets are either entire (without teeth) or have wavy edges. The flowers, in a pyramidal-shaped, showy cluster, with seven-inch-long spikes, sport tiny blue to lilac blooms (or white, in cultivar 'Alba'). The flower stalks are dotted with resinous glands. The chaste tree blooms as early as April in the Deep South, lasting into October in more northerly areas. Typically it blooms from June through August. The small round fruits (seeds) have a pungent scent and flavor.

The shrub was introduced into American horticulture at a relatively early date. It is naturalized in Florida, Georgia (coastal plain), Alabama, Mississippi, Louisiana, Arkansas, Texas, and southeastern Oklahoma. Chaste tree is hardy as far north as southern New York. It could conceivably be cultivated in much of the United States. Cultivars available in the nursery trade include the white form, 'Alba', a pink-flowered form, 'Rosea', and a large-leaved form, 'Latifolia', sometimes sold under the erroneous name *V. macrophylla.*

The name *Vitex* is the ancient Latin name for this plant group. The species name, *agnus-castus,* derives from *agnus* (a lamb) and *castus* (chaste), hence the common name "chaste tree." In medieval European traditions, it was held as a symbol of chastity, and the branches were once strewn before the feet of novices as they entered the monastery or convent.

Unlike most woody plants, chaste tree seeds germinate readily without any pregermination treatments, and soft-wood cuttings root at a near 100 percent success rate. Cuttings can be made from May through July, before flowering begins. A dip of 1000 to 4000 ppm IBA quick dip (rooting hormone) has been suggested for optimum propagation of cuttings in a peat-moss/perlite mix. Mist cuttings to produce more rapid rooting, but reduce or eliminate misting once rooting actually begins, as excessive moisture may result in less-healthy cuttings. Chaste tree can also be propagated by layering. Seed and plant sources are readily available. In short, this shrub can be successfully propagated by a gardening klutz.

There are few woody plants as easy to cultivate as chaste tree. It prospers in a wide variety of soils, thriving in hot, desertlike conditions, and growing luxuriant in fertile, moist soils as well. Plants raised in rich soils tend to have paler blooms. The shrub does not like standing water, and should be planted in a well-drained area. It likes full sun.

Vitex agnus-castus, Chaste Tree

The long, stringy roots of established specimens make it difficult to transplant. Chaste tree has an open-spreading habit, and if it becomes too large and sprawling, it can be pruned back within a couple of feet of the ground each year to create a smaller, more-controlled shrub. It is popularly grown as an ornamental in the South.

The twigs have been valued as a basket-making material, the fruits have been used as a pepper substitute, but chaste tree is best known for its religious symbolism. In the Mediterranean region, the fruits were traditionally thought to be an antiaphrodisiac, and perhaps this idea led to the shrub's connection with chastity. The use of the plant as an antiaphrodisiac can be traced to ancient Greece. Many of the common names of the shrub refer to this chastity motif, including monk's pepper tree, Abraham's balm, chaste lamb tree, and safe tree. It has also been called Indian spice and wild pepper because of the use of its fruits.

Certainly, it has been a long time since chaste tree was popularly regarded as an antiaphrodisiac. The fact that the plant had no power to save monastics from earthly pleasures was officially recognized by medical professionals as early as 1789, when Duncan, the author of *The Edinburgh New Dispensatory,* wrote, "These seeds have been celebrated as antiaphrodisiacs, and were formerly much used by the monks for allaying the venereal appetite; but experience does not warrant their having any such virtues" (119). In 1812, John Hill had something similar to say in his *The Family Herbal:* "The seeds of this shrub were once supposed to ally venery, but no body regards that now. A decoction of the leaves and tops is good against obstructions of the liver" (70).

Dr. Robert John Thorton (1814), also author of *A Family Herbal,* put it more eloquently: "As there are provocatives to procreations, as shell-fish, eggs, and roots of orchises made into salep for the male, and spare dict and use of steel for the female, so it is possible the chaste tree may have a contrary effect; and hence the seeds have been called *Piper monachorum* (Monk's pepper), who flew to them when they found the spirit to be willing, but the flesh weak" (589).

Other European traditions include making a tea of the fruits for the treatment of rheumatic conditions and colds. The fruits have also been employed as a digestive carminative. It is interesting to note that these three uses parallel traditional Chinese practices for closely related species. In the nineteenth century, eclectic medical practitioners suggested a tincture of the fresh berries to increase milk secretions and alleviate menstrual disorders. In small doses, the fruit was said to be helpful in the treatment of impotence, and perhaps even in cases of nervousness or mild dementia.

Modern European scientific research has not bothered with the fruit's supposed antiaphrodisiac attributes, but rather chose to focus on its traditional uses for menstrual and menopausal disorders. Recent German studies suggest that extracts of the seeds can control excessive menstrual bleeding or too-frequent menstruation. One study shows that plant preparations may have the ability to stimulate progesterone production, and may also have a regulating effect on estrogen. Chaste tree products have been used in Germany to help reestablish normal menstruation and ovulation after women stop taking birth-control pills. Comparative clinical studies suggest confirmation of the ability of plant preparations to increase or stimulate milk flow. The preparation had to be used for several weeks before it produced results, however. One proprietary medicine

manufactured in Germany has been shown to reduce water retention during menstruation, and to allay effusions in the knee joints associated with premenstrual syndrome (S. Foster 1989i).

A 1972 retrospective joint communication reported on the use of Agnolyt®, a preparation of chaste-tree fruits manufactured by Madaus, AG, in Cologne, Germany, in the treatment of several thousand cases. One of the physicians reported notable success in the treatment of premenstrual syndrome, polymenorrhea, and hypermenorrhea associated with uterine fibroids. Agnolyt was also reported to be of value in relieving headaches which occurred during intervals between taking packages of oral contraceptives. One of the physicians collected more than five hundred case studies in which a dose of forty drops of the preparation was used on a daily basis. Treatment ranging from three weeks to three months proved helpful in controlling mastodynia and irregular uterine bleeding (Attelmann et al. 1972). In modern phytotherapy in Germany, preparations of the fruits are used to treat primary or secondary corpus-luteum insufficiency, premenstrual syndrome, mastodynia, menopausal symptoms, and inadequate lactation.

Various iridoids, such as aucubin and agnuside, and flavonoids identified from the leaves and seeds, have been shown to have significant antibacterial effects. Other components include a volatile oil, castin (a bitter substance), and fixed oil.

CHERVIL

Anthriscus cerefolium (L.) Hoffm.
(an-thriz'-kus sir-e-foh'-lee-um)
Umbelliferae (Apiaceae)—Carrot Family

Chervil is a hardy annual, little known, yet worthy of a place in every garden of edibles because of its delicate flavor in salads. It is a native of southeastern and south-central Europe, growing to a height of two feet. It is naturalized in most parts of Europe, extending north to Sweden, and east to the Ukraine. The small, finely divided, parsleylike leaves are on erect, branching, wiry stems. Chervil produces umbels of minute white flowers. The fruit is linear, about one-fourth inch long with a one-eighth-inch-long beak. One variety has crisp leaves. Chervil has a decidedly mild anise or tarragonlike flavor. In the northeastern United States, it has escaped from cultivation and grows wild.

Chervil is easily grown from seed sown at intervals from

spring to fall. Plants take six to eight weeks to develop. It does best in the cool of spring and autumn, disliking summer heat. Seedlings should be thinned so that they stand six inches apart.

Chervil likes a well-drained, moderately rich garden soil in partial shade. A pH range between 7 and 8 is optimum. It can be planted among taller vegetables or herbs which will shade it during the hot, dry summer weather. In hot weather, it has a tendency toward rapid bolting. Harvest before flowering. To retain a good green color, it should be dried at temperatures below 90° F.

Fresh chervil is best for cooking. It loses its delicate

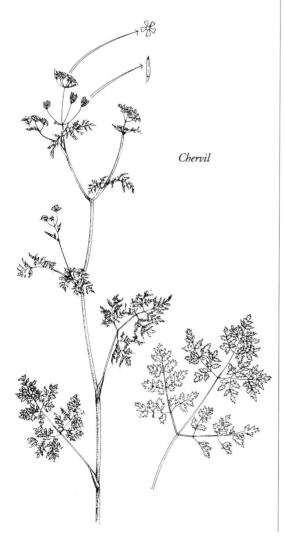

Chervil

tarragon flavor upon drying. Its subtle flavor has to be tasted to be appreciated. Use more chervil than you would other herbs because its mild flavor is easily lost. Add it to food after the dish is cooked to preserve flavor. Add Chervil fresh to soups and sauces. It is also good in egg dishes, with baked potatoes in sour cream, or mixed (two tablespoons of fresh to one teaspoon dried) with a package of cream cheese or a stick of butter. It has great potential, and when combined with other herbs, glorifies their flavor. Its delicate parsley and anise flavor, coupled with its parsleylike appearance, has earned it the name "gourmet's parsley." It is an ingredient of French culinary herb combinations known as "fines herbes." Basil, chives, parsley, sage, savory, and tarragon are also used in such mixtures.

Chervil contains up to 23 percent proteins, and appreciable amounts of calcium, phosphorus, and magnesium, with smaller levels of potassium, iron, and zinc.

Chervil is diuretic, a blood cleanser, and an expectorant, and has traditionally been used to increase perspiration and reduce high blood pressure. In the European tradition, the fresh juice is a treatment for fevers, gout, jaundice, and chronic skin problems.

The essential oil contains estragole (as is the case with tarragon and basil), plus anethole. The leaves contain a fixed oil, and apiin—a glycoside.

CHICORY

Cichorium intybus L., *C. endiva* L.
(si-koe'-ree-um in'-ti-bus; en-dive'-a)
Compositae (Asteraceae)—Aster Family

One person's weed is another person's herb. More often maligned than enjoyed in America, chicory is a culinary herb deserving greater appreciation. Chicory is thought to be native to Europe and Asia, and is extensively naturalized in North America. Two species, *Cichorium intybus* and *C. endiva,* are grown in gardens. *C. intybus,* common chicory, is a perennial, growing from two to six feet high. It has a deep, spiraling taproot, and its lower leaves resemble dandelion leaves, though they are usually larger. The upper leaves are alternate, clasping the stem and becoming progressively smaller toward the top of the plant. They may be with or without teeth. The pleasing, sky blue, rarely pink, ligulate flowers hug the stems in clusters of two or three flower heads, or one head may sit alone on a short branch. They are about an inch and a half in diameter. *C. endiva* is an annual or biennial, growing to three feet high, and its leaves are ruffled and more robust. My seed catalogs list nineteen chicory cultivars, including red-leaf varieties, heading chicories, large-root chicories, and salad varieties.

Both endive and common chicory are grown from seed sown in late spring or midsummer for autumn salad greens. Seedlings can be thinned to six-to-ten-inch spacings. About seven to twelve pounds of seed will sow an acre, if broadcast. A rich, deep-dug soil and full sun provide a good home for chicory. It thrives best in cooler regions. *C. intybus* can be sown in the spring, followed by a successive planting of *C. endiva* in midsummer. Azure blue flowers, edible foliage and root, and medicinal qualities make chicory an alluring plant for the herb garden.

Witloof (a Flemish word for "white leaf"), or blanched leaves forced from winter-stored roots or roots banked with earth in spring or fall, is chicory's best-known leaf product. For winter-grown witloof, the tops are cut just above the ground, then stored in sand, light soil, or sawdust in a warm cellar. Before storage, the lower end of the root is trimmed into eight-inch-long sections, and placed upright in the growing medium. If one covers the crowns with about eight inches of soil, the roots form a "head" three to six inches long of etiolated (blanched) leaves, tender and mild in flavor. Crowns can also be forced by placing the roots in a warm, moist, dark spot or covering them in the field with flowerpots.

If a root harvest is desired, do not allow the plants to go to seed. They should be harvested at the end of the growing season, plowed up and allowed to cure on the ground surface for two weeks. In New Zealand, experimental plantings have produced up to ten tons per acre in a year, though expected yields in other parts of the world are less than half that amount.

Young, unmanipulated shoots and roots may also be eaten as vegetables. The bitter taste of fresh green leaves can be reduced by cooking them in several waters. Before boiling, slice the roots in thin pieces and soak them in water overnight to remove bitter elements.

The greens are high in vitamin A, calcium, and potassium. They also contain appreciable amounts of phosphorus, choline, iron, vitamin C, and B vitamins. The roots contain over 50 percent inulin, choline, tannins, and a host of other compounds.

The root is a well-known coffee adulterant or flavor enhancer. But I prefer to describe chicory as an enhancer of coffee flavor, enricher of color, and acidity balancer. Adulterants are added to disguise things. Coffees containing chicory should flaunt the improvement.

Gathering chicory roots is a task of excavation. The deep taproots, often more than two feet long and two inches in diameter, are difficult to unearth. My shovel pries broken

Chicory

roots in twelve-inch lengths from the Ozark's rock-ridden soil. A double-dug bed makes root harvest easy. Wash and slice the roots into pieces one-fourth inch in diameter and an inch or two long. Roast pieces in an oven at 250°–300° F for one hour or until crisp. Be careful not to scorch the roots. Grind them in a blender and brew a chicory-root tea or add one portion of roasted root to two portions of coffee.

Chicory has stomachic, tonic, cholagogic, diuretic, laxative, and slightly sedative qualities. In laboratory experiments, alcoholic extracts have been shown to slightly depress heart rate and the amplitude of the heartbeat. Antiinflammatory activity is also indicated. An infusion of the root stimulates bile secretion and tones an upset stomach. If taken in excess, chicory is said to cause fullness of blood in the head and reduce the visual power of the retina (Grieve 1931).

The dried (unroasted) roots are high in inulin (up to 58 percent of the root weight). Other components include the sesquiterpene lactones, lactucin and luctpicrin, and a number of coumarins, including chicoriin, esculetin, esculin, and umbelliferone. When chicory is roasted, numerous flavoring components develop in the root, including maltol, a natural taste modifier which intensifies the flavor of sugar. Inulin is largely destroyed by the roasting process. Chicory is also high in fructose, and has been investigated as a potential sugar source (Simon, Chadwick, and Craker 1984; Council of Industrial and Scientific Research 1950).

CHIVES

Allium schoenoprasum L.
(al'-i-um skee-no-pray'-sum)
Liliaceae—Lily Family
Plate 11

The genus *Allium* is represented by over four hundred species and is one of the most important food-producing genera in the plant kingdom. Onions, leeks, garlic, elephant garlic, and chives are all species of *Allium*. *A. schoenoprasum* is a hardy perennial of Eurasian origin that has become naturalized in North America. Chives grow from eight to twenty inches tall, though they rarely reach over a foot in gardens. The leaves are hollow, round, reedlike spears. The globular flower heads are a mass of mauve-pink flowers, encased in paperlike bracts, borne on scapes. Flowers appear from June to August. The tightly crowded bulblets grow in clumps and have the appearance of flattened miniature onions. *A. schoenoprasum* var. *sibericum* differs primarily in that the leaves are more robust and are shorter than the scapes. Chives are very popular in American gardens.

Seeds germinate easily. Sow indoors six weeks before the last frost or directly in the garden as soon as the soil warms up. Chives may also be propagated by dividing the clumps at any time of year, except, of course, when the ground is frozen.

A fairly rich, moist soil, high in humus, is best. Chives will tolerate full sun or partial shade with a pH range between 6 and 8. Keep free of weeds—once grasses become established in a clump of chives, they are difficult to eradicate. The clumps should be divided every four or five years. Chives are completely winter hardy, drought tolerant, and will grow in almost any garden soil. Simply put, anyone can grow chives. In commercial plantings the leaves are harvested three to four times a year, cut about three inches above the ground. The leaves should be harvested before flowering, usually about four to six weeks after the growing season begins.

Ever try to dry chives in the home? You usually end up with a brownish mass, unlike the bright green chives purchased at a supermarket. Commercially, chives are freeze-dried, and it is this product that dominates the dried-chive market. From fresh to dry weight, chives reduce in bulk at a ratio of twelve to one.

The delicate piquancy that chives impart to food makes it an herb of varied use. No garden or galley should be without this little cousin of onions. Chives are primarily used fresh. They usually retain moisture after drying, and therefore are difficult to store. Chives will produce a second, more-tender crop if cut back to about two inches. I usually thin the clumps, taking only what I need at the moment.

Chives are essential to vichyssoise and are good in asparagus, potato, and cauliflower soups. Mix the chopped leaves in cream cheese, cottage cheese, or butter. Chives are great in deviled eggs, omelets, and scrambled eggs. And what better place for them than in a salad!

High concentrations of vitamin A and vitamin C are found in the leaves, along with measurable amounts of iron, calcium, magnesium, phosphorus, potassium, thiamin, and niacin.

Chives can be called a healthful rather than a medicinal herb. They are useful in toning the stomach, reducing high blood pressure, and strengthening the kidneys. Oil of chive is strongly antibacterial.

COLTSFOOT

Tussilago farfara L.
(tus-il-lay'-go far'-far-a)
Compositae (Asteraceae)—Aster Family

The blooming of coltsfoot sparks the beginning of spring and the season of the garden. It is a hardy perennial native to Europe and widely naturalized in the northeastern United States. Occasionally it has escaped from cultivation in the western United States. It should not be confused with the indigenous western coltsfoot, *Petasites* species, though they may be used interchangeably for medicinal purposes. One species of *Petasites* native to Japan is used in a manner similar to *Tussilago*.

The emerging spring blooms of coltsfoot race crocuses to christen the welcome season with color. Coltsfoot flowers appear before the leaves, often in late February to mid-March. The light yellow, dandelionlike flower heads emerge on erect, leafless stems or scapes. Each stem is covered with scalelike bracts of a brownish-pink color. The large (three to eight inches in diameter), angular, heart-shaped leaves unfold as the last flower begins to wilt. They are coarsely toothed, a dull green color above, and covered with a downy cotton underneath. The plant spreads by means of underground runners or stolons.

Coltsfoot is easily propagated by dividing the stolons in the spring or fall. Give it plenty of room to spread in the garden. It likes a heavy clay soil with a fair amount of moisture and a neutral to slightly acid pH. It will do well in sun or shade,

Colt's Foot

and is a good plant for borders.

The leaves, flowers, and roots are useful. The slightly bitter leaves can be eaten as a green in the early spring; but once the emergence of so many delicious spring greens begins, coltsfoot is best reserved as a pot herb for times when there is nothing else to eat. The flowers can be gathered and dried in spring. They have a mild, sweet fragrance even when dried.

Coltsfoot is a medicinal plant known since ancient times. The leaves and flowers are demulcent, emollient, and expectorant. The leaves have long served as a remedy for pulmonary ailments such as bronchitis, laryngitis, asthma, whooping cough, and sore throats. A decoction or infusion of one ounce of the leaves to one pint of water is medicinally effective. In Germany and Scandinavia, the dried roots have been smoked to relieve coughs.

The leaves are rich in polysaccharide-based mucilage (about 8 percent), and contain some inulin, tannins, and flavonoids such as rutin, hyperoside, and isoquercetin. Like comfrey, coltsfoot contains liver-toxic pyrrolizidine alkaloids, among them senecionine, but in minute amounts. Other alkaloids reported from the plant include senkirkine, tussilagine, symphytine, and petasitenine (De Vincenzi and Dessi 1991). Certain pyrrolizidine alkaloids can cause a condition known as hepatic veno-occlusive disease, a rare disorder involving obstruction of the venous outflow tract of the liver. Unsaturated, retro-necine-structured pyrrolizidine alkaloids are the offending group. Saturated pyrrolidines are not implicated in producing liver damage; therefore it is important that the exact chemical classification of each of these alkaloids be known before pointing the finger at all of them.

The effects of toxic pyrrolizidine alkaloids are cumulative. Development of disease is dependent upon the chemical structure of the alkaloids, the total dose ingested, and especially the susceptibility of the individual. A case was reported in 1988 (Roulet et al.) in Switzerland in which a newborn baby had been diagnosed with veno-occlusive liver disease. The infant died on its twenty-seventh day of life. The mother's long-term ingestion of a tea purported to contain up to 9 percent coltsfoot was thought to have caused the problem, though it is possible other plant materials were involved.

This case raised a warning flag about the long-term effects of coltsfoot. Consequently, as of the summer of 1992, for better or worse, sale of the herb has been banned in Germany. Rats fed on high daily doses of coltsfoot have developed liver lesions; however, low doses have not produced hepatotoxicity. Veno-occlusive liver disease is seen mainly in children. I think the main lesson here is that no herbal tea or herb product should be ingested by pregnant women, especially on an extended basis throughout the pregnancy, unless the fetal effects of the herb are clearly established and its use has been recommended by a *knowledgeable* healthcare practitioner. More on the subject of pyrrolizidine alkaloids under comfrey.

COMFREY, RUSSIAN COMFREY
Symphytum officinale L., *S.* x *uplandicum* Nym.
(sim'-fit-um off-iss-i-nail'-ee; up-lan'-di-kum).
Boraginaceae—Borage Family

The genus *Symphytum* of the borage family includes about thirty-five species, most of which are native to Europe or western Asia. *S.* x *uplandicum* and *S. officinale* are commonly grown in North America. Comfreys have erect stems that often branch at the top. The eight-to-twelve-inch-long leaves are entire (without teeth) oval, or lance shaped. The leaves become progressively smaller toward the top of the plant. Both the leaves and stems are covered with rough, bristly hairs. From the axils of the small upper leaves emerge curving clusters of rose, purple, mauve, or sometimes white bell-shaped flowers up to one-half inch long. In some regions, flowering begins as early as April and lasts through September.

Common comfrey (*S. officinale*) is a branched perennial, twenty to forty-two inches tall. The large leaves are broadly lance shaped. The middle and upper leaves are without stems, but the point at which they attach to the stems (point of insertion) extends downward on the stalk. The stalk itself is distinctly winged. The flowers range from cream to yellow, pink, or purple. The flower lobes curve backward, and the anther is about as wide as the filament. The calyx lobes are narrowly lance shaped. The deep taproot has a fleshy, cream-colored interior. 'Variegatum' is a cultivar with white-margined leaves. It is native to moist grasslands and riverbanks throughout most of central Europe, and is naturalized in northern Europe, though rare in the extreme south. It is also naturalized in the eastern United States.

Russian comfrey, *S.* x *uplandicum,* a native of the Caucuses, is a large, coarse perennial that may reach four to six feet in height. *S.* x *uplandicum* (once known as *S. peregrinum*) is now believed to be a hybrid between *S. officinale* and *S. asperum* (commonly known as prickly comfrey). On the main stalk, it only has narrow wings, which end between the internodes. The leaves, which are rounded or heart shaped at the base, narrowly hug the main stalk. The flowers, about three-quarters of an inch long, are dark purple changing to blue, or pinkish changing to pink-blue. The short calyx lobes have pointed tips.

At least seven species are found in American horticulture. In addition to *S. x uplandicum* and *S. officinale,* other species in American gardens include *S. caucasicum, S. grandiflorum, S. orientale, S. tauricum,* and *S. tuberosum.* Most of the latter five species are found in the gardens of collectors.

Comfrey can be started from seed, though it rarely produces viable seed, and bulk seed sources are unknown. It is best propagated by dividing the roots in spring or fall. A little piece of root will produce a plant. At Taylor's Herb Gardens, inch-long roots are used. Generally, I dig a mature plant and split the root into ten equal pieces with a sharp shovel. Once planted in a spot, comfrey will be there forever. Each small root cutting of comfrey (as little as a three-inch-long section) will produce a plant. It is this propensity to grow with great ease from root cuttings that makes the plant difficult to eradicate once it is established; any root pieces left in the ground will produce a new plant. The taproot may stretch six feet into the soil. If you leave a small bit of root after transplanting, another plant will soon emerge. Plant comfrey in a permanent location and space at three feet.

Comfrey will grow in almost any soil, but will produce larger roots and more leaf material in a rich, deep, moist soil, high in organic matter and well supplied with compost or well-rotted manure. An average garden soil is fine. Good drainage is essential. Soil pH should be between 5.5 and 8.7 (an average pH is 7.1). A neutral to slightly acid or slightly alkaline soil is acceptable. Irrigate as necessary during the growing season. Rainfall is usually sufficient, except in areas receiving less than thirty-six inches of rain per year, evenly distributed throughout the growing season. Full sun or partial shade are both okay.

Harvest the leaves as the flowers bud up. In Maine, I made my first leaf harvest on June 1 when most gardeners start planting peas and seasonal vegetables. That summer we harvested the comfrey patch seven times. Each cutting from the quarter-acre plot yielded sixty to eighty pounds of dried leaves. A study by Gary Steuart (1987) suggests that alkaloid development in the leaf is affected by the growth stage of the plant, indicating that timing the harvest is a significant factor in the amount of pyrrolizidine alkaloids in the leaf. In this study, the first spring cutting showed the highest levels of alkaloid content (0.026 percent of pyrrolizidines on a dry-

Comfrey

Symphytum officinale, Comfrey

ians, not only for its high protein content, but also because of its purported vitamin B_{12}, rare in vegetarian diets. However, a 1977 report in the *British Medical Journal* showed that comfrey was virtually devoid of vitamin B_{12}.

Traditionally, comfrey leaves, and especially the root, have been used as expectorants, emollients, astringents, demulcents, and hemostatics. Knitbone is one common name. A poultice of the leaves or root is placed over a sprain or broken limb to aid the "knitting" of the tissue. The root has been used to allay diarrhea, pharyngitis, tonsillitis, bronchitis, pneumonia, and whooping cough. Over the past twenty years, comfrey has become a very popular home remedy.

The root contains allantoin—a cell proliferant. The root, and to a lesser extent, the leaves contain pyrrolizidine alkaloids (PAs). At least eight PAs have been identified from the leaves and stems of Russian comfrey (*S.* x *uplandicum*). According to Dr. Dennis Awang, head of Health and Welfare Canada's Natural Products Section, symphytine and echimidine are the major alkaloids found in comfrey (Awang 1987a, 1991a). Echimidine, believed to be the more toxic of the two alkaloids, is found in prickly comfrey (*S. asperum*) and Russian comfrey (*S.* x *uplandicum*); however, it is not found in common comfrey (*S. officinale*). Symphytine is the major alkaloid in *S. officinale*.

Questions about comfrey's safety and possible carcinogenicity first arose in a report by Japanese researchers published in 1978 (Hikino et al.). In this study, 0.5 to 8 percent of the rats' diet for 600 days was comfrey leaf or root. Liver toxicity was observed within 180 days, and all groups developed liver tumors. The study raised several questions. It is apparent that the authors confused Russian comfrey with common comfrey. So what if a few rats given large amounts of comfrey over a long period of time developed some sort of liver problem? What can you expect? Can that data be extrapolated to humans? After all, comfrey has been used safely for thousands of years!

The concerns raised in the animal study prompted a response from the herbal community. A 1979 press release entitled "Comfrey as Medicine," issued by England's National Institute of Medical Herbalists, opens with the following paragraph:

> The strange saga of comfrey indicates the folly and illogicality of the approach which runs as follows. If a trace of a chemical can be isolated from a large quantity of a plant and be fed or injected into

weight basis). Harvests later in the season showed only minute amounts of alkaloids in leaf tissue (5 ppm). The study confirms that it is best to use the first leaf harvest as mulch or compost.

Comfrey leaf is dried under shade. Leaves dried in the sun rapidly turn black. Weight loss in leaves is 88 to 95 percent upon drying. Comfrey leaf tends to mat up during the drying process and can be very difficult to handle. Leaves must be spread in thin layers to ensure even air circulation. After harvest, piled leaves may be "fluffy" and well ventilated, but in a few hours, they will lose their shape and mat together. Good ventilation is important. The roots can be harvested in the spring or fall. An acre may yield more than a ton of dried roots or leaves.

The young leaves have been boiled as a springtime pot herb. They contain calcium, phosphorus, potassium, vitamin A, and up to 22 percent protein. On a dry-weight basis, the leaves contain as much as 23 to 35 percent protein. Comfrey earned a reputation as a pot herb among vegetar-

laboratory animals, the lethal results may be extrapolated to man who is then told not to take any of the original plant because it contains poison. The plant may have been eaten or made into a tea for centuries during which no single instance of ill-effect has followed its use. Today there is no single man, woman, or child in any country who has been recorded as suffering toxic effects from taking comfrey leaf or as root medicine. *Comfrey has a clean sheet and has no case to answer.* The *onus probandi* lies upon those who denigrate a safe herbal remedy by making assumptions in the absence of any evidence to justify what has tended to become an emotive rather than a scientific issue.

But now, more is known. Today there are published case reports of human toxic reactions from the ingestion of comfrey. It is a long and complex story, but one worth exploring in depth here. The crux of the matter is that before a human consumes enough comfrey to develop liver cancer, he or she would probably have developed another disease—veno-occlusive disease of the liver, caused by comfrey's PAs. Here's some background:

Public-health concerns over the effects of PAs were heightened in the mid-1970s after it was reported that wheat contaminated with the seeds of a PA-containing heliotrope species had caused an outbreak of liver disease in thousands of Afghani villagers. During a two-year drought, a weedy species of heliotrope became common in grain fields in Afghanistan. Heliotrope-contaminated wheat became the staple diet of poor people in the region, resulting in the poisoning epidemic. Over the two-year period, more than seven thousand people developed severe liver impairment, resulting in many deaths.

In 1975, a similar problem occurred in the Sarguja district of Madhya Pradesh in central India. Food cereals had become contaminated with the seeds of a rattlebox (*Crotalaria*) species. Almost seventy people became ill with typical PA poisoning, characterized by liver necrosis. Nearly half of these patients died.

Scientists and public-health officials worldwide began to examine PA toxicity in greater detail. PAs are especially prominent in the borage family (to which comfrey and borage belong), as well as certain tribes in the aster family and the pea family. Famous PA-containing plant groups include aster family members such as groundsels (*Senecio* species) and thoroughworts (*Eupatorium* species), as well

as rattlebox (*Crotalaria* species) in the pea family. Being a popularly consumed herbal product, comfrey, a known PA-containing plant, came under scrutiny.

PAs produce a condition known as veno-occlusive disease of the liver. A liver biopsy is necessary for diagnosis. The condition is seldom recognized by Western physicians. Historically, veno-occlusive liver disease has been isolated to parts of Jamaica, Africa, and India, where PA poisoning cases are more prevalent and better documented. American physicians rarely encounter the condition; therefore it is seldom diagnosed. In veno-occlusive liver disease caused by PAs, blood flow is hampered due to clotting of the large veins that drain from the liver. Now PA toxicity has been directly associated with comfrey (S. Foster 1992b).

PA toxicity is insidious. It generally does not produce acute reactions. Rather, PA-induced disease is more likely to occur if low PA levels are consumed over a relatively long period of time. Symptoms, which are difficult to diagnose without a liver biopsy, may not appear for months or years. The toxicity is cumulative. Veno-occlusive disease may develop into more serious liver disease, which may be mistakenly attributed to other causes. In short, the reason that we have not heard about comfrey toxicity until recently is that the problem has not been easily recognized.

There are numerous variables involved in PA poisoning. Susceptibility to PA toxicity ranges greatly in humans—affected by gender, age, general health, habits, dietary and nutritional factors, the use of other drugs, alcohol, etc. For example, a twenty-three-year-old New Zealand male whose death was attributed to comfrey ingestion was a vegetarian described as a binge eater. He apparently subsisted on single dietary items (such as comfrey leaves) for weeks at a time. Levels of PAs in comfrey are also highly variable. Different comfrey species, and separate plant parts, contain shifting levels of diverse PAs. Comfrey root has about ten times the PA level of the leaves. Young leaves hold about sixteen times the levels of PAs found in mature leaves. The young leaves picked from the first leafy growth of spring may contain about 0.22 percent PAs. Mature leaves, picked at the end of the growing season, have an average 0.05 percent PAs.

At this point, the potential of comfrey to cause problems if ingested by susceptible individuals in small amounts, over a long or short period of time, has been well established. Since the mid-1980s, there have been at least four well-documented case reports on human occurrence of veno-occlusive disease. PAs have to be metabolized by the liver before they become toxic; therefore ingestion is more of a concern than external use of topical products on unbroken skin. Comfrey as a food is now banned in Canada. Phytomedical comfrey products are banned in Germany and Australia. In Australia, however, topical products are allowed.

A.R. Mattocks (1980), writing in the British journal *The Lancet,* has stated, "People who consider the benefit of comfrey to outweigh the (perhaps slight) risk involved may like to know that large, mature leaves carry the lowest concentration of toxic alkaloids." If you insist on contin-

uing to use comfrey, you would be advised not to ingest the roots, and to discard the first leaf cutting of the year. Comfrey should not be ingested for long periods of time. Ultimately, future development of PA-free strains of comfrey, or the removal of PAs by using sophisticated technologies may bring comfrey products back to the herb-consuming public. Until then, approach comfrey with caution and information—not an emotional reaction to science.

The old saying goes, "Everything in moderation." In regard to comfrey, cautious moderation, or perhaps even abstinence, works best.

CORIANDER

Coriandrum sativum L.
(koe-ree-an'-drum sa-tie'-vum)
Umbelliferae (Apiaceae)—Carrot Family

Coriander

Coriander, cilantro, or Chinese parsley, native to southern Europe, western Asia, and naturalized in North America, is a strong-smelling herb, to say the least. It may reach four feet in height, and is a hardy annual. The lower leaves are rounded, toothed, and resemble the young leaves of anise. As the plant matures, the leaves become more finely divided and feathery. The flowers are in graceful, lacy umbels; the individual blossoms are pinkish-white. On each umbel group, the petals are enlarged on the outer flowers. Bees work coriander feverishly. It produces pink pollen, and bees fly about the garden with pink pollen sacs. The seeds (fruits) are about one-eighth inch in diameter, globular, ribbed, and light brownish when ripe. Each fruit consists of two halves (mericaps), both containing a seed. Mature plants may bend under the weight of the pleasant-smelling fruits. Like many herbs, the quality of coriander and the quantities of its chemical constituents depend upon the chemotype grown, environmental factors, harvesttime, and other variables.

Coriander is easily grown from seed sown to a depth of one-fourth to one-half inch in the spring or fall. Thin the plants to stand at four- to eight-inch spacings. Seeds germinate in seven to twenty days, and mature, producing seed, in about three months. Depending on the spacing of the rows, ten to twenty pounds of seed will sow an acre. Plants self-sow freely.

Coriander likes a deep, well-drained, moderately rich loam with a pH between 6 and 8. It needs full sun and plenty of moisture, and will probably require an occasional watering. The plant is generally adaptable, tolerant of cool conditions and heat, and relatively drought resistant.

Coriander is an ancient herb, first mentioned in Sanskrit texts from India nearly seven thousand years ago. It was also found in Egyptian tombs dating back three thousand years (Prakash 1990). It has been used in China for over a thousand years.

Leaves for fresh or dry use should be harvested before the plants bloom. Seeds should be harvested after about two-thirds of the plants have turned from a green to a brownish color. Cut in the early morning while the plants are still moist with dew to avoid seed shattering since coriander can easily become weedy. Yields vary; five hundred to two thousand pounds of seed per acre have been obtained.

Many Americans dislike the fragrance and flavor of fresh coriander (cilantro). It has been described as unpleasant, awful, noxious, and buglike. I have to admit, while tending the Shaker herb gardens, I usually found someone else to weed the coriander rows—until Dr. Shiu Ying Hu taught me to appreciate the flavor of this herb. In China, it is eaten in salads and as a pot herb. Most people, unfamiliar with Chinese parsley, have to acquire a taste for it.

Cilantro is often the secret ingredient that gives Mexican, Turkish, Indian, and certain Chinese dishes their distinctive flavor. Fresh cilantro can be found in markets wherever Mexican, Chinese, Vietnamese, Spanish, or Indian populations abound. In recent years, it has become increasingly common as a fresh herb in American supermarkets. Here in the Arkansas Ozarks, we can occasionally buy fresh cilantro at the local grocery store. Cilantro is now widely used in restaurants throughout the United States.

In Western cookery, the seeds are used primarily for flavoring breads, cookies, and cakes. Use the leaves in rice dishes, refried beans, curries, chutneys, omelets, soups, and salads. This much-ignored herb can enhance the flavor of many foods. I now describe the flavor as sweet, pleasant, and aromatic.

The fresh leaves are a rich source of vitamin C (150–200 mg / 100 g), vitamin A, niacin, calcium, phosphorus, potassium, and iron. Coriander contains 14–22 percent protein and small amounts of fiber, niacin, and thiamin. The whole herb is taken to quiet stomachache and nausea. The fruits will relieve cramping when mixed with laxative herbs. In Chinese medicine, the fruits (known as "yuan-xu-zi") are used to promote sweating, break out the measles, and as an aromatic stimulant to appetite. Coriander is an ingredient in

prescriptions for the common cold, stuffy nose, measles, and dysentery, and can be gargled for toothaches. In India, an eyewash made from the seeds is a treatment for chronic conjunctivitis, and serves as a blindness preventative for smallpox victims. Coriander is carminative, diuretic, tonic, stomachic, and aphrodisiac, and reportedly lessens the intoxicating effect of alcoholic beverages.

The essential oil of the fruits contains 55 to 75 percent coriandrol (delta-linalool), geraniol, borneol, camphor, carvone, anethole, and other constituents. Commercially, the fruit oil is used to flavor tobacco, pharmaceutical preparations, alcoholic beverages, baked goods, and condiments. Experimentally, the fruit oil is antibacterial and larvicidal, and coriander has antiinflammatory and hypoglycemic effects. The leaf oil, which is not used commercially, has the fragrance of decylaldehyde and other fatty aldehydes (Prakash 1990).

COSTMARY

Balsamita major Desf.
(*Chrysanthemum balsamita* [L.] Baill).
(ball-sam-ee'-ta may'-jor)
Compositae (Asteraceae)—Aster Family
Plate 11

Open most herb books and you will find costmary, or bible leaf, as it is also known, listed under the name *Chrysanthemum balsamita*. Taxonomists who have split the once-large *Chrysanthemum* genus into smaller parts have given this plant its very own genus, with just one species represented. It has also been classified as *Tanacetum balsamita*. Costmary is a dull green, densely hairy perennial, growing from one to four feet in height. Leaves at the base of the plant and on lower stems are oblong, four to six inches long, with rounded teeth and long stalks. The leaves on the upper part of the plant are much reduced. The flowers are yellow buttons about one-quarter inch wide. Costmary blooms from August to October. Originating in southwest Asia, it has been cultivated as an ornamental and decorative herb in European gardens since the sixteenth century, perhaps earlier. It is now widely naturalized in many parts of Europe, and sporadically escapes from cultivation in eastern North America.

Costmary is common in herb gardens, but seldom used for much of anything. It has a relatively controlled, pleasing spreading habit that doesn't try to take over a garden, and can be divided every two to three years to keep it neat. It is easily propagated by dividing clumps in spring or fall. The plant is adaptable to most average garden soils, provided the soil is relatively light and well drained. It likes a dry soil. While the leaves produce an essential oil, it has no commercial applications. Bulk dried leaves are available from some herb purveyors who specialize in the obscure.

As John Hill noted nearly two hundred years ago, by that time use of the plant had become obscure: "A garden plant kept more for its virtues than its beauty, but at present neglected" (1812, 91). Today, however, it is kept more for its beauty than its virtues. The leaves can be used as a substitute for bay leaves, but possess a unique, sometimes stronger, balsam fragrance and flavor. It's the kind of flavor that lends itself to desserts. The leaves were formerly used for flavoring beer and ale. The fresh leaves have been added to salads and soups. Perhaps they are best in potpourris. The leathery leaves, dried in a book, make good bookmarks and once served as a wafting herb, perhaps to keep churchgoers from nodding off, hence the name "bible leaf." Historically, a tea of the herb was used for strengthening the stomach, treating headaches, and for conditions of the liver and spleen.

The plant contains sesquiterpenoids, including dehydroisoeivanin, and isoeivanin.

DANDELION

Taraxacum officinale Wiggers.
(tar-ax'-a-kum off-ish'-i-nal-ee)
Compositae (Asteraceae)—Aster Family
Plate 11

Dandelion an herb? Certainly. It fits the definition of a plant used for culinary and medicinal purposes. Of course, it is so common, so pervasive, and so familiar, our association of it is with weeds. After all, we try every means possible to remove it from our lawns. Maybe the better tactic would be to remove the grass from our lawns and encourage the dandelion instead. If one plant group embodies the essence of endless variation, it is the genus *Taraxacum*. There are about sixty species or species' groups recognized in the genus today, but this encompasses well over twelve hundred species that have been described at one time or another, most from northern temperate climates. The *Taraxacum officinale*

group is highly diverse, encompassing over a hundred variations that have themselves been separately described as species in Europe. The common dandelion is, therefore, a highly complex group, rather than a neatly defined single taxonomic entity.

Dandelion is a biennial or perennial herb, with white milky latex exuding from any broken part of the plant, including the taproot. The plant is stemless. The leaves are arranged in a basal rosette, arising from the crown of the root. The flower heads, those crowded, familiar yellow blooms, are actually hundreds of tiny flowers packed together, rather than a single flower. The flower head sits atop a solitary hollow stalk. The leaves are lance shaped, broadest at the top, and lacerated by deep, sharp irregular lobes and teeth. Dandelion usually flowers in early spring or summer, though it sometimes has a secondary flowering period in autumn. Probably native to Europe, it is widespread throughout the Northern Hemisphere. Wherever humans find a home, so does the dandelion.

Dare I include instructions for propagation of the dandelion? Why not. Dandelion is propagated by seed, sown after the last spring frost, or planted six weeks before the first frost of the previous autumn. Cover to a depth of one-half inch. Germination is in seven to twenty-one days at temperatures between 68° and 86° F and germination is better in cool soils. One ounce contains approximately thirty-five thousand seeds.

Dandelion is a hardy perennial crop, generally treated as a biennial for root production. Fall-planted seed, or early spring planting, is used to produce the leaves as a winter annual (harvested in the summer of the first full season). Treated as an annual, the dandelion leaves can be harvested during the summer after spring planting, but before flowering. It does well in climates with an ambient, evenly distributed rainfall of at least thirty-two inches per year.

Dandelion is adaptable to most soil types, but will produce larger roots in a rich, deep, moist soil, well supplied with compost and well-rotted manure. A well-drained, sandy loam with a pH of between 6 to 8 is preferable. Depending upon soil quality, spacing can be as little as six inches per plant, or up to eighteen inches. Addition of phosphorus to the soil significantly increases yields of both leaves and root. One nineteenth-century reference suggests thinning plants to six-inch spacings for root-crop production.

The root is harvested in autumn as the vegetative growth

fades. The timing of the harvest affects the quality of the root. Roots harvested in summer (June–August) are less uniform with a lower content of inulin and other bitter components (the biologically active compounds of the root). Late September–October harvest is preferred. The fall-harvested roots make an opaque extract. Spring-harvested roots (lower in inulin and other bitter elements) produce a clear extract.

Leaves are harvested when they are still tender and sweet during the first year of growth. Leaves harvested after the plant buds tend to be bitter and tough. If you are harvesting dandelion leaves from your lawn, you will want them early in the spring before the flowers bud up. As a specialty crop for fresh-leaf production, three to four million dollars worth of leaves are grown in Texas, Florida, New Jersey, Arizona, and California.

Fresh dandelion leaves have endless culinary possibilities. Just imagine. Dandelion boiled greens, dandelion spaghetti, dandelion quiche, dandelion lasagna, dandelion bread, dandelion pizza: these are just a few of the options. Dandelion flowers offer an even more interesting array of alternatives, from wine to jams. Want to know more? See Peter Gail's *On the Trail of the Yellow Flowered Earth Nail—A Dandelion Sampler* (available from Goosefoot Acres Press, P.O. Box 18016, Cleveland Heights, OH 44118). Fresh dandelion leaves contain protein, fiber, calcium, phosphorus, iron, potassium, thiamin, riboflavin, vitamin C, and are especially high in vitamin A. The dried leaf is very high in potassium (about 4 percent).

Traditionally, both dandelion leaf and root have been used for liver, gallbladder, and kidney ailments, and as a tonic for weak or impaired digestion. They are also considered mildly laxative. The dried root is believed to have weaker benefits than the fresh root or its preparations. In modern phytomedicine, the leaves are used to alleviate water retention resulting from various causes because they have significant diuretic effects. The dried herb can be made into a tea, tincture, or extracts. The fresh juice of the leaf is also considered medicinal. Animal experiments have confirmed that the herb has a strong diuretic action, and because of the high potassium content in the leaf, it replaces this mineral lost through the urine. The root is traditionally employed for the treatment of rheumatism and has experimental anti-inflammatory effects. Its primary use is for conditions associated with bile secretion in the liver, as well as dyspepsia and loss of appetite. Alcoholic extracts of the root increase bile secretion in animal models by over 40 percent (ESCOP 1992). The root is experimentally hypoglycemic, has weight-loss potential due to its diuretic actions and is weakly antibiotic against *Candida albicans* (yeast).

In addition, extracts from the roots are used as bitters in alcoholic and nonalcoholic beverages, and as a "natural flavoring" in candy, frozen dairy products, baked goods, and cheeses. Due to its high sugar content (up to 77 percent fructose), the fresh root has been developed into syrups. The roots are also roasted as a coffee substitute (Leung 1980).

Dandelion leaf contains a number of interesting compounds, including sesquiterpene lactones (germacranolides) such as taraxinic acid glucoside, cycloartenol, phytosterols, and p-hydroxyphenylacetic acid. The root contains eudesmanolide and germacranolide-type sesquiterpene lactones, triterpene alcohols and phytosterols, taraxacoside, caffeic acid, p-hydroxyphenylacetic acid, and in autumn-harvested root, about 40 percent inulin, compared with 2 percent in the spring-harvested root (ESCOP 1992). For a complete review of the history and use of dandelion, see Hobbs (1989b).

DILL

Anethum graveolens L.
(a-neeth'-um gra-vee'-o-lenz)
Umbelliferae (Apiaceae)—Carrot Family

An herb garden without dill is like a car without wheels. Dill's versatile culinary use and easy culture make it the perfect herb for the beginning herb gardener and a favorite of die-hard enthusiasts. *Anethum graveolens* is a hardy, fragrant annual native to southwest Asia and southeast Europe. It is also naturalized in some parts of North America, India, and elsewhere. It grows from two to four feet high, though 'Bouquet', a dwarf form, is bushier and may be one-and-a-half to two feet tall. The stems are smooth, ribbed, hollow, and have a bluish-green cast. The finely divided linear leaves envelop the stem with a thin sheath. The tiny yellow flowers grow on terminal umbels up to eight inches across. The flattened fruits have prominent ribs and are about one-eighth of an inch long. Dill has a carrotlike taproot. It is produced in India, Pakistan, Egypt, Fiji, Mexico, the Netherlands, England, Hungary, Germany, and the United States, especially in California and Oregon. The Canadian provinces of Manitoba and Saskatchewan are also major sources.

Several commercial cultivars are available. Tetraploids produce very large plants that may be susceptible to wind damage. 'Bouquet' is a small cultivar, one-and-a-half to two feet high. 'Vierling' has bluish-green leaves and stems and is sometimes grown as a cut flower. Dill seed is readily available from most wholesale seed sources. The leading commercial dill cultivars planted in the United States are 'Mammoth Long Island' and 'Bouquet'.

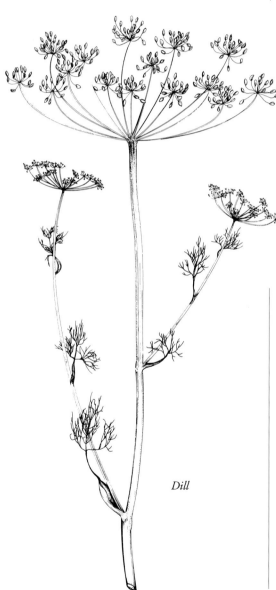

Dill

Dill provides a further example of the diversity of common herbs. There are both qualitative and quantitative differences in the essential oil of dill grown under varying ecological conditions, including soil and climate. The time of harvesting and crop genetics are also important factors. A number of chemical races have been identified in which the leaf oil contains 30 percent carvone and 35 percent limonene, while another chemotype has an essential oil composed primarily of 14 percent carvone, and 45 percent phellandrene, with no limonene (Tétényi 1970).

Seed dill in early spring after a minimum nighttime temperature of 25°F has been reached. Drill seeds in rows at one-to-three-foot spacings, adjusting for equipment used in planting. Cover seeds to a depth of one-eighth to one-quarter inch. Seeds may need some light to germinate. Germination is high and even, in as little as seven or as many as twenty-one days, at 60° to 70° F. Five to ten pounds of seed should sow an acre depending upon planting scheme used. Densities of a hundred thousand plants per acre have been recommended. Highest yields of dill weed have been observed with rows spaced at ten inches, with plants thinned to four-inch spacings (Craker 1987). Plantings can be staggered at one-to-two-week intervals to provide a continuous supply of fresh dill throughout the growing season. I once broadcast four pounds of seed over a half acre of tilled ground. The resulting seedlings were nearly impossible to thin and weed, making harvest difficult. I recommend planting dill as a row crop.

A ready market can be found for fresh dill stalks in most urban areas, making dill a good supplemental cash crop for a family garden. A fifty-foot row will provide a teenager with some extra spending money for summer vacation. If you can find a way to entice an adolescent to do the work, please let me know. A sample "process budget" developed for dill economic projections in 1987 on a quarter-acre plot included costs of $1,013.24, with a return of $1,760.00, providing a net profit of $746.76 (see Pontius 1987).

Dill thrives best in a moderately rich, moist, slightly acid (5.6 to 7.8 pH), sandy loam, well supplied with compost and a good nitrogen content. Good drainage is essential. Dill is best grown under full sunlight, but will tolerate some shade, especially in the South. Its life zone is northern temperate climates in temperatures between 53° and 90° F. Dill likes cool weather and does not do well in the heat stress of southern climates. A recent study (Hälvä et al. 1992) has shown that light affects the quantity of the essential oil and the growth of dill. Accumulation of the essential oil, as well as biomass of the plant, is increased under higher light levels, providing a rational basis for growing the plant in full sun. The plant seems to be very sensitive to decreased levels of sunlight.

A two-week schedule of shallow side cultivation, with appropriate equipment, and hand-hoeing between plants is suggested. In a rich garden soil, dill self-sows in abundance. However, reports of continued self-sowing over a longer period of time are confined to acid soils.

Once the plants reach about two feet in height, it has been recommended that overhead irrigation be abandoned. At this point, furrow irrigation is used as a standard practice. Overhead watering could increase chances of powdery mildew infestation. Dill is sensitive to wind damage as well as hard rains during flowering and fruiting periods which could adversely affect crop harvest. Appropriate windbreaks are suggested in high-wind production areas (Craker 1987; Garrabrants and Craker 1987).

Dill leaves are harvested just before the plant comes into bloom. Seeds can be harvested as soon as the tips begin to turn light brown. Plants produce seed about six to eight weeks after planting. Leaves can be monitored for harvest three to five weeks after they emerge, but before the plant flowers. Dill weed should be carefully spread to dry at a temperature of 90° F. When hung to dry without temperature regulation, dill often turns an undesirable brown color. Leaves should be bright green to dull green. Dill weed and seeds should have relatively high essential-oil content. Seeds should be a rich brown color with about 50 percent carvone in the essential oil. Yields of four hundred to seven hundred pounds per acre of dried dill weed have been obtained. Seed yields vary widely from five hundred to fourteen hundred per acre. Somewhere in the middle would probably be a reasonable expectation (Craker 1987; Garrabrants and Craker 1987).

Dill leaf's delicate, aromatic flavor lends a refreshing spark to otherwise bland foods such as potatoes, scrambled eggs, omelets, carrots, sauces, and fresh cucumbers. Dill is, of course, best known for its use in flavoring pickles—and just because some find the flavor of dill pickles unpleasant doesn't mean they will turn up their nose at dill-seasoned dishes. The seeds have a pungent aromatic flavor great with cabbage dishes, potato salads, fish, stew, soup, and breads.

The leaves contain magnesium, iron, calcium, potas-sium, phosphorus, and Vitamin C.

Dill leaves are little used medicinally, though the seeds possess aromatic—stimulant, stomachic, and carminative properties. Drinking dill tea or chewing seeds will reportedly relieve digestive gas, soothe an upset stomach, and sweeten bad breath. European herbalists use dill in preparations for treating colic in infants. In folk medicine the seeds have been employed for antispasmodic, carminative, sedative, lactogogue, and diuretic properties. The seeds have been used in the treatment of bronchial asthma, neuralgias, genital ulcers and hemorrhoids. The chief medicinal use has been as a carminative in the treatment of colic, and hiccups, as well as allaying nausea (Mahran and co-workers 1992). All of these uses, which persist to the present day, were recorded by early Greek and Roman writers and continued through Medieval times (Stannard 1982).

Recent research has shown that there may be additional uses for the plant. Various plant substances are increasingly becoming linked with an ability to inhibit cancer formation. Epidemiological studies, for example, have shown that the consumption of cruciferous plants, such as broccoli, are linked to a decreased incidence of cancer in humans. Garlic and onion oils have also been linked with their cancer "chemopreventive" activity. Plants with essential oils are of particular interest to researchers. It is believed that compounds that induce an increase in the activity of the detoxifying enzyme glutathione *S*-transferase (GST) may be considered potential inhibitors of carcinogenisis. GST causes a reaction between glutathione and electrophiles forming less toxic compounds for excretion. Chemical carcinogens that are electrophiles may be detoxified if anticarcinogenic compounds induce the reactions of GST with glutathione and electrophiles, ultimately resulting in their elimination from the system. Various components of dill weed oil, including anethofuran, carvone, and limonene have been shown to increase GST activity at least two times greater than controls in the livers of mice (Zheng and co-workers 1992).

Dill weed oil contains anethofuran, alpha-phellandrene, limonene, and carvone. The seed oil contains the same constituents with higher concentrations of carvone. The seed also contains flavonoids including kaempferol and vincenin. Coumarins identified in the plant include umbelliferone, begapten, scopoletin and esculetin. The seed oil is antibacterial, carminative, and has antifoaming action. Various studies have also shown that dill seed oil as well as alcoholic extracts of the fruits are strongly diuretic in a number of experimental models. The seed oil had the strongest effect (Mahran and co-workers 1991).

Dittany, Stone Mint, American Dittany

Cunila origanoides (L.) Britt.
(koo-nie'-la oh-rig'-an-oi-deez)
Labiatae (Lamiaceae)—Mint Family
Plate 11

American dittany, stone mint, mountain dittany, or feverwort, as it is known in the Arkansas Ozarks, is an herb from North American woods ideal for rocky, shaded crevices in the herbal landscape. It grows in dry, open, rocky woods, favoring acid soils on sandstone, chert, and granite, from Florida to Texas, and north to Illinois and New York. It is a

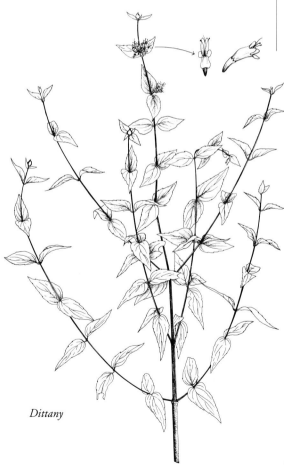

Dittany

hardy, branched, erect perennial, reaching from one to two feet tall. The leaves are nearly sessile (without leaf stalks), oval, almost triangular in shape, with acutely pointed tips. They have small teeth, and as the specific name *origanoides* implies, an oreganolike fragrance. The rose-to-lavender flowers appear in axils around the leaves or in terminal clusters from August to October. This dittany should not be confused with the fuzzy-leaved dittany-of-Crete, which is more commonly grown in herb gardens.

During the first chills of autumn, dittany produces frost flowers at its base—twisting, white, fluted ribbons of ice, sometimes four inches tall and two inches broad. This phenomenon is caused by cell sap rising from the still-alive root into the dead tissues of the leaves and stems. The rising vapors seep through cracks in the stem, crystallizing as they contact the freezing air. Frost flowers have to be seen to be appreciated. Only a few plant species produce these exceptional frost flowers. Besides dittany, these include frostweed (*Helianthemum canadense*), stinkweed (*Pluchea camphorata*), white crownbeard (*Verbesina virginica*), also known as frostweed, and a few other species.

Dittany is easy to grow from seed. It can also be propagated from root divisions made in the spring. Plant it among rocks under 50 percent shade. A sandy, dry soil with a pH around 5 and good drainage is best. The plant is established in the Heritage Herb Garden of the Ozark Folk Center in Mountain View, Arkansas. Under cultivation in this garden, the normally thin, straggly wild plants take on a stately, full, compact form, showing they adapt well to the herb milieu.

Harvest the leaves in late summer when dittany is in bloom, and hang them in bunches. They dry quickly. The dried leaves make a mild-flavored mint tea—a good wintertime beverage. The leaves can be used in cooking as an oregano substitute.

Recorded uses of the plant by the Cherokees included making a tea to treat colds, headaches, fevers, and to increase perspiration. Externally, it was beneficial for the treatment of snakebites. A strong tea of the herb increased labor pains, hence facilitating childbirth. Medicinal folk use of dittany has been as a diaphoretic to reduce fevers, as well as for headaches and snakebites.

This plant has not been well investigated chemically. The plant produces an essential oil with a fragrance resembling oil of thyme. It contains the antiseptic thymol (see thymes). Jim Duke has collected the plant for the National Cancer

Institute's anticancer and anti-HIV chemical-screening programs (Duke 1990a). While it is doubtful that it produced positive results, it is an American herb deserving a place in American herb gardens.

ECHINACEA, PURPLE CONEFLOWER

Echinacea pallida Nutt., *E. angustifolia* D.C., *E. purpurea* (L.) Moench, *E. paradoxa* var. *paradoxa* (Norton) Britton
(ek-i-nay'-see-a pal'-lid-a; an-gust-i-foh'-li-a;
pur-pur-ee'-a; par-a-docks'-a)
Compositae (Asteraceae)—Aster Family
Plate 4

Over the past ten years, my hobby has been echinacea. I have propagated and grown eight of the nine species in the genus, and visited echinacea growers and product manufacturers in the United States, Europe, and Australia. I have read all of the popular, historical, and scientific literature I could find on the plant. I have had lengthy discussions and collaborated with the primary researchers on echinacea, and written extensively about the plant, including a book, *Echinacea—Nature's Immune Enhancer.* The study of this plant group has become a passion, one of endless fascination, sometimes frustration and controversy, new understanding, and concern for the biodiversity of the genus. As echinacea grows in popularity throughout the world, and continues to be harvested from the wild, the gene pool is being reduced, highlighting the acute need for cultivated supplies, especially of *Echinacea angustifolia* and *E. pallida.* Despite this need, there is room for only a handful of dedicated commercial growers in the world marketplace.

What I don't know about echinacea is far greater than what I do know. The more I learn, the more I find there is to learn. This can be said for herbs in general—no matter what plant or what aspect of herbs one studies. To my mind, echinacea is probably the most interesting American medicinal plant from both a historical and modern perspective.

The genus *Echinacea* is represented by nine species and two varieties indigenous to North America, with distribution centered in Arkansas, Kansas, Missouri, and Oklahoma. These coarse perennial herbs occur in rocky prairies, barrens, glades, fields, along railroad tracks and roadsides, and, in the case of *E. purpurea,* in open woods. Echinaceas grow from one to four feet high with erect, simple, or branched stems. Most species have rough,

bristly, stiff hairs on the stems and leaves. The simple, alternate leaves are oval to lance shaped with relatively long petioles (leaf stalks) at the base of the plant. The leaves become progressively smaller and sessile (without leaf stalks) toward the flower head. The leaves are entire (without teeth) or have coarse teeth. The cone-shaped flower head, a hemispherical receptacle with radiating ray florets ranging in color from rose, pink, purple, and white, to yellow, characterizes the plant. Disk flowers range from brownish-orange to reddish-brown. The ray florets are drooping (reflexed), especially in *E. pallida.* Flowering begins as early as mid-May in the South, extending into October in the northern limits of the range. The fibrous, horizontal or vertical rootstocks, pungently aromatic with a bitter flavor, are six to twenty-four inches in length. Several rosettes of leaf and flower stalks may arise from a single root.

Echinaceas in cultivation include the common species *E. angustifolia, E. pallida,* and *E. purpurea.* The Ozark endemics, *E. simulata,* and especially the yellow-flowered *E. paradoxa,* have also been introduced into horticulture. *E. paradoxa,* my favorite garden plant from the genus, is now available from a number of commercial sources. I know of no organizations, public or private, offering seeds of *E. atrorubens,* a species of the eastern edge of the prairies, or the west Gulf Coast plain's *E. sanguinea.*

The federally listed endangered species, *E. tennesseensis,* the Tennessee coneflower, known from only five natural populations in central Tennessee, is available. It sports upturned rather than drooping petals, and its nursery or seed source must be licensed by the U.S. Fish and Wildlife Service to sell plant material in interstate commerce. Three places known to me offer it for sale. It is easily grown from seed, drought tolerant, and a good example of an endangered species that may proliferate under cultivation.

The rare Appalachian endemic, smooth-leaved coneflower, *E. laevigata,* known from only nineteen natural populations and represented by 97 percent fewer individuals in the wild than *E. tennesseensis,* has been available from a number of sources. However, as of 9 November 1992, *E. laevigata* obtained its rightful and long-overdue status as a federally listed endangered species, which may, for a short time at least, limit distribution of seeds, until the sources which previously sold the plant can become licensed. *E. laevigata* is similar to common *E. purpurea* in appearance, though the leaves are relatively smooth, not cordate at the base, and it is taprooted rather than possessing a fibrous root

Echinacea purpurea, Common Purple Coneflower, Cologne, Germany

like *E. purpurea.*

E. pallida, E. purpurea, and *E. angustifolia* are the most common species. *E. pallida* has long, slender, entire leaves, five to twenty times longer than broad. The purple, pink, or white ray flowers are one-and-a-half to three-and-a-half inches long and drooping. The plant stands sixteen to thirty-six inches tall, and ranges from Michigan to Nebraska, south to Georgia, and west to Texas.

E. angustifolia is the species historically listed in most American herb catalogs and books. It is smaller than other Echinacea species, growing from six to twenty inches high. The ray flowers are as long or shorter than the width of the disk (seven-eighths of an inch to one-and-one-half inches long). The stiff hairs on the plant appear swollen at their bases. It is found from Minnesota to Saskatchewan, south to Oklahoma and Texas.

E. purpurea grows from two to four feet (rarely six feet tall). Its leaves are oval with acutely pointed tips and coarse teeth. Ray flowers are rose to deep purple, with orange-tipped palae (the bristles on the flower head). Unlike all other echinaceas, which are taprooted, *E. purpurea* has a fibrous root. This species is the most widely distributed, ranging from Georgia west to Oklahoma, and north to Michigan and Ohio. The seeds of this species are widely available on the horticultural trade, sometimes known as *Rudbeckia purpurea,* a name that has been obsolete since the 1840s! Several cultivars are offered, including 'The King', 'Sombrero', and 'Bright Star'. German seedmerchants offer variants known as 'Alba', 'White Prince', 'White Lustre', and 'White King'. Ronald McGregor (1968), author of *The Taxonomy of the Genus Echinacea,* reports that all these variants have been observed in natural wild stands.

A number of German cultivars of *E. purpurea* are also available in the international horticultural trade, including 'Schleissheim', 'Hybrida', 'Leuchtstern', 'Magnus', and 'Rubinstern'. A recent study by German researchers investigated whether *E. purpurea* cultivars developed for horticulture were suitable for use in pharmaceutical products and field production. Ten cultivars were studied over a three-year period. The cultivars mentioned above were all found acceptable as medicinal plants (Bomme et al. 1992a, 1992b).

In the Ozarks, echinaceas are known as droops, because of the drooping ray flowers. Most *E. purpurea* cultivars in horticulture have been selected for spreading rather than drooping petals, because German gardeners thought the drooping petals indicated diseased plants. *E. purpurea* cultivars in American gardens have primarily originated in Germany. *E. purpurea* has been grown as a garden ornamental in Europe for nearly three hundred years.

Unlike other "purple coneflowers," the paradox of *E. paradoxa* var. *paradoxa* lies in its yellow ray flowers and near-hairless, smooth stems and leaves. It is easily grown from seed, and has become much more common in cultivation. The plant is an Ozark endemic known from seventeen Missouri counties, five Arkansas counties, and has recently been found in two counties in Oklahoma.

There have been historical problems with the identification of echinacea species in the herb trade. *E. angustifolia* supplies have included a mixture of *E. pallida* and *E. angustifolia*. The roots of *E. atrorubens, E. paradoxa,* and *E. simulata* have also been involved, to a limited extent, in the *E. angustifolia* supply. *E. purpurea* leaf and flower products are generally not subject to misidentification, though *E. purpurea* root products have historically been adulterated with prairie dock (*Parthenium integrifolium*). Clear chemical and microscopic identification methods for the echinacea species have now been developed by Dr. Rudolf Bauer at the University of Munich and his coworkers, and this has gone a long way in helping to clear up market confusion.

Propagation is by seed or by carefully dividing branching crowns from the main rootstock in spring or fall. Echinacea seeds sprout better if stratified before germinating. This can be achieved by sowing the seeds on the surface of a sandy soil mix in an open, cold frame during January. *E. purpurea* can be directly sown in the garden without pregermination treatment. If carefully planted outdoors in the fall of the previous year, in a well-prepared and protected seedbed, *E. angustifolia* and *E. pallida* seeds will exhibit relatively good germination the following spring. If stratified, a period of 90 to 120 days is suitable for *E. angustifolia* seed. *E. pallida, E. paradoxa,* and *E. simulata* seeds germinate well after a sixty-day period of cold, moist stratification at about 41° F. Once the weather warms in early spring, the seeds will quickly sprout if provided moisture and sunlight.

Tamp the seeds into the soil mix, but do not cover them. A light dusting of soil or a light straw mulch will help retain moisture.

Sown from seed, echinaceas need to grow for three or four years before sizable roots can be harvested. Plants propagated by division can be harvested two years after planting. If the herbage is desired, *E. purpurea* can be harvested late in the first-through-third year, then the ground can be rotated into another crop.

Most echinaceas grow in poor, rocky, slightly acidic-to-alkaline (pH 6 to 8), well-drained soils. *E. purpurea* likes a moderately rich soil. All species are drought resistant. Full sun is required, except for *E. purpurea,* which enjoys dappled shade during hot summer months. Deep and frequent cultivation encourages healthy growth. Echinaceas do not like weed competition; therefore, keep them well weeded.

Harvest the roots in autumn after the plants have gone to seed. Dry in shade or under forced heat. Roots over one-half inch in diameter can be split before drying. Yields of about twelve hundred pounds of dried root per acre have been obtained for *E. purpurea*.

In his 1919 classic study of Indian groups of the Missouri River region, ethnologist Melvin R. Gilmore wrote of *E. angustifolia*: "This plant was universally used as an antidote for snake bite and other venomous bites and stings and poisonous conditions. Echinacea seems to have been used as a remedy for more ailments than any other plant" (131). Echinacea was one of the more important medicinal plants of the Plains Indians. The root was used as an antidote for all types of venomous bites and stings. A piece of the root was applied to toothaches to relieve pain. The Kiowa Indians chewed the ground root slowly, swallowing the juice for sore throats and coughs. A decoction was employed in steam baths so that participants could endure higher temperatures. The Sioux valued the roots as a remedy for rabies. *E. pallida* was a treatment for mumps, measles, rheumatism, arthritis, bad colds, smallpox, mouth sores, and many other ills. Indians used echinacea to treat cancers. Kiowa women adopted the bristly dried flower heads as hair combs. (S. Foster 1991l; Kindscher 1989, 1992).

Dr. John King of Cincinnati, a leading botanic physician in his day, described the medical uses of *E. purpurea* in the 1852 edition of his *The Eclectic Dispensatory of the United States of America*. In an article in an 1887 issue of the *Eclectic Medical Journal,* Dr. King again became the first to extol the properties of *E. angustifolia* in print. King employed the herb extensively in his private practice and found it to be the only remedy to relieve his wife's "virulent cancer." In the late-nineteenth and early twentieth centuries, tincture of echinacea became the fastest-selling medicine derived from a native American plant, despite denunciations of the herb's benefits in the *Journal of the American Medical Association.* By the late 1920s, echinacea fell into disuse in the United States, as did plant drugs in general, but starting in the late 1930s, it was further developed as a plant medicine in Germany. Today both scientific and popular interest in echinacea is increasing rapidly, thus creating the threat of overharvesting wild populations. Cultivated supplies of the root are needed.

Historically, echinacea preparations have been used to treat dozens of conditions, including gangrene, boils, carbuncles, abscesses, mucous-membrane inflammations, typhoid, burns, wounds, diphtheria, blood poisoning, mouth ulcers, and other ailments related to diseased blood. Its effects were considered antithermic, antibiotic, depurative, alterative, and antiseptic. In modern times, especially in Europe, where nearly three hundred echinacea phytomedicine products are available, preparations are used to support and stimulate the immune system, particularly for diseases of the throat, nose, and larynx, and to back up treatments for colds and influenza. Echinacea is also employed (mostly topically) for inflamed and suppurative injuries, abscesses, herpes simplex, inflammations, and wounds.

Echinacea extracts increase bacteria-destroying cells (phagocytes), inhibit inflammation, and accelerate wound healing. Experiments with *Echinacea* essential oil also suggest tumor-inhibiting capacity (Walker carcinosarcoma and lymphocytic leukemia). Echinacea research shows that this herb possesses resistance to herpes and influenza virus, *Staphylococci* and *Streptococci* bacteria, and allergies.

The phytomedical system of the German government has published several monographs on various echinacea species, plant parts, and product forms. Currently, the aboveground parts of *E. purpurea,* in the form of the expressed juice of aerial portions of the fresh-flowering plant, are the subject of an official German monograph produced by Commission E of the BGA (the German FDA). In Germany the sophisticated standard requirements for registering a plant drug include: the name of the drug, its composition, areas of allowed application, contraindications, side effects, interactions with other drugs,

dosage, mode of administration, duration of administration, and effects of the drug (S. Foster 1991l).

Contraindications for echinacea exclude its use in progressive systemic diseases such as tuberculosis, leukoses, multiple sclerosis, AIDS and related HIV infections, and other autoimmune diseases. While echinacea is sold in Germany as a nonspecific stimulant to the immune system to increase the body's own defenses, it is not used when actual diseases or dysfunction of the immune system are present. In other words, it is used as a short-term stimulant for a healthy immune system—not a treatment for autoimmune disease.

The stimulatory action involves raising properdin levels, increasing phagocytosis, and releasing corticosteroids. For these purposes, oral and injectable forms are used. The dosage of injectable forms should be determined by a physician. Externally, products are allowed which help stimulate regenerative processes, restore damaged tissue, activate phagocytosis, and exert an indirect antiinfective influence, resulting from the effect of the herb on the hyaluronidase/hyaluronic acid system (S. Foster 1991l; BGA 1989).

Surprising new monographs from the German BGA on the aerial parts of *E. angustifolia* and *E. pallida,* and *E. angustifolia* roots state, "Since the effectiveness for the claimed application is not documented, therapeutic use cannot be recommended" (BGA 1992c). Ditto for the root of *E. purpurea* (BGA 1992a). A positive monograph, however, exists for *E. pallida* root, which is recommended for the supportive therapy of influenzalike conditions (BGA 1992b), as well as for *E. purpurea* aerial parts (BGA 1989).

Various polysaccharides which stimulate the immune system have been isolated from the roots, tops, and tissue-cell cultures of echinacea species, especially *E. purpurea.* The polysaccharides are considered to be important components of water-soluble and dried-plant echinacea preparations. Topically and orally, echinacea polysaccharides exhibit strong wound-healing and infection-fighting capacities because of the formation of a hyaluronic-acid polysaccharide complex that helps neutralize inflammation and swelling along with the enzyme hyaluronidase. Hyaluronic acid, found in the ground substance (the material which occupies spaces between cells) of connective tissue, acts as a binding and protective agent.

E. angustifolia roots contain echinacoside (0.3 to 1.3 percent), which has a mild antibacterial activity. Once felt to be a primary active component unique to *E. angustifolia,* echinacoside is now thought to be a relatively unimportant pharmacological constituent. It has also been found in *E. pallida, E. simulata, E. paradoxa,* and *E. atrorubens. E. angustifolia* roots also contain the quinic-acid derivative cynarin, which has so far been identified only in *E. angustifolia* and *E. tennesseensis,* which are closely related species. *E. purpurea* has cichoric acid, especially in the flowers (1.2 to 3.1 percent) and roots (O.6 to 2.1 percent). Various flavonoids have been identified from the leaves of the plant as well. Echinacea species also incorporate polyacetylenes, which in *E. pallida* include ketoalkynes and ketoalkenes which do not occur in *E. angustifolia.* Hence they are useful in identifying the former plant.

The essential oil of *E. angustifolia, E. pallida,* and *E. purpurea* has been studied by various researchers, and the tops of all three species contain borneol, bornyl acetate, germacrene D, caryophyllene, caryophyllene epoxide, and palmitic acid. Typically, the leaves and roots of *E. angustifolia* have less then 0.1 percent essential oil. *E. pallida* roots hold 0.2 to 2.0 percent, while the leaves have less than 0.1 percent. The oil of *E. pallida* contains various ketoalkynes, also typical of *E. paradoxa* and found in *E. simulata.* However, the ketoalkynes are found only in trace amounts in *E. angustifolia* and *E. pallida.* The flowers, however, contain up to 0.3 percent essential oil. The roots of *E. purpurea* may hold up to 0.2 percent essential oil, and the flowers and leaves have up to 0.6 percent. The root oil consists of caryophyllene, humulene, caryophyllene epoxide, and germacrene D, which is also found in the leaves. Germacrene alcohol is a typical component and a characteristic indicator of the essential oil of *E. purpurea* fresh-plant preparations (Bauer and Wagner 1991).

Alkylamides are another group of components in echinacea, represented by isobutylamides of various acids. The isobutylamides are the compounds responsible for the characteristic tingling or numbing sensation produced on the tongue by echinacea. They may also be involved in the immunostimulatory activity of the plant. The research group of Dr. Rudolf Bauer at the University of Munich has found eleven alkylamides in the roots of *E. purpurea,* some of which occur in the leaves. At least fourteen alkylamides have been identified in the roots of *E. angustifolia* (Bauer and Wagner 1991).

Is there one immunostimulating principle of echinacea? The answer is no. In alcohol-soluble preparations, it appears that the isobutylamides and cichoric acid contribute to the activity. Polysaccharides participate in the immunostimulatory activity in the expressed juice of *E. purpurea,* its water extracts, and its whole powdered leaves or root. In other words, the plant's biological activity depends on the combined action of several constituents (Bauer and Wagner 1991).

The question of which echinacea species is the best has often been raised. There is no definitive scientific answer. I have my own bias. The vast majority of pharmacological and clinical studies on echinacea have involved a German product line, Echinacin, which includes a liquid oral-dosage form, salve, and injectable products used by physicians in Germany. These products have been manufactured by Madaus AG in Cologne since 1939. Pharmaceutically, the liquid preparation is termed a "succus." It is the expressed juice of the fresh flowering plant of *E. purpurea,* preserved by the addition of about 22 percent alcohol.

As echinacea has become more popular, there have been increased pressures on wild populations of *E. angustifolia* and *E. pallida,* as well as endemic species such as *E. atrorubens, E. paradoxa,* and *E. simulata.* In my opinion, their wild harvest is not sustainable over the long term, creating conservation concerns, especially because of the continuing depletion of their genetic diversity. On the other hand, the entire world's supply of *E. purpurea* comes from cultivated material. Therefore, *E. purpurea* (or alternately, cultivated supplies of *E. angustifolia* or *E. pallida*) is my echinacea of choice.

For more information on all aspects of this endlessly fascinating plant group, see my book, *Echinacea–Nature's Immune Enhancer* (Rochester, Vt.: Healing Arts Press, 1991), as well as Bauer and Wagner (1991) and Hobbs (1989a).

ELECAMPANE

Inula helenium L.
(in'-you-la he-lee'-ni-um)
Compositae (Asteraceae)—Aster Family
Plate 8

Elecampane is a striking plant, a good focus for an herbal design scheme. This robust perennial generally grows from four to six feet high, but I've seen specimens in double-dug beds that exceeded eight feet. The basal leaves are long and comparatively narrow, being ten to eighteen inches long and about four inches broad. The leaf stems add an additional six to twelve inches to the leaf's overall length. Above, the leaves are rough; below, they're covered with soft, velvety white hairs. Moving up the stem, the leaves become successively smaller, losing their petioles (leaf stalks) at the top. Instead, the upper leaves clasp the stalks with their heart-shaped bases. Abundant, long, slender ray flowers project radially from the splendid golden flower heads, which are sometimes four inches in diameter. The flower heads are sparse and may sit alone or in groups of two or three on top of the stalk. The root is large and fleshy, about six inches long and one or two inches thick, with half a dozen or more lateral rootlets, six to twelve inches long and one-half to one inch across. Elecampane flowers from May to August. It is probably native to southeastern Europe, though it was once widely cultivated as a medicinal herb all over Europe, and has become naturalized throughout much of the Continent. It is also naturalized in eastern North America.

Elecampane is propagated in autumn by dividing buds or "eyes" off two-year-old roots which are being harvested for drying. Plants may also be started from seed sown indoors about seven weeks before the last frost. First-year plants from seed do not flower.

Elecampane thrives on a fairly rich, moist clay loam with an acid pH, 4.5 to 6, in full sun and partial shade. Give plants in rich soil three feet spacing; space those in average soils at eighteen inches. Deeply dug soil will help produce large roots and robust plants. An acre may produce a ton of roots.

Only the root is used, and it should be harvested in the fall of the second year. By the third year, the roots often become woody and pithy. For easy drying, slice roots into half-inch-diameter pieces. Yields of fifteen hundred to twenty-five hundred pounds of the dried root per acre have been obtained. They can be candied like angelica and calamus roots.

Elecampane has a rich tradition of medicinal use, especially as a home remedy for lung ailments like pneumonia, whooping cough, asthma, bronchitis, and vesical catarrh. The efficacy of the plant for bronchial-related conditions has not been experimentally substantiated. It is considered stimulating, diaphoretic, diuretic, expectorant, tonic, emmenagogic, bechic, cholagogic, and mildly anthelmintic. Elecampane has been used for skin afflictions, upset stomach, diarrhea, intestinal parasites, and in Chinese medicine, to treat certain cancers. Topically, elecampane has been applied to facial neuralgia and sciatica. Experiments with mice have shown the tea to be a strong sedative.

The root is prepared by decocting one-half ounce of it in one pint of boiling water. A tincture is made by weight with two parts root and one part alcohol. One-sixth of the alcohol is added to the root and thoroughly mixed, after which the remaining alcohol is added. Let it sit for ten days.

The root contains up to 44 percent inulin. Many plants contain the polysaccharide inulin, which is tasteless to slightly sweet, and is particularly abundant in elecampane, as well as Jerusalem artichoke (*Helinathus tuberosus*). While inulin-containing plants have been associated in folk medicine with the treatment of diabetes, about the only thing that inulin and insulin (a pancreatic hormone) have in common is the similarities of their names. They should not be confused. The essential oil comprises up to 4 percent of the root's weight and primarily consists of the sesquiterpene lactones, alantolactone (helenalin) and isoalantolactone. Alantolactone is a powerful worm expellant still used in Europe. It is experimentally antiinflammatory and has been shown to stimulate the immune system. Both lactones are strongly bactericidal and fungicidal.

Evening Primrose

Oenothera biennis L.
(oh'-noth-er-a bye'-en-iss)
Onagraceae—Evening Primrose Family
Plate 12

Evening primrose, a neglected weed, wildflower, and once-purported cure-all, is an indigenous North American biennial, growing from one to eight feet in height. Jim Duke has termed it a winter biennial—a plant that germinates one year, making a taproot for the winter, then flowers the second season (Duke 1992). The coarse, branched stems have numerous, alternate, lance-shaped leaves. The basal leaves are in a rosette, with red spots, and deeply sinuate lobes. The cream-to-bright yellow, four-petaled flowers, with drooping or outcurved sepals, and a prominent X-shaped stigma, bloom from June through September. The flowers unfold after sunset (hence the name "evening" primrose) or bloom on dark, cloudy days. It is found in ditches, fields, and waste places throughout much of the eastern United States. Elsewhere it is widely naturalized. The plant is extremely variable. Evening primrose, scabbish, scabish, scurvish, scabious, tree primrose, sundrop, wild evening primrose, cure-all, kings' cure-all, nightwillow herb, and German rampion are just a few of its common names.

Evening primrose is propagated by seed which requires light to germinate. If the seeds are planted in the manner of a conventional annual or biennial—covered in a moist growing medium—germination will be poor. If the seeds are scattered upon the soil surface, tamped in, then bottom-watered, they germinate readily at temperatures between 71° and 74° F. The plant is somewhat weedy in habit, often growing in disturbed areas. It seems to do best in a relatively poor garden soil, and if grown for seed production, it produces a lower content of gamma linolenic acid (the desired compound in the seed oil) if given high levels of nitrogen (Nonnecke 1988). Good drainage is essential. It will grow in full sun or partial shade. Evening primrose is a colorful addition to the back border of an herb garden.

Yields of between four hundred to five hundred pounds per acre have been reported, though selected plant lines have produced as much as eight hundred to a thousand pounds per acre. Should you run out and plant a few acres of evening primrose as a cash crop? The answer is no. A number of farm groups developed commercial supplies of the seed for oil production in the mid-to-late 1980s. Overproduction resulted, and many farmers were left with a crop for which there was no market. Furthermore, the commercial interest that has produced most of the research on the plant, and most evening primrose products, has developed high-yielding GLA germplasm that is produced by contract growers. Regulatory action against evening primrose oil products has also reduced the market demand.

Evening primrose is traditionally known as an edible wild plant. The seeds were used as a food by native groups in Utah and Nevada (Yanovsky 1936). The young mucilaginous leaves can be used in salads or as a pot herb. The plant was introduced to European gardens as early as 1614, where it was cultivated in both England and Germany for the edible roots, which were boiled as a vegetable. Evening primrose was developed in Germany as a vegetable, and by 1863 came back to America under the name of "German rampion." The root possesses a nutty flavor (Hedrick 1919). Basically, all parts of the plant are edible. The seeds can be sprinkled on top of breads as a poppyseed substitute.

Among American Indian groups, the plant seems to have been widely used. The Ojibwa treated bruises with it. The forest Potawatomi considered the seeds a valuable medicine, though H. H. Smith (1933) was unable to determine the specific use from his informant. The Cherokee employed an infusion of the plant to treat obesity, and the hot root served

as a hemorrhoid remedy. The Iroquois also treated hemorrhoids with it, and chewed the root, spitting the pulp on the hands, then rubbing it on the arms and muscles of lacrosse players to give them strength.

Medicinal uses date back to the earliest publications on American medicinal plants. Johann David Schöpf (1787) stated that evening primrose was esteemed as a vulnerary. Rafinesque mentioned the benefit of the freshly bruised leaves as a poultice on wounds, and noted that the roots are edible either boiled or pickled. The Shakers, who established the first commercial herb business in the United States, listed evening primrose roots in many of their catalogs as a vulnerary, demulcent, mucilage, and stomachic. A poultice of the fresh or dried leaves, simmered in milk, was a folk remedy for tumors and painful swelling. A decoction of the plant was recommended by Griffith (1847) for "infantile eruptions." It is interesting to note that one of the main components of the seed oil, gamma-linolenic acid (GLA), is found in human breast milk. Sometimes infants removed from breast feeding to artificial-milk formulas are deficient in delta-6-desaturase, and develop atopic eczema. Could Griffith's mention of "infantile eruption" have been an early recognition of the value of the plant for atopic eczema?

Modern use of the plant has focused on the seed oil, and more specifically its GLA (gamma-linolenic acid) content. In England, topical preparations of evening primrose oil are registered for medicinal use in the treatment of atopic eczema. In Canada, the seed oil is an approved dietary supplement for treating deficiencies of essential fatty acids. In the United States, sales are currently restricted. Recent research suggests seed oil may be beneficial for a wide range of conditions associated with imbalances and abnormalities of essential fatty acids, including allergy-induced eczema, asthma, migraine headaches, inflammations, premenstrual syndrome, breast problems, metabolic disorders, diabetes, arthritis, and alcoholism. Conflicting results point to the need for further well-designed scientific studies. Clinical studies in eight research centers have shown that evening primrose oil produces an average of 20 to 25 percent improvement in atopic eczema over results achieved by existing treatments such as steroids. Over 120 studies in university hospitals in fifteen counties have been conducted on evening primrose oil. Its efficacy is linked with deficiencies or imbalances of essential fatty acids and their relationship to prostaglandin production or abnormalities.

The seed produces about 14 percent fixed oil, consisting

of cis-linoleic acid (70 percent) as the primary component, along with about 9 percent gamma-linolenic acid (GLA), a rare constituent of vegetable seed oils. The seed oil contains smaller amounts of palmitic, oleic, and stearic acids. GLA is an intermediate compound between cis-linoleic acid and prostaglandins. The natural conversion of cis-linoleic acid into prostaglandin E_1 is hampered in some individuals, and has been related to aging, alcoholism, cancer, improper nutrition, bad diet, and radiation damage. GLA supplied from evening primrose then could become an important dietary supplement to increase prostaglandin production in the treatment of essential fatty-acid deficiencies (Duke 1988; Briggs 1986).

FENNEL

Foeniculum vulgare Mill.
(fee-nik'-you-lum vul-gay'-ree)
Umbelliferae (Apiaceae)—Carrot Family
Plate 12

Fennel is an annual, biennial, or perennial native to Eurasia. It has become extensively naturalized in south and central California, where it is often called wild anise. Fennel grows to six feet in height, and has an erect, round, smooth, striated, jointed, and branching stem. The leaves are long, linear, and pointed, similar to dill leaves. The tiny yellow flowers grow on flat umbels with fifteen to forty rays. Each umbel is up to seven inches in diameter. The half-inch-long fruits are oval and greenish-gray, with prominent ribs.

Copper or bronze fennel (*Foeniculum vulgare* 'Ruburum') has bronze leaves with a metallic lustre. *F. vulgare* subsp. *vulgare* var. *azoricum* (Mill) Thell., like celery, has edible stalks greatly thickened at their base. It is known as "finocchio" or "Florence fennel." It is often erroneously confused with *F. vulgare* subsp. *vulgare* var. *dulce* Batt. & Trab., whose leaves are not thick at the base and which is primarily grown for the essential oil in its large fruits. *F. vulgare* subsp. *piperitum* (Ucria) Coutinho, which has sharp-tasting fruits, occurs in dry rocky soils in the Mediterranean region.

Finocchio fennel has become increasingly available as a specialty vegetable throughout the United States. Seeds of at least seventeen different cultivars are available from commercial seed sources. Researchers at Purdue University's Department of Horticulture have studied the commercial feasibility of their cultivation and have found wide differences in leaf yield, time needed to mature, and the shape, size, and compactness of the "bulb" of the various cultivars. The bulb is the thickened stem base, or enlarged leaf stalk, harvested as the vegetable product. According to their research, the highest-yielding cultivar line was 'Zefo Fino' (available from Johnny's Selected Seeds). This plant produces a larger bulb, and hence has a greater yield. Harvesting, cleaning, trimming, and packaging of finocchio fennel is done by hand for commercial markets. Once harvested, it is stored at temperatures at or just above freezing. Unfortunately, it has been sold as anise in the American vegetable trade, which has caused some consumer confusion (Simon 1990; Morales and Simon 1991).

Fennel is easily grown from seed sown directly in the garden after danger of frost has passed. Seed usually germinates in fourteen days. It is basically a cool-season crop that can be planted early in the year. Optimum seed germination occurs at temperatures of 59° to 64° F. Thin seedlings to stand at six-to-twelve-inch spacings. Four to seven pounds of seed will plant an acre.

Common fennel likes a light, dry, limey soil with a pH from 7 to 8.5, and full sun. Finocchio (var. *azoricum*) needs a rich soil with lots of moisture to produce succulent, edible stems. Once the stems become about an inch thick, they can be hilled with soil to blanch them and produce a milder flavor. Harvest ten days after hilling. Commercial fields have produced six hundred to fourteen hundred pounds of seed per acre.

The roots are edible and may be harvested in the fall of the first year. Leaves and stems should be harvested for fresh use before the plant flowers. Seeds are harvested in late summer as they begin to turn their characteristic grayish-green color. Seed maturity occurs about 100 to 115 days after planting.

The boiled, blanched stalks make a wonderful vegetable in and of themselves. The filiform leaves are a great addition to soups and salads, and especially complement fish. Fresh leaves can be chopped into a vinegar and oil salad dressing in the blender. The seeds are used in breads and cookies, and a mild, aniselike tea can be brewed from the leaves or seeds.

Fennel is high in calcium, iron, potassium, vitamin A, and vitamin C. It contains some protein and phosphorus.

The seeds are used to stimulate milk flow, as an aromatic stimulant for digestive disorders, and as a carminative, especially to relieve infant colic. Fennel is also an expectorant, diuretic, and antispasmodic. As a carminative, fennel is not as strong as caraway, but has a much more pleasant flavor; hence it has been traditionally used in combination with other digestives. In China, a poultice of the powdered seeds is applied to hard-to-heal snakebites. The seeds are used in tea and in tincture form. Experimentally, the oil has been shown to have antispasmodic and carminative properties, as well as to foster liver regeneration in rats. Extracts of the seeds are antiinflammatory and have a slight estrogenic effect in animal experimental models.

The fruits may contain up to 28 percent by weight of a fixed oil, consisting mainly of petroselinic acid, oleic acid, and linoleic acid. The essential oil, comprising up to 8 percent of the weight of the fruit, contains trans-anethole, fenchone, estragole, limonene, camphene, and other substances. Fennel is another example of a chemically diverse plant which shows high variation in the quality and quantity of its essential oil. In some chemotaxa, the oil is composed chiefly of anethole (60 to 80 percent), while other races are without anethole, and contain 80 percent estragole. The latter tend to be bitter and unsuitable for use. Fenchone is another variable component in fennel's essential oil. The oil reportedly checks spasms of smooth muscles in animal experiments and is antibacterial.

FEVERFEW

Tanacetum parthenium (L.) Schultz Bip.
(tan-a-see'-tum par-then-ee'-um)
Compositae (Asteraceae)—Aster Family
Plate 12

Feverfew is a strongly aromatic perennial with ridged stems, originating in the mountain scrub and rocky soil of the Balkan peninsula. It grows from one-and-a-half to four feet in height. The leaves are yellowish-green, more or less oval in outline, and up to three inches long, with three to seven oblong elliptical lobes, further divided into smaller segments with an entire (without teeth) or round-toothed margin. The white-petaled, small, daisylike flowers, usually with yellow disk florets, are in a dense corymb. Several cultivars are available. Some have all-yellow diskettes, or are double flowered, with only white ray florets. Feverfew blooms from June through November. In Europe, it has been grown as a medicinal and ornamental plant for many centuries and has become naturalized in hedges and waste places throughout the Continent. It is naturalized in both North and South America. In the United States, it escaped

from gardens sometime in the mid-nineteenth century, and is now found naturalized in waste places, roadsides, and borders of woods from Quebec south to Maryland, and west to Missouri and Ohio.

Best known in modern botanical literature as *Tanacetum parthenium*, feverfew is often found in horticultural and herbal literature under the name *Chrysanthemum parthenium* (L.) Bernh. *Tanacetum* is an altered form of "athanasia" (athanatos), meaning immortal, referring to the everlasting nature of dried flowers. *Parthenium* is derived from the Greek "parthenos" (virgin), originally applied to another plant by Hippocrates. The name "feverfew," of course, honors the traditional use of the plant for treating fevers.

Feverfew is best propagated by seeds or division. The seeds should be pressed into the growing medium (rather than covered) as light enhances their germination. In soil maintained at 70° F, the seeds germinate in ten to fifteen days. Seedlings should be given one-foot spacings. Once established in the garden, feverfew will self-sow freely. Plants can be divided in spring or fall. The flowers should be pinched back as they begin to form because the plant will die after going to seed. If topped, the roots will remain perennial, and since it is the leaves that are used, pinching back the flower buds will encourage a more bushy and vigorous leaf growth. The plant does well in any good garden soil. A sunny, south window can be used to maintain it as a houseplant year-round.

The leaves are harvested just before the plant flowers, then dried under shade. At two-foot spacings, an acre could be expected to produce over a ton of dried leaves.

Since the time of the first-century Greek physician Dioscorides, the plant has been used for stomach ailments, fevers, menstrual irregularities, and headache. In the 1633 edition of Gerarde's *Herball,* there is a hint of the value of the plant for headache: "It is good for them that are giddie in the head" (653). The 1787 Dublin edition of Culpepper's famous (or infamous) herbal affirms it as traditional treatment for headaches: "It is very effectual for all pain in the head coming of a cold cause, the herb being bruised and applied to the crown of the head" (150). Feverfew has traditionally been considered a tonic, carminative, emmenagogue, vermifuge, and stimulant, used primarily for fevers and menstrual regulation. In South America, where feverfew is naturalized, it has been effective for colic, stomachache, morning sickness, and kidney pains. In Costa Rica, it has also been employed as a digestive aid and emmenagogue. Mexicans have used it as a sitz bath to regulate menstruation as well as an antispasmodic and tonic (Duke 1985). While the herb has been utilized since the beginning of Western civilization, we are only at the beginning stages of understanding its efficacy as a medicinal plant. Prior to the last decade, twentieth-century application of the plant had been relegated to folk medicine and popular herbals.

Few ailments result in the number of trips to medical practitioners in search of relief as do migraine headaches. As many as one in eight people suffer from them. Feverfew is now being promoted as a welcome relief for migraine sufferers. Several articles published in British medical journals in the past decade have catapulted feverfew to the forefront as a potential treatment for migraine headache as well as a possible palliative in arthritis. Adopting a unique approach, researchers have bypassed animal studies. Instead they have sought volunteers who were already using feverfew for self-treatment of migraine. The 1985 study by Johnson and coworkers on the efficacy of feverfew for the prophylactic treatment of migraine was conducted at the City of London Migraine Clinic in collaboration with the Chelsea College of the University of London. Seventeen patients who had been self-treating with feverfew were involved in the double-blind study, which examined the effects of withdrawal of the herb from users who thought it to be beneficial. The nine patients who received a placebo reported an increase in the frequency and severity of migraines and its associated symptoms, such as nausea and vomiting. This provided indirect evidence of the efficacy of feverfew. Another clinical trial by Murphy and coworkers (1988) reported on the value of feverfew to prevent the symptoms of migraine among the seventy-two volunteers who took part. Fifty-nine patients were assessed at the end of the randomized, double-blind, placebo-controlled study. The researchers observed significant improvement in the reduction of mean number of headaches, severity of migraine attacks, and vomiting associated with migraine. These two studies provide a reasonable basis for evaluating the benefits of feverfew in managing migraines.

One side effect of chewing the leaves is development of sores in the mouth, but some who suffer from migraine are more than willing to put up with this inconvenience. Like chamomile, some individuals may also be allergic to feverfew. Others may experience inflammation of the mouth or tongue from chewing feverfew. As many as 18 percent of those who use the herb develop oral inflammation.

A sesquiterpene lactone, parthenolide, is believed to be the primary active component of feverfew responsible for mitigating the severity and frequency of migraines. Properly-identified, dried feverfew leaf (with at least 0.2 percent parthenolide) has been proposed by Canadian regulatory authorities as a minimum standard for feverfew products. French authorities have proposed a level of 0.1 percent.

After the clinical trials from England were reported in the popular and scientific literature, many feverfew products appeared in herb markets. Much misinformation has accompanied popular reports and product literature. According to Awang (1993), it has been erroneously asserted in various articles and books that freeze-dried material is superior to the dried leaf, that air drying destroys parthenolide, and that single-flowered forms are preferable to double-flowered ones. In fact, the study at the University of Nottingham (Murphy, Heptinstall, and Mitchell 1988), the best clinical study to date, used encapsulated, whole, dried feverfew leaf, with a mean of 0.66 percent parthenolide—not freeze-dried leaf. Furthermore Awang, Dawson, and Kindack (1991) found that the highest level of parthenolide ever recorded in feverfew came from *T. parthenium* f. *flosculosum*—a double-flowered form, containing 1.27 percent parthenolide. The same study also determined that North American commercial feverfew products contained as much as 0.1 percent parthenolide, let alone the 0.2 percent proposed for a predictable level of efficacy by Health and Welfare Canada.

Health and Welfare Canada has just issued a DIN (Drug Identification Number) to a feverfew product made by an English firm. This is an important regulatory development, since it is the first DIN issued to an herbal product which makes substantive claims about relieving a relatively significant medical condition. The product will be required to be standardized to 0.2 percent parthenolide. Extrapolating parthenolide content and dosage from the various clinical trials, Dennis Awang proposed the 0.2 percent parthenolide content for Canada based on a daily dose of 250 milligrams of feverfew leaf.

The parthenolide content of feverfew sources has been found to be highly variable (Awang, 1987b, 1989a, 1989b, 1990a; Awang, Dawson, and Kindack 1991; Heptinstall et al. 1991). What's more, there are several different chemotypes. One contains about eighty parthenolide as the total sesquiterpene fraction, with smaller amounts of germacranolides, guaianolides, and other components. A second chemotype includes the eudesmanolides, reynosin and santamarin. The third is a mixture of eudesmanolides and guaianolides. The second two types contain no parthenolide.

All of this shows the importance of attention to detail, or as Dr. Awang puts it, "further vigilance and education." Feverfew, and its recent development as an antimigraine agent, provides the best documented example of the need for herb products that have been properly identified (both botanically and chemically), that have predictable levels of active constituents, and that are delivered in appropriate dosage forms and amounts so that herbal medicines can take their rightful place in modern healthcare.

For detailed information on feverfew, see the reviews by Awang (1989a), S. Foster (1991h), and Hobbs (1989c).

FOXGLOVE

Digitalis purpurea L.
(dij-i-ta'-lis pur-pur-ee'-a)
Scrophulariaceae—Figwort Family

Foxglove, a biennial or short-lived perennial, is a well-known ornamental for flower and herb gardens. It is native to Europe and widely cultivated throughout the world. In the American Northwest and Northeast, it has become naturalized along roadsides. When flowering, foxglove may reach six or seven feet. In the first year, the leaves form a dense basal rosette. In the second year, the plant shoots up a thick, erect, round, downy stem. Leaves on the stem are alternate with long stalks. Leaf blades are oval to lance shaped, with small, round teeth, prominent veins, and a wrinkled appearance. They are six to twelve inches long and three to four inches wide, green and woolly on the upper side, and covered with a white or gray pelt of hairs beneath. Their flavor is extremely bitter, which should be a good warning flag for the plant's high toxicity. The showy, bell-shaped flowers appear on one-sided spikes. They are usually one-and-a-half to three inches long, have flared lips, and are purple, cerise, and sometimes white. The flowers, too, are poisonous. The lower inside surface is whitish, covered with purple dots. Numerous cultivars are available.

Foxglove is grown from its tiny seeds, sown indoors in flats in February or March. Transplant outdoors after the last spring frost. Plants will self-sow.

An acid or slightly alkaline soil (pH 5 to 8) is acceptable. A loose, well-drained, moist, rich soil produces lush growth.

Foxglove will tolerate full sun or light shade. Seedlings need to be kept free of weeds, and the soil should be well cultivated throughout the plant's growth cycle.

In Great Britain and on the European continent, the leaves have been used as an expectorant, as a remedy in epilepsy, and as a poultice on scrofulous swellings for centuries. In 1775, William Withering, an English physician, brought foxglove's diuretic and dropsy-relieving properties to light. By the late nineteenth century, it was widely

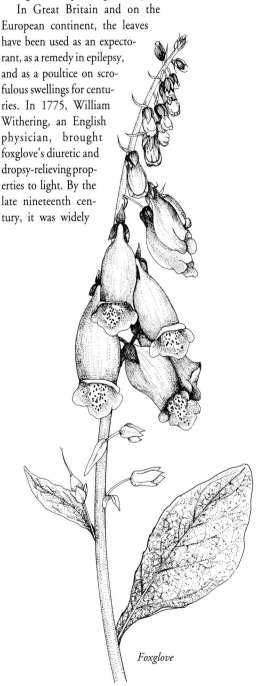

Foxglove

prescribed by physicians as a cardiotonic and diuretic.

In modern South America, an infusion of the leaves or foxglove pills are used for asthma relief, sedatives, or heart tonics. Colombians make a tea out of three or four corollas of a white-flowered variety to treat epilepsy in infants. In India, wounds and burns are treated with an ointment containing digitalis glycosides. Digitalis glycosides are used to treat congestive heart failure, as they increase the force of heart contractions while providing rest between them. They also raise low blood pressure. Foxglove contains more than thirty glycosides. Two are precursors to digitoxin and gitoxin.

Several years ago, a newspaper reporter interviewed me for an herb article. After the interview, the reporter arranged to trade some herb plants with me. He wanted to show me some comfrey, which he had tried in salads and found extremely bitter tasting. The next day I went to his office, and there, sitting on a file cabinet, was a box of first-year foxglove plants! To the novice, comfrey and foxglove have a similar appearance. Earlier that same year (1979), an elderly couple had eaten what they thought were comfrey leaves. It was foxglove, and both died within twenty-four hours. Foxglove

Allium sativum, Garlic

should be well marked in an herb garden or not planted at all. Its utility to herb gardeners is purely ornamental. The plant and its preparations are highly toxic. Poisoning is characterized by nausea, vomiting, dizziness, severe headache, irregular heartbeat and pulse, convulsions, and death.

GARLIC

Allium sativum L.
(al'-i-um sat-eye'- vum)
Liliaceae—Lily Family

Allium sativum is perhaps the most popular and pungent herb of world cuisines. This perennial, close relative of onions is not found in the wild, but has evolved, over millennia, in cultivation. It was cultivated in the Middle East some five thousand years ago. Its wild ancestors are thought to have originated on the high plains of west-central Asia, perhaps in the Kirghiz Desert of the former Soviet republic of Kirghizia and adjacent regions. In 1875, a wild progenitor of garlic, similar in morphological appearance to the modern top-setting ophio garlic, was discovered by the German-born botanical specialist of Russian flora, Eduard von Regel (1815–1892). He named it *Allium longicuspis.* It is believed today to be the closest wild relative to the plant we have come to know as garlic.

Garlic has been used for at least as long as humans have recorded historical events. From the time of the Egyptian pharaohs and the earliest Chinese dynasties, garlic, *A. sativum,* has been widely consumed as both food and medicine. Garlic may even have played a role in the building of the Egyptian pyramids. The Greek historian Herodotus (484–425 B.C.) wrote that an inscription of Egyptian characters on a pyramid records the quantities of radishes, onions, and garlic consumed by the laborers who constructed it. Garlic was also discovered in the tomb of Tutankhamen, as well as at the sacred-animal temple precinct at Saqqâra. Even King Tut had garlic breath.

Garlic belongs to the genus *Allium* of the lily family. There are more than seven hundred species of *Allium*, a genus which includes many important food plants such as onions, leeks, and chives. *Allium* is the ancient Latin name for garlic. The word is believed to be derived from a Celtic word meaning "hot" or "burning." The species name, *sativum*, signifies cultivated or planted. "Gar-leac" or "spear-plant" is an Anglo-Saxon designation for the plant now known as garlic.

Garlic has four or more flat, grayish-green leaves about one foot long and one-half inch wide. The flower stipe may reach three feet in height. Globular clusters of white flowers unfold from a papery, beaklike envelope; bulbels—miniature seed bulbs—may develop in place of flowers. If planted in early spring, flowers emerge in midsummer. The root is a fleshy bulb, one or two inches broad. A thin white sheathing encases five or more pointed, oblong cloves. Several varieties are grown commercially. In central California, "early" garlic is planted in the fall and harvested the following May or June. The bulbs are large and flat; the delectable cloves are enclosed in white sheathing. "Late" garlic is planted soon after the "early" harvest and has medium-sized cloves with light pink to reddish sheathing. The whole bulb is covered with a thin, white skin. Late has a longer shelf life than early. 'Creole' is a hardy variety with small red-skinned cloves.

According to a spokesperson of the Fresh Garlic Association, there are approximately eighteen thousand acres of garlic under cultivation in the United States. California is, of course, the largest garlic-producing state. In 1989, the crop was about 250 million pounds. About 80 percent is used for various dehydrated garlic products. Twenty percent of the crop is sold as fresh garlic, representing about fifty million pounds of the California harvest in 1989. Nearly 40 percent of the fresh garlic used in the United States is imported. It is estimated that in 1989 Americans consumed eighty million pounds of fresh garlic (S. Foster 1992a).

Garlic can be grown from nursery sets (bulbels), or by planting individual cloves. Cloves are perhaps the most convenient way. The outer cloves will generally produce superior plants. Place them point up in one-inch-deep holes at six-inch spacings. Fall plantings can be made in the Deep South and on the West Coast where the ground does not freeze in winter. In other regions, garlic can be planted as soon as the ground thaws or in the previous autumn before it freezes.

A moist, sandy soil, moderately rich in humus, is perfect for garlic culture. Full sun is essential, and slightly alkaline soil is best. Garlic plants take very little space and can be planted throughout the garden among other herbs and vegetables. As a companion plant, garlic is said to help keep away cabbage moths, Japanese beetles, and aphids. Aphids can be controlled with a garlic spray made by blending a handful of unpeeled cloves with three cups of water. Strain and spray on affected plants, being sure to cover undersides of leaves and stems. Repeat as necessary until the vermin travel to more fragrant shores.

Harvest garlic when the leaves turn brown and die down. Shake off loose dirt and cut off stringy rootlets. Let the bulbs dry for a day or two, then bring them in to braid. Soak the tops in water for about an hour or until pliable. Braid the leaves tightly together, adding another bunch with each twist, and knot at the top. Hang in the kitchen and remove cloves as needed.

If there is one herb that defies categorization, it is garlic. Here the product form and end use determine whether you consider it a food or condiment, culinary or medicinal herb, dietary supplement or drug, food or medicine. Garlic crosses, often indiscernibly, all of those barriers. Garlic is a most versatile culinary herb. However, there are two schools of thought when it comes to garlic breath—emphatic fans and equally energetic disdainers. The Lovers of the Stinking Rose, a garlic fan club, have a remedy for garlic breath—socializing with other garlic lovers. The fresh cloves can be used with an endless variety of meats, vegetables, soups, sauces, and salad dressings.

A highly nutritious herb, garlic abounds in fiber, calcium, iron, magnesium, phosphorus, potassium, protein, thiamin, niacin, riboflavin, vitamin C, and especially vitamin A. It also contains folic acid, iodine, germanium, copper, selenium, zinc, and other nutrients. At least seventeen amino acids have been identified in garlic. According to Indian studies reported in *Wealth of India*, incorporating moderate (but unspecified) amounts of garlic into the diet produces a favorable effect on intestinal microflora. It apparently benefits lactic organisms, helping to enhance the absorption of minerals in the diet.

If one plant can be termed a medicine chest in and of

itself, garlic lays claim to that reputation. Expectorant, diaphoretic, diuretic, carminative, vermifuge, stomachic, antispasmodic, rubefacient, and intestinal-antiseptic qualities have been attributed to it. It proves beneficial in fevers and colds, lung ailments, intestinal disorders, and general health maintenance. It has been employed in dozens of forms by cultures throughout the world. Traditionally, the fresh cloves, a tea, syrup, tincture, and other preparations have been used to treat colds, fever, flu symptoms, coughs, earache, bronchitis, shortness of breath, sinus congestion, headache, stomachache, high blood pressure, arteriosclerosis, hypertension, diarrhea, dysentery, gout, rheumatism, whooping cough, pinworms, old ulcers, and many other conditions or ailments (Foster and Duke 1990). At the onset of a cold, I chew two or three cloves of garlic, and without fail have been cured. To quote a bumper sticker, "Fight mouthwash—eat garlic."

Over the past twenty years, garlic has been the subject of intensive, and sometimes conflicting, research. More than a thousand papers on all aspects of the chemistry, pharmacology, and clinical uses of *Allium* have been published. A major focus of research has been high-tech odorless garlic products, available in many Western countries, some of which are now advertised on prime time television, and their impact on cardiovascular disease. Studies using fresh garlic and other products have researched its effects in lowering blood pressure in hypertension, thinning the blood (anti–platelet aggregation), and lowering serum-cholesterol levels. Like aspirin, some researchers feel the blood-thinning properties of garlic may hold a key to its potential value in reducing risk factors in heart disease. According to A. Y. Leung's *Encyclopedia of Common Natural Ingredients Used in Foods, Drugs, and Cosmetics,* garlic holds promise for the prevention or treatment of high blood pressure, arteriosclerosis, hypoglycemia, digestive ailments, colds, flu, and bronchitis; it is also antibacterial and antifungal (S. Foster 1991i, 1992a).

In 1989, Florida and Louisiana researchers measured the activity of natural killer cells and helper/suppresser ratios in a pilot study involving ten AIDS patients, though results were available for only seven of them. They were given a garlic product as a food supplement for six weeks. Six out of seven patients were found to have normal killer-cell activity at the end of that time. Four of seven patients showed an improvement in helper/suppresser ratios. An improvement in AIDS-related conditions, including diarrhea, genital herpes, candidiasis, and pansinusitis with recurrent fever was also reported. The study involved a statistically insignificant number of patients, so it is inconclusive, but it paves the way for more research in the future (Abdullah, Kirkpatrick, and Carter 1989; S. Foster 1992a).

The volatile oil of garlic contains compounds believed to be responsible for its characteristic flavor and fragrance, as well as its biological activity. More than thirty sulfur compounds have been identified from garlic's volatile oil, with allicin, diallyl disulfide, and diallyl trisulfide considered primarily responsible for its biological activity. Hence, a number of odorless, capsulated garlic products have been designed for optimal delivery of allicin to the small intestines, bypassing breakdown by stomach enzymes. Another active component is called ajoene. It is formed by combining allicin and diallyl disulfide. Ajoene has experimental anti–platelet aggregation (anti–blood clotting) and antibiotic effects. In 1988, chemists at the University of Qatar revealed evidence that prostaglandins could be produced by homogenized garlic extract.

Allicin is the principal source of garlic's characteristic odor. By itself, an uncrushed, fresh garlic bulb does not have a strong odor, but that smell, or fragrance, if you will, appears when the cloves are crushed. Allicin is a chemical byproduct which results when the cloves are bruised or crushed. When the odorless, sulfur-containing amino acid known as alliin comes into contact with an enzyme, allinase, it produces the biologically active, strongly garlic-scented compound allicin. When steam-distilled to produce essential oil, allicin breaks down into diallyl disulfide. Allicin is unstable when heated; therefore, if you roast garlic cloves, or add them as a condiment at the early stages of cooking, the characteristic flavor and fragrance of garlic dissipates.

Allicin is strongly antibacterial. In 1858, Louis Pasteur, immortalized as the developer of pasteurized milk, became the first scientist to experimentally confirm the antibacterial property of garlic. Since that time, numerous studies have shown that garlic has broad-spectrum effects against various forms of bacteria. In a 1984 study, scientists in India found garlic to be a promising agent against eight of nine bacteria forms that were highly resistant to antibiotics. The study points to the need for further research on possible antibacterial clinical applications for garlic.

For more information on garlic's history, use, and research, the interested reader is referred to Stephen Fulder's and John Blackwood's *Garlic—Nature's Original Remedy* (Rochester, Vt.: Healing Arts Press, 1991) and Benjamin Lau's *Garlic for Health* (Wilmot, Wis.: Lotus Light Publications, 1988). For detailed information on garlic cultivation, see Ron L. Engeland's *Growing Great Garlic* (Okanogan, Wash.: Filaree Publications, 1991).

GERMANDER

Teucrium chamaedrys L.
(too-kree'-um kay-mee'-dris)
Labiatae (Lamiaceae)—Mint Family

Germander is a dwarf, semievergreen, perennial shrub producing annual flowering stems and growing from six to twelve inches tall. The small, dark green, glossy, oblong-ovate leaves, about twice as long as wide (three-fourths of an inch long by three-eighths of an inch wide), are entire (without teeth) or toothed. Sometimes they may resemble miniature oak leaves. Usually they have soft hairs on the underside, though not always. Germander produces small pale to deep purple flowers; occasionally they are pink, or rarely white. This is a highly variable plant, occurring in much of Europe, north to the Netherlands, westward to southern Poland and south-central Russia.

The species name, *chamaedrys,* is from the Greek "chamai," meaning "on the ground," referring to the plant's low growing habit. Generally there are two forms of *Teucrium chamaedrys* in American gardens. One is the typical upright form; the other is a prostrate variety, with a somewhat creeping spreading habit.

Germander is propagated from softwood tip cuttings, seed, or by dividing the clumps. The seeds germinate readily, usually in about two weeks at 70° F. The best way to propagate is by dividing the clumps in the spring of the second or third year of growth. A sharp spade can be used to divide the plant. Planted in a sunny situation, it will take on a neat, compact growth. While it will grow in partial shade, it tends to get leggy. Germander will grow in any well-drained average soil with a slightly alkaline pH. It is quite adaptable, and can be trimmed to produce neat, tiny hedges. In northern climates, a mulch at the base of the plant will help it get through a harsh winter. Germander is easy to grow.

The best use for germander is as an ornamental minihedge for the herb garden. It is especially nice in knot gardens or formal herb-garden planting schemes. The plant is usually

Germander, *Teucrium chamaedrys*

not aromatic, and if it is, its fragrance is not particularly pleasant.

Traditionally, the plant has been used as an astringent, diuretic, stomachic, and fever-reducing herb. It was once employed for digestive and gallbladder ailments. Germander was also one of many less-than-successful herbal remedies for gout.

Germander has been the recipient of intensive scientific attention in 1992. Unfortunately, that attention is not positive. One longtime folk tradition recommended germander to treat obesity. That habit had become relatively popular in recent years in a number of European countries. Germander had been approved in France as an ingredient in weight-loss products, as well as a treatment for mild diarrhea, and topically as a remedy for infections of the oral cavity. Those practices have been suspended.

Germander as an ingredient in weight-loss products has resulted in several well-documented cases of toxic reactions. A collection of case studies by Larrey and coworkers (1992) reported on seven cases where germander products were chosen to help facilitate weight loss. The patients may have lost weight, but they also developed hepatitis. The herb produced liver injury, characterized by jaundice and high serum aminotransferase levels. The type of nonspecific acute hepatitis involved resembles that induced by viruses and various drugs. Causes other than the presence of germander were ruled out in the patients, all of whom were women, perhaps reflecting the fact that women use weight-loss products more intensively than men, rather than a gender-specific factor.

Germander's ability to cause hepatitis has only been recognized in the early 1990s. It prompted the French government to take a closer look at the herb. After twenty-six cases of acute hepatitis were collected by French Department of Health officials, they prohibited the sale of germander products in April of 1992. Tragically, in September of 1992, the first fatal case of hepatitis from the ingestion of a germander product was reported from France in the British journal *The Lancet* (Mostesa-Kara et al. 1992). There is a remote possibility that contamination by pesticides or fungal molds could have caused toxic reactions, but the jury is still out on this. Obviously, it is no longer wise to ingest germander.

Other *Teucrium* species such as *T. canadense,* a North American plant that has been reported to be an adulterant to commercial supplies of scullcap (*Scutellaria lateriflora*), may be implicated in reports of hepatotoxicity. There are over a hundred species in the genus *Teucrium.* Once again, this reinforces the need for correct botanical identity of the plants used in herbal preparations (Huxtable 1992).

Germander contains tannins, bitter principles, an essential oil, and other components, including diterpenoids such as teuchamaeydryins A, B, and C; 6-epi-teurcin A, teucroxide, and teugin. These diterpenoids help the plant adapt to its environment. They are antifeeding agents, which deter animals and insects from eating its leaves.

GINSENG, AMERICAN GINSENG

Panax quinquefolius L.
(pan'-acks kwin-kwe-foh'-li-us)
Araliaceae—Ginseng Family
Plate 1

There are about nine species in the genus *Panax,* all but two of which are native to eastern Asia. American ginseng (*Panax quinquefolius*) and dwarf ginseng (*P. trifolius*) are native to North America. American ginseng is a perennial herb which grows in eastern North America, favoring north- or east-facing slopes in a well-drained, humus-rich soil. It reaches a height of fifteen inches. One- or two-year-old plants—"strawberry ginseng"—produce three strawberrylike leaflets. Two- or three-year-old plants often develop characteristic five-fingered, palm-shaped leaves. Older plants have two to five prongs with five leaflets on each prong. The leaflets are oblong, coarsely toothed, and two to six inches long. The flowers are tiny and greenish-white, appearing in June to July. Bright red two-seeded berries ripen in late July to October. The white, fleshy taproot often evolves into a humanlike form. The plant dies back to the ground every fall, leaving a scar on the "neck" at the top of each root. The age of the root is determined by counting the scars.

Father Petrus Jartoux (1668–1720), a Jesuit missionary in North China, related his experience on a mapping expedition near the Korean border undertaken for the Emperor Kanghi in the year 1709 (Jartoux 1714). Jartoux observed the harvest of *Panax ginseng* and provided the first technical description and drawing of the plant. He described the range and habitat of ginseng, concluding, "All of which makes me believe, that if it is to be found in any other country in the world, it may be particularly in Canada, where the forest and mountains, according to the relation of those that have lived there, very much resemble these here" (S. Foster 1986, 1989f).

In 1715, subsequent to the publication of Jartoux's remarks in a Jesuit newsletter, Père Joseph Francois Lafitau (1681–1746) began a search for American ginseng. Lafitau, also a Jesuit missionary, had come to Canada in 1711 to work among the Mohawks above Montreal for a period of six years (Fenton 1941). After three systematic months of searching for the plant in 1716, he stumbled upon it quite by accident outside his cabin. In 1718, his labors were detailed in the now-rare publication, "Memoire . . . concernant la precieuse plante du Ginseng, decouverte en Canada, an eight thousand-word letter to his superior, the Duke of Orleans, Regent of France" (Fenton 1941; S. Foster 1986, 1989f). Lafitau is also credited with being one of the earlier authors to develop the theory of the Asiatic origin of the American Indian. He conjectured that both the Chinese and Iroquois (Mohawk) name for the plant had the same sound and meaning, referring to the humanlike form of the root. The Mohawk word "Gar-ent-oguen," meaning "hips and legs," plus "cleft or bifid," according to Lafitau's way of thinking, was analogous to the Chinese name for the plant, meaning "body of man" or "essence of man root." Within a year after Lafitau's discovery of *Panax* in North America, the root was harvested in large quantities and exported to the Orient (Fenton 1941; S. Foster 1986, 1989f).

Lafitau sent samples of the roots to Jartoux, and within a few years export of American ginseng began from Canada to China. Most shipments went by way of Europe, but after the Revolution, a New York merchant, John Jacob Astor, began direct American exports to China in 1782. There is little information on ginseng exports through the nineteenth century, but it is clear that the entire supply was harvested from the wild. Ginseng cultivation was begun in the United States in the 1870s by Abraham Whisman of Boones Path, Virginia. Just fifteen years later, there were only twenty ginseng growers. In 1895, the USDA published a how-to pamphlet on ginseng cultivation which resulted in many farmers entering the market.

Over two hundred years later, the exports continue. In 1989, 2,359,510 pounds (1,070,267 kg.) of cultivated ginseng root was exported from the United States, valued at $54,299,600, while 203,440 pounds (92,280 kg) of wild-harvested root, valued at $18,867,000, was exported (Foster 1991f). Ninety percent of the cultivated ginseng comes from Madison County, Wisconsin, while wild-root harvest continues in many eastern states where the plant occurs. In the early 1980s, someone sold a quantity of American ginseng seed to Chinese interests. Now there are over five hundred acres of American ginseng grown in northeast China. The Chinese-grown American ginseng hit the Hong Kong market around the fall of 1990. The low-priced, low-quality "Chinese white," as traders call Chinese-grown American ginseng, has caused problems for the American market, resulting in the state of Wisconsin establishing a certification program in Hong Kong to help guarantee that American ginseng labeled "Wisconsin grown" is indeed grown there. This author has personally observed American ginseng growing in China, as well as start-up American ginseng operations in New Zealand.

We have just passed the five hundredth anniversary of Columbus's arrival in the New World. That event marked the beginning of what has become a nearly unabated transoceanic dispersal of seeds and live plants. American ginseng is among them, but opportunities still exist for growers in the United States. Wild populations, unfortunately, continue to decline.

The United States is a party to an international treaty known as CITES (Convention on International Trade in Endangered Species). Ginseng international commerce is regulated under the provisions of Appendix II of the treaty "in order to avoid utilization incompatible with survival." The ginseng harvest is controlled by state and federal agencies, and since the harvest began to be monitored in 1975, it has become clear that wild roots entering commerce have become smaller, suggesting that younger plants are being harvested. In the future, there will have to be tighter controls placed on the harvest; otherwise the wild supply will become nonexistent, especially as both demand and the price of the root increase. In autumn 1992, wild American ginseng prices hit all-time highs. Diggers of wild root made more than $250 per pound during the 1992 season. Once considered common in eastern North America, ginseng is now becoming a threatened, rare, or endangered species in many areas due to overzealous harvests of the root (Lewis and Zenger 1982).

Ginseng is not the easiest herb to cultivate. Propagation is by seeds, which may take six to twenty months to sprout. It should be stratified before planting. Prestratified seeds are available from most seed sources. One- two- or three-year-old roots can be purchased for planting, but the buyer risks introducing diseased stock into his or her beds. Freshly harvested seed that has not been stratified can be planted one-half inch deep, six inches apart, in well-prepared beds in September. Seeds may germinate the next spring or the following year. If seed is purchased from a large grower, it is a good idea to disinfect them by soaking them in a mixture of nine parts water and one part chlorine bleach for five to ten minutes. This will kill diseased organisms. Stratified seed may be planted in the spring. Fifty to one hundred pounds of seed will sow an acre.

A light-textured woods loam, high in humus, is best for ginseng culture. Heavy clay or sandy soils will not promote healthy plants. Maintain a pH of around 5 to 6. Shade of 70 percent or more is required for ginseng and can be provided by natural tree canopies, a shade screen, or a lath shed. The design of the shade structure should allow rain to reach the beds. Ginseng grown under a natural tree canopy is, of course, the least expensive. Beds can be double-dug and provided with blood meal, bonemeal, and leaf mold as soil amendments. If these substances unbalance the pH, use a light application of lime or wood ashes. After plants die back in autumn, they should be mulched with a four- to six-inch layer of straw or leaves.

Plants are subject to attack by leaf blight, insects, root rot, and rodents, who consider the roots a delectable treat. Preventative control measures for the organic grower are the most effective. To avoid diseased stock, gather wild seeds when possible. Remove and destroy all affected plants in beds. Vertical metal barriers placed around the bed's perimeters can control rodent attacks. Half of a twenty-four-inch sheet of aluminum should be below the soil's surface. Commercial ginseng growers use herbicides such as Phytar 560 and Paraquat. Diathaine, M–45, Captan 50, Malathion, and Sevin are among the pesticides employed in ginseng production.

The roots are harvested in the fall of the fifth or sixth year after planting from seed. The timing of the harvest is important, affecting both the active constituent level (ginsenoside) and the size of the root. A study by Soldati and Tanaka (1984) notes that the highest yields of ginsenosides (770 mg per root of *P. ginseng* grown in Korea) were obtained at the end of the summer of the fifth year, as the root doubles in weight between the fourth and fifth years. After the fifth year, root size and ginsenoside content increased only slightly. Therefore, the best time to harvest the roots seems to be at the end of the fifth year of growth. Carefully dig the roots with a garden spade, taking care to keep the whole root intact. Remove loose soil by spraying with a hose, then spread the roots on racks to dry. Stir as needed to provide adequate air circulation. Drying time varies depending upon weather conditions and size of roots. Air curing may take as long as a month. Harvest seeds after berries ripen.

The mysterious powers of ginseng are shrouded in folk fact and fiction. "The root of life" is believed to invigorate, rejuvenate, and revitalize the system. Over the past thirty years, Russian, Japanese, and, most recently, American research suggests a scientific basis for the use of ginseng as a general body tonic. Ginseng also increases work efficiency by raising the capacity for mental and physical performance and allowing for better adaptation to high and low temperatures and darkness. Ginseng also increases tolerance to stress. Its effect is termed adaptogenic. The life of X-ray irradiated mice has been prolonged with ginseng.

Staba and Chen (1979) reviewed major pharmacological activity associated with ginseng. Small doses of the ginsenoside Rg_1 tend to stimulate the central nervous system (CNS), while large doses are a CNS depressant. Antifatigue and antistress effects have been suggested, perhaps due to the peripheral and neurogenic stimulation of the adrenal cortex. External use of ginseng regenerates the skin and inhibits wrinkling. Preparations of ginseng can counteract the toxic effects of chloroform, amphetamines, and other toxins. Ginseng has been reported to increase the weight of seminal vesicles and prostate glands, and increase sperm counts and pregnancies. Small doses have a tendency to increase body weight; large doses tend to decrease it.

In Chinese medicine, ginseng is combined with other herbs to treat a wide range of illnesses. Future research may provide important new applications for ginseng in disease prevention and cure.

Saponin glycosides are responsible for ginseng's biological activity. They are called panaxosides by Russian researchers and ginsenosides by the Japanese. Ginsenosides in American ginseng include Rb_1, Rb_2, Rb_3 (0.03 percent), Rc, Rd, Re, Rg_1 (0.15 percent), Rg_2 (0.008 percent), Ro, and F_2 (Thompson 1987).

Research on American ginseng is still in its infancy. As Professor Staba noted in a letter to the editor in *The Lancet* (1985), "Evaluation of existing studies is not going to establish ginseng as a useful therapeutic agent. What we need now are long-term, controlled human studies of ginseng to identify predictable beneficial or harmful physiological effects. If such effects were to be found we might be better able to find out how ginseng works." To date, there are over twenty-five hundred modern studies, the vast majority of which are on Asian ginseng (*P. ginseng*) rather than American ginseng (*P. quinquefolius*). For further information see B. Braly (1987), and Jim Duke's *Ginseng: A Concise Handbook.* (Algonac, Mich.: Reference Publications, Inc., 1989).

GOLDENSEAL

Hydrastis canadensis L.
(hi-dras'-tis kan-a-den'-sis)
Ranunculaceae—Buttercup Family
Plate 1

Goldenseal is a perennial with an erect, hairy stem about a foot in height with three to four yellowish scales at its base. Each plant has two leaves which seem to fork about three-fourths of the way up the stem. One branch supports a larger leaf; the other, a smaller leaf and flower stalk. The leaves, which are up to twelve inches wide and eight inches long, have prominent veins on their lower surfaces. They are

Hydrastis canadensis, Goldenseal under cultivation, Nature's Cathedral, Blairstown, Iowa

palmate with five to nine lobes, and have sharply pointed, irregular teeth. At flowering time, the leaves partially expand, and are very wrinkled. The flowers appear in late April to early May, lasting only three to seven days. They are one-half inch in diameter and petalless. A round spray of forty to fifty stamens characterizes the flowers. The globular, fleshy, bright red fruits, resembling a large raspberry, ripen in July or August. They contain ten to twenty black, hard, shiny seeds. The horizontal rhizome is knotty, about one-half to three-fourths of an inch thick, two to three inches long, with numerous fibrous rootlets. The root is intensely yellow. The plant, which usually dies down after the fruits mature, grows in rich, moist woods favoring beech canopy from Vermont to Minnesota, south to Georgia, Alabama, and Arkansas. The highest concentration of population has traditionally been in the Ohio River Valley in Ohio, Kentucky, and West Virginia.

Goldenseal (also seen as golden seal) is the common name under which the plant is best known. It has had numerous other names, including orange root, yellow puccoon, ground raspberry, eye-balm, and eye-root. As a dye plant, it was known as Indian paint, yellow paint, Indian dye, golden root, Indian turmeric, wild turmeric, curcuma (kurkuma), Ohio curcuma, wild curcuma, jaundice root, and yellow eye. The name "goldenseal," adopted in the 1880 revision of the United States pharmacopeia, was introduced by the Thomsonians (adherents to the medical system of Samuel Thomson, 1769–1843), because small cuplike scars on the top of the rhizome resembled wax seals, once used on envelopes (J. U. Lloyd and C. G. Lloyd 1884–85; Foster 1991g).

Various botanical writers note the rarity of the plant in various parts of the country where it once flourished, due to overcollection of the root. As early as 1884–85, J. U. Lloyd and C. G. Lloyd documented dramatic declines in wild populations, to some extent as a result of root harvest, but even more as the result of habitat loss through deforestation. While overharvesting may be blamed for some shortages, the Lloyd brothers paint a complex picture of economic and social reasons for others, indicating that fewer areas or populations are not necessarily responsible for a decreased supply. Historically, farm laborers or poor people collected the roots during times of economic hardship, but fewer persons gather herbs during periods of economic prosperity. Since goldenseal was a minor commodity, sometimes the entire supply would be exhausted in one season, causing shortages and a rise in price. This would stimulate more harvest the following season, causing market gluts and price drops. Collectors or dealers would then be left with overstocks which were sold at low cost, again producing less incentive for harvest of the root the following season. Collectors would turn their attention to other substances or pursuits. The price would stabilize, but overstocks would be exhausted, and then, as the Lloyds put it, "history repeats itself" (J. U. Lloyd and C. G. Lloyd 1884–85; Foster 1991g).

Similar supply shortages and gluts to those of a hundred years ago, with their concurrent price fluctuations, have been experienced in the past decade. Reasons for recent shortages include: 1) harvesters shifting to higher-priced commodities; 2) a recent three-year period of drought in the Southeast, which made digging difficult; 3) disinterest due to price fluctuations; and 4) lack of sufficient wild populations (Foster 1991g). I would estimate that something in the neighborhood of 150,000 pounds of goldenseal is currently consumed on the American market. Given current patterns of scarcity, the plant seems to be a prime candidate for commercial cultivation.

What is clear is that the supply of goldenseal has been unstable for over a hundred years. One theory is that, even after the main rhizome is harvested, these buds may help to regenerate a population; hence there would be a possible biological basis for continued redevelopment of plants. However, no studies on population dynamics have confirmed this theory (Foster 1991g). Causes for year-to-year changes in population sizes include differences in climatological conditions, and factors influencing the development of the biomass (Eichenberger and Parker 1976).

In its native haunts, goldenseal grows in similar habitats to ginseng—moist, rich, deep-shaded woods. As a potential cash crop in woodland cultivation conditions, it has several advantages over ginseng. Goldenseal can be harvested in as little as three years as opposed to ginseng's four to five years. Goldenseal can also be propagated vegetatively, and is not subject to the disease and pest problems which plague ginseng, at least under current cultivation levels. It may also be possible to grow goldenseal without shade in certain parts of the country. USDA researcher Jim Duke has said that his goldenseal thrives in the sun in Maryland. John Uri Lloyd (1912) spoke of an Ohio goldenseal grower who had success cultivating the plant in full sun. While it may be possible to grow it in the northern limits of its range with more exposure to sunlight, perhaps in highly favorable soils, it remains best to grow goldenseal in deep shade.

Propagate by seed, division of rhizomes, or by planting the "eyes" or buds from vigorous root fibers. The pulpy red fruits can be harvested as soon as ripe. They should then be rubbed through a strainer and thoroughly rinsed to remove all the fleshy pulp. Cleaned fresh seeds (which should not be allowed to dry out) can then be mixed with ten parts of fine, clean sand, placed in well-drained containers, and stratified in a cool, moist cellar or similar situation until ready for planting. Seeds that are dried will not germinate. Seeds can be sown in October in a protected bed (preferably a cold frame, or some other arrangement that protects them from animals and birds). Seeds or seedlings should not be trampled upon because they are very tender. Seeds in moist sand can also be stored for the winter months and planted the following spring. They need to be stratified before germinating. A mixture of two parts moist sand and one part leaf mold—finer than the seeds—serves as a good medium. Place in a refrigerator for three months and plant the following

spring. The seeds lose their viability very rapidly, so they need to be processed and planted as soon as the fruits ripen. Most first-year seedlings only develop cotyledons. One true leaf is produced the second year; two leaves plus a flower develop in the third. It is estimated that there are approximately 28,000+ seeds per pound, 1800 seeds per ounce.

Each rhizome is studded with rootlets and undeveloped buds. Any piece with a bud or eye and a few strands of fibrous root will produce a plant. On an average, about five plants can be divided from each mature rhizome. Plant one inch deep, eight inches apart. Break the roots into pieces and plant in September. Often tops will not appear until the *second* summer after planting. Being a goldenseal cultivator requires patience.

A deep, loose, friable soil, high in organic matter, such as compost, well-rotted manure, or especially composted leaf mold, is best. Composted manure may introduce weed seeds to the bed, increasing weeding time. Four-inch layers of leaf mold can be added to the beds, along with well-composted manure, wood ashes, and rock phosphate. Good drainage is important. Though the plant likes a good supply of moisture, boggy, poorly drained ground will not produce a crop. Bonemeal can be added at the rate of ten pounds per thirty square yards. Wood ashes are not beneficial, and may even hamper root production. A liberal application of rock phosphate has been recommended by one source. Soil pH should be around 5.5 to 6.5. About 75 percent shade is necessary. Goldenseal can be grown as a row crop in raised beds under artificial shade (lath sheds or a shade cloth) or, simulating the woods, under a natural hardwood canopy. Oak, maple, sycamore, and basswood are preferable. Pine, spruce, hemlock, red cedar, and other conifers should be avoided. Woodslike situations require more frequent amendments because tree roots compete for nutrients. Beds must be kept free of weeds.

Botrytis blight (fungus) may attack the entire plant during wet seasons. Symptoms include rotting of petioles (leaf stalks) at the base and blighting of leaves. Root gall is another potential problem. Goldenseal should not be planted in ginseng beds that have suffered from root gall. Altenaria blight, a major problem with ginseng, apparently does not affect goldenseal. The best way to avoid potential fungal problems is good ventilation; make sure that air moves freely through the beds. Moles, slugs, or earthworms can also adversely affect goldenseal plantings. Slugs may eat the root crown down to the rootstock, killing the plants.

Seed-sown plants are harvested after four or five years. Plants grown from root divisions may be harvested after three or four years. Spring harvest may produce roots with a higher moisture content, greater shrinkage, and poorer quality. September/October harvest is probably preferable. Estimated shrinkage is about 70 percent from fresh weight. Roots should be cleaned, then dried until brittle. When they are dry, the fibrous rootlets can easily be removed from the main rhizome by rubbing.

In an experimental bed, John Uri Lloyd (1912) reported producing 345 divisions from 70 mature plants. Lloyd suggests that it takes about 250 plants to produce one pound of dried root. A portion of each root harvested can be replanted. At six-inch spacings, average yields of fifteen hundred pounds per acre can be expected. Yields of as much as twenty-five hundred pounds per acre have been obtained.

American Indians used goldenseal for eye ailments, skin diseases, gonorrhea, cancers, and as a dye and skin stain. The Cherokee made a root wash to treat local inflammations, and drank a decoction for general debility, dyspepsia, and to stimulate appetite. The Iroquois found a decoction of the root beneficial for whooping cough, diarrhea, liver trouble, fever, sour stomach, flatulence, pneumonia, and added whiskey to it for heart trouble (Moerman 1986).

In the first part of his *Collections for an Essay towards a Materia Medica of the United States* (1798), under his discussion on *Heuchera americana,* Barton makes one of the earliest observations about the occurrence of cancer among American Indian groups: "I am informed that the Cheerake [*sic*] cure it with a plant which is thought to be the Hydrastis Canadensis, one out of five native dies [*sic*]" (8). In the third part of his *Essay* (1804), Barton notes that "the Hydrastis is a popular remedy in some parts of the United States" (13). As recorded by Barton, the root was used as a bitter tonic (in "spirituous infusion") and as a wash for eye inflammations in a cold-water infusion (Barton 1798, 1804). These traditions have persisted to the present day (Foster 1991g).

The popular use of goldenseal was first encouraged by the Thomsonians, but an eclectic physician, John King (1813–1893), is credited with the first critical review of its therapeutic applications, thereby bringing it into general acceptance. King first wrote about goldenseal in the first edition of *The Eclectic Dispensatory of the United States of America* (1852).

Goldenseal has numerous functions including, but not limited to, that of antiseptic, hemostatic, diuretic, laxative, and tonic/antiinflammatory for the mucous membranes. It has also been recommended for hemorrhoids, nasal congestion, mouth and gum sores, and eye afflictions; externally, it helps heal wounds, sores, acne, ringworm, and other ailments (Leung 1980). Duke (1985), who has probably listed the greatest number of applications for the plant found in modern literature, notes that goldenseal extracts and hydrastine hydrochloride are still components in eye washes. Traditionally, a wash made from the roots is valuable for conjunctivitis and other eye ailments. Goldenseal is a beneficial tonic and astringent for inflamed mucous membranes of the vagina, uterus, mouth, throat, and digestive system. Gonorrhea, jaundice, bronchitis, pharyngitis, ulcers, and many other ailments have also been treated with goldenseal.

Despite its continued popularity, very little scientific research has been conducted on goldenseal over the past forty years, or at all in this century. The most recent comprehensive review of the pharmacology and therapeutics of *Hydrastis* and its alkaloids was by Shideman (1950), who noted the dearth of other studies.

One modern folk superstition has it that consuming goldenseal can mask urine tests for illicit drugs. The notion that goldenseal affects drug testing has its basis in fiction. To be specific, the source is the plot of John Uri Lloyd's third novel, *Stringtown on the Pike,* published by Dodd Mead in 1900. Red Head, the major character, is accused of poisoning an uncle with strychnine. A native of Stringtown, Samuel Drew, the book's narrator, is a noted chemist and is retained by the prosecution to give expert testimony against Red Head. Based on alkaloid color reagents, Drew determines strychnine to be present in the stomach of the dead man. This testimony results in the conviction of Red Head for murder. Red Head, a hill boy, has competed with Samuel Drew for the love of the novel's heroine, Susie. Susie refuses Drew's hand in marriage after the incident in the courtroom. She has studied chemistry with Drew, as well as in Europe. Upon returning from Europe, she shows Drew that a mixture of hydrastine and morphine produce the same color reaction as the then-established assay for determining the presence of strychnine. Susie reminds the surprised Samuel Drew that the dead uncle had, as was his habit, drunk bitters containing goldenseal on the morning of his death. Drew, realizing his error, takes small doses of a toxic root which slowly cause his suicide (Simons 1972 S. Foster 1989h).

Soon after publication of the novel, expert chemical witnesses became commonplace in the American courtroom. Had the novel been written by a novelist with no knowledge of chemistry, the experiments in the book would have passed into obscurity, but John Uri Lloyd was an internationally renowned plant pharmacist. The testing procedures published in the novel were subjected to professional peer scrutiny. In the context of a novel, Lloyd had indeed shown that what was thought to be an infallible reagent methodology of the day, using bichromate-sulphuric to react to strychnine, was not foolproof after all.

There is no scientific evidence to support the idea that hydrastine masks tests for illicit drugs. In fact, attempts to use goldenseal to mask the presence of morphine have backfired because they may instead promote false-positive readings (Tyler 1987; S. Foster 1989h).

The alkaloids hydrastine (2 to 4 percent) and berberine (2 to 3 percent) are the major biologically active compounds in goldenseal, along with smaller amounts of canadine and hydrastinine. Berberine is responsible for goldenseal's yellow color and bitter taste. It has a strong antibacterial effect, increases bile secretion, is anticonvulsant, and stimulates the uterus. In laboratory animals, it has acted as a sedative and lowered blood pressure. Pharmacological evidence suggests that berberine may be helpful in correcting high tyramine levels in patients with cirrhosis of the liver (Foster and Duke 1990). The properties of hydrastine resemble berberine. It has decreased blood pressure and stimulated involuntary muscle activity in animal models. Canadine stimulates the uterine muscles.

HOPS

Humulus lupulus L.
(who'-moo'-lus loop'-you-lus)
Cannabinaceae—Cannabis Family

Hops are native to Europe, Asia, and North America. The genus's two species are grown in gardens—*Humulus lupulus,* which has a perennial rootstock and annual shoots growing thirty feet or more in a season, and *H. japonicus,* a rapid-growing annual which creates a graceful festoonery. The leaves of *H. lupulus* resemble those of grapes. They are rough, hairy, three- to five-lobed, coarsely toothed, about as broad as wide (three to five inches), and are in opposite arrangement, though leaves at the end of shoots may be arranged singly. The twining stems, spiraling clockwise, are tough, flexible, and fibrous. Some plants produce racemes of male flowers from the leaf axils. Others develop female flowers and the plump, rounded, conelike fruits called

strobiles. The strobiles are about one-and-a-quarter inches long and are characterized by translucent, yellowish-green, papery bracts, each covering a seed (unless the variety is seedless). Hops flower from July to August.

Hop growing is big business in the Pacific Northwest, where most of the hop supply used in brewing is produced in Idaho, Washington, and Oregon. Specific cultivars such as 'Cascade' and 'Willamette' have been developed for this region of the country. Those in the eastern United States and Canada may have better luck with European cultivars such as 'Perle', 'Hersbrucker', and 'Tettnanger', which are said to perform well as far north as Quebec. The hop industry once flourished in the eastern United States, particularly New York, but by the turn of the century, fungal blights had virtually wiped it out.

Hops can be grown from seed, but are generally propagated by dividing the young shoots from the main crown in spring or fall, or by cuttings rooted from older shoots and suckers in late summer. The first-year, seed-grown hops usually develop slowly. Plant root cuttings in a hill—three roots per hill, spaced eighteen inches apart at the corners of an equilateral triangle. Keep them well cultivated and free from weeds.

Hops require a deeply dug, rich, moist soil with full sun. Soil pH should be between 5 and 8. By midsummer, the prickly vines may stretch from fifteen to thirty feet. Once rapid growth begins, water frequently. Cut the stems back after they are hit by a fall frost and add the refuse to your compost pile. In autumn, dress the roots with compost. Hops may require more care than some herbs, but they are worth the effort. Trained over a trellis, they create enclosed spaces in the garden—to say nothing of their food and medicinal value.

Harvest in early fall on a clear day when the strobiles begin to feel firm, turn an amber color, and are covered with a yellow dust. The strobiles will spoil rapidly if not quickly dried after harvest. To preserve them, the moisture must be reduced from 65 to 80 percent to about 12 percent. Place them in an oven no warmer than 150° F and leave its door ajar.

As the young shoots appear in the spring, they can be eaten as an asparagus substitute. Blanch the shoots by hilling the crowns with dirt the previous fall. This makes milder-flavored and more tender shoots. Eat only young shoots. The older ones tend to be tough and bitter. The flavor is nutty and pleasing, though the texture is often dry and gritty. At one time, a hill of hops was part of every English vegetable garden.

Hops are stomachic, tonic, nervine, diuretic, anodyne, sedative, and soporific. A pillow stuffed with hops will help an insomniac sleep. Moisten the hops with water before going to bed so rustling strobiles don't keep you awake (assuming you're either the insomniac or sleeping in the same bed with one). An infusion of the strobiles helps relieve muscle spasms. A poultice can be used externally as an anodyne on rheumatic joints and muscle pains. The bitter-tasting tea helps stimulate appetite and calm nervous tension. The tea is soothing and serves as an antispasmodic in delirium tremens. Add one-half ounce of the herb to boiling water and give four-ounce doses of this infusion. The most reliable benefits are those of a sedative, antispasmodic, and digestive stimulant for the treatment of nervous

Humulus lupulus, Hops

tension, restlessness and sleep disturbances, and lack of appetite. No side effects, contraindication, or adverse drug interactions from the use of hops are known.

Ripe hops contain a yellow granular powder called lupulin. It holds the plant's active principles—an essential oil mainly composed of humulene, myrcene, beta-caryophyllene, and farnesene. Resinous bitter principles comprise up to 12 percent of the weight of the strobiles—mostly bitter acids, including lupulone and humulone. Over a hundred compounds have been found in the essential oil. A trace component of the fresh essential oil, which increases

in storage of the dried strobiles after two years due to the degradation of humulone and lupulone, is 2-methyl-3-buten-2-ol. It has been found experimentally to depress the central nervous system. Antispasmodic effects of alcohol extracts of hops have been experimentally confirmed to stimulate gastric secretions.

Hops are best known as a flavoring and preservative for beer, but the plant has many uses. The spent hops left over from beer production make a good compost and mulch, especially for nursery trees. The ashes have value in glass manufacturing. A pulp of the stems is employed to make paper and cardboard. Textiles such as yarns and strings are made from the stem fiber, and the stalks are practiced for weaving baskets.

HOREHOUND

Marrubium vulgare L.
(mar-rue'-bi-um vul-gay'-ree)
Labiatae (Lamiaceae)—Mint Family

Horehound is a hardy perennial herb native to Europe, southward from England, southern Sweden, and central Russia. Throughout its range, it occurs in waste places. It is naturalized in many parts of the United States. The genus *Marrubium* contains thirty species found in Asia and Europe, twelve of which occur in Europe. White horehound (*M. vulgare*) is the best known herb in the genus. Another member of the mint family, *Ballota nigra,* a Mediterranean plant, is traded as "black horehound" and has sometimes appeared as an adulterant to *M. vulgare. Ballota* possesses a fetid odor.

Horehound is a bitter aromatic herb, standing about one foot tall, with a bushy spreading habit. The whole plant is covered with a soft, woolly felt, giving the plant a whitish-gray appearance. The thick, somewhat-leather-textured leaves are round or oval shaped and arranged opposite one another on square stems. They are about an inch long, and have slight teeth and short petioles. The tiny white flowers occur in tight whorls around the leaf axils. The calyx has ten sharp-pointed, recurved teeth; when dried, they cling to clothing like burdock pods. Horehound flowers from June to September.

Horehound is easy to grow from seed sown in shallow drills in fall or early spring. Resulting seedlings should be spaced eight to fifteen inches apart. Horehound may also be propagated from stem cuttings or root division. Plants grown from seed may take two years to bloom.

Horehound is one of those hardy herbs that grows in places other plants shun. A poor, dry, sandy soil with a wide pH range (4.5 to 8) and full sun are all horehound needs, though it thrives best in a light, dry, well-drained, calcareous environment. It's a good herb to plant around a border which doesn't need much attention. An acre of horehound has been reported to produce three-fourths to one ton of dried herb.

The leaves and flowering tops are harvested in peak bloom, but before flowers begin to fade. Horehound is easy

to dry, but difficult to process by hand because of its prickly calyces. To retain a bright green color, it should be dried in shade under low heat.

Medicinally, this bitter-tasting herb is a stimulant, bitter stomachic, resolvent, deobstruent, expectorant, tonic, and mild vermifuge. Its primary value is to break up phlegm,

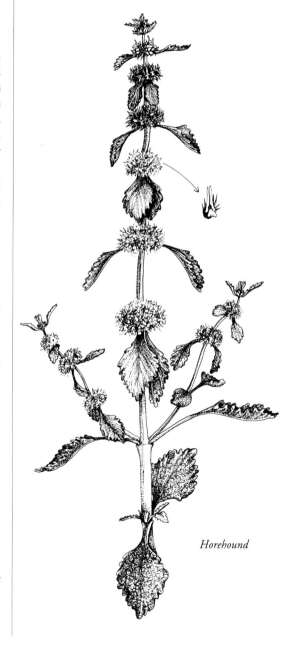

Horehound

relieve coughs, soothe sore throats, and ease bronchitis and other upper-respiratory ailments. Horehound has also been beneficial with jaundice, chronic hepatitis, amenorrhea, and luecorrhea. An ointment made from freshly bruised leaves can help heal cuts. Large doses have a laxative effect.

Marrubiin, a bitter diterpene lactone, has long been considered to be the main active constituent of horehound. It possesses expectorant qualities and influences the flow of liver bile. It has also been reported to stimulate secretion by bronchial mucosa (Tyler 1987). The leaves also contain tannin, mucilage, a resin, ursolic acid, minute amounts of alkaloids (betonicine), and an essential oil (0.05 percent, containing alpha-pinene, sabinene, limonene, camphene, etc.). The volatile oil is a vasodilator and expectorant, and is antimicrobial. In addition, flavonoids such as apigenin, luteolin, and quercetin have been isolated from the plant, along with alkanes, phytosterols, diterpene alcohols, and other components.

A tea can be made by adding one ounce of the herb to a quart of water. Sweeten with honey before drinking.

HORSERADISH
Armoracia rusticana P. Gaetn., B. Mey. & Scherb.
(ar-mor-ay'-see-a rus-ti-cay'-na)
Cruciferae—Mustard Family

Horseradish is a deep-rooted, robust perennial, native to southeast Europe and naturalized in North America. It is believed to have originated in eastern Europe, then spread westward through cultivation. Commercial cultivation is centered in the Mississippi Valley near St. Louis in Missouri and Illinois, as well as in Wisconsin. An international horseradish festival is held each year in Collinsville, Illinois. The plant has been known in cultivation for about two thousand years. Henry J. Heinz, founder of the H. J. Heinz Company, is believed to have been the first to develop a commercial horseradish product in 1844. The English name "horseradish" first appeared in the 1597 first edition of Gerarde's *The Herball*. The name is an apparent corruption of the German "meerrettich" (sea radish). "Meer" is derived from "mähre" (an old mare), referring to the tough roots (Courter and Rhodes 1969).

In bloom, horseradish may reach a height of five feet. The docklike lower leaves have wavy scalloped edges and may be two feet long and nine inches wide. By the sixteenth century, at least two different leaf-type cultivars were known. One has an acute leaf base with smooth leaves, and the other has a cordate (heart-shaped) base with crinkled leaves. Various commercial cultivars have been selected by growers. Sometimes the leaves are divided into jagged linear segments. As the leaves progress up the flower stalk, they become miniaturized and scarcely recognizable as horseradish. The flowers are tiny and white, and appear in June. The rootstock may be two feet long and two to four inches wide.

Propagate by root cuttings in the spring or fall. The large taproot will produce numerous lateral rootlets. Take those that are pencil-thick and about two to eight inches long, and cut them square at the top and slanted at the lower end. Place one foot apart, six to twelve inches below the soil's surface. Leaves will soon appear. Plants can be grown from any division of the root, though cuttings from the top crown are best. Horseradish may also be grown from seed, but it is not readily available.

A rampant, energetic grower in a deep-dug, rich, moist soil, horseradish likes full sun or partial shade. Keep the soil loose and free of weeds. Dig compost around the roots in autumn. A pH of 6 to 8 is best. Horseradish is very hardy and thrives in a deep, rich loam, high in organic matter.

Harvest in the fall of the second year. After that time, the roots may become pithy and bitter. Plant anew every year or two, but reserve one spot in the garden for horseradish. Like comfrey, once established, it will always be there unless every scrap of root is removed. The fresh roots can be stored in a cellar in moist sand, or outside, covered by earth that won't freeze in winter as you use them. Smooth-leaved cultivars such as 'Sass' have produced an average of 4.81 tons of fresh root per acre.

The young, tender spring leaves can be boiled like spinach. The fresh root can be grated and used as a condiment on meats or fish. I make a horseradish spread by blending a cup of chopped root with one-fourth cup vinegar, one-fourth cup olive oil, two teaspoons of honey, and two cloves of garlic. When you lift the lid off the blender, don't stick your nose into the cloud of fumes. The combination of sulfur compounds can literally knock you out!

The root is high in potassium and vitamin C, and contains appreciable amounts of calcium, phosphorus, iron, and vitamin B. It will stimulate appetite and aid digestion. It is laxative, diaphoretic, strongly diuretic, rubefacient, and antiseptic. If applied externally, it will give some people a rash with blisters. A cataplasm has been used to break up chest colds and relieve rheumatic muscle pain. One teaspoon

Armoracia rusticana, Horseradish

The root contains an essential oil, almost identical to mustard oil, plus asparagine and sinigrin. Mustard oil has antibacterial and antifungal properties. The fresh root has little odor. The pungency is released upon crushing or mincing due to the reaction of the enzyme myrosinase (thioglucosidase) with gluco-sinolates, producing the highly pungent isothiocyanates. Since the oil is extremely volatile, commercial preparation of the root often occurs under refrigeration. Freeze-drying is another way to preserve the root. A peroxidase enzyme extracted from the root has novel commercial applications as an oxidizer in chemical tests to evaluate blood glucose, and a molecular probe in studies on rheumatoid arthritis. Horseradish peroxidase has also been investigated for its ability to remove pollutants from wastewater (Simon, Chadwick, and Craker 1984; Courter and Rhodes 1969).

HYSSOP

Hyssopus officinalis L.
(hiss'-op-us
off-iss-i-nay'-lis)
Labiatae (Lamiaceae)—
Mint Family

of the root in a glass of water with a little honey makes a good gargle for sore throat. While the root is generally recognized to be safe as a food ingredient, ingestion of large amounts have caused bloody vomiting and diarrhea. Inhalation of the highly volatile constituents or contact with mucous membranes can cause irritation.

Hyssop is a hardy, shrub-like perennial, native to southern, south-central and eastern Europe. Elsewhere it has been cultivated and has locally escaped from gardens, including in North America. The erect stem, woody at the base, has a controlled growth, making it a good plant for edging and borders. It grows from one-and-a-half to two feet tall, and is either with or without

Hyssop

hairs. The leaves are also three-fourths to one-and-a-half inches long, lance shaped, and have short petioles. The flowers occur in six-inch spikes with whorls of six to fifteen blossoms emerging from each axil. The flowers are generally a bright blue. White-, pink-, or rose-flowered cultivars also exist. Flowering is from June to October.

Hyssop is easily grown from seed sown directly in the garden, or is propagated from spring or fall root divisions, or from cuttings made from the vigorous summer tips. Plants should be given one- to two-foot spacings.

A calcareous, light, rocky soil and full sun are best. Hyssop will grow under partial shade, but becomes leggy. It will lose its pungent aroma if grown in a rich, moist soil. An acre of hyssop may produce one-and-a-quarter tons or more, but the market for dried leaf is limited.

The young shoots and flowering tops can flavor tomato soups and sauces, but use sparingly. The fresh herb contains iodine at a concentration of fourteen micrograms per kilogram. Plant extracts and the essential oil, used in minute amounts as commercial flavorings in foods, are generally recognized as safe.

The flowering tops or whole herb in flower are harvested just as blooming begins, usually in midsummer. Tied in bunches, hyssop dries easily.

The tea is considered stomachic, diaphoretic, carminative, stimulative, sedative, and expectorant. Along with horehound, hyssop is used for lung ailments including bronchitis and asthma, as well as pectoral symptoms associated with coughs and colds. A gargle made from the leaves relieves sore throats. Externally, a tea, poultice, or strong bath of the leaves helps relieve muscular rheumatism, wounds, sprains, and strains. One-fourth ounce of the herb to a pint of boiling water makes a medicinal infusion.

The essential oil contains pinocamphone, isopinocamphone, pinenes, camphene, linalool, bornyl acetate, and other substances. The plant also has up to 8 percent tannin, a glucoside—hyssopin, and oleanolic and ursolic acids. Various flavonoids, including diosmin and hesperidin, have been isolated from the plant. Marrubiin, also in horehound is a terpenoid found in the leaves. Extracts of hyssop have had antiviral effects against herpes simplex and are also antiinflammatory. The oil is used to flavor Chartreuse and Benedictine, and as a fragrance in eau de cologne. The primary modern value of hyssop, however, is as an ornamental bee plant for the herb garden.

LADY'S MANTLE

Alchemilla xanthochlora Rothm. (*A. vulgaris* auct.).
(al-kem'-il-a zan-tho-klor'-a)
Rosaceae—Rose Family

Lady's mantle is a hardy perennial with elegant foliage and lacy mists of yellow blooms. It grows to a foot-and-a-half tall and is native to western and central Europe, extending north to south Sweden and Latvia, and south to central Greece. It is sporadically naturalized in North America, in New England, New York and southeastern Canada. The rounded leaves, two to eight inches in diameter, have plaited folds with seven to eleven lobes and tiny teeth. Sprays of small yellow, petalless flowers bloom in June, lasting in the far north to August. Folded, leaflike stipules collar the stem. The taproot is stout and black. When we think of the lady's mantle of herb gardens, we generally consider only one plant. In Europe, on the other hand, the genus containing this plant is large, complex, and diverse, consisting of more than three hundred species.

Drops of dew form in the leaf folds and cups of stipules, giving lady's mantle an early morning, jewellike sparkle. This dew was thought to extract subtle medicinal virtues from the leaf—the stuff of alchemist's potions. *Alchemilla* derives from an Arabic word "alkemelych," meaning "alchemy."

Alchemilla species are highly variable and are divided into many microspecies. They are often apomictic, that is they produce fruits without seeds, much like a navel orange or a seedless grape. Lady's mantle can be propagated in the spring or fall by carefully dividing the sections of the crow with eyes or a bud, leaving some attached root.

Lady's mantle's taproot likes a deep-dug soil with good drainage. A poor, slightly acid soil will suffice for this plant. It grows in full sun or partial shade, and is completely winter hardy. Once established, it requires little care. Plant on rocky inclines that may be hard to reach and maintain.

The root, harvested in spring or fall, and the leaves, harvested as the plant blooms in June, are used medicinally. A decoction of the fresh root is a powerful styptic which stops bleeding. The leaves are also astringent and styptic owing to their tannin content. Applied internally or externally, they can control bleeding or profuse menstruation. One ounce of the dried leaves is added to a pint of water for medicinal purposes. While the plant is generally considered of historical interest in America, it has a long, continuing tradition as a popular European herb medicine. Its astringency, and hence medicinal benefit, is attributed to the tannin content, though the plant has been little studied. In Europe, decoctions or infusions of lady's mantle are valuable to treat diarrhea and other gastrointestinal conditions. Tinctures or gargles of the herb can help soothe irritated mucous membranes of the mouth and throat. A recent study (Geiger and Rimpler 1990) identified the ellagitannins, agrimoniin

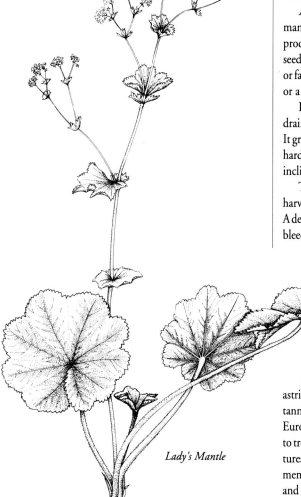

Lady's Mantle

and pendunculagin, in the herb. These compounds may be partly responsible for the plant's biological activity. A trace of salicylic acid is also found in the plant.

LAMB'S EARS, WOOLLY BETONY

Stachys byzantina C. Koch (*S. lantana* Jacq. & *S. olympica*).
(stay'-kiss biz-an-tie'-na)
Labiatae (Lamiaceae)—Mint Family
Plate 5

If there is one plant that has received an appropriate common name, it is lamb's ears. When you have the chance, close your eyes and rub this plant's leaves while imagining the texture of a lamb's ear. It's almost impossible to distinguish between the two, except perhaps that a real lamb twitches. *Stachys byzantina* is a hardy perennial native to Turkey and western Asia, and is much enjoyed in North American gardens. Inevitably, upon first sight, a person unfamiliar with this plant will ask for its name.

In a rich soil, lamb's ears may reach a height of two-and-a-half feet. The densely woolly, grayish leaves, about four inches long and one inch wide, are oblong to spatular shaped. They grow in rosettes, forming a dense spreading mat of silvery white foliage. In May or June, fuzzy, pencil-thick stalks shoot up, bearing almost-hidden mauve-rose flowers, each an inch long. About a month after flowering, the plant goes to seed.

Lamb's ears can be propagated from seed, or better, by dividing the roots in spring or fall. Give plants six-inch spacings. It takes a sharp spade to cut through the thick mass of spreading rhizomes that lamb's ears produces.

Lamb's ears need full sun, a moist, moderately rich soil, and good drainage for optimum growth. The soil should be slightly alkaline. This is a wonderful, light-colored foliage plant for border plantings, especially along pathways. It satisfies the eyes, nose, and sense of touch, and is best grown as an ornamental.

The leaves, however, can be harvested just before flowering. They have a mild, aromatic taste, which becomes applelike upon drying, and make a mild-flavored tea. After seeding, the leaf stalks should be cut to the height of the basal leaves.

Woundwort is another name for lamb's ears. The leaves are mildly astringent and have historically been applied to cuts to stop bleeding and used as an absorbent dressing.

Mainly, however, the plant functions as an easy-to-grow, carefree perennial ornamental which adds a touch of soft color and texture to the herb garden.

LAVENDERS

Lavandula angustifolia Mill., *L. dentata* L., *L. multifida* L., *L. stoechas* L., *L.* x *intermedia* Emeric ex Loiseleur, *L. latifolia* Medicus.
(la-van'-doo-la an-gus-ti-foh'-li-us; den-tay'-ta; mul-tif'-i-da; stee'-kas;)
Labiatae (Lamiaceae)—Mint Family

The lavenders have long been appreciated by herb gardeners for their silver-gray foliage, sweet perfume, and delicate flowers. Lavender was probably introduced to England by the Romans hundreds of years ago. Commercial production began by 1568. The name "lavender" probably derives from the Latin "lavo" or "lavare," "to wash" or "to bathe." The flowers and their oils and derivatives have long been appreciated in perfumes and toiletries for their clean or refreshing scent. There are about twenty species and numerous varieties of lavenders, occurring mainly in the Mediterranean region, though some hail from as far east as India.

English lavender *Lavandula angustifolia,* is a two- to three-foot-tall perennial Mediterranean shrub with slightly hairy linear or lance-shaped leaves up to two-and-a-half inches long. This is the most widely grown lavender, and is often erroneously sold in the horticultural trade as *L. vera* or *L. officinalis.* It produces one-half-inch-long blue-violet flowers, arranged in whorls of six to ten blooms on loose, three-and-a-half-inch-long spikes. Leaflike bracts are in an opposite arrangement below each whorl. They are usually shorter than the three-sixteenths-inch calyces. Flowering is generally from mid to late June in USDA Zone 7.

According to Tucker and Hensen (1985), lavenders can be distinguished by the bracts. Those of *L. angustifolia* are ovate-rhombic in outline, with a length/width ratio of 0.83 to 2.20. Bracteoles (a small bract borne on the flower stalk above the bract and below the calyx) are absent or up to 2.5 millimeters long. There are dozens, if not hundreds of genotypes, all with subtle and sometimes great genetic variation, both in the morphology and the chemical composition of the essential oil.

English lavender has many cultivars, including the white-flowered dwarf, 'Nana Alba', growing to nine inches in height. 'Alba', listed in a number of herb books, is actually quite rare and seldom seen in American gardens. According to A. O. Tucker (1985), he had not seen it in cultivation, though it was first described in 1826, and was grown in Switzerland as early as 1623. Tucker found pink cultivars designated 'Rosea', 'Jean Davis', and 'Loddon Pink' to be virtually identical in appearance and essential oil composition. He says that 'Rosea' is probably the oldest name, hence the correct one.

Cultivars with dark violet flowers include 'Dwarf Blue', 'Hidcote', 'Loddon Blue', 'Middachten', 'Nana Atropurpurea', 'Mitcham Gray', 'Munstead', and 'Summerland Supreme'. Lavender blue–flowered cultivars in the horticultural trade include 'Backhouse Purple', 'Bowles Early', 'Compacta', 'Folgate', 'Graves', 'Gray Lady', 'Gwendolyn Anley', 'Irene Doyle', 'Maillette', and 'Twickel Purple'. All of these cultivars are described and evaluated by Tucker and Hensen (1985), to which the reader is referred for complete details.

Of the more than a dozen lavender blue cultivars available, Art Tucker finds 'Irene Doyle' unique, given its ability to flower twice (late May and September in Zone 7), its excellent fragrance, and its essential oil with a range of constituents suitable for commercial lavender products (Tucker and DeBaggio 1984, Tucker 1985). 'Irene Doyle' was the first recurrent-blooming lavender discovered by Thomas DeBaggio of Earth Works Nursery in Arlington, Virginia. Another recurrent bloomer introduced by DeBaggio is 'W.K. Doyle', which he calls "dark supreme lavender." It differs from 'Irene Doyle' in having slightly darker lavender blue flowers and green buds suffused with violet, which add color to the herb garden an extra week before opening. The Doyles, incidentally, are DeBaggio's in-laws.

French or dentate lavender, *L. dentata*, grows to three feet in height. The leaves are grayish in color and covered with a soft fuzz. They are about an inch and a quarter long, linear-oblong with well-defined rounded teeth at the margins. The tight spikes are up to one-and-three-quarters inches long and one-half inch in diameter. The one-fourth-inch-wide, purple, oblong to oval-shaped bracts are up to one-half inch in length. One variety has green rather than gray leaves. It grows in southern and eastern Spain and is widely cultivated elsewhere in warm, temperate regions.

L. multifida, fern-leaf lavender, has lacy, finely divided, fernlike leaves. Each segment is one-fourth to three-fourths of an inch long. The spikes are often in threes or solitary, up

to two-and-a-half inches long with one-half-inch-long bluish corollas. It is found in the western Mediterranean region and southern Portugal.

L. stoechas, Spanish lavender, is a shrub growing to four feet tall with linear to oblong, lance-shaped leaves about three-fourths of an inch long. The spikes are short and plump, up to an inch and a half long and one-half inch in diameter. The three-eighths-inch flowers are dark purple. This lavender is native to France, Spain and Portugal. Spanish lavender tolerates more acid soils than English lavender.

L. x intermedia, lavandin, which is widely cultivated and offered by American herb nurseries under a variety of names, as well as grown commercially as a source of lavender in France and elsewhere, is a natural interspecific hybrid of *L. angustifolia* with *L. latifolia* (spike lavender). Art Tucker (1981) notes that the correct name of lavandin is *L. x intermedia* Emeric ex Loiseleur. Lavandin is a sterile hybrid that must be propagated vegetatively. It was first described as a natural hybrid in 1828 (Tucker 1985).

Like *L. angustifolia*, lavandin has ovate-rhombic bracts, but the width to length ratio is 1.33 to 3.00. It always has bracteoles which are one to four millimeters long. It flowers from early to mid-July, typically blooming three to four weeks later than *L. angustifolia*. It is also larger and rounder than *L. angustifolia*, growing to three feet in height. The leaves, according to Tom DeBaggio, are wider, longer, and grayer. Lavandin cultivars are generally hardy.

There are numerous cultivars which, according to Dr. Tucker, are distinguished by chemical characteristics of the oil, rather than morphological features. Commercial lavandin oil- and flower-producing cultivars include 'Abrialii', 'Super', 'Grosso', 'Standard', and 'Maime Epis Te'. Most of these have been selected in France, the principal producer of lavandin oils. Horticultural cultivars include 'Dutch', 'Grappenhall', 'Hidcote Giant', 'Old English', 'Provence', 'Seal', and 'Silver Gray'. Lavandin is best known to perfumers, though has become better known in American horticulture, thanks to Art Tucker's efforts in working to clear up the murky taxonomy and identification of lavenders in cultivation.

L. latifolia, often called "spike" lavender, is native to the Mediterranean region and Portugal, and is generally only found in the gardens of the dedicated lavender collector. It has linear to lance-shaped bracts, with a length to width ratio of 4.67 to 7.00. Its bracteoles are one to six millimeters long, and it flowers late in the season, from late July to mid-August in USDA Zone 7 (Tucker and Hensen 1985). Apparently, no named cultivars of this species exist in the United States. Like English lavender, *L. angustifolia,* spike lavender is one of the parents of lavandin. Spike will tolerate more acid soils than English lavender.

Lavenders can be grown from seed, cuttings, or root divisions. Cuttings taken in spring or fall are the best means of propagation. Since most English lavender and lavandin grown in American gardens are clones, Art Tucker has asked lavender growers to make sure that they are propagated vegetatively, rather than grown from seed, to retain their unique characteristics. Seed propagation of cultivars creates overlapping traits and further variation, intensifying an already-confused situation. Plants from cuttings or seeds grow very slowly the first year, often reaching only six to eight inches in height. They must be mulched or otherwise protected through the first winter. According to Art Tucker, the best time to take cuttings is from August to November, when the stems are semihardened, but have not been subjected to a freeze. He recommends a mix of one part coarse perlite to one part sterilized, baked clay frit (such as kitty litter). The trays are placed in a partially shaded greenhouse and left uncovered, so that neither the atmosphere nor rooting medium becomes too moist. Tucker warns that the leaves should not come in contact with the root medium, as this can cause burning on the leaves. Following these simple guidelines, Tucker gets a 95 to 100 percent success rate with his lavender cuttings (Tucker 1985). New transplants like plenty of moisture to get a jump-start on the first growing season.

Lavenders like a light, well-drained, gravelly soil, well supplied with lime; pH should be between 6.4 and 8.3. The addition of well-decomposed manure, compost, or other humus sources will produce the best results. *L. angustifolia,* lavandin, and spike are the only species I've listed that will survive a hard, cold winter. The other species will hardly stand a freeze. Wet soils will inevitably winter-kill the crown. A protected, south-facing location is best. A heavy mulch should be provided after the ground freezes in late fall. For a detailed account of lavender growing, see DeBaggio (1989).

Fine lavender-oil production is best known in southern France, at elevations of about two thousand feet. Here, on approximately eighty-six hundred acres, about fifty metric tons of lavender oil is produced a year. Lavandin production also occurs in France, where there are over 28,000 acres, producing more than 850 metric tons of oil each year. The lavandin cultivar 'Grosso' accounts for about 70 percent of this amount. Lavender is also grown commercially in Bulgaria and Russia (Verlet 1988). There is also a large lavender farm in Tasmania. The United States imported over four hundred thousand kilograms of lavender oil in 1991.

Some lavender plantations are maintained for as long as thirty years, though the typical productive life in the case of English lavender is ten years, and five to six years for lavandin. A number of commercial cultivars have been selected and bred from erect flower stalks that tower above the foliage to facilitate mechanical harvesting. An acre of lavender turns out between three hundred and eighteen hundred pounds of dried flowers per acre (twelve to fifteen pounds of essential oil), while lavandin, a heavier producer, yields thirty-five hundred to forty-five hundred pounds per acre (fifty-three to sixty-seven pounds of essential oil).

Harvest the buds just as the flowers are about to open. Dry in a well-ventilated space with subdued light. Creating high-quality lavender oils depends on a wide range of variables, including the stage of blossoming, harvesting at the right time of day, weather conditions, and methods of harvest and storage. Flowers for oil production are harvested when at about 50 percent blooming. The harvest takes place on dry, warm, sunny days. Cold or rainy weather can hamper the development of esters in the essential oil.

Lavender is one of the most appreciated of herbs. Its oils are used as fragrance in pharmaceutical preparations and in cosmetic creams, lotions, soaps, perfumes, and colognes. I distinctly remember my first cup of lavender tea. It tasted more like a bar of soap than a beverage. Both *L. angustifolia* and *L. stoechas* are commercially grown for dried flowers and essential oil.

The development of the high-yielding lavandin cultivars in commerce was a mixed blessing. Fine lavender oils, once highly prized in perfumery, have ketones belonging to the amyl group, while in the hybrids and other lavender species besides *L. angustifolia,* the ketones take on the form of camphor. Consequently, the lower-priced oils from the hybrids have become the norm in the marketplace and sales and production of higher-priced, fine lavenders have dropped off. The Bridestow Estate in Tasmania is now the largest world producer of fine lavender oils (Denny 1981).

Lavender has a steady tradition of medicinal use since

the time of Dioscorides, a first-century A.D. Greek naturalist. It possesses tonic, stimulant, antispasmodic, carminative, sedative, stomachic, and diuretic qualities. In folk traditions, lavender has been used for nervous-tension headaches, insomnia, neuralgia, and other ailments. Lavender tea, oil (externally), or inhalants are treatments for headaches, neuralgia, migraines, muscle spasms, rheumatism, and many other problems. In tests with mice, the oil has been found to be a central nervous system depressant. The oil is also antibacterial and antiseptic.

L. *angustifolia* oil contains linalyl acetate (up to 40 percent), linalool (about 25 percent), geraniol and its esters, nerol, lavandulol, cineole (up to 33 percent), lavandulyl acetate, pinocamphone, limonene, cadinene, caryophyllene, and as many as a hundred other components. L. *latifolia* oil has alpha-pinene, camphene, beta-pinene, sabinene, beta-myrcene, 1,8-cineole (up to 33 percent) beta-cymene, linaloyl oxide, camphor (about 5 percent), linalool (up to 25 percent), among other constituents. L. *stoechas* oil is high in camphor (24 to 72 percent), borneol, cineole, fenchone (up to 34 percent), linalool acetate, and others (De Vincenzi and Dessi 1991). L. *angustifolia, L.* x *intermedia, L. latifolia,* and L. *stoechas* all contain the antioxidant, rosmarinic acid. There are more than thirty different types of lavender oils traded on commercial markets. Buying a high-quality one is an art known only to a few experienced specialists.

LEMON BALM
Melissa officinalis L.
(mel-iss'-a off-iss-i-nay'-lis)
Labiatae (Lamiaceae)—Mint Family

Every herb garden should harbor this herb with its strong but delicate lemon scent. It is an upright, tender perennial, native to southern Europe and naturalized in England, France, and the eastern and western United States. Lemon balm grows to two feet high. Its stems are branching and hairy. The two-to three-inch-long leaves are oval or heart shaped, deeply wrinkled, and have scalloped edges. The light blue to white flowers occur in whorls around the leaf axils. They are about one-half inch long and appear in May to August. One cultivar has variegated leaves.

Melissa officinalis, Lemon Balm

Lemon balm is easy to grow from seed sown in the spring or early fall. Plants self-sow freely; lemon balm can become a weed if young seedlings aren't transplanted or given to a needy herb gardener. Cuttings can be made from the vigorous summer growth, or the roots can be divided, preferably in the springtime. Give seedlings one-foot spacings.

A fertile, moist, slightly acid to alkaline soil (pH 5 to 7.8) is best for lemon balm. It likes a cool habitat and thrives in moist, open spots in California's redwood forest. If grown under full sun, lemon balm may wilt during hot, dry spells. Plants grown under shade tend to be larger and more succulent than those grown in direct sunlight. Light, dry soils cause the leaves to yellow. In regions where the ground freezes and heaves, the crowns should be mulched during the winter months. An acre may produce eight hundred to one thousand pounds of the dried herb. Higher yields can be obtained when rows and individual plants have closer (about fourteen inches apart), rather than wider spacings. Side-dressing with a nitrogen source can also increase yield and oil content.

Harvest just as the plant comes into bloom. Care should be taken not to bruise the leaves through drying. Lemon balm dries quickly and easily, but loses much of its lemon scent. When dry, store in tightly closed containers. If hung to dry in bunches, lemon balm can be rapidly processed by rubbing each bundle across a half-inch mesh screen. The leaves crumble and fall through the screen, leaving the processor with a handful of stems.

The fresh leaves make a refreshing tea, either iced or hot. The leaves are underutilized as a culinary herb. The fresh leaves are a delicious addition to salads if used sparingly. Simply snip them with a pair of scissors into small slivers.

Carminative, diaphoretic, febrifuge, and mild sedative properties are attributed to lemon balm. A hot tea promotes sweating in colds accompanied by fever. While little known as a medicinal herb in the United States, according to Purdue University's Varro Tyler, lemon balm was selected as the medicinal plant of the year in Europe in 1988. Its essential oil is recognized as sedative, spasmolytic (relieving spasms), and antibacterial. In Germany, it is used as a mild calmative and carminative. A lemon balm-containing cream is sold in Germany for the treatment of cold sores and related herpes simplex conditions. Studies have shown that it reduces the healing time of herpes lesions and lengthens the time between recurrences of the condition (Tyler 1992).

The volatile oil contains citral, citronellal, eugenol acetate, linalool, limonene, and geraniol. Citronellal is the primary terpene to which sedative action is attributed. In laboratory testing, hot-water extracts possessed strong antiviral action against Newcastle disease, herpes simplex, mumps, and other viruses. The oil also has antibacterial properties. Tannins in the plant may be responsible for its effectiveness against herpes simplex.

LEMON VERBENA

Aloysia triphylla (L'Her) Britt. (*Lippia citriodora* [Ort.] Hbk.).
(al-oiz'-i-a try-fil'-a)
Verbenaceae—Verbena Family

Lemon verbena is a deciduous shrub—it loses most of its leaves in fall—native to Argentina, Chile, and Peru. In American gardens, it seldom grows to more than ten feet, but I've seen a twenty-five-foot-tall specimen. It is rather scraggly. The long, lance-shaped leaves (three to four inches) are entire (without teeth) or slightly toothed, have a strong lemon fragrance, and are arranged in whorls of three or four leaves. The flowers are small and inconspicuous, of a white to pale lavender color, and appear on axillary spikes or terminal panicles in July to September. The plant has been introduced to various parts of the world, and historically was cultivated on a small commercial scale in southern France, Algeria, and Tunisia. It is widely grown in warm, temperate areas of Europe, and naturalized in the Mediterranean region, where it has escaped from cultivation. Introduced to India, it is a common subject in Indian gardens.

Lemon verbena is best propagated from stem cuttings. Kent Taylor of Taylor's Herb Gardens takes cuttings from pencil-sized or smaller, green wood. The cuttings have two leaf joints: one with leaves above the rooting medium, the other below. Three leaves are left on the upper joint; the outer half of each leaf is cut off. Mid- and late-summer stems take best.

This fragrant shrub likes a moist, moderately rich, sandy soil with good drainage and full sun. Lemon verbena is not winter hardy where temperatures dip below 20° F. In preparing for a Maine winter, I cut plants back to the ground, dig up the roots, and heel them in moist sand in a cellar. Water the roots every few weeks to keep them from drying out. Once danger of frost has passed the following spring, replant the roots. If you use this method, plants grow up to four feet high each year. They may also be put in a large

Aloysia triphylla, Lemon Verbena

The essential oil, found at about 0.5 percent in the leaves, contains borneol, limonene, dipentene, cineole, citral (up to 35 percent), geraniol, linalool, nerol, isovalerianic acid, and other substances. Mucilage, tannin, and flavonoids have also been identified in the plant. The oil is experimentally antispasmodic, and has been found to have antibacterial and insecticidal activity. On essential oil markets, it has been traded as "true verbena oil," which is expensive because of limited production. The oil has been used as a fragrance in bath salts, toilet waters, perfume formulations, and eau de cologne.

Licorice

Glycyrrhiza glabra L.
(glis-sir-ize'-a gla'-bra)
Leguminosae (Apiaceae)—Pea Family

Licorice is a fairly hardy perennial native primarily to the Mediterranean region. In Europe, it is found in dry, open habitats in the south and east, and has been cultivated throughout the Continent, where it is naturalized in almost all countries except Scandinavia. It is herbaceous or slightly woody, and grows to a height of three to seven feet. The leaves are divided into oval leaflets, one inch long, opposite-arranged along a midrib similarly to acacia. Each leaf is placed alternately on the main stalk. The small, light yellow, bluish, or purple pealike flowers are borne on four- to six-inch spikes arising from the leaf axils. The small pods, containing two to four kidney-shaped seeds, look like immature pea pods. The main rootstock is a deep, penetrating taproot, burrowing from three to six feet below the soil's surface. Creeping horizontal stolons branch from the main root, traveling up to six feet just under the ground. In the second year, shoots emerge from the stolon buds. Licorice reportedly grows best along river and stream banks subject to periodic inundations.

The genus *Glycyrrhiza* includes twenty species native to Eurasia, North America, and Australia. Five species are found in Europe, and at least six species are the source of Chinese licorice ("gan-cao" or sweet herb). *G. lepidota* is native to the United States, and the common European licorice (*G. glabra*) has sporadically escaped from cultivation

pot and brought indoors for the winter, though often the change in climate will cause the leaves to drop. Large plantings have produced three-fourths to two tons of dried herb per acre.

Lemon verbena makes a fine herb tea and can be added to potpourris, floated in iced mint tea, or just hung about the kitchen for its lemon fragrance. Traditional culinary practices include it as a flavoring for fruit salads, melons, jellies, beverages, and desserts.

It has limited medicinal use, primarily as a folk medicine in Latin America for cold, colic, diarrhea, dyspepsia, and fever. It has also been adopted to treat colds and fever in North Africa (Duke 1985). Sedative, febrifuge, stomachic, and antispasmodic properties have been attributed to the herb. It also works to settle indigestion or dyspepsia.

in North America.

Licorice was always harvested from the wild until the first European plantings almost a thousand years ago. Though not native to Germany, it was well known there by the eleventh century, and extensively grown in Bavaria by the end of the sixteenth century. Cultivation is recorded in Spain by the thirteenth century. Edward I of England placed a tax on licorice imports in the year 1305 to finance the repair of London Bridge.

Licorice can be grown from seed sown in spring in well-prepared seedbeds, but seedlings are slow to develop. As with other hard-seeded legumes, the seeds should be soaked overnight in cold water, then dipped in water of 160° F for ten minutes or scarified before attempting to germinate them. However, licorice is usually propagated by dividing the root crown or by stolon cuttings. Eight-to-twenty-inch stolon cuttings with a bud or eye can be planted vertically about an inch below the surface, spacing the plantings at eighteen inches. This is best done in the spring. Plants will grow to a one-foot height the first year, and onions or other shallow-rooted crops can be sown with first-year licorice plantings. Root cuttings should be well watered until plants are firmly established.

Soil should be dug to a depth of two feet or more and manured well the autumn prior to planting. A moist, fairly rich, well-drained sandy loam is best. Soil pH should be slightly alkaline (7 to 8). Licorice is a plant for warm climates, with a long photo period, and it will die in a hard freeze. Warm regions and mild climates ensure vigorous growth.

The main root and stolons are harvested in the fall of the third or fourth years—preferably the latter—once the leaves have died back. All pieces of the root must be removed from the ground, for like comfrey and horse-radish, once established, licorice can become weedy. It is best to harvest plants that haven't gone to seed as the sweet sap is exhausted by the flowering process. Pinch flowers back as they develop. An acre has been reported to produce two-and-a-half to five tons of root. The main root should be split since it is slow to dry. Depending upon soil conditions, root weight is reduced from 10 to 50 percent upon drying.

An extract of licorice is made by crushing the fresh or stored roots, then boiling or passing steam through them and evaporating the liquid, leaving a thick paste or solid black, glossy substance with a sharp fracture. Medicinally, the dried, peeled root has been decocted to allay coughs, sore throat, laryngitis, and urinary and intestinal irritations. The root is expectorant, diuretic, demulcent, antitussive, antiinflammatory, and mildly laxative. It has proven helpful with inflammatory upper-respiratory disease, Addison's

Licorice

disease, and gastric and duodenal ulcers. Its cough-suppressant effect is likened to that of codeine. Side effects may develop in ulcer treatment. Licorice may increase venous and systolic arterial pressure, causing some people to experience edema, cardiac asthma, and hypertension. In some countries, licorice has been used to treat cancers. In China, licorice root is valued as an antacid. Licorice stick, the sweet, earthy-flavored stolons, are chewed. Licorice chew sticks blackened Napoleon's teeth.

Up to 24 percent of the root weight is glycyrrhizin, the plant's major active component. Glycyrrhizin (glycyrrhizic acid), a sweet, foaming triterpene glycoside, may cause hypertension from potassium loss, sodium retention, and an increase of extracellular fluid and plasma volume. It is fifty times sweeter than sugar. It stimulates the excretion of hormones by the adrenal cortex, and has been suggested as a possible drug to prolong the action of cortisone. Glycyrrhizin has a similar chemical structure to corticosteroids released by the adrenals, and research has suggested that it might one day be helpful in improving the function of hormone drugs, or relieving withdrawal symptoms from corticol hormones. Licorice has shown estrogenic activity in laboratory animals, and is experimentally anti-inflammatory, antirheumatic, and antibacterial. The flavonoids liquiritin, isoliquiritin, liquiritigenin, and isoliquiritigenin found in the root are thought to be responsible for its antiulcer benefits.

Licorice extracts are used to flavor tobacco, chewing gums, confections, soft drinks, liqueurs, ice cream, and baked goods. It is also an ingredient in cough medications, laxatives, and antismoking preparations. Licorice increases the foam in beer. It is one of the more widely consumed herbs in the world.

LION'S EAR, LION'S TAIL

Leonotis leonurus (L.) R. Br.
(lee-on-ah'tis lee-on-ur'-us)
Labiatae (Lamiaceae)—Mint Family
Plate 2

Lion's ear is a tender, branching shrub native to South Africa. There are about fifteen species in the genus *Leonotis*, most of which are found in Africa. Both the generic and common name come from the fanciful resemblance of the flowers to the ears of a lion. Lion's ear's vibrant orange whorls of velvety flowers make it one of the mint family's most

striking ornamentals. It usually grows to five feet in the garden, though it may reach seven feet. The plant is covered by short hairs. The opposite oblong or lance-shaped leaves are two to five inches in length, and are coarsely toothed. The whorls (verticillasters) of the fuzzy two-and-a-half inch-long orange blossoms emerge from the leaf axils. Blooming may begin as early as June in southern California, lasting into autumn. The plant has been widely grown throughout the world, including Asia, the United States, Africa, and Europe. It was one of the first plants introduced from South Africa to European gardens, and was grown in the Netherlands as early as 1663.

Lion's ear is best propagated by spring cuttings. They sprout more readily than those made in summer or fall. Full sun and a dry, sandy, slightly alkaline soil, with good drainage, suits *Leonotis* culture. To encourage more blooming when the plants are young (six to nine inches high), pinch back the stalks, which causes branching. This is a subtropical species and will not survive a hard freeze. Where temperatures dip below 20° F in winter months, lion's ear will have to be brought indoors. Before an autumn frost, cut the plant back to the root, pot it, and bring it into the greenhouse. If given enough sun, lion's ear can be forced to bloom there during winter months. It is a fabulous border plant in temperate climates. At Taylor's Herb Gardens, a hundred-foot row of lion's ear graces the west end of the display garden.

Lion's ear has been employed to promote menstruation, as a snakebite antidote, and to relieve epilepsy, cardiac asthma, and leprosy. In South Africa, several species of *Leonotis* are referred to as "dagga-dagga." Its leaves or resin are smoked alone or with tobacco for a feeble euphoric effect similar to, but weaker than, marijuana. The plant is also considered mildly anthelmintic, once used for the treatment of tapeworm, but is considered too weak for practical value. It has also functioned as a cough and cold remedy. The Zulus of South Africa have supposedly made a decoction of the leaves and sprinkled it around housing to repel snakes.

The plant contains a resin and essential oil. Two phenolic compounds have been identified from the leaves. The diterpenoids marrubiin and leonitin have also been found in the plant. First and foremost, lion's ear is an ornamental, and one of the most brilliant flowering residents of the herb garden from the mint family.

LOBELIA

Lobelia inflata L.
(loh-beel'-i-a in fla'-ta)
Campanulaceae—Bellflower Family

Lobelia is an erect, hairy annual growing in the wild to one foot in height, though often reaching two to three feet in cultivation. The leaves are mostly sessile, oval, about two inches long and half as broad. The pale, blue-white, irregular flowers, one-half by one-fourth inch long, are arranged on a spike at the end of the plant's stalk, blooming from July through September. Typical of the *Lobelia* genus, the top throat of the corolla is split its entire length. The seed capsules resemble an inflated bladder (hence the specific name *inflata*) and are filled with tiny black seeds. Lobelia grows in fields, open woods, and along the banks of streams and ponds from Labrador to Georgia, and west to Arkansas.

The seeds are very small and must be sown on sifted, or very well-prepared, soil. Plant indoors in late February, sprinkling seed on the surface of the soil mix, lightly tamping it with a spatula. Place flats in trays of water to moisten soil through capillary action, which prevents the seeds from becoming displaced by surface watering. Seeds germinate in ten days and must have light at the red end of the spectrum to emerge. This can be supplied by sunlight or a couple of two hundred–watt incandescent bulbs mounted about thirty inches above the flats. When seedlings are about two months old, transplant them to larger flats at two-inch spacings, or to individual pots. It's important not to crowd the seeds too closely together. While germination rate is usually high, the tiny seedlings are subject to drying out, but if given too much water, they will suffer from damping off. About one month later, plant them in the field with eighteen-inch spacings. Seeds can also be carefully sown directly in the garden in spring or fall.

Lobelia will grow in a slightly acid clay loam, but does best in a rich, moist loam. It will tolerate full sun or partial shade. Higher yields of active constituents are obtained from plants grown in full sunlight. An acre may produce a thousand to seventeen hundred pounds of dried herb. An interesting study by Krochmal, Wilken, and Chien (1972) showed the value of cultivated material over wild-harvested plants. A poorly drained cultivated field kept clear of weeds for two years produced an average lobeline content of 1.05 percent (dry weight), about 40 percent higher than the

lobeline content of wild plants. The average fresh weight of cultivated plants was fifty-three grams, while that for wild plants was as little as one-and-a-half grams. The cultivated plants also generated up to 129 seed capsules, while wild plants produced between 5 and 25 seed capsules. The field-grown plants averaged 409 seeds per capsule, while wild

Lobelia

material produced a high of 246 seeds per capsule. Since the highest concentration of lobeline is in the seeds, cultivated plants had substantially higher yields. Irrigation increased the harvest weight of field-grown plants. Under a planting scheme that would hold 21,780 plants per acre (planted on one-foot centers in rows spaced two feet apart), a yield of 1,700 pounds per acre was obtained. The weight of field-grown plants was reduced by 30 percent after drying.

Harvest the whole herb while still in flower after a few seed capsules develop. Lobelia dries easily.

Over the past two hundred years, lobelia has sparked much controversy. Samuel Thomson (1760–1843), the guru of nineteenth-century botanic physicians, claimed to have discovered lobelia's medicinal virtues in 1793. However, in 1785, the Reverend Dr. Manasseh Cutler of Hamilton, Massachusetts, made the first mention of lobelia in "Account of Indigenous Vegetable," a paper delivered before the American Academy of Arts and Sciences. Thomson was an exceptionally popular empirical physician who popularized the use of lobelia, calling it his "No. 1" herb in a "course" of medicine which included induced vomiting, sweating, stimulating, and correcting the "morbid" action of the system.

In 1809, Thomson was arrested for murder for allegedly administering a fatal dose of lobelia. In a colorful trial, he was acquitted due to lack of evidence that he willfully intended to harm the deceased, and lack of satisfactory proof that lobelia was, in fact, a poison. As there were no laws at the time against practicing medicine without a license, that was not an issue. The trial sparked a great deal of interest in Thomson, lobelia, and the lack of legislation defining who was eligible to practice medicine. Today Thomsonian medicine is perpetuated in such popular books as Jethro Kloss's *Back to Eden*.

The plant's efficacy and toxicity ratio is still open to question. Its strong emetic action earned it the names "emetic herb," "gag root," and "puke weed." Simply chewing a leaf or seed capsule stimulates the vagus nerve, leaving the stomach and throat with an acrid, burning sensation. You may feel nauseous without vomiting, or experience violent vomiting. The reaction depends on the dose and the potency of the herb, which deteriorates rapidly after drying; much commercially available lobelia is weak.

Lobelia has been smoked or used in powdered form or as a tea to relieve asthmatic paroxysms. It is also strongly diaphoretic, expectorant, and sedative. Fevers, whooping cough, insect bites, bruises, and sprains have been treated with lobelia.

Lobelia contains over fourteen alkaloids, including the pyridine alkaloid, lobeline, found at rates of .36 to 2.25 percent of the dried plant. These alkaloids come from the same chemical grouping to which nicotine belongs. It is interesting to note that even before alkaloids closely akin to nicotine were isolated from the plant, lobelia was known as "Indian tobacco." Other alkaloids present include lobelanidine, lobelanine, and isolobinine. Like nicotine, lobeline acts first as a central nervous system stimulant, then as a depressant. Overdose can cause convulsions and collapse. Lobeline sulphate has been part of commercial over-the-counter antismoking lozenges. Apparently it replaces physical addiction to nicotine without its addictive effects. Lobeline and its preparations have been used as a respiratory stimulant, especially in newborn infants and in drug poisonings accompanied by a depressant effect on the central nervous system. The effect of lobeline as a respiratory stimulant is considered unreliable because the dose necessary to produce the desired results varies greatly from patient to patient. The action is sometimes too short to be effective. Consequently, lobelia is seldom used.

Because of the conflicting nature of the information available on lobelia, it must be administered with caution, and preferably by a healthcare practitioner.

LOVAGE

Levisticum officinale W.D.J. Koch
(le-vis'-ti-kum off-iss-i-nail'-ee)
Umbelliferae (Apiaceae)—Carrot Family
Plate 12

There are few culinary herbs with as many hidden secrets as lovage, *Levisticum officinale*. It is familiar to the consummate herb grower, but unknown to the common palate. Like cilantro, there are those who love its flavor and fragrance and those who simply can't stand it. It is one of those creations of the vegetable kingdom for which one must develop a taste. Though sometimes likened to celery, its flavor is best described as "lovagelike."

Lovage is a stout, hardy perennial, native to southern Europe and naturalized in some parts of North America. It generally grows from four to six feet tall, though I've seen it stretch to over eight feet. The stems are smooth, hollow, erect, and thick. The compound, divided leaves have long

PLATE 1

Goldenseal (page 102) and Ginseng (page 100)

PLATE 2

Sweet Goldenrod (page 183), Pleurisy Root (page 166), and Lion's Ear (page 120)

PLATE 3

Lavendula stoechas, L x *intermedia, L. dentata, L. multifida, L. angustifolia* 'Munstead', *(page 113)*

PLATE 4

Echinacea paradoxa, E. pallida (emerging),
E. pallida, and *E. purpurea, (page 85)*

PLATE 5

Lamb's Ears (page 113), Cat Thyme (page 189), and Salvia divinorum (page 172)

Plate 6

Spiderwort (page 182) and Passion Flower (page 159)

PLATE 7

Monarda russeliana, M. fistulosa,
M. didyma and M. punctata, (page 45)

PLATE 8

Elecampane (page 89), Calendula (page 56), and Rue (page 169)

PLATE 9

Laurus nobilis, Bay, page 43

Cimicifuga racemosa, Black Cohosh, page 47

Sanguinaria canadensis, Bloodroot, page 50

Chamaemelum nobile, English Chamomile, page 64

PLATE 10

Capsicum, Capsicum, page 62

Mentha x *piperita,* Peppermint Harvest, Trout Lake, Washington, page 148

Herb Drying Catnip/Spearmint; Sister's Shop, Sabbathday Lake, Maine, page 148

PLATE 11

Allium schoenoprasum, Chives, page 72

Balsamita major, Costmary, page 79

Taraxacum officinale, Dandelion, Trout Lake, WA, page 80

Cunila origanoides, American Dittany, page 84

PLATE 12

Oenothera biennis, Evening Primrose, page 90

Foeniculum vulgare, Fennel, page 92

Tanacetum parthenium, Feverfew, page 93

Levisticum officinale, Lovage, page 138

PLATE 13

Althaea officinalis Marshmallow, page 143

Silybum marianum, Milk Thistle, page 146

Leonurus cardiaca, Motherwort, page 151

Artemisia vulgaris, Mugwort, page 152

PLATE 14

Mentha pulegium, European Pennyroyal, page 161

Rosmarinus officinalis, Rosemary, page 167

Salvia officinalis, Sage, page 170

PLATE 15

Tragopogon porrifolius, Salsify, page 175

Santolina chamecyparissus, Gray Santolina, page 176

Artemisia abrotanum, Southernwood, page 200

Thymus vulgaris var. *citriodora,* Variegated Lemon Thyme, page 189

PLATE 16

Thymus spp., Thyme (various varieties), page 189

Hamamelis vernalis, vernal Witch Hazel, page 197

stalks (to twenty-four inches). The leaves are alternate on the stalk and individual leaflets are broad, flat, and wedgeshaped, much like celery leaves. Tiny yellow flowers occur on loose umbels. The elliptical, curved seeds have three prominent wings on each mericap. The vertical rhizome is strongly aromatic, white, and fleshy, three to five inches thick, with lateral rootlets up to eight inches long.

Linnaeus first named the plant *Ligusticum levisticum* L. N. L. Britton (1859–1934) and J.N. Rose (1862–1928) gave it the name *Hipposelinum levisticum.* Henri Ernest Baillon (1827–1825), another nineteenth-century botanical worker in the Umbelliferae, endowed it with the name *Angelica levisticum.* In the 1880s, the German botanist G.K.H. Karsten (1817–1908) called it *Levisticum levisticum.* W.D.J. Koch (1771–1849) classified it as *Levisticum officinale,* the name that remains with it today.

Lovage is easily grown from seed sown in the early spring or fall. Fall-sown seed may not germinate until the following spring. They are best planted in early fall soon after they ripen. Like angelica, their viability is short-lived. If you plan a spring planting, store the seeds in a refrigerator over the winter. Germination will usually begin in about ten days, but may take as long as four weeks. Seeds sown in a bed in autumn can be transplanted in early spring as the seedlings begin to emerge. If you plant in a cold frame or well-prepared seedbed, transplant when the seedlings are about three inches high, after two true leaves have appeared, and when danger of frost has passed.

In early spring or late autumn, the roots can also be divided to increase stock. It is best done, of course, while the plant is dormant. Different authors conversely say spring is best, while others say fall division is optimum. I think the best time depends upon your schedule. If divided in spring, dig the plants just as the first reddish leaves emerge from the crown. Don't wait until stalks begin to develop. Divide the roots, making sure each division has an eye. Plant sections about two inches beneath the soil surface. Give plants two-foot spacings.

Lovage will do well in almost any garden soil, but thrives best in a deep, rich moist loam with good drainage. Soil pH range is between 5.5 and 7.5. Full sun or partial shade is acceptable. In the North, plant in a sunny situation. In the South, the plant prefers partial shade and attention to watering. The plants seem to like to be crowded together. Lovage does not like a heavy clay soil with poor drainage. A deep, well-drained soil that will produce a good crop of

potatoes or corn has been recommended as suitable for lovage. Heavy applications of manure or compost, will, of course, stimulate heavy leaf and top growth. Whether or not to add manure should be relative to your intended use of the plant. If you plan to harvest and use the fresh leaves, a heavy manure would be advantageous. The plant is very hardy and will not require a mulch in a well-drained soil. If you're in the habit of mulching, a light straw mulch couldn't hurt. I have found it easier to winter-over some plants in the cold, snow-covered Maine weather, than the open, mostly snow-free winters of Arkansas. Experimental plantings have shown an acre may produce about a thousand to fourteen hundred pounds of root in the third year.

If you desire the roots for product material, they can be harvested in the second or third autumn after planting. Numerous offshoots from the roots will be found. These can be divided and planted. The main root, like angelica, often twists upon itself, so careful attention should be paid to cleaning the roots before drying. To create larger roots more quickly, I would recommend a Chinese practice used in commercial production of most root crops. Pinch back the flower tops as they begin to develop. The energy of the plant then goes "back to the root," rather than into the development of seeds. You can let a few plants go to seed if you want to collect the seed for planting, or if the seeds are the desired crop.

Dry the roots in the sun or shade, but not at temperatures higher than 125° F. Those interested in commercial production of the plant are referred to the excellent paper by Galambosi and Szebeni-Galambosi (1992).

The leaves, stems, roots, and seeds are all useful. Leaves may be harvested and dried in the second or third year before plants bloom. Stems and leaves can be used fresh. The roots are best harvested in the fall of the third year. In autumn, harvest the seeds as they begin to turn light brown. Like angelica, lovage seeds are subject to aphid infestations. Its succulent leaves are best dried on screens under low, forced heat rather than being hung to dry.

The fresh leaves and peeled stems can be chopped into salads. The leaves make a rather pungent and unique-flavored celery substitute. Use half as much lovage as you would celery. I like a sprinkling of the chopped leaves on carrots, cabbage, potatoes, and in tomato dishes. The root can be candied like calamus root. A Bloody Mary should, of course, be sipped through a lovage-stem straw. Those celery stirrers, served in bars throughout the country, are an impostor.

Medicinally, the root is an aromatic stimulant, carminative, diaphoretic, emmenagogue, and diuretic. Indigestion, colic, flatulence, menstrual problems, bladder ailments, cramps, stomachache, eczema, gout, insomnia, lumbago, sciatica, toothache, and worms are among the ailments treated with an infusion of lovage root. Extracts of lovage root, as well as the oil, have strong diuretic effects in mice and rabbit experiments. The major components of the essential oil are also reported to have sedative activity.

It is interesting to note that lovage has been classified in the genus *Ligusticum* as well as *Angelica. Angelica,* in addition to producing the common angelicas of European and American herb gardens, is also responsible for the best-known Chinese herb, "dong-gui," *A. sinensis.* In the mid 1960s, in the early days of China's ill-fated Cultural Revolution, unforeseen demand for dong-gui exhausted wild supplies which came traditionally from the province of Qinghai in north-central China. At the time, dong-gui was not commercially cultivated in China as it is today. Until commercial supplies became available a few years later, the Chinese grew lovage as a substitute for dong-gui. The Chinese name for lovage translates to "European dong-gui" (Foster and Yue 1992).

The western North American medicinal plant, osha (*Ligusticum porterii*), belongs to the genus *Ligusticum.* Osha, a Pueblo Indian term, is becoming a popular native medicinal from the Mountain West. In essence, osha was used for similar purposes by native peoples of the western United States as dong-gui is in China. It was utilized for female maladies, and as a general strengthening tonic during convalescence, among other things. In a study on uses of plants by Hispano-Americans in the valley of San Luis in south-central Colorado, Robert A. Bye (1986) noted that lovage can be a substitute for osha. They call lovage "osha del jardin" (osha of the garden). Here it is important to define the difference between substitute and adulterant. An adulterant is a substance knowingly (and usually secretly) added to another material to stretch a supply and add to profit. A substitute is an acceptable alternative to an established botanical (S. Foster 1988c).

The root contains up to 1.8 percent essential oil, primarily composed of compounds known as phthalides, with lesser amounts of terpenoids. The oil incorporates butyl-phthalidine, umbelliferone, bergapten, and terpineol. The root also has some volatile acids, as well as coumarins. The coumarins include umbelliferone, bergapten, and psoralen. Bergapten and psoralen are known to cause photodermatitis. The same components that cause photosensitizing have been proven valuable in the treatment of psoriasis and other skin ailments. Psoralens are even being researched as potential anticancer and anti-AIDS fighters. Lovage oil is generally believed to be nonsensitizing to human skin, though reports of at least one reaction are noted in the literature. Phototoxic effects of lovage oil in humans have not been adequately researched.

When the dried root is distilled, it produces, in addition to the oil, a sticky, yellow resin which partly separates from the oil, but dissolves in it as well. This resin is nearly absent from the fresh root oil. The variations in composition of the oils from different parts of the plant make each oil a separate commodity. The root oil is widely employed in perfumery, as a fragrance component of soaps and creams, and even to flavor tobacco products. The seed oil is often added as a flavoring agent for liqueurs, baked goods, and confections. The oil distilled from the leaves and stems of the flowering plant is now seldom used for flavoring manufactured food stuffs. Lovage oils are primarily produced in the herb-growing regions of central Europe. Lovage and its essential oils are deemed "GRAS" by the FDA (Generally Recognized as Safe).

MAIDENHAIR FERNS
Adiantum pedatum L., *A. capillus-veneris* L.
(a-di-ayn'-tum ped-ay'-tum)
Adiantaceae—Maidenhair Fern Family

Northern maidenhair, one of the most well-known and appreciated ferns, is not often considered an herb, but this illusive inhabitant of dim-lit, rich, moist woods has a long history of medicinal and practical use by Europeans and American Indians. The genus *Adiantum* has over two hundred species, mostly native to tropical America, though a few of them grow in North America. *A. capillus-veneris,* known as southern maidenhair or Venus hair is the only species found in Europe, occurring in much of the western and southern regions on damp, calcareous rocks. It generally frequents warmer areas of the Old World, including China. In the United States, it is located in similar habitats in Virginia, Kentucky, and Arkansas, ranging north to South Dakota, and west to Utah.

The lacy fronds of *A. pedatum* stand up to a foot and a

half high and the leaves (pinnae) may be a foot and a half across. Sometimes called five-finger fern, *Adiantum*'s leaves fork at the plant's summit, making five or more hand-shaped divisions. The individual pinnules (leaflets) are four-sided, oblong, and wedge shaped. Two edges of the pinnule are deeply notched. Spores develop at the tips of the notched edges, which roll back to cover the spores, forming indusa. The stems are wiry and slender with a brownish-black luster. Fine, bluish hairs cover the uncurling spring fronds (croziers), and the young leaflets are tinted red. Creeping rootstocks send up fronds at intervals throughout the growing season. The roots are slender, branched, and dark. Maidenhair occurs throughout the United States in moist woods. There are several varieties and forms.

A. capillus-veneris is a smaller, and perhaps less showy, fern. The stem, nearly one-foot tall, is purplish black and shining, and is about as long as the entire leaf blade. The leaflets are two or three pinnate, oval to oval-lance shaped, bright green, and of a delicate texture. They are about two to four times as long as wide, and the divisions are alternate. The lower edges are deeply parted with dentate lobes, and lack a midrib. The overall shape of the leaf blade is somewhat triangular. The short-creeping rhizome has dark scales.

Perhaps no other fern enjoys cultivation as much as maidenhairs. They are easily propagated from root division in the spring or fall, when the plant is dormant. Rhizome sections should be at least two inches in length and have a bud or eye. If you do divide the roots during the vegetative period, the root divisions must be carefully watered and protected from drying out. Trim back all but one frond on the division. Plant in a spot where the rootstocks can spread.

The adventurous grower can collect the spores on the backside of the leaflets, once they turn dark, and the leaf edges begin to curl back. The spores can be propagated in a moist, sterile potting medium in a closed case. Once they begin to produce young plants, they can be misted with distilled water. Young sporelings can be transplanted to a sterile medium in another closed environment. They should be spaced at one-inch centers.

Maidenhair favors deep to light shade in a moist, rich, well-drained soil. A north-facing location, protected from wind, is best. Northern maidenhair will tolerate a pH of 4.5 to 7. A slightly acid soil is preferred. Southern maidenhair likes an alkaline situation, constant moisture, and excellent drainage. Ground limestone can be added to the soil. In cooler regions, the plant can be grown in a greenhouse or as a houseplant.

The whole plant can be gathered for fall use. Wild plants should be left alone, both for propagation and harvesting purposes. Nursery-propagated plants are easily obtained from fern sources. If you intend to harvest the plant, harvest only those that you have grown in your own garden. Maidenhair dries quickly and easily.

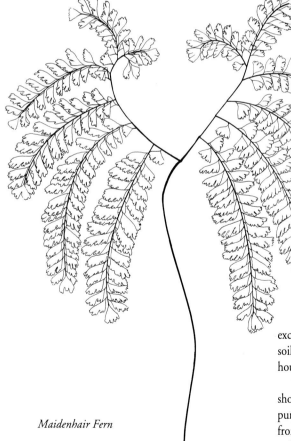

Maidenhair Fern

Some Indian tribes used the dark polished stems of northern maidenhair for basket weaving. Ashes of the leaves were rubbed on the hair to make long, shiny, black strands. Some Indians tried an infusion of the leaves as a hair wash. To add body and luster to hair, boil a handful of the leaves in a pint of water for ten minutes. Cool, strain, and use as a final rinse. Northwest tribes chewed the leaves to stop internal bleeding. The Iroquois made a poultice of the fresh, smashed plant to treat sores on the backs of babies, and for snakebite. A handful of the roots, steeped in water, relieved excessive menstruation.

In Arab countries, a mix of olive oil, vinegar, and the ashes of southern maidenhair will regrow hair on bald scalp patches caused by ringworm. Northern maidenhair is considered to be a stimulant, demulcent, expectorant, and mild astringent. It will activate the lungs' mucous membranes, causing the expectoration of accumulated wastes. A tea of the leaves helps soothe a sore throat, allay coughing, and break up the congestion of asthma or other pulmonary ailments. This herb is mild, so the tea needs to be strong. Infuse an ounce of leaves in a pint of water. The taste is slightly aromatic and sweet, with bitter overtones.

Southern maidenhair is used in Europe and elsewhere in parallel ways to *A. pedatum*. Traditionally it is considered to be an expectorant, antitussive, and demulcent. It is a part of preparations to treat cough and bronchitis, as well as a hair rinse. Extracts of the plant have shown experimental diuretic and hypoglycemic activity. In India's Punjab region, where the fern is common, the fronds are combined with pepper to treat fevers. Mixed with honey, they act as an expectorant. Pulmonary symptoms associated with colds are relieved by smoking the leaves. Boiled in wine, the plant has functioned as a treatment for hard tumors of the spleen and liver. It will also stimulate menstrual discharges. A maidenhair cough syrup formerly made in France, "Sirop de Capillaire," flavored with orange flowers, was once a popular remedy for coughs, throat infections, and bronchial disorders. In China, the leaves have been employed to treat snakebites, as well as impetigo; they can also act as a bronchial expectorant. In the Philippines, maidenhair has also been valued as a pectoral and for menstrual difficulties. Western applications for asthma, splenetic disorders, snakebites, and as a falling hair treatment date to the first-century Greek physician Dioscorides. The plant is subsequently discussed in most European herbals which followed.

Northern maidenhair contains a little tannin and minute traces of an essential oil. Southern maidenhair, which has been much more thoroughly studied by Chinese, European, and Indian scientists, has a number of flavonoid glycosides, including rutin, isoquercetin, astragalin, kaempferol, 3,7-diglucoside, and kaempferol 3-sulphate. Adiantone, a terpenoid, has also been isolated, along with four hydroxycinnamic-acid sulphate esters (Wren 1988). The plant incorporates a volatile oil, a bitter principle termed capillerin, tannins, gallic acid, mucin, and other components.

MARJORAM
Origanum majorana L. (*Majorana hortensis* Moench).
(or-i-gay'-num ma-jor-ay'-na)
Labiatae (Lamiaceae)—Mint Family

Marjoram is a tender, bushy, slender-stemmed perennial which must be grown as an annual in most parts of the United States, except coastal California or Florida, where it is hardy. It reaches a height of two feet and is smooth or hairy. The leaves, with tiny white woolly hairs, are one-fourth to one inch long, oval, and entire (without teeth), with short petioles on the lower leaves, and sessile upper leaves. The veins are somewhat raised. The spikelets are borne in terminal panicles on short branches. Each spikelet is one-fourth to one-half inch long. The bracts are small, rounded, and glistening with oil glands. The calyx has one lip with a deep slot down one side. The one-eighth-inch-long flowers are white, pale lilac, or pale pink.

Marjoram should not be confused with the hybrid, sold on the American market as hardy sweet marjoram or Italian oregano. This herb is designated *Origanum* x *majoricum*, and arises from a hybrid between *O. majorana* and *O. vulgare* subsp. *virens*. A hardy shrublet which develops a woody base when older, it retains the flavor and fragrance of sweet marjoram.

Marjoram, native to North Africa and southwest Asia, and naturalized in southern Europe, blooms in late summer. It is commercially cultivated in the United States and Egypt, as well as France, Greece, and Hungary. Like other *Origanum* species, there is a wide range of chemotypes and variation in *Origanum majorana* due to ecological conditions.

Marjoram is easily propagated by seeds sown in the spring or by summer cuttings. Seeds germinate readily in about ten days. Winter indoors in pots and replant in spring after danger of frost has passed. A light, fairly rich, well-drained, slightly alkaline soil (pH 7 to 8) in full sun is favorable.

Harvest as soon as blooming commences, generally in late July or early August. A second cutting is often possible in October, depending upon the growing region. Harvest plants about three inches above ground. Marjoram dries easily, but to retain a bright green color, it should be dried under relatively low heat in shade. As much as fifteen hundred pounds of dried herb have been produced per acre.

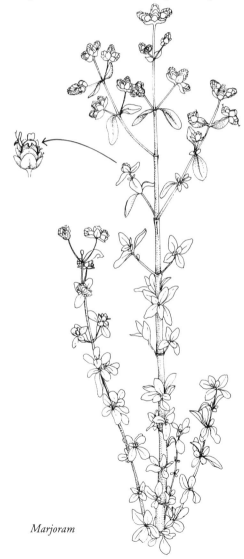

Marjoram

Marjoram is sweeter, somewhat more piquant than oregano. It's great with tomato dishes, meats, onions, brussels sprouts, and mushrooms, and is a pleasant surprise in salads. Fresh or dried leaves have wide and varied use in seafood, soups, egg dishes, poultry, fish, salads, and sauces. Sweet marjoram is an extremely versatile culinary herb.

The leaves contain up to 13 percent protein and are high in vitamins A and C. They also have varying amounts of minerals, including calcium, phosphorus, iron, magnesium, and trace amounts of manganese.

Carminative, diaphoretic, antispasmodic, and diuretic properties have been attributed to marjoram. In laboratory experiments, extracts of marjoram were reported to inhibit herpes simplex. The oil has been beneficial for toothache, and marjoram was once employed for cancer. The oil has also been used as an embrocation to treat rheumatism.

The essential oil contains terpinenes, sabinene, linalool, carvacrol, cis-sabinene hydrate, trans-sabinene hydrate, and over forty other components. Cis-sabinene hydrate is responsible for sweet marjoram's typical fragrance. The plant also has rosmarinic acid (3.3% dry weight). Extracts have antioxidant and antiviral effects.

MARSHMALLOW

Althaea officinalis L.
(al-thay-ee'-a off-ish-i-nay'-lis)
Malvaceae—Mallow Family
Plate 13

Marshmallow is a densely gray, pubescent, erect, branched perennial growing to over six feet in height. The often-somewhat-folded, undivided or three- to five-lobed leaves are triangular-ovate in shape, with acute tips and toothed margins. The pale lilac-pink flowers are borne singly or appear in clusters in leaf axils or terminal groups. The purple-red anthers stand out against the lighter background of the petals. It flowers from July through September. It occurs in damp soils in most of Europe from England to Denmark and central Russia and southward. Marshmallow has become naturalized in the United States, occurring in salt marshes from Massachusetts to Virginia, and sporadically inland. It is not as well known in American herb gardens as it might be.

The plant grows readily from seed, which can be sown directly in the garden or raised in a seedbed for transplanting. Seeds germinate in about thirty days. The easiest way to propagate marshmallow is simply by dividing the roots in spring or fall when the plant is dormant. Plants can be spaced on fifteen-inch centers.

Marshmallows will do fine in the average garden soil, but flourish in a deep, fertile sandy loam with good drainage. A light, well-drained sandy soil will reportedly produce more mucilage (the active component) in the plant than clay soils. Moister soils will produce less mucilage than drier ones, and the mucilage content is higher in the fall and winter than in the spring or summer.

If grown from seed, marshmallow root can be harvested in three years. Once the roots are dug in midautumn, offsets can be divided or cut from the main crown for replanting. Each root section should have a bud or eye. If offsets are planted in autumn, the roots can be harvested the following fall. If planted in spring, harvest in the fall of the second year. The dried root is subject to insect infestations, so it should be stored in protected containers. Yields of about four hundred pounds of root per acre have been reported.

The tender leaves and young tops are edible and can be added sparingly to salads. In times of famine, the roots have served as a food.

The roots have been used in the cosmetic and confectionary, as well as the drug trade. Like many mallow family members, marshmallow is valued as a demulcent and emollient. It helps to alleviate local irritation, stimulate phagocytosis (mild immunostimulating activity), and inhibit mucociliary activity. The dried leaves and dried peeled or unpeeled roots are employed in modern Germany to treat irritations of the mucosa of the mouth and throat, and associated dry cough. It is also beneficial for the treatment of mild gastric mucosa inflammation. Because of the "slimy" nature of the root or leaf preparations, they act to coat mucous membranes and may delay the absorption of other remedies taken at the same time.

Traditionally, it has also been applied externally as a poultice to heal bruises, muscle aches, sprains, burns, and other local inflammations. Infusions act as an expectorant for coughs, hoarseness, bronchitis, and whooping cough. The fresh leaves have been administered to burns and insect bites. They have also been eaten for the treatment of kidney disorders. The generic name *Althaea* is derived from "altheo," meaning "to cure," referring to the plant's traditional medicinal uses.

The leaves and root both contain varying amounts of mucilagin, which is responsible for the plant's primary biological activity. The leaves have as much as 16 percent mucilage, while the roots have 25 to 35 percent. The mucilage consists of galacturonic acid, galactose, glucose, exulose, and rhamnose. Sugars, including glucose and sucrose, are present in the root as well. In Germany, marshmallow syrups state their percentage of sugar as a warning for diabetics. The root also contains a polysaccharide, named althaea mucilage 0.

Marshmallow has served as a source of fiber for coarse fabrics and rope. It has also been the basis of a pulp to make wrapping papers and bags. The cut, dried stems, harvested when the plant is flowering, are soaked in seawater for three weeks, then beaten and combed to obtain the fiber.

Mayapple
Podophyllum peltatum L.
(po-doe'-fil-lum pel-tay'-tum)
Berberidaceae—Barberry Family

Under the shade of pines and oaks in damp woods from Quebec to Florida, west to east Texas and Minnesota, lives the indigenous perennial mayapple or American mandrake. It grows to a foot and a half high and one foot broad. Smooth, roundish leaves with three to seven lobes unfold like umbrellas in the early spring. One leaf sits atop first-year plants; on older plants, two leaves are borne on a forked petiole. Drooping from the axil of the forked petioles, one white, waxy flower, one to two inches with six petals, blooms in May to June. Its odor is nauseating. The fruits, the mayapples, are the shape and size of large rose hips; they are pale banana yellow, rarely red, and about an inch and a quarter long. They have a sweet, slightly acid, hint-of-strawberry flavor. The root is a slender, knotty, creeping rhizome about one-fourth inch thick and several feet long.

In spring, mayapples are easily propagated by dividing any portion of the root. The seeds are very difficult to germinate, so root propagation is certainly preferred.

A warm, shaded location, in light but moist soil with a pH of 4 to 7, is preferable. Mayapple spreads in clumps, and should be given a space where it will not crowd more delicate plants.

When ripe, the fruit is edible, but all other parts of the plant can be fatally toxic. The highest biological activity is from spring-dug roots.

When early settlers reached American shores, they found

Indians using the root as a strong purgative, liver cleanser, emetic, and worm expellant. The Penobscots of Maine treated cancers and warts with the root. The Cherokees considered drops of the fresh plant juice beneficial for deafness.

In the last century, mayapple was widely used as a cathartic, emetic, and vermifuge. The root was valued to treat constipation, jaundice, hepatitis, fevers, and syphilis. Ingesting the root may cause vomiting, diarrhea, headache, bloating, stupor, and lowered blood pressure.

The root contains a resin—podophyllin—consisting of lignan glycosides, 20 percent of which is podophyllotoxin. Alpha-peltatin and beta-peltatin are also found in the root. Derivatives of podophyllotoxin are now used as analogs to produce semisynthetic drugs to treat refractory testicular tumors and small-cell lung cancer.

The genus *Podophyllum* (Berberidaceae) presents conservation problems in international trade. The genus,

Mayapple

represented by the North American *P. peltatum* and the Asian *P. hexandrum*, as already mentioned, is the source of a semisynthetic anticancer drug, etoposide. This drug generates revenues of between a hundred and two hundred million dollars annually for the manufacturer, Bristol-Myers Oncology. Significant declines of wild populations of *P. hexandrum* as well as of *Rauwolfia serpentina* (Indian snakeroot, the source of the tranquilizer drug reserpine) prompted India to propose these species for protection at the seventh conference of the Convention on International Trade in Endangered Species of Wild Fauna and Flora (CITES), held in Switzerland in 1989. The plants were afforded the protection of the monitoring provisions of CITES's Appendix II "in order to avoid utilization incompatible with their survival." However, chemical components derived from the plants were excluded from the listing. In essence, the listing procedure only brings attention to a conservation problem, while it does little to assure future adequate supplies of the drug or to protect wild populations of the plant. The North American *P. peltatum* does not seem to be a significant part of commercial supplies. It is an easily cultivated species that could become a future source, though it contains lower levels of biologically active constituents than *P. hexandrum* (Olin 1992).

Podophyllotoxin has been used in drugs to treat venereal warts and some skin cancers. The peltatins are responsible for mayapple's purgative effects. Ingestion of podophyllin resin and its derivatives, as well as the root of mayapple, can be fatally toxic.

MILK THISTLE

Silybum marianum (L.) Gaertner.
(sil-eye'-bum mar-ee'-ah-num)
Compositae (Asteraceae)—Aster Family
Plate 13

Milk thistle is a stout, branching annual or biennial growing from three to seven feet in height. The leaves are alternate, mottled, smooth, shiny, and scalloped, with sharp spines on the margin lobes. The common name "milk thistle," as well as the species name *marianum*, refer to the white mottling of the leaves, which medieval legend holds was caused by a drop of the Virgin Mary's milk. Accordingly, the plant is often depicted in medieval sculptures of Mary and the martyrs. The purple flower heads, up to two-and-a-

half inches in diameter, are solitary atop the tall flower stalks. The black shiny seeds are crowned with a spreading silky pappus, similar to that atop a dandelion seed. Milk thistle is native to the Mediterranean region and southwest Europe, but has been cultivated for centuries as a food, medicinal, or ornamental plant in many parts of Europe. It was generally naturalized in England in the days of John Gerarde, whose famous herbal was first published in 1597. It is now naturalized throughout much of the European continent. Milk thistle was introduced to American gardens at an early date, and has escaped from gardens in the eastern United States. In California, however, the plant has become a common naturalized weed, finding a suitable home in the Mediterraneanlike climate, where it is prolific in abandoned fields, old pastures, and roadsides throughout the state. It is also found in South America, naturalized from Uruguay to Chile and Ecuador, where it is common and well known along roadsides and in waste places. Ecuadorians know it as "Cardo Santo," a name given to other plants with prickly leaves such as the prickly poppy, *Argemone mexicana*. In Australia, it is a nuisance weed forming large thickets.

The genus name, *Silybum*, is attributed to Dioscorides, the first-century Greek physician who gave the name to a number of edible thistles. Also known in older works as Our Lady's thistle or holy thistle, *S. marianum* is one of two species in the genus. The other, *S. eburneum*, known as elephant thistle, ivory thistle, and ivory milk thistle, not found in American horticulture, is native to northeast and central Spain as well as northwest Africa.

As a specimen plant for the herb garden, with ornamental and edible possibilities, milk thistle is easily grown from seed which germinates readily. In its native haunts in the Mediterranean, it thrives in poor, dry soils. The plant is very adaptable to growing conditions, provided the soil is well drained. Seeds are sown in early spring or late fall, and germinate in one to two weeks. They are generally harvested in the second year.

Today milk thistle is grown commercially for seed production in Germany. It is one of those specialty crops that present difficult problems for the commercial grower interested in harvesting the seed, especially in timing the harvest. In the same field, individual plants may flower and go to seed when they are from three to seven feet high. In addition, some plants will bloom as early as May, or as late as August. Therefore, in a single field you may have seeds produced at height variations of four feet as much as twelve weeks apart. Once the seeds are ripe and ready for harvest, they easily shatter from the receptacle, making handling difficult. Consequently, there is a tremendous amount of loss, both in the harvest itself, as well as because of the timing problems. The seed must also be rubbed or threshed to remove the plume of pappus from its crown.

On top of these difficulties, once ready to shatter from the receptacle, the seeds can be airborne by a brisk wind and parachute into an adjacent field, perhaps causing a weed problem in future years—or a public-relations problem, if the seeds end up at a neighboring farm. Only a few highly specialized growers in Europe and South America have succeeded in developing milk thistle as a commercial crop.

All parts of the milk thistle are edible and have been used as food. It was once cultivated in gardens of Europe as a vegetable, and was still grown in "old-fashioned" British gardens at the end of the nineteenth century. The young leaves with their spines cut away can be added to spring salads. The older leaves can be eaten if the spines are trimmed off the edges. They can also be boiled or steamed as a spinach substitute. Young stalks have been peeled, soaked, and eaten like asparagus. The second-year roots can be harvested, then soaked in water overnight to remove bitterness and eaten like salsify. The roots have also been baked in pies. The bracts of the fleshy flower receptacles spread outward, and are armed with sharp spines. Historically, the unopened flower receptacle has been boiled and eaten like an artichoke. The seeds were once a part of birdseed mixes and were considered a favorite food of goldfinches. The roasted seeds have also served as a substitute for coffee (S. Foster 1991c, 1991n).

The plant has emerged as an important herb in world markets in the past twenty-five years. Its use as a liver-protecting agent dates to the earliest Greek references to the plant. The first-century Roman writer, Pliny the Elder (A.D. 23-79), who died in the eruption of Vesuvius, tells us the plant was known in Sicily, Syria, and Phoenicia, and notes that its juice, mixed with honey, is excellent for "carrying off bile."

A thousand years later, milk thistle was already well known in Germany. It is mentioned in an important medieval German manuscript, the *Physica* of Hildegard of Bingen, the first herbal written by a woman, composed about 1150 and first published in a 1533 edition, printed at Strassburg by Johann Schott. Hildegard was born in 1098 in a small German town called Böckelheim. At the age of eight, she entered the Benedictine convent at Bingen. She left Bingen

in 1148 to found a new convent at Rupertsberg, where she remained until her death in 1179. Hildegard wrote about the uses of the roots, whole plant, and leaves of milk thistle, which she called "vehedistel" or "Venus thistle." She also recorded the scientific name of milk thistle as *Carduus Mariae officinalis*. Some German publications still refer to the plant as *Carduus Mariae*. Milk thistle, she noted, was good for tumors and erysipelas (a bacterial disease causing fever, localized inflammation, etc.). However, the plant decoction was never kept on the stove for long—superstition held that this could lead to household quarrels.

In one form or another, various milk-thistle seed preparations have been used for the treatment of liver disease for over two thousand years. Historical references to it are particularly abundant in the herbal literature of the Middle Ages, especially German books. By the turn of the century, it had become an obscure medicinal plant at best. "[It] is an old remedy which had nearly passed out of use and has more recently been revived," write authors Harvey Wickes Felter and John Uri Lloyd (1906), who also noted that "congestion of the liver, spleen and kidneys is relieved by its use."

In 1929, a German researcher, H. Schulz, began to reinvestigate the potential value of old herbal remedies. He found a number of references to the use of milk thistle for liver ailments, which sparked further interest in the plant. In his 1938 *Textbook of Biological Remedies* (in German), Dr. Gerhard Madaus, (cofounder of Madaus, AG, Cologne), noted that milk-thistle seeds were the famous liver preparation advocated by the eighteenth-century German physician Rademacher, who employed it for chronic liver diseases, acute hepatitis with side aches, jaundice, and other conditions. By the 1930s, interest in clinical use of milk-thistle preparations for liver disease had again begun to grow.

Modern preparations of the seeds, including oral and injectable dosages, are made in Germany to treat liver disease, including alcohol-induced cirrhosis, as well as amanita (deathcap) mushroom poisoning. Numerous studies conducted since the late 1960s have established an experimental basis for the pharmacological efficacy and safety of silymarin, the active component in milk thistle, in a number of laboratory models. This has led to a relatively large number of double-blind clinical trials of milk thistle, primarily published in the German literature. Studies include those dealing with the effect of silymarin on toxic liver damage (mostly induced by alcohol and psychopharmaceuticals) and chronic liver disease. The scientific data shows that silymarin is a therapeutically sound medicinal plant deriva-tive. According to Rudolf Fritz Weiss (1988), few plant principles have been as extensively researched as silymarin in recent years.

The German version of the FDA (BGA) has published a positive monograph on milk-thistle seed phytomedicines, which allows the clinical use of the preparations for the supportive treatment of chronic inflammatory liver disor-ders such as chronic hepatitis, cirrhosis of the liver, and fatty infiltration of the liver by alcohol and other chemicals. Further studies have noted that pretreatment with silymarin inhibits alcohol-induced liver damage, suggesting that milk thistle is beneficial in both a preventative and curative sense.

According to the monograph, the effectiveness of silymarin is based on several spheres of activity. It has the ability to alter the outer-membrane cell structure of the liver so that certain toxins, like the highly poisonous deathcap fungus, cannot enter the cell. Silymarin stimulates RNA polymerase A (also known as polymerase I), enhancing ribosome protein synthesis, resulting in activating the regen-erative capacity of the liver to develop new cells. It also acts to scavenge free radicals and leukotrienes. In simple terms, silymarin has three-fold benefits: it helps to stabilize liver cell membranes, simulate protein synthesis, and accelerate the process of regeneration in damaged liver tissue (S. Foster 1991c, 1991n).

A water-soluble chemical fraction derived from the seeds of milk thistle, known as silibinin (not to be confused with silymarin or other oral forms), is now available in virtually every poison-control center in western Europe as an adjunct therapy in treating deathcap mushroom poisoning. The deathcap mushroom (*Amanita phalloides*) is responsible for between 10 to 50 percent of mushroom poisoning cases in Europe. Mortality rates from ingesting deathcap mush-rooms in adults are conservatively placed at a little over 22 percent. If administered in time (during the first eight hours), silibinin in intravenous drip-injection therapies has helped push these rates below any previous levels (S. Foster 1991c, 1991n).

Any adverse effects from ingesting any plant part, except for the possibility of choking on the leaf spines or a mild laxative action from the seeds, are not reported.

As early as 1958, attempts were made to isolate the active component of milk thistle, though the components were not characterized until the late 1960s. A research team headed by H. Wagner at the University of Munich was successful in identifying silymarin, which was then believed to be a single compound. Improved chemical-separation methods later revealed that silymarin was not a single entity, but a complex of chemicals known as flavonolignans. The primary compo-nents structurally characterized from silymarin include silybinin, silydianin, and silychristin. Collectively, these isoflavonolignans are found in concentrations of 4 to 6 percent in the ripe seeds. European milk-thistle products, some of which are available on the American market, are standardized to 80 percent silymarin. A number of other flavonolignans have also been located in the seeds, including apigenin, silybonol, and myristic, palmitic, stearic, and oleic acids (S. Foster 1991c, 1991n).

MINTS

Mentha spicata L., *M.* x *piperita* L., *M. suaveolens* J.F. Ehrh., *M. requienii* Benth.
(men'-tha spy-kay'-ta; pie-per-ee'-ta; swa-vee-oh'-lenz; rek-quee-en'-ee-ey)
Labiatae (Lamiaceae)—Mint Family.

There are only about twenty true species in the *Mentha* genus, but hybridization has created at least twenty-three hundred named variations, half of which are synonyms, while the rest are legitimate infraspecific names (Tucker et al. 1980). Most of these species are Eurasian natives.

Spearmint, *M. spicata*, is a perennial growing to two-and-a-half feet high, spreading by underground root run-ners. Its leaves are smooth, shiny, wrinkled, lance shaped, sharply toothed, and about two inches long. The white, pink, or lilac flowers appear in midsummer.

M. x *piperita*, peppermint, once thought to be a distinct species or a hybrid between *M. aquatica* and a cross of *M. spicata* and *M. rotundifolia* (Ruttle 1938), is now believed to be a hybrid between spearmint, *M. spicata* L., and water mint, *M. aquatica* L. (Murray, Lincoln, and Marble 1972). Peppermint is a perennial growing to three feet tall, spread-ing by runners traveling across the soil's surface. The stem is usually reddish purple, and smooth. The leaves are similar to spearmint's, though often longer and less wrinkled. The pink or lilac flowers appear in mid or late summer. *M.* x *piperita* var. *citrata*, orange or bergamot mint, has a distinctive odor like that of orange rind. Historically, pep-permint has variously been considered a botanically unstable species, subspecies, or type of *Mentha* spp. which has a high percentage of menthol in its essential oil, or contains oils possessing the properties of peppermint oil.

M. suaveolens, apple mint, is a perennial that grows to four feet tall with hairy, oval-shaped, toothed leaves. The tight flower spikes branch and produce tiny white or pink flowers in midsummer. A smaller, variegated cultivar, 'Variegata', has a pineapplelike fragrance and is often sold under the name "pineapple mint."

M. requienii, Corsican mint, is native to Corsica and Sardinia. It is a creeping perennial herb which forms a dense ground cover. The stems are threadlike and the leaves are entire (without teeth), nearly round in shape, and no more than three-eighths of an inch long. It produces tiny, inconspicuous flowers in midsummer.

Mentha x *piperita,* Peppermint Harvest, Trout Lake Farm, Trout Lake, Washington

Because of mint's propensity to hybridize, buying and planting seeds is a futile effort in my opinion. You never know what will come up. Begin with stem or root cuttings. At the Sabbathday Lake Shaker community, I started a peppermint bed using ten seedlings in two-inch pots purchased from a local nursery. By the second summer of growth, the plants covered a hundred square feet. In the third spring, I dug one quarter of the roots from the bed and planted them in ten 250-foot rows, spaced four feet apart. After two months of growth, the plants completely covered the entire 250-by-50-foot area. It was impossible to distinguish the original rows. Any piece of root with a joint or node (about every inch) can produce a plant. Divide the root runners in spring.

Mints require a rich, moist soil with good drainage; pH should be neutral to slightly alkaline. Full sun is necessary except for Corsican mint, which requires at least 50 percent shade. If planted in a small garden, mints should stand alone or have some kind of growth barrier like metal or tile placed below the soil around the beds. This will prevent the roots from taking over the garden.

The largest organic herb farm in North America, Trout Lake Farm in Trout Lake, Washington, has about fifty acres

of peppermint, twenty-five of spearmint, and twenty of catnip, to name just a few crops. The farm is nestled about ten miles south of Mount Adams, a twelve-thousand-foot peak. Lon Johnson, the farm's owner, plants certified mint stock from a state university experiment station. Young plants are cultivated with a special harrow until they reach a height of about four inches, when they are cultivated with tractor-mounted beet hoes and hand hoes. As the runners fill in between the rows, hand-hoeing becomes particularly important. Trout Lake's fields are virtually weed-free without the use of herbicides. The mints are sometimes harvested twice each season, as they reach full bloom. Harvesting is performed with a cutter bar, similar to that used for harvesting hay, then windrowed with a hay rake, and allowed to dry in the field for a day, weather permitting. The following morning, when the dew has dried from the leaves, the rows are turned with a windrow turner and allowed to dry for another day. When the leaves have dried until they easily "crack" from the stems, a combine is run through the field to separate stem and leaf material. The leaves are transferred from the combine's bin into heavy-gauge plastic bags, where they are stored until cut and sifted at the farm's milling facilities. Trout Lake Farm's herbs are the highest quality available. Between eight hundred and two thousand pounds of mint can be produced on an acre.

Peppermint and spearmint are often neglected as culinary herbs, but can be added to tossed and potato salads, desserts, beverages, carrot dishes, or sautéed with parsnips. Peppermint and spearmint should be used more often. I think the fresh or dried leaves definitely enhance the flavor of steamed carrots. A couple of teaspoons of finely chopped fresh leaves, or a sprinkling of dried leaves, are a wonderful addition to any tossed salad. While many people turn up their noses at parsnips, peppermint leaf, dried or fresh, can turn it into a gourmet delight. Slice parsnips very thin, sauté in butter or peanut oil, and liberally add finely chopped peppermint leaf for flavor.

Peppermint is probably the most heavily consumed herb tea in North America, and it is one of the best. Peppermint tea products are widely available from health-food stores and supermarket shelves. You can buy bulk dried peppermint leaf for making your own tea. Simply put a couple of teaspoonfuls of dried mint leaf in a tea ball and steep in hot (not boiling) water for ten minutes or so, to suit your taste buds. Fresh peppermint harvested from your garden makes a good sun tea. Cut a large, full handful, then bruise the leaves in your hands or twist the bunch of leaves as if wringing out a washcloth, releasing the essential oil. Place in a gallon of water in the sun for about an hour. The tea will be very light in color, but will have a strong peppermint flavor. Iced, it is a refreshing summer beverage.

Mints are high in calcium, vitamin A, vitamin C, and riboflavin, and contain phosphorus, potassium, and niacin.

Peppermint leaf, dried and fresh, and the essential oil distilled from fresh or dried leaves are widely used in foods, pharmaceuticals, cosmetics, and folk medicine. Medicinally, peppermint is antispasmodic, carminative, stomachic, stimulative, and tonic. A tea will help allay insomnia, upset stomachs, indigestion, nervous tension, headache, colds, cramps, diarrhea, nausea, and many other minor ailments. The major use of the oil is for flavoring toothpastes and other mouth-care products, as well as chewing gums. The high price of peppermint oil thwarts its potential as raw material for the production of menthol. Peppermint oil has antimicrobial activity. Peppermint extracts have shown antiviral behavior against Newcastle disease, herpes simplex, and other viruses. Oil of peppermint is experimentally antispasmodic (Leung 1980). Other studies have revealed that peppermint oil inhibits gastrointestinal smooth-muscle spasms in humans and reduces colonic motility (Sigmond and MacNally 1969; Taylor, Luscombe, and Duthie 1983;

Duthie 1981).

Attention on peppermint oil is now focusing on its therapeutic value, rather than its assets as a flavoring ingredient. Rees, Evans, and Rhodes (1979) reported results of a clinical trial with eighteen patients with active irritable bowel syndrome, characterized by recurrent colicky abdominal pain, a feeling of distention, and variations in bowel habits. Patients were given either one to two enteric-coated (hard-coated), peppermint-oil capsules (to prevent absorption in the stomach) three times a day for three weeks or peanut-oil capsules. Patients felt considerably better and experienced relief from abdominal symptoms while taking the peppermint-oil capsules as compared with the placebo. Occasionally peppermint oil was released into the stomach, causing heartburn. The treatment was given between meals rather than with meals (S. Foster 1991d).

A study by Somerville, Richmond, and Bell (1984) suggests that the oil is released in the colon in enteric-coated capsules, while it is absorbed in the stomach with gelatin-coated capsules. To be effective in the treatment of spastic-colon syndrome, the oil must reach the colon before it is metabolized; therefore the dosage must not break down in the stomach.

Another British research team, Leicester and Hunt (1982) found that a diluted suspension of peppermint oil, sprayed on endoscopes and inserted in the colon during colonoscopies, reduced colonic spasm during the procedure in the twenty patients on which the technique was tried. Antispasmodic drugs usually associated with the diagnostic procedure have to be administered intravenously while the patient is in an uncomfortable position. Recognizing that peppermint oil is a safe substance and produces local smooth-muscle relaxation, these researchers sprayed the diluted oil onto the endoscope itself as a more convenient means to relax the colon during colonoscopy (S. Foster 1991d).

Ironically, while the rest of the world is increasing therapeutic application of peppermint oil, the FDA, in its ongoing over-the-counter (OTC) drug-review process, has removed peppermint from its list of effective digestive aids. During the OTC review process, manufacturers submit new data on safety and efficacy to support OTC drugs. Since no company came forward with information on peppermint, it was simply dropped from the list of safe and effective remedies. In Germany, on the other hand, peppermint oil is allowed in products for cramplike discomfort in the upper gastrointestinal tract and bile ducts, as well as irritable colon, catarrh of the upper lungs, inflammation of the mouth, and externally for muscle and nerve pain. The Germans consider peppermint oils to be spasmolytic, carminative, cholagogic, antibacterial, expectorant, and cooling. Peppermint oil is also employed in Europe to treat gallbladder inflammation and gallstones; however, for these conditions or bile-duct obstruction, it is advised only under the direction of a physician. It is not placed on or around the nose of babies and small children, as peppermint oil may cause spasms of the larynx or bronchi (S. Foster 1991d).

Peppermint oil contains menthol, menthone, menthyl acetate, and menthofuran, along with viridoflorol, which is known only in peppermint. Menthol is the primary component of its essential oil (29 to 48 percent). Ingestion or external application of synthetic menthol (artificially produced by the hydrogenation of thymol) are well known for their toxic effects, so information on synthetic menthol should not be mistakenly associated with peppermint oil. Peppermint herb also has flavonoids, phytol, tocopherols, carotenoids, betain, choline, azulenes, rosmarinic acid, and tannins (Leung 1980).

Spearmint oil is characterized by a high content of carvone (67 to 80 percent) with lesser amounts of pulegone, limonene, menthone, menthol, cineol, and many other compounds. The oil is extensively used for flavoring toothpaste, mouthwash, chewing gums, and candy.

The United States produces more than 80 percent of the world's peppermint and spearmint oil. Peppermint does not seem to have been known in commerce until the eighteenth century. The herbarium of the English botanist John Ray (1628–1705) has one of the oldest peppermint specimens, collected in Hertfordshire County in the south of England. Ray first described the plant in his *Synopsis Stirpium Britannicarum* (1696), and by the time of publication of the third edition, he declared that it was superior to all mints for stomach weakness and diarrhea (Flückiger and Hanbury 1879).

Commercial cultivation of peppermint began in England about 1750, and on the European continent, it was grown near Utrecht in the Netherlands by 1770. English production peaked by 1850, after which American markets began to provide stiff competition. The first commercial peppermint appeared in the United States in the 1790s in Cheshire, Berkshire County, Massachusetts. By 1812, peppermint was being cultivated commercially for its oil in Ashfield, Massachusetts. Production then spread to New York, Ohio, and Michigan, where from 1839–1889 mint growing became a big business (Landing 1969). Peppermint is now raised commercially, mostly for its essential oil, in Indiana, Wisconsin, Oregon, Washington, and Idaho (Foster 1991d).

In 1991, United States peppermint oil generated $86.9 million in revenue. That year, 2,934 metric tons of peppermint oil were produced in Idaho, Indiana, Oregon, Washington, and Wisconsin on 44,800 hectares (110,700 acres). In the same year, the spearmint-oil crop, centered in Idaho, Indiana, Michigan, Oregon, Washington, and Wisconsin, was valued at $42.4 million. Over 1,300 metric tons of oil were processed from 16,470 hectares (40,697 acres).

MOTHERWORT
Leonurus cardiaca L.
(lee-on'-or-us card-ee-ay'ca)
Labiatae (Lamaiceae)—Mint Family
Plate 13

Motherwort is a smooth-stemmed to slightly hairy perennial growing from two to as much as ten feet tall. The main stem, often branching at the base, is stout and strongly four-angled. When not in flower, the plant may be mistaken for mugwort. The opposite leaves, unlike most mint family members, are lobed, with three to seven unequal, toothed lobes. The upper leaves are lanceolate to three-lobed. The flowers occur in tight whorls at the leaf axils, giving the plant a showy wandlike, spike appearance in the garden. The calyx teeth are almost as long as the tube, and are very distinctly five-veined. They include white or pale pink flowers, often with purple spots. The upper lip of the flower is densely hairy on the back. A ring of hairs can be observed inside the flower tubes. Motherwort blooms from June through August. The strongly pointed calices, which surround the four nutlike one-seeded fruits, persist once the plant has dried. This feature, coupled with the rather stout stems, makes it a good filler for dried flower arrangements.

Motherwort is found through much of Europe except for the far north, northern islands, and the Mediterranean region. The plant is highly variable throughout Europe. It has casually established itself as a scattered weed, escaped from cultivation, throughout much of the United States and southern portions of Canada. It has a strong fragrance, though not a pleasant one, unlike so many of our mint-family herb-garden subjects.

The plant is easy to cultivate; in fact, it may become weedy in some garden situations. It is easily grown from seed and self-sows freely. Seeds, planted in midautumn or spring, after danger of frost has passed, germinate in about ten days. It may also be propagated from division of the roots in early spring or midautumn. Space plants about one foot apart. Motherwort prefers a sunny situation (though it will tolerate some shade), and likes a slightly alkaline, well-drained sandy loam. It will do well in any average garden situation. Motherwort is hardy in all parts of the United States and does not require any special attention (other than weeding it out of the garden if it self-sows too freely). The gardener should be aware that the plant will produce contact dermatitis in some individuals.

Traditionally, motherwort is harvested in full bloom in mid to late summer. Chinese studies indicate that the active chemical components are at their highest concentrations when the plant is in bloom. Before flowering, the quantity of active components is much reduced. The whole fresh herb or dried herb can be used.

European motherwort and its Chinese counterparts have been valued for sedative, antispasmodic, emmenagogic, cardiotonic, hypotensive, and slightly astringent properties. In *A Modern Herbal* (1931), Maude Grieve states that it is diaphoretic (induces sweating), nervine, and is especially useful in "female weakness and disorders" (2:555). She also informs us that older writers mention there is no better herb for strengthening and gladdening the heart, or for palpitations of the heart "that arise from hysteric causes" (2:555).

While the historical traditions of China (several thousand years) and Europe (several hundred years) show parallel patterns employing motherwort for treatment of menstrual disorders, and its sedative effects, uterine-tonic benefits in childbirth, diuretic attributes, heart-regulating qualities, and ability to increase blood circulation, our understanding of the scientific basis for these parallels is sketchy. In this regard, it is interesting to note, too, that several North American native groups adopted European motherwort as a medicinal plant. The Cherokees used the herb as a sedative for nervous afflictions. The Delaware, Micmac, Mohegan, and Shinnecock (Montauk) tribes all valued European motherwort as a treatment for gynecological diseases or ailments. A review of experimental data in the Chinese literature shows that *Leonurus artemisia* extracts stimulate the uterus, increase blood circulation by dilating blood vessels, "excite" the central nervous system, and in an inject-

able form, have diuretic effects (S. Foster 1988a).

In a country where heart disease is still the number-one killer, it is nothing short of amazing that public funds are not directed toward researching this and other herbal drugs of historical benefit in the management of heart problems. Here we have clearly established patterns of use from cultures on opposite sides of the world. What's more, the plant kingdom already provides some of the main agents used in the management and treatment of heart disease—the cardiac glycosides of foxglove (*Digitalis*).

Both European motherwort and its Chinese counterpart (*L. artemesia*) share the alkaloids leonurine, stachydrine, and leonurinine, as well as rutin. European motherwort contains tannins, an essential oil, and fixed oils in the seeds, as well as palmitic, oleic, stearic, linoleic, and linolenic acids (S. Foster 1988a; Foster and Yue 1992).

MUGWORT

Artmisia vulgaris L., *A. douglasiana* Bess.
(are-te-miz'-i-a vul-gay'-ris; dug-las-i-an'-na)
Compositae (Asteraceae)—Aster Family
Plate 13

Artemisia vulgaris, mugwort, is a six-foot perennial with a creeping rhizome, native to Eurasia. The four-inch-long, oval, divided leaves are dark green on the upper surface with tiny whitish hairs underneath. The purple-red, one-eighth-inch wide flowers occur in loose panicles in late summer. Its close relative, *A. Douglasiana*, is similar in appearance and native to the western United States. *A. vulgaris* is found in most of Europe, though it is rare in both the extreme north and south. In the United States, mugwort has become naturalized and is established throughout most of the eastern United States and adjacent Canada.

Mugwort is easily propagated by dividing the rhizomes while they are still dormant in spring. Dig up the clumps and break them by hand into sections. Plant in rows on eighteen-inch centers.

Mugwort is an adaptable plant, growing in a wide variety of situations, but prefers full sun and a relatively rich, moist soil. It is tolerant of cold and does not need winter protection. The leaves are collected as the plant comes into bloom. Typically the leaves are dried in the shade, though in China they are dried in the sun. Turning them carefully to make sure that they dry uniformly.

Both mugwort herb and mugwort root are used in

they are black. They are mixed evenly with vinegar before stir-frying. About one hundred pounds of the dried herb are mixed with fifteen pounds of vinegar. During the process, the leaves are stirred frequently to make sure that they don't begin to smoke. The whole mass is dried at room temperature. The herb is used sparingly in China. Some people may have a toxic reaction, including dry throat, thirst, stomach and intestinal discomfort, nausea, vertigo, ringing in the ears, and other symptoms (Foster and Yue 1992).

The most famous use for the dried herb in China is as a moxabustion. Moxa is made from the leaves by beating and rubbing them between the hands until only fine woody fibers remain. The mass is combed to remove the fibers, then formed into little cones. For many centuries, these cones have been placed on the skin at certain acupuncture points, then burned to stimulate circulation for the treatment of various conditions.

The leaves, which are highly variable in both the content and quality of the essential oil, generally contain linalool, 1,8-cineole, beta-thujone, borneol, pinenes, vulgarole, and many other components. A sesquiterpene lactone, vulgarin, is also found in the leaves along with flavonoids and coumarin derivatives.

Urtica dioica, Stinging Nettle

modern phytotherapy in Europe, primarily for the treatment of gastrointestinal complaints such as colic, diarrhea, constipation, intestinal spasms, and indigestion. They help to stimulate the secretion of gastric juices and bile. Traditionally, the leaves have been employed to expel worms, treat menstrual disorders and irregular periods, promote blood flow, and as a mild sedative. Some people have an allergic reaction to the plant, and given its effect on menstruation, it is, of course, not recommended during pregnancy or lactation. Despite its continued use, many therapeutic claims for the plant have not been substantiated.

In China, mugwort allays bleeding of the womb and treats threatened abortion, as well as regulates the menses. Externally, a decoction of the herb is a treatment for eczema. Some Chinese prescriptions call for the "charcoaled leaves." The processing method involves stir-frying the leaves until

NETTLE
Urtica dioica L. and related species.
(er-ti'-ka die-oh'-i-ka)
Urticaceae—Nettle Family

About fifty species of nettles grow throughout the world. *Urtica dioica* is a Eurasian native widely naturalized in North America. Most people neglect this plant—until they walk through a patch while wearing short pants. Nettle is a perennial growing from two to six feet tall. The ovate, sharp-pointed leaves have a heart-shaped base and are deeply toothed. Leaves may reach six inches in length. Both the leaves and the fibrous stems are covered with tiny, hollow, silica-tipped hairs which release an irritant when touched. Drooping from the leaf axils, racemes or panicles of inconspicuous greenish flowers emerge from June to September.

The plant has a creeping persistent rootstock, forming extensive patches.

Nettles can be grown from seed, cuttings, or root divisions. Divisions are best made in autumn after the leaves have dried back.

A damp, rich soil under full sun or partial shade is preferable. In their native habitat, nettles will often grow along edges of streams or in moist pastures. Reportedly, when one nettle is planted among ten seedlings of such aromatic herbs as valerian, marjoram, sage, peppermint, and angelica, the nettle will substantially increase the oil content of these herbs. When added to compost piles, nettles activate the decomposition process. Nettles themselves compost into a rich humus. In commerical plantings, it has been determined that adding nitrogen to the soil produces greater amounts of growth. Three to four harvests a year can be obtained. The second harvest generates the highest yield.

Harvest in May or June before nettles begin flowering. Handle fresh plants with gloves. The leaves dry quickly. Once cooked or dried, nettles lose their sting, which is caused by the ends of the sharp fragile hairs penetrating the surface of the skin, breaking off, then releasing their irritating toxins. The sting can be neutralized by rubbing the affected area with either mashed jewelweed leaves (*Impatiens pallida* or *I. biflora*), yellow dock leaves (*Rumex crispus*), or the juice of the nettles themselves.

The spring shoots make a tasty green when cooked. The dried herb can be sprinkled in salads, soups, vegetables, and other foods for a subtle saline flavor and a rich supply of iron, magnesium, potassium, calcium, vitamin A, protein, and dietary fiber.

The leaves have diuretic, astringent, blood-building, depurative, and galactogenic properties. An infusion reportedly improves blood hemoglobin. The powdered leaves and juice will lessen bleeding from excessive menstruation, nosebleeds, and hemorrhoids. Smoke inhaled from burning leaves is a treatment for asthma and bronchitis. Nettles stimulate blood circulation and have been employed as a spring tonic to clear chronic skin ailments. In Europe, nettle-leaf tea or extracts have been of value in the treatment of skin eruptions such as eczema. Traditionally, nettle has been used for rheumatism and gout.

French researchers published results of a clinical study (Belaiche and Lievoux 1991) that explored the effects of fluid extract of the root of two species of stinging nettle (*U. dioica* and *U. urens*), which was administered to sixty-seven patients suffering from varying degrees of severity of prostate enlargement. The patients were divided into three groups, depending upon the number of times they had to pass urine in the night. The first group of twelve patients, who had to get up twice a night, showed considerable improvement after three weeks of treatment. Ten of the patients no longer had to get up. In the second group of twenty-seven patients who had to get up three times a night, thirteen no longer had to

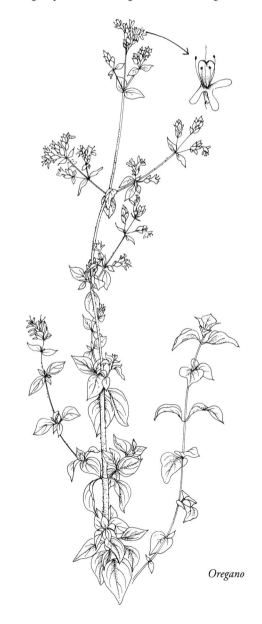

Oregano

get up, and nocturia was reduced to twice a night for ten patients. Four patients had no improvement. The third group of twenty-eight patients, who at the beginning of the study had to urinate more than three times a night, showed less improvement. Therefore, the extract of stinging nettle was found to reduce frequency of nocturia primarily in patients with less severe conditions.

A recent study looked at the effects of a freeze-dried stinging-nettle preparation in the treatment of allergic rhinitis. Of the sixty-nine patients who completed the study, 58 percent reported moderate or good improvement in their symptoms (Mittman 1990). In addition, extracts of water-soluble fractions of stinging nettle have significant antibacterial activity against *Staphylococcus aureus* and *S. albus.*

The stinging hairs contain formic acid, histamine, and acetylcholine. The herb also has a coumarin which was found to have a toning effect on smooth uterine muscles in mouse experiments and a slight depressive impact on the central nervous system.

Nettles were developed as a fiber plant, and once commercially grown for that purpose in Germany, France, and Sweden. The fiber, contained in cultivated plants up to 15 percent by weight, could be combed to about a yard in length, and when processed was considered soft and flexible. If prepared with special care, the material was considered to be as fine as silk. The fiber has been used for cordage, fishing lines, and sailcloth.

OREGANOS

Origanum vulgare L., *O. vulgare* subsp. *hirtum* (Link) Ietswaart (*O. heracleoticum* auct., non L.),
O. onites L., *O. dictamnus* L.
(or-i-gay'-num vul-gay'-ree;
oh-nye'teez; dik-tam'-nus)
Labiatae (Lamiaceae)—Mint Family

Oregano more properly refers to a flavor than to one particular plant. Plants known as "oregano" have an essential oil dominated by a phenol known as carvacrol, which has a characteristic fragrance that many associate with pizza. Trying to figure out the correct botanical designations of the plants sold as oregano in American horticulture has presented a nightmare until only recently. Fortunately, herb taxonomist Art Tucker, a research professor at Delaware State College, along with Elizabeth Rollins, past president of the Herb Society of America, have sorted out the American

oregano scene in several popular and technical publications (Tucker 1974, 1986, 1992; Tucker and Rollins 1989; Rollins and Tucker 1992). They have documented sixteen named species of *Origanum* (including hybrids) as well as two garden hybrids, all of which are under cultivation in the United States. The treatment of oreganos in *Herbal Bounty* followed *Hortus Third. Herbal Renaissance* is based on the work of Tucker and Rollins.

The genus *Origanum* is represented by thirty-six species native to Eurasia. Thirteen species originate in Europe, primarily the Mediterranean region. This is where most of our cultivated oreganos come from. A member of the mint family, this genus is characterized by tight cylindrical heads of sessile flowers called spikelets or spicules. Leaflike bracts cover the flowers just as shingles overlap on a roof. Plants in the genus *Origanum* are dwarf shrubs, or annual, biennial, or perennial herbs native to the Mediterranean region and central Asia.

In his first attempt to unravel the oregano saga, Art Tucker bought a bottle of commercial oregano, and found a few seeds in it which he planted out. What sprouted from the seeds was a surprise. He found *O. vulgare* subsp. *hirtum,* as well as pot marjoram (*O. onites*), a hairy form of spearmint, European pennyroyal, and a scentless lemon balm (*Melissa officinalis* subsp. *altissima*). Tucker discovered that oregano used to be harvested wild in the mountains of Greece. As wild populations declined, commercial interests turned to Turkey, where peasants picked anything that smelled or looked like oregano. Realizing that little of the *O. vulgare* subsp. *hirtum* was actually cultivated in American herb gardens, he introduced it via Well-Sweep Herb Farm in 1979 (Tucker 1992). Now it is readily available.

True Greek or Turkish oregano (*O. vulgare* subsp. *hirtum*) is a perennial up to two feet high, which spreads to form a dense cluster. The green, rounded leaves are less than one inch long. Beneath the small, not-very-showy whorls of small white flowers are green bracts. The calyces have five teeth of nearly equal length. The flowers are three to eleven millimeters long, and two-lipped for about a third of their length. The stamens, with filaments about half as long as the flower, protrude slightly outside the flower's mouth. The leaves and calyces are usually covered with glandular dots, and the stems with rough, coarse, glandular hairs. The branches and spikes are not slender. Art Tucker describes the plant's odor as a very pungent, penetrating smell, almost like creosote. Much material sold under the name *O. heracleoticum* is now known as *O. vulgare* subsp. *hirtum.*

One of the most commonly encountered plants sold as oregano, both by seed and plant sources, is actually wild marjoram, *O. vulgare* subsp. *vulgare.* It is similar to Greek oregano in that it is a perennial to two feet high also spreading to form dense clumps, with rounded green leaves less than an inch long. The bracts beneath the pink or sometimes reddish flowers are purple. Its leaves and calyces do not have the conspicuous glandular hairs typical of Greek oregano. Art Tucker describes its fragrance as "weak musty." It is the species that is naturalized in much of the United States, but unfortunately, when grown from seed, it has a very weak fragrance and makes a poor culinary herb. It is best suited for an ornamental.

A number of additional subspecies and cultivars of *O. vulgare* are available for American gardens. One is *O. vulgare* subsp. *virens,* which, unlike typical subspecies of this plant, has membranous yellow-green bracts. *O. vulgare* subsp. *vulgare* 'Aureum' is a cultivar with yellow-green leaves and a light fragrance. It is often sold under the name of "golden creeping oregano." Another cultivar, *O. vulgare* subsp. *vulgare* 'Humile', sometimes known by the name 'Compactum Nanum', is a dwarf ground cover which reaches eight inches tall and has small dark green leaves. To honor the Dutch botanist Dr. J. H. Ietswaart, whose 1980 publication on the taxonomy of *Origanum* serves as the basis for their work, Tucker and Rollins named a cultivar with golden yellow, round, wrinkled leaves *O. vulgare* subsp. *vulgare* 'Dr. Ietswaart.'

O. onites L., pot marjoram, is a hairy dwarf perennial shrub, with woody stems at the base, which grows to one foot tall. The leaves are oval or rounded, slightly pointed, one-fourth to three-fourths of an inch long, sessile, and sparsely toothed. The flowers are in a dense terminal corymb up to three inches across. Each spikelet is about three-fourths of an inch long. The bracts are pointed and about one-eighth of an inch long. The one-fourth-inch-long flowers are pale creamy white. This is a tender plant and not cultivated as widely as other species. It is a close relative of sweet marjoram; both have calyces rounded at the top with a deep slit down one side. The calyx is bractlike in appearance. Pot marjoram is a Mediterranean native.

In its native habitats in the mountains of southern Greece and on the Greek islands of the Aegean Sea, extending to western and southern Turkey, *O. onites* produces two types of leaves. In order to adapt to the long dry summers, it puts out small leaves, while growing larger leaves during the winter months. A study of native Greek populations of the wild plant has revealed quantitative and qualitative differences in the essential oil. Some populations yielded 1.84 percent essential oil, while one had 4.37 percent. The carvacrol content in the oil ranged from 51 to 84.5 percent. While the major compounds in the oil were always consistent, wide variation was observed in its minor components. Compared with the highly variable *O. vulgare, O. onites* is relatively stable in its oil yield and quality, probably due to the overall consistency in its habitat (Vokou, Kokkini, and Bessière 1988).

O. dictamnus L., dittany of Crete, is the genus's most distinctive looking plant. It is a tender perennial growing to a foot in height, with opposite, rounded or oval, white, woolly leaves. The loose panicles of three-eighths-inch-long bracts have a hoplike appearance. Flowers are pink, and about one-half inch long. It blooms in the summer or autumn, and hails from the isle of Crete.

Other oreganos cultivated in American gardens include *O. x majoricum,* also known as hardy sweet marjoram or Italian oregano. It arises from a hybrid between *O. majorana* (sweet marjoram) and *O. vulgare* subsp. *virens.* This small shrublet, which reaches two feet tall, has small oval, gray-green leaves, and cylindrical upright spikes with small white flowers. Its fragrance is more like that of sweet marjoram than oregano. One cultivar, *O. x majoricum* 'Well-Sweep', introduced at Well-Sweep Herb Farm, is a variegated form. A unique ornamental is *O. rotundifolium,* which as the species name implies, has distinctly round leaves. Its cultivar, 'Kent Beauty', sports attractive pink to purple bracts. Most of the other species available, including *O. calcaratum, O. dayi, O. laevigatum, O. libanoticum, O. microphyllum, O. sipyleum,* and *O. syriacum* are primarily found in the gardens of collectors. *O. syriacum,* sometimes used as a commercial species of oregano, is actually the "hyssop" referred to in Luther's translation of the Bible, not *Hyssopus,* the common garden hyssop.

Other plants with an oregano fragrance, sometimes a part of commercial supplies of the herb, include *Lippia graveolens,* a member of the verbena family grown in Mexico and sold as "Mexican oregano." Additional plants include members of the genera *Coleus, Salvia, Satureja, Thymus, Monarda, Hedeoma, Calamintha,* and *Lantana.* As many as forty different plant species have been reported as present in commercial oregano sources. In essence, plants containing high percentages of the phenol carvacrol (over 55 percent) and lesser amounts of thymol in their essential oils have an oregano flavor and aroma.

Oregano is propagated from seeds, stem cuttings, or root division. Seeds are sometimes slow to germinate. Both dittany of Crete and pot marjoram are not hardy in cold climates, and must be started anew each year, or wintered indoors. It is best to propagate oreganos asexually, as seed-grown plants may not be true to flavor or may even be completely flavorless. When buying plants, stroke the leaves to make sure the plant has some fragrance.

For best success in cultivating oreganos, you should keep in mind the origins of many of the *Origanum* species in American horticulture—they come primarily from the dry, rocky, limy soils of the mountains of southern Europe. Oreganos like a light, well-drained, slightly alkaline soil with full sun. In a rich, moist soil, their aroma and flavor may be weaker. Most oreganos are tender perennials. They require a very well-drained soil. According to Rollins and Tucker, oreganos are more likely to survive cold temperatures than high humidity or poor air circulation. Composition of the essential oil, and hence the plant's flavor and fragrance, vary, depending upon the species, the genetic makeup, the origin of the plant, and the geographic area in which it is grown. Harvest oregano as plants begin to bloom. An established planting can be cut back two to six times during the growing season. Yields of twelve hundred to twenty-five hundred pounds of dried leaf per acre are reported. For the fresh market, oregano should be stored at 32° F for optimum shelflife.

Oregano contains vitamin A (beta-carotene), niacin, phosphorus, potassium, iron, calcium, magnesium, and traces of zinc.

I sometimes wondered why my grandmother wasn't familiar with oregano from childhood, until I discovered that the postwar baby-boom generation was the first group of Americans to grow up with oregano. After World War II, GIs who had tasted oregano-rich pizza in Italy made it popular in the United States. Oregano is good with tomato dishes, meats, omelets, beans, and deviled eggs, and has a special affinity with basil.

Stimulative, carminative, diaphoretic, diuretic, nervine, and emmenagogic properties have been attributed to oregano. It has been employed to treat indigestion, headaches, diarrhea, nervous tension, insect bites, toothache, earache, rheumatism, and coughs due to whooping cough and bronchitis

(primarily for its antispasmodic effects).

The oil contains carvacrol and thymol as the primary components. These two phenols may constitute as much as 90 percent of it. They possess fungicidal and worm-expellant properties. *O. vulgare* subsp. *vulgare* has up to 5.5 percent (dry weight) rosmarinic acid (more than twice as much as rosemary). Rosemarinic acid is antiviral, antibacterial, antiinflammatory, and antioxidant. Before hops were introduced into the brewing industry, oregano was used as a flavoring for ale and beer.

PARSLEY

Petroselinum crispum (Mill.) Nym. ex A.W. Hill.
(pet-ro-sel-eye'-num kris'-pum)
Umbelliferae (Apiaceae)—Carrot Family

Perhaps no other herb is as familiar in its fresh form as parsley. What plate of restaurant food is served without a sprig tucked to the side of the main course? At meal's end, it is often the only thing left on the plate, even though it may well have been the most nutritious part of the meal. In the United States, it is the most heavily consumed fresh herb. A 1983 survey of shipments to twenty-three major metropolitan areas showed a consumption of over twenty million pounds of fresh parsley in those cities alone each year! Major production states include California, New Jersey, Florida, and Texas.

Parsley has been cultivated for many centuries, and is now naturalized in much of Europe. It is probably native to southeastern Europe and western Asia, though its exact origin is uncertain. It is a biennial growing to six or eight inches in height the first year, then reaching three feet when in flower. The smooth, bright green leaves are deeply divided. Tiny yellowish-green flowers are borne on loose, compound umbels. Parsley can be divided into three basic varieties: curled parsley (var. *crispum*); flat-leaved or Italian parsley (var. *neapolitanum*); and the large turnip-rooted parsleys (var. *tuberosum*). Within each of these groups, there are several cultivars. *P. crispum* var. *crispum* has curled and crisp leaves. Its cultivar, 'Perfection', has stiff, erect stems, creating a clean bunch which is easy to harvest. 'Triplecurled' has tightly crisped, dark green leaves, which look from a distance like broccoli heads. *P. crispum* var. *neapolitanum,* Italian parsley, has flat leaves similar to celery. *P. crispum* var. *tuberosum,* turnip-root parsley or Hamburg parsley, produces thick parsniplike taproots and tall fernlike leaves.

Petroselinum crispum, Parsley

inches in raised beds.

Close planting in an enriched soil will produce higher yields of fresh parsley. If a spring cutting is desired, parsley can be planted in the autumn, then wintered-over for spring harvest. Six pounds of seed will sow an acre in a carefully planted small-scale operation. In larger areas, where it is more difficult to control conditions, as much as twenty to sixty pounds of seed may be needed to fill an acre. The wide variance in seeding rates is due to many factors. In cold, wet soils, the seeds germinate unevenly. Poor-quality seed, and natural factors such as nonuniform maturation of embryos in the seed, and the presence of a water-soluble germination inhibitor, heraclenol (a coumarin), can also adversely affect rates (Rabin 1987).

A technique known as "seed priming" has been used to overcome problems associated with parsley-seed germination. Priming involves the controlled osmotic injecting of seeds with moisture. In experiments, primed seeds have enhanced early planting of parsley by as much as 78 percent (Rabin 1987).

A fertile, moist, sandy loam with 5.3 to 7.3 pH is best. Good drainage is essential, especially if you intend plants to survive a winter so you can collect seeds the following year. A friable, double-dug bed serves parsley culture well.

Harvest the leaves once they reach a height of about eight inches and at anytime thereafter. Parsley-leaf harvest on a commercial scale is labor intensive. A bunch can be grasped in the hand, cut about an inch and a quarter above the crown (if further cuttings are desired), and then a rubber band slipped over the leaf stems to create a bundle. Bunches should be washed if the leaves are dirty. Any yellow or discolored leaves should be culled and discarded. If the parsley is stored for shipment to market, studies have shown that the optimal temperature should be between 32° to 36° F at 95 percent relative humidity. Hamburg roots are dug

The crisp-leaved forms are the familiar garnish of restaurants, and are grown commercially for dried or dehydrated parsley-leaf products. The Italian parsley is used as a flavoring in sauces, soups, and stews. The large-rooted Hamburg parsleys are grown only for specialty markets, and are seldom seen in the United States.

Parsley leaves stay green during winter. When in Maine, I mulched parsley with straw and in the middle of January, excavated through snow to uncover fresh leaf bunches for salads.

The key to growing parsley from seed is patience. Seeds may take three to six weeks to germinate. Plant anytime from spring to autumn; but for an early crop, sow parsley one-fourth inch deep at the same time peas are sown. A frost or two won't deter young seedlings. Parsley can be sown indoors, but seedlings transplant with difficulty. Seeds can be soaked in water overnight to speed up germination in small-scale plantings. Directly sown plantings are best for larger crops. Treat parsley as an annual, planting anew each year. The second-year leaves tend to be tough and bitter. Once germinated, thin seedlings to stand at six-to-eight-inch spacings. Rows can be spaced at eighteen to twenty-two

in the fall of the first year or the following spring. They can be stored in a cellar in moist sand. Italian parsley is grown for dried leaf or "parsley flakes." The stems are removed, then the leaf is dehydrated. Twelve pounds of fresh parsley will produce about one pound of dried leaf. Leaves must be dried quickly under forced heat to retain a rich green color.

If fresh parsley is desired, the plant should be treated like other leafy green vegetables. A dark green color, and a familiar parsley aroma and flavor are desirable. Long leaf stalks are helpful for bunching fresh parsley for market. A straw of plastic mulch will help keep leaves clean and prevent mechanical injury. Mature leaf harvest occurs about three months after planting this cool-weather crop. Yields for fresh parsley range from five to eight tons per acre. Those interested in detailed information on parsley production should see Simon and Overley (1986), Rabin and Berkowitz (1986), Rabin (1987), and Simon, Rabin, and Clavio (1990).

What better herb for culinary use than parsley? Add it to salads, tomato dishes, baked potatoes, fish, meat, peas, egg dishes, and branch out into parsley butter and parsley sauces. The list is endless. The roots of Hamburg parsley can be grated into salads or soup stocks and cooked like parsnips. Harvest roots in early spring, slice them very thin, and sauté them in butter with the first fresh mint leaves of the season—delicious!

Parsley contains up to 22 percent protein. It is high in vitamin A, vitamin C, fiber, calcium, iron, magnesium, potassium, and riboflavin, and contains some niacin, thiamin, and phosphorus.

The seeds and leaves have been used medicinally to treat indigestion, jaundice, menstrual problems, gallstones, coughs, asthma, and dropsy. They are diuretic, stomachic, carminative, depurative, expectorant, and emmenagogic. The seeds are most often recommended by European herbal practitioners, primarily as a diuretic, in doses of one to two grams, taken three times daily. Ingesting the seeds, as well as excessive consumption of the leaves, should be avoided during pregnancy and lactation. The leaves can be chewed as a breath freshener.

The essential oil from the seeds contains apiol, myristicin, and alpha-pinene, among other substances. A fixed oil in the seed is comprised mainly of petroselinic acid, and has other fatty acids such as oleic, linoleic, and palmitic. The leaf oil includes bergapten, and is used in oriental perfumes and men's colognes. Parsley preparations are reported to be antimicrobial and slightly laxative. Apiol, in part respons-

ible for the characteristic fragrance of celery seed and also known as "parsley camphor," is the main component of the essential oil, comprising as much as 50 to 80 percent of its weight. It has urinary antiseptic qualities, and acts as a stimulant to uterine muscles. Parsley is carminative, and studies have shown that it has a stimulating effect on the secretion of stomach acids and gastric activity. Perhaps, then, parsley should be consumed at the beginning of the meal rather than at the end.

PASSIONFLOWER, MAYPOP

Passiflora incarnata L.
(pass-i-flor'-a in-kar-nay'-ta)
Passifloraceae—Passionflower Family
Plate 6

The genus *Passiflora,* with only a handful of temperate species, explodes in diversity in the American tropics with over five hundred of them. An additional twenty species occur in Indo-Malaysia and the South Pacific islands. Some have edible fruits; others do not. About thirty species of passionflower are edible. At least forty species and numerous cultivated varieties are found in American gardens, primarily in warmer areas. Only two hardy species, *P. incarnata* and *P. lutea,* are indigenous to the southern United States. *P. incarnata* is a perennial climber found from Virginia to Florida, west to Texas and Ohio. The fast-growing vines climb with tendrils, and often reach thirty feet in length. They die back to the root when hit by frost. The dull green leaves are four to six inches long, with three to five broad, deep lobes, which have serrated margins. The fantastic floral assemblage is one of the most intricate and remarkable of the plant world. Above the ten-part receptacle is a corona with white-purple threadlike filaments. Five stamens with hammerlike anthers surround a three-parted style, topped with reddish stigmas protruding from the flower's center like the antennae of a spaceship. The flowers are two to three inches across. The yellowish edible fruits—called maypops—are about the size of a hen's egg, and are filled with seeds surrounded by a sweet mucilaginous flesh.

While passionflower is regarded as a southern plant, it will grow as far north as the Boston area, and I suspect, if placed in a well-protected situation and mulched through the winter, it would even survive as a perennial in central Maine. Here in the Arkansas Ozarks, the native passionflower withstands temperatures of -25° F without protection. Try to obtain seeds or plants from an area with a similar climate to that in which you intend to grow it. Passionflower seeds or plants from south Florida are less likely to survive in New England than plants originating in more northerly areas.

Passionflower spreads from root runners and can be grown from seeds, cuttings, layering, or by dividing the runners in autumn. Cuttings about six inches long can be taken from mature plants, then rooted in sand. Given patience, passionflower grows readily from seed. After the fruits are harvested, clean the seeds from the mucilaginous, fleshy aril surrounding them, then dry them in the shade. Plant the following spring in light soil, preferably in flats. Germination should occur late in the summer, or the seeds will sit dormant until the following spring.

Passionflower growers have different techniques for achieving success. David Evans, a passionflower enthusiast in central Arkansas, suggests storing the seeds in peat moss in the refrigerator for the winter, taking care not to let them freeze, then planting them about the first of April (or after the last frost in your area). Plant about one-quarter inch deep and cover with fine loose soil, keeping the seeds moist until emergence, which should take about thirty days. Care should be taken not to damage the delicate rootlets when transplanting. First-year plants develop slowly, expending much of their energy in developing an extensive root system which can be damaged with careless hoeing. A black plastic mulch can be used to help protect the shallow root system of young plants.

Describing his technique of starting passionflowers, Delaware State College research professor Arthur O. Tucker (1989) takes cuttings in September, then roots them in perlite in eight-ounce Styrofoam cups with holes punched in the bottom. After dipping them in a rooting hormone/fungicide, he places them in a warm, north-facing window for two to three weeks until they root. He then repots them, and gradually moves them to a sunny location until they are well established. Dr. Tucker also warns about buying passionflower plants at farmers' markets.

Once well established, passionflower develops a tuberous root, which stores food to help it through the winter. If suckers are taken from the plant without a section of the tuber attached, they must be treated like a cutting, rather than a transplant. The suckers, even if they have fibrous roots attached, should be placed in a rooting medium such as perlite, and allowed to develop good root systems before

transplanting. If transplants have some of the main tuber attached, they can be placed directly in the garden and kept well watered until they recover from transplant shock. Such transplanting is, of course, best accomplished when the plant is dormant.

Propagation by layering can be achieved simply by removing the leaves from a small section of a stem in late summer, and placing a portion beneath the soil with a leafy end sticking out of the ground. Kept well watered, the buried stem should produce roots. It is best to keep the layered section in the ground through the dormant months, allowing it to develop a full root system before transplanting. The layered cutting can then be severed from the mother plant and placed in a new location (S. Foster 1991a).

Passionflower grows in waste places, thriving in relatively poor, sandy, acidic soils. Good drainage is essential. Full sun is necessary. Passionflowers need a place to climb. They often grow along fence rows, or climb trees along railroad tracks. A slightly acidic sandy loam with full sun will create a good patch. In the South, maypop is considered a farm weed. It is controlled by destroying the shallow root system through tillage, or if necessary, digging it out by hand. In most of the eastern United States, plants will thrive with natural rainfall, though if you live in a dry climate, watering once a week will be necessary.

In his "Thousand Mile Walk to the Gulf," John Muir speaks of the apricot vine (passionflower) as having a superb flower "and the most delicious fruit I have ever eaten." The fruits ripen in late summer, becoming yellowish-brown. The slimy aril covering the seeds is sweet and delicious. The hard seeds can be separated from the pulp by using an applesauce strainer. Perfectly ripe fruits are delicious—overripe fruits ferment into a foul paste.

At the annual fund-raising auction of the Arkansas Native Plant Society a few years ago, I was the fortunate high bidder on two jars of maypop jelly. I know of no other native fruit whose flavor is best described as "indescribable." The best maypop jam recipe can be found in *Billy Joe Tatum's Wildfoods Cookbook and Field Guide* (New York: Workman Publishing Co., Inc., 1976).

Archaeological evidence shows that maypop seeds could be found at Indian campsites over five thousand years old. Seventeenth-century visitors to Virginia such as the Englishman William Starchey observed the Algonkian peoples harvesting the fruits from their cornfields. It is unclear whether Indians intentionally planted the maypop as a crop, or whether it simply occurred naturally on the disturbed ground at the edge of their plots (Gremillion 1989).

Passionflower extracts are regarded by the FDA as "Generally Recognized as Safe" (GRAS) as a flavoring additive. In the food industry, passionflower extract is employed for flavoring alcoholic and nonalcoholic beverages as well as frozen dairy desserts. The fruits contain some calcium, iron, and phosphorus.

The aboveground plant parts are harvested when in bloom. Passionflower is a gentle herbal tranquilizer and antispasmodic. A tea is beneficial for insomnia caused by worry and overwork, tension headaches, and neuralgia. Passionflower will slightly reduce blood pressure while increasing respiration and depressing motor activity. Extracts of the rhizome were formerly used to treat hemorrhoids, burns, and erysipelas.

Passionflower never became an important medicinal plant in the United States. Like many American plants, it is more highly revered in modern Europe than in its homeland. In Europe, passionflower products act as mild nerve sedatives and sleep aids. Passionflower extract, once available as an over-the-counter (OTC) sleep aid in the United States, was given a "Category II" listing in 1978 after an FDA review of OTC drugs, which has been operational since 1972. Category II listings represent substances that are not generally recognized as safe and effective and are misbranded if labeled for drug use. During the OTC review process, more than two hundred botanicals were dropped, not necessarily because they are not beneficial, but because no commercial interest stepped forward to support their safety and efficacy. Thus, prunes can no longer be labeled as a laxative, even though consumers still buy them for that purpose (S. Foster 1991a).

In Europe, passionflower is the basis of a number of proprietary phytomedicines (plant medicines). Germany's FDA, the BGA, publishes monographs on acceptable or unacceptable labeling for phytomedicines. They allow passionflower to be labeled for "conditions of nervous anxiety." The monograph lists the dosage at six grams of the herb per day in infusion (tea) or other methods of preparation for internal use. Products are made from the fresh or dried whole plant, excluding the root (BGA 1985).

A number of chemical components have been identified from the dried leaves, including flavonoids such as vitexin and isovitexin, maltol, coumarin derivatives, and a small amount of an essential oil. In addition, passionflower contains varying amounts of harmala alkaloids, which according to the BGA monograph must not exceed 0.01 percent in products. Lutomski and Malek (1974) reported isolating four alkaloids from the plant, and suggested that both the alkaloids and flavonoids must be present for a sedative effect.

Several pharmacological studies have confirmed sedative, antispasmodic, and anxiolytic (antianxiety) activity of different passionflower chemical fractions at various dosage levels. Scientists have not been able to attribute the herb's effects to a single chemical compound. Limited research suggests that the synergistic action of several chemical components may account for the plant's performance. Clinical research on passionflower extracts is notably absent from the literature, except for several studies focusing on products containing passionflower in combination with other plant materials. Most of the supply of dried leaves, either cultivated or wild-harvested in North America, goes to the European market. No doubt continued use of passionflower products in Europe will spark further research. And once again, to obtain information on an indigenous medicinal plant, Americans will have to turn to European scientific literature.

PENNYROYAL

Mentha pulegium L., *Hedeoma pulegioides* (L.) Pers. (men'-than pul-ee'-ji-um; head-ee-oh-ma pul-ee-ji-oi'-dees)
Labiatae (Lamiaceae)—Mint Family
Plate 14

European pennyroyal, *Mentha pulegium*, is a perennial member of the same genus to which peppermint and spearmint belong. The genus *Mentha* includes twenty-five true species, but is highly variable. European pennyroyal is very unpredictable itself, both in terms of its morphological features and its chemistry. It is native to southern and western Europe, with a range extending northward to Ireland and central Poland, and westward to western and southern Ukraine and western Asia. It is found in much of Europe except the northern regions. This somewhat-smooth to hairy herb grows to about a foot tall, and has rather a sprawling habit. The entire (without teeth) or slightly toothed, opposite leaves are at least minimally hairy beneath, oval or roundish, and about an inch long. Tight whorls of small, irregular lilac flowers bloom from July to August. The plant spreads by underground runners. *M. pulegium* var. *gibraltarica* has fuzzy white leaves. *M. pulegium* has become naturalized in a wide variety of California plant communities.

Hedeoma pulegioides, American pennyroyal, is an annual plant of open woods and fields native to eastern North America. It grows to fifteen inches in height with leaves three-fourths of an inch wide and about one inch long,

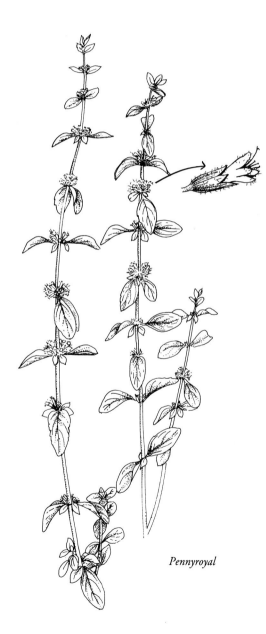

Pennyroyal

resembling those of *M. pulegium.* The one-fourth-inch-long bluish-purple flowers appear in summer in whorls around upper leaf axils. The genus *Hedeoma* includes thirty-eight species primarily found in the southwestern United States and South America.

H. pulegioides must be grown from seed sown in the spring or fall. *M. pulegium* is best propagated by dividing root runners in spring or early September, and by summer stem cuttings. Space plants eight to twelve inches apart.

Pennyroyal needs fairly rich, sandy loam, with a good supply of moisture and a pH range from 5.5 to 8. Full sun or partial shade are tolerable. European pennyroyal must have room to spread. After the plant flowers, it shoots out root runners from the crown. A pennyroyal lawn needs only occasional mowing. North of Pennsylvania, pennyroyal will need a winter mulch. At the Sabbathday Lake Shaker gardens, we had three 250-foot rows, from which we harvested about eighty pounds of dried herb. One winter I decided not to mulch the bed. Even though most of the pennyroyal was winter-killed, enough runners survived to more than double the size of the original planting. An acre of either species may produce a thousand to fourteen hundred pounds of dried material.

Pennyroyal's historical and folk medicine traditions include two primary uses—as a menstruation-effecting or abortifacient agent, and insect repellent. From classical antiquity through the Middle Ages, there is no doubt that pennyroyal was known as an antifertility herb. Paraphrasing the lines of Aristophane's plays *Lysistrata* (411 B.C.) and *Peace* (421 B.C.), medical historian John Scarborough (1989) shows how the ancient playwright played puns on the name of the herb, suggesting that his audience was familiar with it. Aristophane's ancient Athenian audiences knew that the herb was employed by women of all social groups from nobility through slave prostitutes as an antifertility agent. According to Riddle (1985) when Dioscorides (A.D. 40–80), whose first-century *De Materia Medica* was the basis of herbal medicine for sixteen centuries, omitted location descriptors for a plant, it was because that plant was very well known. It needed no descriptors. Therefore, Dioscorides wasted no words.

Unfortunately, what was common herb knowledge twenty or twenty-five centuries ago has been handed down to our generation only in a convoluted form. There is no clear, unbroken lineage. We are a lost generation of herbal users. We have learned bits and pieces of what once was. Ancient innuendo and pun, understood by all who once heard, are misinterpreted by our untrained ears. Herbal knowledge that comes to us through word of mouth today is not the oral tradition of mother to daughter. Rather it is the quoting of Culpepper and Gerarde ad infinitum in lots of poorly researched popular herbals. We learn from what our neighbor reads, not what she knows. Americans have generally lost touch with the ancient ways of nature. And now that herbs are becoming popular, we sometimes employ them inappropriately, either in too-high doses or incorrect dosage forms. Such is the case with pennyroyal.

That pennyroyal has an abortifacient effect has been established in ancient literature and modern scientific research. The ketone pulegone, a chief chemical component of pennyroyal oil is a known abortifacient. The oil contains as much as 80 to 94 percent pulegone. The dried leaf of European pennyroyal yields about 1 percent essential oil. American pennyroyal has up to 2 percent. All essential oils which are readily available are highly concentrated—and highly toxic. An acre of pennyroyal will produce more than half a ton of dried leaves. That same acre will yield only ten to thirty pounds of pennyroyal oil!

Unfortunately, the ancient association of *pennyroyal herb* with abortion has been translated by the unwitting modern mind into the use of *pennyroyal oil* as an abortifacient—with tragic results, including several deaths. In 1978, a Denver woman died after ingesting a one-ounce dose of pennyroyal oil reportedly to induce abortion—though she apparently wasn't pregnant. A rash of newspaper articles condemning pennyroyal herb followed. Speaking at the third International Herb Symposium held in 1979 at the University of California, Santa Cruz, Dr. Norman Farnsworth of the University of Illinois, Chicago, put the case in proper perspective. You would have to ingest about seventy-five gallons of strong pennyroyal tea (within a short time) to equal the effect of a one-ounce dose of pennyroyal oil. He also noted that almost any plant-derived essential oil in a one-ounce dose could be fatal. Pennyroyal herb by association has gotten a bum rap. The oil of pennyroyal, however, can be toxic in very small amounts. Ingestion of only one-half teaspoonful of the oil has resulted in convulsions and coma. Doses of the oil capable of inducing abortion are likely to cause irreversible kidney damage. The oil has been known to produce acute liver and lung damage as well (De Vincenzi and Dessi 1991).

European pennyroyal herb has carminative, diaphoretic, and emmenagogic properties. It has been effective in settling upset stomachs and soothing nervous headaches. In recent years, pennyroyal tea has become popular to promote menstrual flow, relieve cramps, and, in some instances, to induce abortion. Tyler (1987) states, "Pennyroyal tea possesses no therapeutic properties which could not be obtained from more pleasant and effective medicaments (178)." This wisdom, I think, explains why the plant is seldom used in modern European phytomedicine.

American pennyroyal was valued by the Iroquois as a treatment for headache. A small bunch of the herb was steeped in three quarts of water. Two cups were drunk before mealtime. When returning from the outdoors in winter with chills, the Indians drank the tea. The Iroquois also enjoyed a beverage tea of the herb with winter meals. The Delawares made a tea of the leaves to relieve stomach pains (Tantaquidgeon 1942; Herrick 1977).

European and American pennyroyal are often considered to be interchangeable. Both have a somewhat checkered reputation as insect repellents. In his *Medical Botany* (1847), Griffith, writing of American pennyroyal, comments, "It is said that the plant or its oil is an effectual remedy against the attacks of ticks, fleas, and musquitoes [*sic*]; but, from many trials made with it, it does not appear to possess any more effect than the other aromatics" (509).

Oil of European pennyroyal has long been an ingredient in insect repellent formulas to deter mosquitoes, fleas, mites, and ticks from the skin and clothing. The species name *pulegium* derives from the Latin "pulex" (flea), which honors use of the plants as a flea repellent for dogs since ancient times. Pulegone does appear to repel ants and other insects that live in proximity to pennyroyal. The oil is an effective antifeedant agent for the fall armyworm (*Spodoptera frugiperda*) at concentrations of five thousand parts per million (Zalkow, Gordon, and Lanir 1979). Pennyroyal oil was found to kill the eggs of the screwworm, *Cochliomyia americana* (Busland 1939). The oil also has a relatively potent antifungal effect (Maruzzella and Balter 1959; Maruzzella et al. 1960). Its insecticidal impact depends upon the concentration of the oil and the tolerance of the target organism.

On a practical level, I have found oil of pennyroyal, dabbed onto the cuffs of pants, the top of socks, and canvas shoes (not directly on the skin), to be helpful in deterring ticks and chiggers in the Arkansas Ozarks. As for mosquitoes, I think that those species that live in areas where I've tried pennyroyal as a repellent have a particular fondness for the oil.

Pulegone is cited as the main chemical component of pennyroyal oil. Quantitative and qualitative differences have been observed in European pennyroyal. Typically, the oil contains 80 to 94 percent pulegone. In the Sicilian variety *hirsuta,* the major constituent of the oil is piperitone, with pulegone comprising only 9 to 16 percent. In India, pulegone content has been placed at 71 to 84 percent. Seven separate chemical taxa were observed by Soviet scientists in the mid-1960s, characterized by oils high in isomenthone, menthone, and piperitenone types (Tétényi 1970). Other components of pennyroyal oil include carvacrol, thymol, menthol, isopulegone, menthone, isomenthone, alpha-pinene, beta-pinene, limonene, and over forty additional

constituents (Duke 1985). The pulegone obtained from European pennyroyal is used commercially as a starting material for the synthesis of menthol. Essential oil of pennyroyal is added in minute amounts (1.5 to 24 parts per million) as a flavoring ingredient in nonalcoholic beverages, ice cream, candy, and baked goods, as well as tea.

Perilla

Perilla frutescens (L.) Britt.
(per-il'-la frou'-tes-senz)
Labiatae (Lamiaceae)—Mint Family

Perilla is an erect, branching, tender annual (or sometimes perennial), native to and cultivated from the Himalayas of India, through Burma to China, Japan, and Korea. Introduced to Europe by the 1750s, it has long been grown in European gardens, and has become naturalized in the Ukraine. It seems to have been introduced to North America in the mid-nineteenth century. By 1889, the plant had escaped from gardens and become naturalized in southern Illinois. By the turn of the century, it had become a widespread weed, occurring from Illinois to New York and south to Georgia. Now it is a common weed of the southern states growing in a variety of habitats, and commonly raised in herb gardens under the names "perilla," "beefsteak plant," and "shiso" (a Japanese name).

Perilla reaches a height of four feet. The leaves are about three inches broad, oval or rounded, up to five inches long, and toothed, with hairs especially on the veins and leaf undersides. The foliage is ruffled with a metallic luster. The flowers are white to light lavender, hidden by longer calyces, and borne on a terminal raceme up to six inches long. In autumn, the dried calyces rattle as you walk through a wild patch, earning perilla the name "rattlesnake weed" in the southern United States. It blooms from August to October. *Perilla frutescens* 'Atropurpurea' has dark purple leaves. *P. frutescens* 'Crispa' has strongly wrinkled leaves, somewhat more rounded and with coarser teeth than the normal species.

It is known that in members of the mint family the essential oils are generally concentrated at hairlike glands called glandular trichomes. They develop from the epidermal cells on the leaf and are the sites where essential oils are accumulated or where their biosynthesis takes place. A

Perrilla

recent study found a direct correlation between the number of glandular trichomes on the leaves of perilla and the amount of essential oil it produces (Nishizawa et al. 1992). This shows the importance of selecting specific traits in developing medicinal and aromatic plants for markets, especially in highly variable plants such as perilla.

Perilla can be sown in the spring, but even though it's an annual, if you let it go to seed in your garden, you will undoubtedly spend more time weeding it out than you ever will planting it. To say it self-sows freely is an understatement. The seeds need light to germinate, and should be sprinkled over the soil surface, then gently tamped in.

Perilla will grow in a variety of soils. In the wild, it grows in dry woods, pastures, and meadows, or along sand and gravel bars near creeks, or in the adjacent moist, rich woodland. For best culture, the soil should be light and well drained with a pH of 5.3 to 6.3. Perilla will tolerate full sun or partial shade.

The Japanese consider perilla a culinary delight. The fresh leaves are eaten in salads, and the flower stalks flavor fresh fish. Purple perilla imparts its fragrant piquancy and color to Japanese pickled apricots. As the flowers fade, the inflorescence is fried or used to season soups. The salted seeds are eaten as an after-dinner cordial. The young leaves of the mild-flavored, green-leafed variety have been eaten as a vegetable in China, and used for tea. In oriental groceries throughout the United States, one can find seasoned perilla leaves from Korea packed in sardine cans. The leaves are seasoned with salt, MSG, sugar, red pepper, soy sauce, garlic, and sesame seeds. These pickled whole leaves are packed flat in the tins and are used for flavoring rice dishes. This strong-tasting condiment requires a trained palate to appreciate it. Frankly, the leaves taste awful. Food preferences in East Asia are many and varied.

The leaves are high in calcium, iron, potassium, riboflavin, and fiber. They are a rich source of vitamins A and C, and contain niacin, phosphorus, thiamin, and protein in measurable amounts. The seeds are high in calcium, niacin, iron, thiamin, and proteins.

In Chinese medicine, perilla has found a place as a carminative, stimulant, and antinauseant. It has been employed to stimulate appetite, expel phlegm, relieve cold and flu symptoms, and quiet a restless fetus. Recorded medicinal use of the plant in China dates back more than fifteen hundred years. Perilla seeds ("zi-su-zi"), leaves ("zi-su-ye"), and stems ("zi-su-geng"), are separate official drugs

in the 1985 edition of the *Pharmacopoeia of the People's Republic of China*. The seeds are primarily prescribed for asthma, and as an expectorant in chronic bronchitis. The leaves are taken internally for headache, coughs, asthma, stuffy nose, fullness of the chest and abdomen, and excessive fetal movement. The leaf tea, combined with fresh ginger, is an antidote to eating too much crabmeat or fish. The juice of the fresh leaves is sipped, in addition to poulticing, to treat snakebites as well as mastitis. The leaf tea is also a part of prescriptions to treat the common cold. The stems are prescribed for conditions characterized by an oppressed feeling in the chest, abdominal fullness and distention, stagnation of vital energy, difficulty in digesting food, stomach pains, morning sickness, and excessive fetal movement (Foster and Yue 1992).

Development of commercial food and medicinal applications of perilla in the West has been hampered by an increasing body of information on its potential toxicity. Attempts to commercially develop perilla in Illinois in the 1930s and 1940s were halted because the volatile constituents and dust of the dried plants caused illness in some workers, and dermatitis from handling the plant. Perilla has been implicated in causing the death of cattle in the eastern and southern United States. A 1963 report attributed the deaths of several thousand cattle in Arkansas to perilla invasions of pastures. Perilla ketone, a three-substituted furan, is a highly lung-selective toxin that is known to cause pulmonary edema and emphysema. Another component, l-perillaldehyde, is also implicated in toxicity (Morton 1991).

The essential oil of the leaves and flowering tops contains up to 55 percent of the monoterpene perillaldehyde. This chemical is easily converted to perillartine, which is two thousand times sweeter than sugar and used commercially in Japan to sweeten tobacco.

The seed oil, comprising up to 51 percent of the seed weight, is known commercially as "shiso" or "perilla oil" and contains linoleic, linolenic, oleic, and palmitic acid. Some strains of perilla produce seed oil very high in linolenic acid (up to 70 percent). The oil is processed commercially in China, Japan, Korea, and northern India. After harvest, the seeds are roasted, then the oil is obtained by expression or solvent extraction. The oil is glossier, tougher, harder, more durable, and more water resistant than linseed oil and dries in about a third the time. However, the oil has a tendency to yellow, shrivel, and crack when exposed to heat. It is an ingredient in Asia for paints, varnishes, printing inks,

Japanese oil papers, waterproof cloth, artificial leather, enamels, linoleum, and cheap lacquers. The seeds also have antioxidant activity. The seed cake, remaining from oil production, has been used as a fertilizer in Japan for mulberry trees and rice (Council of Scientific and Industrial Research 1966, vol. 7).

Since perilla ketones have been determined to be potentially toxic, causing pulmonary disease, the herb should be used sparingly.

Pleurisy Root, Butterfly Weed

Asclepias tuberosa L.
(as-klee'-pi-as tube-er-oh'-sa)
Asclepiadaceae—Milkweed Family
Plate 2

Of the two hundred or so species of *Asclepias, A. tuberosa* is one of the showiest. Butterfly weed or pleurisy root is, in fact, one of the most glorious flowering roadside weeds of America. It well earns both its common names. Historically, it is considered one of the best herbal remedies for pleurisy, and it attracts hordes of butterflies. It is a perennial growing from two to three feet tall, native to dry, gravelly soils from Maine to Florida, west to Arizona, and north to Minnesota. Unlike other milkweeds, it doesn't produce a milky juice, and its leaves are alternate rather than opposite or whorled. The plant is hairy and rough. The lance-shaped to oblong leaves, two to six inches long, are entire (without teeth), sessile, or have short leaf stalks, dark green above, and paler beneath. The one-fourth inch hooded and horned orange flowers are borne on showy, erect umbels, appearing in late May in the southern part of its range, and lasting through September in the north. Occasionally flowers may be reddish or yellow. The slender, furry seedpods are three to four inches long.

Pleurisy root is propagated from root cuttings made in the spring or fall, by seeds sown in late autumn to germinate the following spring, or by stem cuttings taken before flowering. Each section of root should have a bud or eye. The thick, fleshy, horizontal roots break easily when dug, but if you're careful to excavate as much root and surrounding soil as possible, the plant transplants well. This may be easier said than done, however, because the roots are huge—about the size of a man's forearm. It is always best to purchase wild plants from nurseries specializing in such stock, rather than deplete wild populations.

Plants grown from seed may take two to three years to flower. While seed germination is enhanced by a cold, moist stratification period of ninety days at 41° F, the seeds will germinate readily without pretreatment, and can be sown in fall, soon after collection. Seeds germinate well at a temperature of about 75° F. They can be planted about one-quarter inch deep. Young seedlings develop their large root quite rapidly, so if started in pots, they should be transplanted to a permanent location soon after they produce two true leaves.

A dry, sandy, well-drained, slightly acid soil is best. Full sun is essential. Pleurisy prefers an acid soil with a pH of 4.5 to 6.5. Once it becomes well established, it thrives in poor, dry soils, and is drought tolerant. If the flower buds are pinched back before they begin to unfold, plants will branch and sustain a longer blooming period of up to six weeks. Butterfly weed is an excellent choice to add brilliant color to the herb garden.

Harvest roots in the fall. Older woody roots may have to be split with a small ax.

The young seedpods of this and other milkweeds can be cooked as a vegetable. The Sioux made a crude sugar from its flowers.

Pleurisy root has been used more extensively for medicinal purposes than any other milkweed. Plains Indians ate the raw root for bronchial and pulmonary afflictions. The root was also chewed and put on wounds, or dried and powdered, then blown into wounds. The root has diuretic, tonic, diaphoretic, expectorant, and antispasmodic properties. Doses as small as a tablespoon of chopped root boiled in water may have emetic and laxative effects. This plant was historically considered effective as an expectorant and diaphoretic in pleurisy, bronchitis, pneumonia, and other lung inflammations. Flu, asthma, stomach problems, colic, and rheumatic pains have been treated with this plant. It was once employed to treat uterine problems. A recent study has shown estrogenic activity in rats. A teaspoon of the dried root can be boiled in a cup of water and taken one or two times a day.

A glycoside—asclepiadine—is contained in the root, along with asclepione, a bitter principle, an essential oil, and resin. Flavonoids such as rutin, kaempferol, quercetin, and isorhamnetin have been isolated from the root. Despite its historical reputation, the biological activity of this plant has not been well researched. For most herb gardeners, its principal value will be ornamental.

ROSEMARY

Rosmarinus officinalis L.
(rose-ma-rye'-nus off-ish-i-nail'-iss)
Labiatae Lamiaceae—Mint Family
Plate 14

This pine-scented evergreen perennial shrub has been a favorite plant of herb gardeners for centuries. Pliny wrote of its virtues. The often-repeated notion that rosemary sharpens the eyesight seems to have originated with him. Charlemagne ordered the plant's cultivation on imperial farms. Since it is mentioned in Anglo-Saxon herbals of the eleventh century, it is believed that it was grown in Britain prior to the Norman Conquest. Rosemary is native to the western Mediterranean region, especially Spain, Portugal, southern France, Tunisia, and Morocco. Some is produced commercially in California. Current imports come primarily from Portugal, Spain, Morocco, France, Albania, and the independent states of the former republic of Yugoslavia.

Rosemary grows from two feet to more than six feet tall. Its appearance largely depends upon the originating gene pool, varying from creeping or drooping prostrate forms, to rigidly erect ones which may tower to over six feet. The taller cultivars are best grown outdoors where frosts are few. The young branches are hairy. The opposite, leathery, lance-shaped, needlelike leaves are glossy on the upper surface with grayish fuzz beneath. The margins curve downward. The leaves are up one-half to one-and-a-half inches long. The three-eighths-inch-long flowers, usually blue, but sometimes pink or white, appear in whorls on short racemes arising from upper leaf axils. Rosemary flowers from May to July in warmer climates. Plants in the north may not bloom.

Cultivars abound in American horticulture. 'Arp' is one that has proliferated in recent years, with its light blue flowers and thick, widely spaced leaves, though its chief attribute is its ability to withstand temperatures to -10° F. 'Arp' is the hardiest of rosemaries. Madalene Hill of Hilltop Herb Farm in Cleveland, Texas, discovered this hale cultivar in 1972 during an arctic blast in the northeast Texas hamlet of Arp. It was later introduced into the nursery trade by the National Arboretum in Washington, D.C. Rosemary aficionado Tom De Baggio of Earthworks Herb Garden Nursery in Arlington, Virginia, introduced 'Joyce De Baggio', a rosemary cultivar with gold-variegated leaf margins. Other popular cultivars include the white-flowered 'Alba'; the delicate pink-amethyst 'Majorica Pink'; 'Collingwood Ingram', with bright blue flowers and graceful curving, crowded foliage; 'Lockwood de Forest', a prostrate variety with delicate foliage and vibrant blue flowers; 'Prostratus', with a creeping or arching habit; and the rigid, upright 'Tuscan blue', with rich green foliage and bright blue-violet flowers.

Rosemary is propagated from seeds, stem cuttings, layering, or division of older plants. Seeds are best started in early spring. They will germinate in about three weeks, but resulting seedlings are very slow to develop. Propagation from seeds is tenuous at best, and cultivars will not be true to form. Most of the cultivars are best propagated from stem cuttings taken from vigorous spring growth. Three- to four-inch-long stem cuttings, with leaves plucked from the lower half, can be placed in a standard rooting medium. Dip them in a rooting hormone to ensure success. The selected stems should be vigorous, nonwoody, healthy growth. Place in a sunny window with a plastic bag loosely covering the cuttings. Mist by hand daily. After three to four weeks, strong roots should be developed, and the cuttings can be planted in containers or hardened off for planting outdoors. Plants can be layered at any time during the growing season. Transplant or pot resulting offshoots in autumn. Root divisions are the least-recommended propagation method. Give young plants a spacing of two feet if planted in rows. If you're just starting out, forget trying to propagate rosemary. Simply buy a plant at a nursery where rosemary is easily found.

Rosemary is one of the few herbs that I maintain as if it was a pet. The often-harsh, unpredictable Ozark winters force me to grow rosemary as a houseplant. It does well in containers. Soilless mixes high in vermiculite, perlite, and peat moss, spiked with necessary nutrients such as a little lime and trace elements, suit the plant. An occasional dose of liquid seaweed or fish-emulsion fertilizer sparks vigorous growth. I ease my plants into the indoor environment about two weeks before the first hint of autumn frost. Bringing the plants in after a cold spell to a warm, heated house can be a shock. I place the plants in a prominent south-facing window, where they enjoy four to six hours of full sun. If there's not enough light, they soon become leggy. Don't overwater, which will produce symptoms such as brown leaf tips, or shedding leaves. Allow the soil to dry between waterings. If the leaf tips droop in thirst, water immediately. Mist the leaves once or twice a day, especially if you're heating with wood. The trick is to find a happy medium between too moist and too dry. Remember, rosemary will tolerate drought much easier than it will "wet feet." Experience will prove to be your best instructor. Prune the plant for frequent kitchen use, severely if you like (leaving about half the length of the leaf stems). This benefits the appearance and encourages branching. Rosemary grows quickly so repot container-grown plants each spring.

A light, sandy, chalky soil with good drainage, and a wide pH range of 5 to 8 are good for rosemary culture. Full sun is essential. If overwatered, rosemary may develop root rot. It is a tender perennial, even though I've known it to survive without cover where temperatures reach -10° F. Where temperatures dip into the teens, rosemary should be mulched heavily, or better yet, potted and brought indoors for the winter months.

Rosemary is a good hedge plant, border, or ground cover in California gardens. The prostrate cultivars make excellent plants for hanging containers, or ground covers for banks and slopes, or along walls in warm, temperate areas. Under such conditions, rosemary is prolific in California. The plants can be trimmed to encourage bushy growth. Remember to keep the trimmings to dry and use. (See De Baggio (1988) for exacting details on rosemary culture.)

In its indigenous haunts, both wild and cultivated plants are harvested when in flower for their essential oil. The oil is extracted by steam distillation of the newly harvested twigs and flowering tops. For home use, harvest the leaves as needed. Commercial rosemary fields are trimmed on a continuous basis for fresh herbs. For dried-leaf production, the herbage is harvested one or two times during the growing season once it is two years old. The leaves should be dried under shade for best color and fragrance.

Rosemary is great with pork, beef, poultry, fish, wild game, veal, peas, carrots, onions, and soups. One potted rosemary plant has served my kitchen for many years. I pinch back sprigs nearly every day. It is one of the most versatile herbs to the palate. Rosemary contains vitamin A, vitamin C, phosphorus, potassium, iron, magnesium, zinc, and is high in calcium.

Rosemary has a multitude of medicinal benefits. It is reported to be diuretic, diaphoretic, stimulative, astringent, stomachic, carminative, cholagogic, emmenagogic, and antispasmodic. The tea has long been drunk to relieve headaches and soothe nervous tension. Rosemary stimulates digestion, circulation, and bile secretion. It will bring on

menstruation and has been reported to be abortive in large doses. A gargle will heal mouth ulcers and canker sores. Externally, rosemary is used in liniments and ointments for rheumatism, neuralgic pains, bruises, sprains, and as a cosmetic rubefacient.

The list could go on ad infinitum. It is enlightening to see how the plant is used in Europe, where the German government allows labeling of rosemary products for specific medicinal purposes, including improving digestion and aiding circulatory problems. According to Weiss (1988), rosemary is helpful in states of chronic circulatory weakness, such as in cases where slender young people are pale and energyless without apparent disease. For older patients, it is considered a tonic to stimulate appetite and improve poor circulation. A proprietary rosemary extract is a treatment for patients with cerebral arteriosclerosis. Externally, the oil (which can produce skin irritation in some persons, and should not be taken internally) has value as a liniment for rheumatic conditions. If rosemary really does stimulate circulation, perhaps there is something to the old "rosemary for remembrance" axiom.

Rosemary has been reported as a folk cancer remedy in numerous historical European texts. A study published in 1991 showed that a 1 percent extract of rosemary fed to laboratory animals caused a 47 percent decrease in the incidence of experimentally induced mammary-gland tumors when compared with controls (Olin 1992). This certainly does not prove that rosemary can prevent or heal cancer, but it indicates a need for further research.

Rosemary also repels insects. If you are one of those California gardeners (whom I envy) who can harvest rosemary leaves by the bushel, while I nurture my single container-bound specimen, you can stew the fresh leaves to repel ants.

Major constituents of the oil include cineole (up to 50 percent), alpha-pinene (up to 30 percent), borneol (up to 20 percent), and camphor (up to 20 percent). Another component, verbenone, is an important fragrance ingredient. Rosemary oil contains at least fifty additional components. Depending upon the region of origin, the oil composition will vary greatly. Tunisian rosemary oil has high levels of cineole. Spanish-produced oils are high in camphor. While horticulturists classify rosemary cultivars according to morphological characteristics, chemists have separated them into six chemotypes based upon the oil composition. For example, the cultivar 'Arp' has high levels of cineole so it has more of a cool, fresh, eucalyptuslike fragrance.

Rosemary oil is widely employed in cosmetics and perfumery. It is an ingredient of rubefacient liniments, as well as scent for soaps and hair-care products. A strong infusion of the leaves makes a good rinse for dark hair. Fine grades of rosemary oil are valued for flavoring food as well as blending perfumes.

Flavonoids in the plant include apigenin, diosmetin, diosmin, genkwanin, hispidulin, luteolin, and many others. They may be responsible for some of the reported biological activity. According to Leung (1980), the capillary permeability- and fragility-decreasing capacity of diosmin is stronger than that of rutin, a glycoside reputed for this effect. The plant's rosmarinic and ursolic acids may be responsible for its reported antiinflammatory benefits.

Rosemary extracts are powerful antioxidants or preservatives comparable to BHA and BHT due to the action of their rosmarinic, carnosic, and labiatic acids. Rosmarinic acid, which is found in many species of the mint family, has antiviral, antibacterial, antiinflammatory, and antioxidant properties. Hydroxycinnamic derivatives like rosmarinic acid are responsible for the antioxidant activity of many medicinal members of this family (Lamaison et al. 1991). The oil has antifungal and antibacterial properties as well.

While rosemary has been utilized for centuries, its greatest virtues may still await discovery.

RUE

Ruta graveolens L.
(root'-a grave-ee-oh'-lenz)
Rutaceae—Rue Family
Plate 8

Rue is a beautiful, lacy, herbaceous perennial with a woody base. Native to the Balkan peninsula and the Crimea, and perhaps other parts of the Mediterranean region, it is naturalized in south and south-central Europe, having escaped from gardens. It grows to a height of three feet. The finely divided, fernlike leaves distinguish the plant, earning it the name "herb of grace." The leaves are in alternate arrangement on the stems. The dissected leaf segments are oblong or spatula shaped, up to one-half inch long, smooth, glaucous, bluish green, and dotted with oil glands.

The comblike inflorescence of yellow-green flowers appears from late spring to autumn. The one-half-inch-diameter, five-parted corolla surrounds a green center,

appearing on close examination to be similar to citrus-fruit skin. Citrus fruits are in the rue family. The cultivar 'Variegata' has creamy, white-mottled leaves. 'Jackman Blue' has a dense, compact growth and blue foliage.

Propagate by stem cuttings or root division in spring, or plant the seed, which germinates readily and self-sows freely. In southern regions where plants may become several feet wide, give seedlings two-foot spacings. In the north, space plants at one-foot intervals.

Rue is not particular about soil conditions. A poor, well-drained soil with a pH of 5.8 to 8 will suit it. Full sun is preferable. In fact, it is probably easier to grow rue by abandoning it than by giving it too much attention. I left a garden site on a sunny, very sandy, south-facing hillside in north-central Arkansas, and when I returned four years later, rue was the only one of more than two hundred species that had not just survived, but thrived. Here, it endures summer temperatures of 110° F and winter cold to -10° F.

Traditionally, the herb is gathered before it comes into flower. However, many gardeners must approach this plant with caution, as the juice can cause a rather unpleasant dermatitis with irritating burning, reddening, and blistering. The condition looks much like poison-ivy rash. This is caused by photosensitization resulting from a reaction of the furocoumarins in the fresh leaves to sunlight. When the fresh leaves are handled or intentionally rubbed on the skin, followed by exposure to sunlight, an unpleasant rash can result. One friend described her experience with rue dermatitis. She worked for fifteen minutes picking snails off her rue plants. Several hours later, her skin was red and hot as if she had a first-degree burn, and it later blistered. The condition did not show up right away and lasted for two weeks.

Rue's culinary use is limited. The leaves have been added in minute amounts to salads, and as a flavoring component in pickles. Rue has a bitter flavor suggestive of black pepper.

Rue's primary reputation is that of an antispasmodic for smooth muscles. This pharmacological activity is well documented, and has been observed in isolated gastrointestinal and cardiac smooth muscles. Antispasmodic action is attributed to the alkaloids arborine and arborinine, as well as to the coumarin rutamarin, and components of the essential oil. Medicinally, rue has been valued for its diaphoretic, antispasmodic, emmenagogic, stimulative, and mild sedative properties. Rue has a reputation as an anaphrodisiac (reducing sexual excitement) and an abortifacient due to its uterine-stimulant effect. It has been beneficial in expelling worms, breaking fevers and colds, relieving toothache, and as an antidote for insect and snakebites.

Since the time of the Greek naturalist Dioscorides in the first century A.D., it has been known that consumption of rue may be dangerous to pregnant women. In the folk medicine of Europe, Latin America, India, Pakistan, Vietnam, China, Ethiopia, and South Africa, rue has traditionally been employed as an emmenagogic and abortifacient. A tea of the herb has been reported to produce abortion within twelve to twenty-four hours after ingestion; however, it is highly toxic, causing vomiting, digestive pain, delirium, tremors, and frequently death. The World Health Organization's antifertility plant research program selected folk abortifacient plants as possible subjects. Since the ethnomedical literature contains numerous references to rue as an abortifacient, it became a high-priority topic. The research group of Y.C. Kong at the Chinese University of Hong Kong conducted animal experiments which showed that a chloroform-soluble component, chalepensin, is probably responsible for the antifertility action of rue. Unfortunately, the active dose of various extracts of the plant, as well as the isolated component, is at the same level as a toxic dose. Therefore, it is unlikely that rue can ever be developed as a natural antifertility agent (Kong et al. 1989).

The plant contains numerous alkaloids such as arborine, arborinine, graveoline, graveolinine, and gamma-fagarine. More than two dozen coumarins have been isolated, including bergapten, psorsalen, rutamarin, and umbelliferone. Flavonoids such as quercetin and rutin, which is the food supplement vitamin P, are found in the leaves. Rutin itself has had a wide range of pharmacological properties attributed to it, most notably its ability to decrease capillary permeability and fragility. It was once an official drug for the treatment of capillary hemorrhage in degenerative vascular diseases. Rutin has also been used in treating varicose veins and disorders of the retina. Studies with X rays in mice have shown that rutin protects against radiation. The essential oil of rue contains 2-undecanone (methyl-*n*-nonyl ketone) as its main component, which is a starting material for valuable perfume chemicals. Rue oil has been reported to be an effective worm expellant, though consumption can be fatal.

In practical terms for the home gardener, rue is best left to the ornamental and historical-interest realms. While it does have legitimate medicinal and industrial applications, the risk versus benefits warrant that it be left alone.

Sage
Salvia officinalis L.
(sal-vee'-a off-ish-i-nay'-lis)
Labiatae (Lamiaceae)—Mint Family

The genus *Salvia* contains about nine hundred species distributed throughout the world. Common garden sage, *S. officinalis*, a Mediterranean native from southern Europe and Asia Minor, is a shrub growing to two-and-a-half feet high, with white, woolly stems and grayish-green leaves. It has a texture which reminds me of reptile skin. The oblong, entire (without teeth), or slightly toothed leaves are about one-and-a-half to three inches long and about one-half inch wide. The whorls of white, pinkish, or blue-violet one-half-inch-long flowers occur in racemes, blooming in May to June. *Salvias* have two stamens with two-celled anthers, connecting to a point at the summit of the filament. On each stamen the anterior anther is not fully developed, forming an appendage bees hit when they enter the flower for nectar. This tips the fully developed anther, rubbing pollen into the hairs on the insect's thorax. Thus pollen is distributed to adjacent flowers.

Numerous cultivars are available. 'Tricolor' has variegated white leaves with purple margins; 'Purpurea' ('Purpurascens') has purple leaves; 'Albiflora' has white flowers; 'Icterina' possesses beautiful golden yellow leaves; 'Holt's Mammoth' has large, robust leaves. Other cultivars include 'Aurea', 'Crispa', 'Latifolia', 'Milleri', 'Rubiflora', 'Salicifolia', 'Sturnina', and 'Tenuior' (Tucker 1986).

Sage is commercially produced in the United States, Canada, Argentina, Germany, and France, and is collected from the wild and grown for export in Albania, Crete, Greece, Herzegovina, Italy, Montenegro, Spain, and Turkey (Simon, Chadwick, and Craker 1984; Prakash 1990).

Sage can be propagated by seeds, cuttings, layering, or root divisions of older plants. Seeds germinate within three weeks, and should be sown to a depth of one-half inch. Resulting seedlings should be spaced six to twelve inches apart. Plants from seed tend to vary in size and color. One to four pounds of seed will sow an acre. Most of the cultivars should be propagated from stem cuttings taken in the spring. Tips can be layered in September, then removed from the parent plant and transplanted the following spring. Fully mature plants should be spaced at two-foot intervals.

Sage will grow in almost any soil, but requires good drainage, a fair amount of nitrogen, and full sun. It flourishes on a heavy, moist soil, but under such conditions will most likely winter-kill in the North. Where temperatures dip below 0° F, sage should be mulched in winter months. A pH between 6.2 and 6.4 is best for sage, though it will grow in a pH range from 5 to 8. Plants from seed grow slowly, and only a tenth of them fully mature the first year. Commercial plantings are planned to take from two to six years. After the first year, as many as two to three harvests may be made during the growing season prior to flowering. The highest-quality product comes from cutting the tops to five inches in length. Sage is best harvested in the afternoon when the essential oil content is at its peak. An acre has yielded up to a ton of dried herb.

Weather conditions may affect the color of the dried leaf in a given season. A wet season produces greenish leaves, whereas they will be grayer during a dry season. You should pick leaves carefully by hand just before the plant comes into bloom, and later in summer after they have fully matured. Leaves may blacken if not dried quickly under a steady airflow. If hand-harvested, the leaves can be tied in loose bundles and hung to dry. Leaves spread to dry will often turn darker than those that are hung. Forced hot air at 100°F will usually dry a crop in about four hours, depending upon humidity and airflow. It is dried to an 8 to 13 percent moisture content.

Sage is best known as a flavoring for poultry stuffings, sausages, and commercial ground meats. Fresh or dried leaves enhance lamb or pork dishes. It's good in cheeses—try a few leaves in a toasted cheese sandwich. Use it in soups or by itself for teas. The Dutch formerly traded one pound of sage to the Chinese for four pounds of tea. Sage contains vitamin A, vitamins B_1 and B_2, niacin, Vitamin C, potassium, calcium, and iron.

Sage has been used as a folk remedy for centuries, serving as a digestive and nerve tonic, a gargle for sore throats and bleeding gums, an antiseptic in vaginal infections, a poultice for insect bites, and a cure for diarrhea. Sage is astringent, antibacterial, fungistatic, antiseptic, and antispasmodic. Experimentally, the oil of sage has been found to be antispasmodic in laboratory animals, providing a basis for its reputation as a gastrointestinal remedy. Sage tea will dry up milk flow, stop perspiration about two hours after drinking, and relieve gastritis. In Germany, fresh or dried leaves and their preparations in effective doses are allowed to be labeled for external use in the treatment of inflammations of the oral and laryngeal mucosa. Internally, accepted uses include the

treatment of dyspeptic discomfort and relief of excessive sweat secretions. Because of its potential toxicity, the oil of sage, like all essential oils, should only be used in very minute quantities. German authorities recommend an internal dosage level of one drop of the essential oil per cup of water in infusion, perhaps taken up to three times per day. A tea made from one to one-and-a-half grams of the dried herb is acceptable. As a gargle or mouth rinse, up to two-and-a-half grams of the dried herb is beneficial, or two to three drops of the essential oil in a cup of water.

Sage

It should be noted that some of the sage on commercial markets in the United States is not *S. officinalis,* but a related species, *S. fruticosa* (formerly known as *S. triloba*). A study by A. O. Tucker of Delaware State College (1980) showed that 50 to 95 percent of the dried sage-leaf supply in the United States is *S. fruticosa,* and only 5 to 50 percent is *S. officinalis!* In the commercial trade, *S. fruticosa* is known as "Greek sage," while *S. officinalis* is generally termed "Dalmatian sage." All commercial sage produced in the United States is properly identified *S. officinalis.* The leaves of *S. fruticosa* are easily distinguished by two lateral "earlike" lobes at the base of the leaf (hence the former specific epithet *triloba*). A scientist in Portugal informed me that two mint family members, *Phlomis lychnitis* and *Phlomis fruticosa,* are both harvested in the wild in Portugal and exported to the United States as "sage." However, this report has yet to be confirmed.

The essential oil of sage tends to be highly variable in composition and quantity (up to 2.5 percent), depending upon its genetic origin and growing conditions. It contains alpha- and beta-thujones (also found in wormwoods and yarrow), 1,8-cineole, borneol, and other components. Like rosemary, sage extracts are strong antioxidants, primarily resulting from the action of labiatic and carnosic acid. The essential oil suppresses fish odors.

SAGE OF THE SEERS

Salvia divinorum Epling and Jativa
(sal-vee'-a div-in-or'-um)
Labiatae (Lamiaceae)—Mint Family
Plate 5

Salvia divinorum is known in Spanish as "hojas de la Pastora" or "hojas de María Pastora" ("leaves of the shepherdess" or "leaves of Mary the shepherdess"). It was first described by Carl Epling and Carlos D. Jativa of UCLA in 1962 from dried specimens supplied by R. Gordon Wasson. Wasson (1898–1986) is the amateur mycologist whose work on the hallucinogenic mushrooms of Mexico largely ushered in public awareness of psychedelics, first chronicled in a 1957 *Life* magazine article, "Seeking the Magic Mushroom." A Wall Street investment banker, Wasson was self-taught in his avocation. He became a leading scholar in ethnomycology, and the author of numerous seminal works on the subject. Wasson first began visiting the Sierra Mazateca in the state of Oaxaca in 1953, returning each year until

1962. Early in his explorations, he had learned of a psychotropic plant that the Mazatecs of the region referred to as "hojas de la Pastora," or "hojas de María Pastora," which was used by them when mushrooms were not available. Finally, in September and October of 1962, Wasson and his companions obtained flowering plant material that provided the description and name for this new species—*Salvia divinorum* (Wasson 1962; Riedlinger 1990).

The plant is a tender, fast-growing perennial, three to seven feet high, with oval, light green, acuminate leaves, three to nine inches long with slightly curved tips. The serrated leaf margins have hairs between the teeth's sinuses. Leaf stalks are seven-eighths to one-and-a-half inches long. The stems are decumbent and square, with thin, wavy wings at the corners. Epling and Jativa originally said the flowers were blue, but in his *Narcotic Plants,* William Emboden (1979) corrected the description to pure white and densely tomentose, set in a violet calyx tube. The hairy seven-eighths-inch-long flowers are borne on spectacular panicles eleven to fifteen inches long. It has been alleged that the illusive Aztec psychotomimetic "pipilzintzintli" may well have been this plant, though evidence points toward other species.

Until the early 1980s, Western scientists had not seen the plant in the wild. L. J. Valdés observed the plant growing in the Mazatecan highlands, and believes that the Mazatecs collect material from remote areas, then plant it in accessible areas where it has become naturalized. Before this, the plant was thought to be a cultigen surviving only in well-protected stands overseen by Mazatec Indians in Oaxaca, Mexico.

S. divinorum is not known to produce viable seeds, but is grown from cuttings which readily strike in a moist rooting medium or water. Plants may also be produced by layering the long, sprawling stems.

In its native habitat, it grows in rich, black soil of forest ravines at five-thousand-foot elevations. It needs a constant supply of moisture. Leaf mold from deciduous trees is the best growing medium. A black, rich loam or potting mix (without peat, vermiculite, or perlite) is preferred. About 75 percent shade is required. The soil should be slightly acidic. The plant will stand a freeze of 20° F, dying back to the root when hit by frost. Bring it indoors in severe climates. This is an exceedingly rare, cultivated plant. A buyer usually has to join a waiting list before securing one.

S. divinorum flowering specimens collected by Valdés bloomed only between late August and March. Realizing that this was a time period when days were short, Valdés designed a series of experiments to determine the relationship between a certain critical dark period and day length as they relate to the development of flower buds. The experiments showed that in order to develop buds, the plants needed short-day (eleven hour) exposure to sunlight. An increase to over twelve hours of light caused budding plants to abort their flowers and revert to vegetative growth. Plant height was not an important factor influencing the development of flowers. While in bud, the typically scentless plant became strongly aromatic on the upper leaves and flowering stalks (Valdés et al. 1987).

The plant is apparently self-sterile, and in cultivation in the United States, has rarely set seeds. Nothing is known about natural pollinators of the plant. A single living plant introduced to the botanical garden at the University of California, Los Angeles, by Carl Epling was apparently the parent of all of the *S. divinorum* grown in the United States, until Valdés introduced new germplasm from his collections in Mexico in the early 1980s. Since the plant is believed to be self-sterile, this explains why no cultivated specimens in the United States ever produced seed prior to Valdés's experiments.

The Mazatecs use *S. divinorum*—the sage of the seers—as a hallucinogen when more potent mushrooms are unavailable. *Curanderas* (medicine men) have special rituals and chants for its use. Under the plant's influence, patients state the cause of their illness, the whereabouts of lost items, and the truth behind thefts. Intoxication is characterized by a feeling of weightlessness, euphoria, and visions of dancing colors. Effects last only for a short period of time. In small doses of from four to five pairs of the fresh or dried leaves, the plant has been claimed to be a tonic or panacea. Traditionally the plant has treated anemia, headache, and rheumatism, as well as regulate eliminatory functions.

The leaves are harvested in pairs, then crushed in a metate to extract the juice, which is then mixed with water and drunk. Fifty to one hundred fresh leaves can also be nibbled with the incisor teeth. However, as few as three pairs of leaves reportedly induce the desired results. The leaves are extremely bitter. Drinking the juice or eating the leaves often precipitates vomiting. I've nibbled my way through twenty leaves—leaving me with an upset stomach, a dry, acrid mouth, and a great respect for the Mazatecs who can work their way through a hundred. The effect on me was hardly noticeable. Craig Dremmond of Redwood City Seed

Company suggests that plants cultivated outside of Oaxaca may not develop the active constituents. Given its scarcity, extreme bitter taste, and unpleasant side effects, it is clear that *S. divinorum* will never become a popular subculture euphoric.

Between 1963 and 1980, chemist Albert Hoffman, the discoverer of LSD, unsuccessfully attempted to isolate and identify the biologically active compounds in the plant. In 1984, L. J. Valdés and his coworkers at the University of Michigan successfully isolated two diterpenes, called salvinorine A and B respectively, to which psychotropic activity has been attributed.

St. Johnswort
Hypericum perforatum L.
(hi-per'-i-cum per-for-ay'-tum)
Hypericaceae—St. Johnswort Family

St. Johnswort is a plant of many faces. It is at once ornamental, weedy, useful, or harmful. *Hypericum* is a large genus with about three hundred species. *H. perforatum* is a much-branched perennial herb growing from one to three feet high. The stems are ridged or two-sided, smooth, erect, and branching toward the top. Black glands are found along the ridges, with distinct dark rings at the lower nodes. The oblong, entire (without teeth), opposite, pale green leaves are sessile and about an inch long. The leaves are covered by translucent dots easily seen by holding the leaves up to a light; these are the perforations of *H. perforatum*. The star-shaped, golden yellow blossoms appear on terminal corymbs from June through August. The flowers are about an inch across and marked, especially along the margins, with minute dark dots and lines. When the fresh flowers are crushed, they exude a blood-red juice, staining the fingers blue violet.

St. Johnswort is native to Europe and naturalized in waste places and along roadsides in Asia, Africa, North America, and Australia. The plant was likely introduced to America by early European settlers as a medicinal plant. By 1793, the first recorded specimen, grown without cultivation, was collected in Pennsylvania. Especially vigorous populations in western North America and Australia have made the plant a serious weed problem. It is particularly aggressive in rangelands with dry summers. Despite its value as a medicinal plant, eradication programs have been developed in Canada, California, and Australia to eliminate this invasive foreigner. The *Chrysolina* beetle has been used in California and introduced into Canada as a natural biological control on the plant (Crompton et al. 1988).

The eradication programs were sparked in part because of St. Johnswort's potential toxicity to livestock, particularly sheep. There are questions about the "photosensitizing" or "phototoxicity" of the plant. A condition known as "hypericism" was first recorded in 1787. When light-skinned livestock, such as sheep, goats, horses, and cattle, ingest the plant and then are exposed to bright sunlight, they develop welts on their skin and other symptoms. This reaction has not been reported in humans. It is the result of the interaction of sunlight and oxygen with the pigment hypericin, after it has been ingested, absorbed through the intestinal wall, and reached the blood without being eliminated by the liver or kidneys. The photosensitization does not occur from external contact with the plant.

St. Johnswort

St. Johnswort is best propagated from root divisions made in spring or fall, or by spring cuttings. In nature it reproduces from seed or from rhizomes at the base of the stem. Seed germination can be enhanced by brief exposures to temperatures from 212° to 250° F. The germination of new seeds (1 to 6 months old) is accelerated by washing them in water. Seeds will remain viable for many years. Fifteen-year-old seeds in dry storage have maintained a 50 percent germination rate (Crompton et al. 1988).

The plant is not particular about soil conditions, growing in any average garden soil. It does like good drainage, a slightly acid situation, and full sun.

The herb is harvested just as the plant comes into bloom. A medicinal oil can be prepared by soaking a handful of the fresh flowers in olive oil. The fresh herb should be finely cut or crushed, covered with the oil, then placed in the sun or a warm area for two to three weeks until the herb imparts its qualities to the oil. Take about eight ounces of the fresh flowers, adding a sufficient quantity of olive oil to just cover them. Shaking the mixture once a day helps to bring more plant-cell surfaces in contact with the menstruum, enhancing this simple extraction process. Once the allotted time has passed, the herb should be pressed, strained from the oil, then stored in a dark, closed container in a cool place.

If you pick the fresh, bright yellow flowers in mid to late summer, then soak them in a vegetable oil, they impart a bright red color to the oil. Basically you are extracting the pigment, hypericin, considered one of the biologically active compounds of the plant. The fresh herb is used, as hypericin is mostly lost during drying. St. Johnswort oil is often used by herbalists to help speed healing of bruises, wounds, and sores because it is antiinflammatory. I make a bottle of St. Johnswort oil once a year, discarding any that I have left over. I apply it to bruises and to help heal nagging sores. St. Johnswort oil has antiphlogistic qualities; in other words, it helps to reduce swelling.

This is not a New Age herbal treatment, but one that has been handed down for hundreds of years. Once known to pharmacists as "red oil" or "hypericum liniment," it was still available in pharmacies in the early twentieth century. According to Christopher Hobbs's comprehensive review of St. Johnswort (1988/1989), the German government allows external preparations to be labeled for the treatment or aftertreatment of sharp or abrasive wounds, myalgias (muscular pain), and first-degree burns. St. Johnswort oils are listed in the official drug compendiums of Czechoslovakia,

Poland, Romania, and the former Soviet Union and are widely used in western Europe. Externally, the oil is applied to bruises, sprains, burns, skin irritations, or any laceration accompanied by severed nerve tissue.

St. Johnswort preparations have been a popular domestic remedy since ancient times. Internally, a tea or tincture, or standardized powdered extract, is beneficial for lung ailments, bladder infections, depression, dysentery, diarrhea, bed wetting, and worms. In Turkish folk medicine, St. Johnswort is reputed to protect the liver against toxins. Recent investigations have shown positive liver-protectant activity in experimental models, though the mechanism of operation is not understood (Öztürk and Aydm 1992). St. Johnswort oil can be taken for the treatment of gastritis and gastric ulcers in doses of one teaspoonful on an empty stomach in the morning, and another in the evening. An enema of the oil has been used in inflammatory conditions of the large intestine, as well as for hemorrhoids (Hahn 1992).

St. Johnswort is also highly esteemed as an antidepressant and sedative. The German government allows therapeutic claims for St. Johnswort preparations to relieve depressive states, fear, and/or nervous disturbances. The suggested average daily dose is equivalent to 2 to 4 grams of the powdered herb, calculated to contain .02 to 1.0 gram of hypericin (Hobbs 1988/1989). Recent evidence suggests that the herb's action is primarily that of an antidepressive, not a sedative. The mood-enhancing activity is a long-term effort, which takes two to three months to produce results. The earliest-reported response times have been two to three weeks.

According to Mark Blumenthal (1989), one of the most widely accepted theories on the cause of depression is decreased or deficient effectiveness of brain chemicals that act as neurotransmitters. Monoamine oxidase (MAO) inhibitors are chemicals that retard enzymes which break down monoamine. In appropriate dosages, MAO inhibitors will theoretically leave a larger concentration of neurotransmitters in the brain. Recent experiments have shown that hypericin is an MAO inhibitor in animal experiments, though the results are not conclusive (Blumenthal 1989; Hobbs 1988/1989).

The most important new research on the plant focuses on its antiviral effects. In 1988, research at Israel's Wiezmman Institute of Science and New York University discovered potential antiretroviral properties for hypericin. St.

Johnswort's constituents, hypericin and pseudohypericin, are being explored for their impact against the human immunovirus (HIV) as a possible treatment for AIDS. Preliminary studies have shown that the compounds can reduce the spread of HIV in animal models when administered in injections or orally. Hypericin apparently interferes with the virus's reproduction. No serious side effects were observed in these preliminary animal experiments. The compounds can cross the blood-brain barrier, which is considered important in the treatment of retroviral infections. Clinical trials of St. Johnswort derivatives are in progress at this time. The jury is still out on whether or not the compounds will ultimately prove helpful for the prevention or treatment of AIDS (Awang 1991b; Hobbs 1988/1989).

St. Johnswort contains phototoxins which may cause photodermatitis in fair-skinned persons who take the herb internally, and then are exposed to bright sunlight. Because of this possibility, in 1977 the FDA put this herb on the "unsafe herb list." Despite this potential, there are no reports of human photodermatitis as the result of ingesting St. Johnswort.

St. Johnswort has a complex chemistry, containing tannins (up to 16 percent in the flowers, 10 percent in the herb); napthodianthrones, especially the active constituents, hypericin and pseudohypericin; and flavonols such as the glucoside hyperin (hyperoside), quercetin, isoquercetin, quercetrine, isoquercetrine, rutin, and kaempferol. St. Johnswort also has small amounts of an essential oil, as well as choline, pectine, alkaloids, vitamin C, vitamin A, and beta-sitosterol (Awang 1991b).

SALSIFY
Tragopogon porrifolius L., *T. pratensis* L.
(trag-oh-poh'-gon por-i-foh'-li-us; pra-ten'-sis)
Compositae (Asteraceae)—Aster Family
Plate 15

Although not generally regarded as an herb plant, salsify deserves a place in the herb garden for its colorful flowers and useful culinary root. This genus contains about fifty species native to southern Europe, North Africa, and parts of Asia. Several species occur in North America. *Tragopogon porrifolius* and *T. pratensis* are erect biennials with a milky sap, growing from two to four feet high. The latter is known in England as Johnny-go-to-bed (-at-noon), since the flowers close up in the midday sun. The smooth, narrow, grasslike leaves are alternate and clasp the stems. Plants bloom in the second year, sending up a single flower head— a wheel of yellow (*T. pratensis*) or purple (*T. porrifolius*) ray flowers. Beneath the flower heads, long yellow bracts extend beyond the petals, making the flower appear larger. Flower heads may reach four inches in diameter. Blooming begins in June or July of the second year. The seed heads are billowy tufts similar to, but not much larger than, those of dandelions. The white fleshy roots, about one foot long, resemble a small parsnip. Both species have a special role in the history of genetics, since Linnaeus, in 1759, made the first deliberate and scientifically conceived interspecific cross by hybridizing *T. porrifolius* with *T. pratensis*.

Salsify is grown from seed sown in spring as soon as the ground can be worked. Sow seeds to a depth of one-half inch. Thin seedlings to stand at six-inch spacings. Seeds germinate in about a week. One ounce will plant a one-hundred-foot row, and produce about sixty pounds of root.

A double-dug bed with a rich, light, moist soil provides a perfect home for a good crop of salsify. It likes full sun and will tolerate soil pH from 5 to 8, preferring a neutral one. If the crop is side-dressed with fresh manure, roots will branch and take on an earth flavor. Keep plants well cultivated and free from weeds. Irrigate during dry weather. One hundred twenty days of growth are required for harvestable roots.

The roots can be harvested in the fall of the first year and stored in moist sand in a cellar for winter use. A stronger, more oysterlike flavor will develop if plants are left in the ground and allowed to freeze through the winter. Harvest the following spring before the flower stalks begin to develop. Once flower stalks develop, the root becomes woody and the flavor is very bitter.

Salsify is also known as "vegetable oyster," because if you stretch your imagination a little, the root tastes something like oysters. Many people who have tried wild salsify roots can't understand why anyone would want to eat them. The flavor is too bitter. To be enjoyed, the roots have to be prepared properly. They should be scraped, then soaked in water for about an hour to remove the bitter, milky sap. The roots can be eaten like parsnip. Boil them until tender, or grate and shape them into small balls. Dip the balls into a batter made from egg whites and flour, then roll them in bread or cracker crumbs and fry—delicious! The young three-to-five-inch second-year sprouts, salsify chords, can be eaten as an asparagus substitute.

The plant is no longer used medicinally, but once was regarded as an antibiliant, diuretic, emollient, expectorant, mild laxative, and deobstruent, said to liquefy bile that has become too thick (Steinmetz 1957).

The roots contain a fair amount of vitamin C and potassium, plus measurable amounts of calcium, iron, niacin, thiamin, riboflavin, phosphorus, and protein.

SANTOLINA
Santolina chamaecyparissus L., *S. virens* Mill.
(san-toe-lie'-na kam-e-sip'-a-ris-us; veye'-renz)
Compositae (Asteraceae)—Aster Family
Plate 15

There are eighteen species in this genus, two of which— *Santolina virens* and *S. chamaecyparissus* — are found commonly in American gardens. Both are shrubby, growing to about two feet high, and are native to the Mediterranean region. The first, green santolina, has smooth green leaves. The latter, gray santolina or lavender cotton, has downy silver-gray leaves. The alternate, finely cut leaves are about an inch and a quarter long with lateral segments one-sixteenth inch long or less. In midsummer, santolinas shoot up solitary flower heads on a stem taller than the rest of the plant, with yellow buttons resembling the heads of tansy, though more rounded. They are about three-fourths of an inch across.

Cultivars of lavender cotton include 'Nana', a dwarf form, and 'Plumosus', with lacy foliage. A santolina or two at the Farm and Garden Project at the University of California, Santa Cruz, are six feet in breadth. Large santolina plants like these tend to part into divided bunches, giving the plant an unkempt appearance. Some gardeners like to keep the plant trimmed back. I think the wavy divided wisps of the uncut plant have a character worth retaining.

Santolina can be started from slow-to-germinate seeds in the early spring, but is best propagated from spring cuttings or layering. Mature roots can also be divided before new growth begins.

Santolina likes a sandy, limy soil with good drainage and full sun. It will tolerate drought. The soil pH should be close to neutral or slightly alkaline. In northern climates, santolina will need a heavy mulch to make it through the winter. In any region with winter snows, santolina will die back to the root, but will grow again in the spring. In temperate climates, santolina is evergreen. *S. virens* is the hardiest species. It makes a good low hedge. Neatly trimmed, it is widely used in knot gardens. Gardeners in regions with intense summer sun should not cut it back too severely in the summer.

The leaves and flower heads can be harvested as the plant comes into bloom. Both the leaves and dried flowers can be used as moth repellents. The flowers are pretty in dried arrangements.

Santolina was once a popular worm expellant, and has been employed as a stimulant, for stomachaches, and as an emmenagogue and antispasmodic. Extracts of the flowers, leaves, and roots have been reported to be effective against Gram-positive bacteria.

The leaves contain tannin, an alkaloid, resin, and an essential oil (about 1.15 percent of the weight) with santolineone. The plant is not presently used for commercial purposes.

SASSAFRAS

Sassafras albidum (Nutt.) Nees.
(sas'-a-fras al-bye'-dum)
Lauraceae—Laurel Family

Sassafras is a small scraggly shrub or large tree, eighty to one hundred feet tall and up to six feet in diameter, native to eastern North America from Maine to Florida, and west to Texas and eastern Kansas. Two other species occur in the world—*Sassafras tzuma* from central China and *S. randaiense* from Taiwan. On older trees, the deeply furrowed bark is grayish with reddish-brown fissures. Young branches are smooth and light green. The aromatic leaves are entire (without teeth) or three-lobed, alternate, petiolate, oval, or mitten shaped, four to five inches long and two to four inches broad. Half-inch-diameter yellow-green flowers bloom early in spring in raceme clusters as the leaves emerge. The half-inch-long, oval, dark blue fruits ripen from September to October. Trees must be about ten years old before beginning to flower and fruit. The fall foliage is a brilliant yellow or dull orange, streaked with red. The wood is coarse grained, brittle, aromatic, and dull orange. It has been popular for fencing, ox yokes, smaller joints of fishing rods, cooperage, and light boats such as dugout canoes.

Sassafras can be grown from seed or root cuttings. Seeds have a viability of about two years, and often take that long to germinate. Soon after they ripen, remove the pulp from the seeds and place them in moist sand for cold stratification for four months at 35° to 42° F. Sow seeds outside in well-prepared seedbeds at eight-to-twelve-inch spacings, one-half inch below the soil. Don't expect a good germination rate.

However, the roots of sassafras send out runners. Cut young seedlings from the parent plant, then let them sit for a year to develop a good set of roots. Transplant the following year—and give new plants plenty of water. Four-to-six-inch offshoots with sprouts can also be removed from the parent tree to increase stock.

Sassafras is often found growing in dry, infertile soils. In the garden, a moderately rich, sandy, well-drained soil with a pH of 6 to 7 will do. In the North, where sassafras becomes a moderate-sized shrub, a warm, sunny location with winter protection is required. Southern trees become very large and will tolerate partial shade.

The bark of the root, trunk bark, leaves, pith of the twigs, flowers, and fruits can be used variously. Harvest the bark of the root in spring before leaves appear, or in the fall after leaves have dropped. Harvest the leaves after spring blooming.

The leaves have abundant mucilage and were used by the Choctaws to thicken their pottage. Subsequently, sassafras leaves became a prime ingredient in Cajun gumbo. A sprinkling of crumbled flowers adds color and spicy flavor to spring salads. The young tips of sassafras—those emerging, erect leaves—have a soft, delicate texture and pleasing flavor, with a hint of a mild anise taste, followed by a touch of light citrus. The emerging leaf tips are great in salads. The root bark is a famous herb tea.

A decoction of the bark was made by the Cherokees to bathe open or infected wounds. The Mohawks employed an infusion of the twig pith for eye ailments. Sassafras was one of the first export crops from the New World to European shores. Many early English colonies were in part founded on promises of financial return from speculation on sassafras. The tea of the root bark is considered a stimulant, tonic, diaphoretic, stomachic, and blood purifier. In folk medicine, it has been helpful in thinning blood, as well as for high blood pressure, gout, arthritis, rheumatism, kidney ailments, and skin eruptions.

Sassafras contains an essential oil with safrole (comprising up to 80 percent of the oil weight), alpha-pinene, phellandrenes, asarone, camphor, myristicine, thujone, anethole, eugenol, and other compounds. Sassafras oil has carminative, anodyne, diaphoretic, antiinfective, and lice-destroying properties.

In the *Federal Register* of 3 December 1960, the FDA banned safrole as an element in human foods because in laboratory tests with mice, safrole caused liver cancer. In the *Federal Register* of 11 May 1976, the FDA clarified the earlier ruling, banning the sale of sassafras bark and leaves for herbal teas, stating that the intended purpose of making sassafras tea was to infuse safrole (a food additive) into water (a food). Since that time, sassafras has been sold in health-food stores labeled "not for food use" or "for external use." In 1978, the then-fledgling, now-defunct, Herb Trade Association held a tea party at the Boston Tea Party Ship and Museum. In response to the FDA's sassafras ban, a symbolic toss of sassafras was offered to the famed harbor. Safrole is also found in basil, nutmeg, star anise, cinnamon leaf oil, black pepper, and witch hazel, which seem to be none the worse for its presence.

Legal restrictions on the sale of sassafras continue to be in place, though the bark and leaves are still widely available, primarily through health and natural-food stores. In fact, fresh sections of sassafras root can be found in the produce section of grocery stores in the Ozarks in early spring. Toxicity seems to be the result of ingesting large amounts of the tea of the root bark. A recent paper in the medical literature reported on the case of a seventy-two-year-old hypertensive woman who was breaking out with perspiration and experiencing hot flashes similar to those she had had during menopause twenty years earlier. The physician discovered that she had recently begun drinking ten cups of sassafras tea a day as a "tonic and blood purifier." She was advised to stop drinking the sassafras tea and the symptoms disappeared (Haines 1991).

Sassafras

In animal studies, sassafras extracts produced similar symptoms, such as ataxia, ptosis, hypersensitivity to touch, general depression of the central nervous system, and hypothermia (Segelman et al. 1976). Segelman calculated that a possible hazardous dose of safrole may be 0.66 milligrams/kilogram, extrapolating data obtained from animal experiments. Assuming a sassafras-bark tea bag contained 2.5 grams, as much as 3.0 milligrams/kilogram might be imparted to a cup of water, but the actual amount consumed would depend upon many variables, such as the safrole content of the sassafras, the duration of infusion, and the amount of tea drunk.

Sassafras oil has historically been a treatment for lice and is also reported to cause dermatitis. Being a Yankee transplant in the South, I think there's nothing more disgusting than the mention, or even thought of, head lice. But with public schools in the rural South, it's usually a once-a-year reality—inevitably about two weeks after school pictures are taken, when the harried elementary teacher has used the same comb to neaten the hair of all of the kids in the classroom, then a note, and a little instruction booklet, comes home to all the parents from the principal: "Look for head lice".... Horrible! Ever wonder where the word "nit-picking" came from? Nits are the eggs of those little critters that hatch into head lice. They are whitish-translucent ovals, about one-thirty-second of an inch long, and attach to the hair follicle just above the hairline. They have to be manually "picked" out. I don't wish nit-picking on anyone.

I just knew there had to be an herbal solution, and found an obscure reference to sassafras oil killing lice and their eggs. So I tried it. And I suffered the consequences. Using pure essential oil of sassafras, I managed chemical burns of my head and other body parts. And the critters were still alive. The alternative is nothing to write home about either—a medicated shampoo containing the highly toxic insecticide Lindane. The moral—avoid topical (and certainly internal) use of essential oils in concentrated forms.

The lesson here, once again, is everything in moderation. A cup or two of sassafras tea a year is not likely to put you in the hospital—but I would refrain from drinking ten cups of sassafras tea a day.

SAVORIES
Satureja hortensis L., *S. montana* L.
(sat-you-ree'-a hor-ten'-sis; mon-tay'-na)
Labiatae (Lamiaceae)—Mint Family

This genus has about thirty species, including both yerba buena and calamint, which are treated separately in this book. *Satureja hortensis,* summer savory, and *S. montana,* winter savory, are discussed here. Summer savory is a hardy annual growing to one-and-a-half feet tall, native to the Mediterranean region of southern Europe. Its leaves are linear to lance shaped, up to an inch long, entire (without teeth), with the edges slightly rolled back underneath. They are tightly arranged on the leaves. The slender, hairy stems have a purple cast. The one-fourth-inch-long, light lavender to white flowers are borne on separate whorls. They appear about ninety days after planting from seed and last until frost. Winter savory, also a Mediterranean native from southern Europe and North Africa, is a fairly hardy perennial, growing from six to twelve inches tall. The leaves are similar to summer savory, though they are shinier and thicker. The white or pink flowers are shorter than summer savory's. It blooms from midsummer through frost.

Summer savory is easily grown from seeds sown directly in the garden in spring as soon as the ground can be worked. It self-sows freely. Seeds germinate in a week or so. Winter savory can be started from seeds sown six to eight weeks before the last spring frost, but is best propagated from cuttings or layering.

Summer savory likes a moderately rich, sandy soil with a good supply of moisture for the seedlings and full sun. Soil pH should be around 6.5 to 7.5. Winter savory prefers a light, chalky soil with good drainage. It makes a nice, low border. An acre may produce as much as three tons of summer savory.

Harvest the flowers as they begin blooming, usually about ninety days after planting. Winter savory has a woody stem which needs to be removed from the dried leaf. Summer savory should be dried quickly with adequate circulation.

Savory is best known as a flavoring for beans—from lentils to green beans. The fresh or dried leaves are good with cabbage, turnips, brussels sprouts, potato salads, pea soup, and tossed salads. Winter savory has a stronger, biting flavor. Both make good pepper substitutes. Commercially, savory leaf and essential oils have been used to flavor baked goods, liquors, bitters, and vermouth, as well as dry soup and gravy mixes.

The leaves of summer savory are high in vitamin A and calcium, and contain niacin, iron, and potassium.

Medicinally, savory is carminative, antispasmodic, and expectorant. The tea is gargled for sore throat, and is valued for diarrhea, indigestion, and as an aphrodisiac. An infusion of summer savory leaves probably acts as a carminative rather than a true antidiarrheal agent. It has been used in Europe for the treatment of acute enterocolitis. Fresh leaves rubbed on

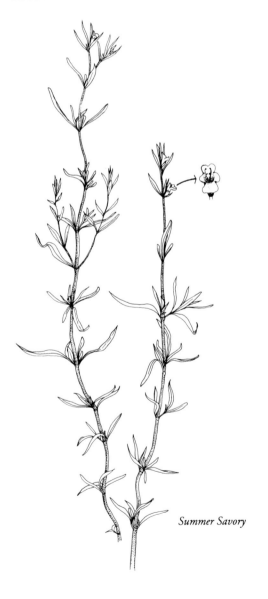

Summer Savory

an insect sting will relieve pain. Medicinal application is almost entirely limited to the historical realm.

The essential oil contains carvacol (the chief component comprising 30 to 45 percent of the oil), rho-cymene, beta-phellandrene, beta-pinene, limonene, and other monoterpenes. Winter savory oil also has thymol. The oils are antifungal, antibacterial, and antioxidant.

SPICEBUSH
Lindera benzoin (L.) Blume
(lin-der'-a ben'-zoin)
Lauraceae—Laurel Family

About eighty species in this genus are native to Asia, with two from North America. One of the species, pondberry (*Lindera melissifolia*), is a federally listed endangered species known only from nineteen populations in six states in the southeastern United States. *L. benzoin* is an aromatic deciduous shrub, three to eight feet tall, found from Maine to Ontario, and south to Florida and Texas. The oblong-to-elongated oval leaves are entire (without teeth), thin, abruptly pointed at the tips, tapering at the base, and up to five inches long. Tiny yellow flowers appear in axils in early spring before the leaves emerge. Male and female flowers usually appear on separate plants. A field study begun in 1980 of two populations of spicebush in Massachusetts showed that in a small percentage of individuals within a population, the shrub may have an altered sexual expression. That is, plants that produce male flowers in one year may produce female flowers in another! This occurrence is rare, however (Primack 1985). One-half-inch-long, oval, scarlet red, shiny, one-seeded fruits ripen after the brilliant yellow fall foliage has dropped. Spicebush is found in moist, rich woods, along banks of streams, and under taller deciduous trees. It is a close relative of sassafras.

Propagate from seeds, layering, or cuttings made from green wood. The seeds have a short viability and should be placed in cold stratification at 35° to 42° F for about four months. Plant in the spring or fall at six-to-twelve-inch spacings to a depth of one-half inch. Seeds germinate two to four weeks after planting. There are about forty-five hundred cleaned seeds to a pound. A good germination rate of between 85 to 90 percent can be expected. Root suckers can be removed and replanted like those of sassafras. Cuttings are best done in a greenhouse and take several months to root.

A soil which is fairly moist the year-round, yet well

drained, high in humus, and with a pH of 4.5 to 6.0 is suitable for spicebush. It likes light shade and a warm situation. Expect twelve to twenty-four inches of growth per year.

Harvest and dry the fruits when ripe. Twigs and bark are strongest when harvested in late winter before very early spring flowering. Leaves are ready in midsummer.

The leaves make a good tea. Wild food expert Billy Joe Tatum makes the world's best venison by roasting a haunch with spicebush twigs. The berries can be crushed in a mortar and pestle and added to meats, soups, salad dressings, and

Spice Bush

vegetables. During the American Revolution, the berries became an allspice substitute.

In Colonial America, the highly pungent plant naturally attracted interest. The spice-leaf tea was used as a stimulant, detoxicant, and tonic. It was considered beneficial against worms. The red berries were applied externally to treat bruises, itch, and rheumatism. Internally, as tea, the leaves and berries were a dysentery treatment. The infusion of the twigs was popular for fevers and colds. The tea also had a reputation as a good carminative.

The flowers were eaten instead of those of sassafras as a springtime digestive aid. The Rappahannocks brewed a tea from the split twigs to bring on the menses. The Cherokees traditionally employed the leaves for colds, coughs, female obstructions, and other purposes. An infusion of the branches was taken internally or used as a steam bath to induce sweating to treat aches and pains. The leaves and twigs were decocted by the Iroquois for colds and measles.

The seeds contain an essential oil plus a fatty oil with capric, lauric, and oleic acids. An alkaloid, laurotetanine, has been isolated from the pulverized stems. A recent study by researchers at Purdue University (Anderson et al. 1992) resulted in the isolation of four new compounds from the leaves, twigs, and fresh ripe berries of spicebush, including isolinderanolide, isolinderenolide, and linderanolide. Six additional compounds, most previously isolated from the Asian species *L. obtusifolia,* were also found. They were evaluated in various assay systems which showed that they may affect the pheromonal secretions of several insects and plants, and play a role as potential chemical defensive mechanisms. These compounds may have evolved to aid the plant's survival by both attracting or repelling insects. The plant does not seem to be bothered by pests, and the crushed fresh leaves rubbed on the skin act as an insect repellent.

Spiderwort

Tradescantia virginiana L.
(trad-es-kan'-ti-a vir-gin-ee-ay'-na)
Commelinaceae—Spiderwort Family
Plate 5

There are about sixty-five species represented in this genus and numerous varieties originating in North and South America. The spiderwort is a close relative of the familiar houseplant, the wandering Jew. *Tradescantia* x *Andersoniana* is a hybrid with numerous cultivars that are often sold as *T. virginiana*. Spiderwort is a perennial growing to three feet in height with smooth, delicate, grasslike leaves about a foot long and one inch wide. The flowers are usually blue, though sometimes rose, pink, or white, and are characterized by three petals alternately arranged with three sepals. Flowers are about an inch in diameter and bloom from May to August. Blooms open in early morning and close around noon.

Tradescantia has six stamens whose filaments are unusual because each stamen has between fifty and ninety hairs. The stamen hairs are elongated chains of between twenty and thirty-five cells so large they can be seen with the naked eye and easily observed under a 20x-powered microscope. A single flower may have between eight thousand and fifteen thousand stamen hair cells. In certain clones of spiderwort, the normally blue stamen hair cells turn pink when exposed to chemical or radiological mutagens.

Spiderworts can be propagated from seeds, cuttings of offshoots, and spring divisions of the rootstocks. Clones propagated for test use should be derived asexually to maintain genetic homogeneity. Spiderworts hybridize readily, changing their genetic stability.

These are easy plants to grow—so easy, in fact, that the well-known late botanist Dr. Edgar Anderson, in his *Plants, Man and Life* (1952), calls spiderwort "the kind of plant not even a botanist can kill" (21). A light, well-drained, humus-rich soil with a neutral pH is preferable. Spiderworts will tolerate full sun or partial shade.

The spiderwort is edible. The young leaves and stems can be added to salads or boiled for ten minutes as a pot herb. The flower petals make a colorful addition to salads.

This interesting garden perennial has a number of laboratory and educational applications. The beginning botany student may well have used the root tips or pollen grains to study chromosome structures. Compared with other plants, spiderworts have a relatively low number of large chromosomes. The spiderwort was chosen as a passenger on the first United States biosatellite, sent up in the late 1960s to explore the effects of weightlessness on living organisms. As early as 1950, spiderworts were employed to indicate the effects of radiation on living organisms. In 1977, this plant was selected by the Brookhaven National Laboratory and the Environmental Protection Agency to monitor the effects of air pollutants in eight high-risk areas of the United States. Spiderworts close to petroleum refineries and mixed-chemical processing plants have exhibited the greatest increase in mutation rates.

How does the spiderwort's detection system work? A percentage of the normally blue stamen hair cells turn pink when exposed to mutagens. The spiderwort clones used in such testing possess a dominant gene for blue and a recessive gene for pink. Upon exposure to even minute levels of radiation or chemical mutagens, a mutation may occur, causing the loss of the dominant blue gene, which shows up as a pink mutation cell. The pink cells appear eight to eighteen days after exposure to the mutagen. The same kind of somatic (body cell) mutation in humans, from short-term exposure to low levels of radiation, may only be noticeable after several decades.

Techniques for using the spiderwort system were developed at the biological department of the Brookhaven National Laboratory and the Laboratory of Genetics, Kyoto University. In conjunction with Dr. Sadoa Ichikawa, a major *Tradescantia* researcher, a Japanese high school teacher, Motoyuki Nagata, placed spiderworts near a nuclear power plant in Japan, and, over a period of nearly five months, spent about six hours a day, in addition to teaching full-time, recording data on over a half million stamen hairs. He counted about 17,600,000 stamen hair cells and detected 2,778 pink mutation cells in the forty plants. Interpretation of the data by Dr. Ichikawa revealed that somatic mutations occurred only when the reactors were in operation and mostly from the leeward side of the power plants. Spiderworts have also been planted near other Japanese, European, and United States nuclear power plants, producing similar results.

Traditionally, the root of spiderwort was used by the Cherokees as a folk cancer remedy. A tea of the root was considered laxative. It was also mashed, and applied as a poultice on insect bites. A tea of the leaves was drunk by the Cherokees for stomachache from overeating. The root of *T.*

occidentalis served the Meskwaki (Fox) as a diuretic. A rather bizarre option was treating insanity with spiderwort. A gum exudes from the root. The treatment consisted of making an incision on the head, then inserting a piece of the gum into the wound as a remedy for craziness.

Some might ask what spiderworts are doing in an herb book. I have included them because of their biological ability to indicate mutagens in our environment. If we heed those warnings, then spiderworts are, in the broadest sense of the term, a preventative medicine.

Sweet Cicely

SWEET CICELY

Myrrhis odorata (L.) Scop.
(mer'-iss oh-dor-ay'-ta)
Umbelliferae (Apiaceae)—Carrot Family

Sweet cicely is a hardy perennial growing to a height of two to three feet. It is native to the Alps, Pyrenees, and the Appennini of Italy. It has been cultivated throughout Europe for many centuries. The leaves are finely divided, fernlike, about one foot long, and covered with downy hairs. The leaf segments are coarsely toothed. The stem is hollow and striated. Inconspicuous white flowers are borne on compound umbels in May and June. The shiny, dark brown fruits are like those of chervil, only larger, reaching a length of one inch.

Propagate by planting the seeds as soon as they ripen in late summer, or divide the crowns of the roots in the fall. Each piece of root should have a bud or eye. Give plants one-foot spacings. The seed is viable only a short while.

Sweet cicely makes a good border plant in a moderately rich, well-drained, slightly acid to alkaline soil. Partial shade is required. The delicate foliage makes it a delightful bright ornamental, especially in the springtime herb garden. The plant persists for many years with little care.

The leaves can be harvested as they develop and the seeds when ripe. The leaves have a mild aniselike flavor and are good with cabbage, carrots, parsnips, and fruit dishes. The young shoots can be eaten raw or cooked as a spring pot herb. Chop the leaves finely and add them to salads. The boiled roots have an excellent flavor.

The roots have been used as a cough remedy and diuretic. The seeds and leaves possess mild expectorant, carminative, stomachic, emmenagogic, and diuretic qualities. The essential oil contains anethole.

SWEET GOLDENROD, BLUE MOUNTAIN TEA

Solidago odora Ait.
(sol-i-day'-go oh-door'-a)
Compositae (Asteraceae)—Aster Family
Plate 2

I've tried dozens of herb teas—some nauseating, others tasty—but my favorite is unequivocally sweet goldenrod. I feel this North American native should be grown in every herb garden, here and abroad.

More than a hundred species of *Solidago* grow in North America, but only *S. odora* has a fragrance and flavor suggestive of anise or tarragon. It is an erect, sometimes-sprawling perennial, three to six feet high, found in thickets, along roadsides, and in dry, open, rocky woods from New Hampshire to southern Ontario, south to Florida, and west to eastern Texas. The leaves are sessile, entire (not toothed), and sharply pointed, about four inches long and half an inch wide. They become successively smaller toward the top of the plant. When held up to light, the leaves are spotted with translucent dots. The stems have a purple cast. The bright yellow flower heads are arranged on one side only of a stem in tight, long panicles. Sweet goldenrod flowers from July to September.

Sweet goldenrod can be grown from spring- or fall-sown seed, but it is most easily propagated by dividing the crowns in spring after the plants become three to four inches tall. In three or four years, the crowns will spread, producing clumps six to ten inches in diameter. These older clumps can be divided into ten or more seedlings.

Sweet goldenrod will grow in rocky or sandy soil with good drainage and a fair amount of humus in either full sun or partial shade. The soil should be slightly acid. It will generally thrive in any good garden soil, and requires little moisture. In the 1940s, there was an attempt to develop the plant as an essential oil-producing crop in Texas, and researchers at a Texas agricultural experiment station found that it would be economically feasible.

Harvest just before the plant comes into bloom because later the leaves take on a more astringent, bitter flavor. The quality and quantity of the essential oil are also greatest when the plant has just bloomed. Tie in bundles. Sweet goldenrod dries quickly, and the leaves can be easily removed from the stem with one stroke. Highest yields of essential oil have been obtained from distillation of the fresh plants.

Sweet goldenrod should be grown as a commercial tea crop. It is easy to grow and produces well. Frederick Pursh (1774–1820), a well-traveled botanical explorer, highlighted its potential economic value at an early date. "The flowers, gathered when fully expanded, and carefully dried, give a most agreeable substitute for tea, which for some time has been an article of exportation to China, where it fetches a high price" (1814, 539). While this quotation is often repeated in the literature, Griffith (1847) raises doubts about it. "Pursh states that they are exported of Canton, where they

bring a high price, but we have been unable to verify this assertion, and feel very doubtful of the accuracy of his information" (396).

There was some interest in the medicinal applications of the plant in the early nineteenth century, which has since waned. Jacob Bigelow was its first champion, and wrote on its potential to replace imported drugs with similar qualities. He was also a keen observer of the plant's pleasant and still underappreciated fragrance:

The leaves of the *Solidago odora* have a delightfully fragrant odour, partaking of that of anise and sassafras, but different from either. When subjected to distillation, a volatile oil, possessing the taste and aroma of the plant in a high degree, collects in the receivers. This oil apparently has its residence in the transparent cells, which constitute the dotting of the leaves, for the root is wholly destitute of the peculiar fragrance of the herb, and has a rather nauseous taste. . . . The claims of the *Solidago* to stand as an article of the Materia Medica are of a humble, but not despicable kind. We import and consume many foreign drugs which possess no virtue beyond that of being aromatic, pleasant to the taste, gently stimulant, diaphoretic and carminative. All these properties the Golden rod seems fully to possess." (Bigelow 1817, 1: 190–91)

The uses for the plant enumerated by Bigelow persisted in the medical literature throughout the nineteenth century. In his own medical practice, he employed an essence made by dissolving the essential oil in grain alcohol to allay vomiting, "and to relieve spasmodic pains in the stomach of the milder kind, with satisfactory success" (190). The same "essence" Bigelow reports "is used in the eastern states as a remedy in complaints, arising from flatulence, and as a vehicle for unpleasant medicines of various kinds" (190). He himself used it to cover the taste of castor oil and laudanum.

Rafinesque (1830), as was his propensity with other herbal medicines of the day, invented new ways to employ the plant. He recommended the essential oil (presumably as an external application) for headache. Little ethnobotanical information on the use of the plant exists, though Rafinesque notes that the Cherokees treated fevers with it.

Sweet goldenrod's medicinal applications remained limited and were best summarized by Johnson (1884): "Golden-rod is a gently stimulant, diaphoretic and carminative. The decoction and warm infusion are used in domestic practice to produce diaphoresis, to relieve colic, and to promote menstruation. The oil is used for similar purposes" (175). Externally, the leaf tea or essence was helpful for rheumatic pains and neuralgia.

The oil contains delta-limonene (15 percent) and estragole (methylchavicol), which is the primary constituent at 75 percent. Other components include borneol, pinenes, and traces of volatile fatty acids. The oil never seems to have been produced commercially, though it has been suggested that it could be a flavoring for chewing gums and candies, and a fragrance addition in deodorants or insecticides. The plant remains one of the less studied, more interesting, and little grown aromatic indigenous herbs.

SWEET GUM

Liquidambar styraciflua L.
(lik-wid-am'-bar stie-ray'-si-flu-a)
Hamamelidaceae—
Witch Hazel Family

Four species of deciduous trees in this genus are native to North America and Asia. *Liquidambar styraciflua* is a North American native with wide distribution from Connecticut, south to Florida and Central America. Sweet gum attains a height of 150 feet or more, with a five-foot di-ameter and a foliage spread over a hundred feet. It grows straight and tall. Young trees are more or less cone shaped. The bark of twigs often has corky wings an inch or more wide. Old trunks have a light gray bark with deep, irregular fissures. The lustrous leaves are almost star shaped, with five to seven lobes and toothed margins. The fruits are globular, up to an inch and a half in diameter, and covered with projecting points. The "sweet gumballs" are composed of many small capsules with two short projecting beaks. They often persist throughout the winter.

The plant is not as popular as it might be, because of the globe-shaped, spiked fruits, which tend to be a nuisance on driveways, sidewalks, and underfoot in general. Some gardeners have discovered that this is a blessing in disguise. If the fruits of the sweet gum are placed around

vegetable gardens, they can serve as a physical barrier to keep rabbits out.

The brilliant autumn foliage varies from yellow through red to golden bronze or purple. The handsome, dark, straight-grained, and close-grained wood has a reddish tint that takes an exceptionally fine polish. It has proved to be a popular tree in American arboriculture, with more than thirty-five named cultivars available from commercial sources.

The seed has a short dormancy period. Germination is improved by cold, moist stratification for thirty days. Plant seeds one-half inch deep in well-prepared seedbeds in spring. Sometimes seeds may take more than a year to germinate. Transplant six to ten feet apart. Since the tree's range is from New England to Central America, when selecting a young tree or seed for planting, it is wise to choose one from a

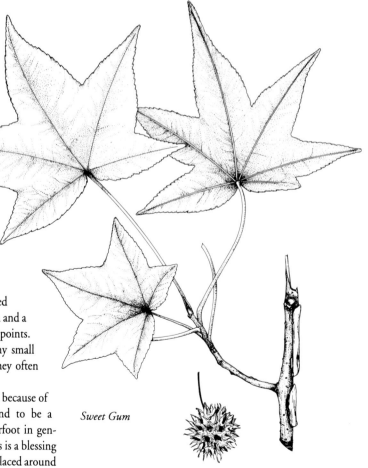

Sweet Gum

similar climatic zone to your own. Seeds or trees from the Deep South may not be hardy in the North.

Sweet gum is planted as a street shade tree throughout the United States. It rarely attains a height of more than fifty feet in cultivation. A neutral to slightly acid, rich, moist soil with good drainage is best. Like oaks, it grows moderately fast, straight, and tall under the shade of other trees.

In Central America, the exudate from the bark is collected in hanging buckets, often producing forty to two hundred pounds of gum per tree. Usually a pocket of gum is found in the tree, then slashed and allowed to drip. I once came across a stand of old-growth sweet gums that had been girdled by beavers. Gum was running down the sides, and I spent an hour scraping a few pounds from the damaged bark. The gum or balsam, called American storax, is liquid as it comes from the tree, but hardens when exposed to air.

Antiseptic, expectorant, antimicrobial, and antiinflammatory qualities are attributed to the gum. It has been chewed for sore throats, coughs, colds, and used for diarrhea, dysentery, ringworm, and other skin ailments caused by parasites. The gum is applied to sores and wounds to promote healing. It is an ingredient of hemorrhoid ointments and compound tincture benzoin. I've chewed the gum on occasion. The taste is fine, but the more it's chewed, the more resilient it becomes.

The gum contains storesin, styracin, phenylpropyl cinnamate, vanillin, borneol, bornyl acetate, and tannins. The leaf oil has at least thirty-six terpenoid components. The major constituents are terpinene-4-ol, alpha-pinene, and sabinene. The leaf oil also contains vitispirane, valerone, and valeranal. Interestingly, the essential oil of the leaves is very similar in composition to that of the tea tree (*Melaleuca alternifolia*), an Australian member of the eucalyptus family that has become popular as an antibacterial in recent years. That similarity suggests that the leaf oil of sweet gum may someday emerge as a commercial antibacterial agent.

Syrian Rue

Peganum harmala L.
(peg-ay'-num har-may'-la)
Zygophyllaceae—Caltrop Family

Syrian rue is a relatively tender perennial native to southern Russia, the Balkans, North Africa, the central Asian steppes, and the Iranian plateau. It grows from one to two feet tall and has a somewhat sprawling habit. The stems are smooth, rather succulent, and blue green. The finely divided, linear, alternate leaves resemble deer antlers. The five-pointed star flowers have creamy white petals streaked with green veins. Flowers are about an inch and a half in diameter. The ovary is spherical, surrounded by eighteen stamens. It blooms from June to September, and produces an abundance of seeds that are dark brown, about three-sixteenths of an inch long, and one-eighth inch in diameter. In some areas, the plant is considered a serious weed. The seeds are the source of the colorfast Turkish red dye used in Persian and Turkish rugs.

Syrian rue grows easily from seed sown in spring, taking about two weeks to germinate. The plant self-sows freely.

Soil should be fairly rich, sandy, and well drained. Full sun is required. The plants die back to the crowns every winter, and should be mulched where temperatures dip below 10°F. An alkaline pH between 7.3 and 8 is preferable. In some states, county extension agents frown upon the cultivation of this plant as it may escape and become weedy in pastures. It is reportedly toxic to livestock.

The seeds are used as a narcotic and worm expellant in

Syrian Rue

Pakistan and India. In recent years, *Peganum* has been noted as a possible source of the Vedic Soma (the drug cariso prodol). It has also been employed as an aphrodisiac, to increase lactation, to bring on the menses, to treat genitourinary disorders and fevers, as a diuretic, and, in large doses, as an abortifacient.

Ingesting the seeds can reportedly cause paralysis and even death. Poisonous doses depress the central nervous system. Smaller doses stimulate the motor tract of the cerebrum. Syrian rue contains the alkaloids harmine, harmaline, and harmalol. In minute doses, harmine has been used to treat encephalitis lethargica (sleeping sickness) and Parkinson's disease. The Nazis turned it into a narcotic truth serum. Harmine is also the chief constituent of a hallucinogenic jungle vine in the genus *Banisteriopsis,* used by natives of the upper Amazon basin.

TANSY

Tanacetum vulgare L.
(tan-a-see'-tum vul-gay'-ree)
Compositae (Asteraceae)—Aster Family

Tansy is a hardy, strong-scented, aromatic perennial native to most parts of Europe, occurring along roadsides, waste places and river gravel. It has been extensively cultivated in Europe over the centuries, which may in part account for its present wide distribution on that continent. It is also found in many parts of North America, particularly the eastern United States (from Maine to North Carolina, west to Minnesota and Missouri) and the Pacific Northwest. Tansy grows to four feet tall and has coarsely divided leaves three to five inches long. The leaves are deeply incised and toothed. The quarter-inch-diameter, buttonlike, yellow flower heads appear from late July to September in flat clusters.

Tansy has a creeping rhizome that can spread and take over a garden if not kept in check. It is a long-lived perennial whose commercial plantings have survived as long as twenty to twenty-five years. The genus *Tanacetum* includes about seventy species of aromatic herbs, primarily native to northern temperate regions of the Old World. *T. vulgare* var. *crispum* has more finely divided leaves and luxuriant foliage. These divided-leaf cultivars originate in Corsica, Sardinia, and Sicily in the Mediterranean.

Tansy is grown from seed, or better, from spring or fall root divisions. Any piece of root with a bud will produce a new plant. Seeds can be sown indoors in early spring. Give young plants twelve- to eighteen-inch spacings. Plants may self-sow.

Tansy

Tansy is not particular about soil conditions as long as there is good drainage. A moist, rich soil makes for lush growth. Tansy tolerates a pH range between 5 and 7. For commercial essential-oil production, a muck soil, favorable to peppermint, is appropriate for tansy. Tansy produces thick growth, and thus does not require much hand weeding. It is a tough plant not generally subject to disease, insect or pest problems. An acre may produce fifteen hundred to two thousand pounds of dried leaves, but any grower would be hard put to sell a ton of tansy leaves.

The plant is harvested and spread or hung to dry when in full bloom. The best crop is achieved by separating the main stem from the leaves and flowering tops, then drying the herb under shade to retain a bright green color.

Tansy is said to be of some help as a moth or ant repellent, but I've never found this to be the case. Its primary historic medicinal use is as an intestinal worm expellant. Tansy oil and tea have also been of value to bring on the menses, as diaphoretics in fevers, and as a digestive tonic. A crystallized tansy preparation has been beneficial in treating gout. Tansy is also an ingredient in an Irish sausage made of sheep's blood, known as drisheen. It has been suggested as an abortifacient, but any internal use should be discouraged because of its high toxicity even in low doses.

Tansy represents a remarkable example of the diversity of medicinal and aromatic plants, not in its variation in flower or leaf structure, but in the unseen realm of its chemistry. Among its chemical constituents are alpha-thujone and beta-thujone, and parthenolide. The presence of thujone prevents wormwood, tansy, and yarrow from being classified "generally recognized as safe" food ingredients. To be sold, they must be thujone-free. A bit of a double standard exists, because other plants relatively high in thujone (such as common sage) are considered safe food ingredients. Thujone, a terpenoid compound, is considered the source of wormwood's toxicity. It is believed that thujone may interact with the same brain receptor sites as the active constituent of marijuana (tetrahydrocannabinol, better known as THC). Wormwood has long been known to cause dementia, trembling, stupor, and convulsions, thus absinthe, a wormwood alcoholic beverage, was banned by many countries in the early part of the twentieth century.

Interestingly, a recent study by Dutch researchers showed that some populations of tansy contain varying amounts of thujone, while others contain parthenolide. In parthenolide-producing tansy, no thujone was detected. Parthenolide is a sesquiterpene lactone considered to be the active constituent of feverfew (*Tanacetum parthenium*) and responsible for its benefits in treating migraine. One cannot detect these divergent chemical patterns by simply looking at the plant—a chemical analysis is necessary. Given this fact, it is conceivable that thujone-free, parthenolide-containing strains of tansy would be a suitable phytomedicine, while thujone-containing tansy should be avoided. Tansy has been recommended in European products for the treatment of migraine and neuralgia. Historically, the efficacy of tansy could be restricted to parthenolide-producing strains (Hendriks and Bos 1990).

The essential oil has thujone, with varying amounts of borneol and camphor, thujyl alcohol, piperitone, umbellulone, camphene, pinene, cineole, and other components. According to the principal constituents of the essential oil, the highly eclectic and ubiquitous tansy can be separated into eleven different chemotaxa.

TARRAGON
Artemisia drancunculus L.
(are-te-miz'-ee-a dray-kun'-kyou-lus)
Compositae (Asteraceae)—Aster Family

There are two varieties of tarragon: *Artemisia drancunculus* var. *sativa*, French tarragon, and *A. drancunculus*, Russian tarragon (formerly known as *A. redowskii*). They are native to southern Europe, Asia, and western North America. The stems are usually shiny and smooth, though sometimes hairy. The linear to lance-shaped leaves of French tarragon are one to three inches long and a darker color than Russian tarragon. I have rarely seen it flower. It grows to about three feet tall. Russian tarragon stretches to five feet tall, and its leaves may be as long as six inches. It has tiny (one-eighth-inch-diameter) greenish-white flowers blooming in loose clusters in June or July. Both varieties spread by creeping rhizomes.

Russian tarragon does not have the fine flavor of French tarragon so often appreciated by French chefs. When buying plants, bruise the leaves and smell them. If they have a rich, aniselike fragrance, buy them. If they don't, you don't want the plant, as it is Russian tarragon. Unfortunately, Russian tarragon plants are often offered as French tarragon. Let your nose make the choice. If you buy seeds, you are going to get undesirable Russian tarragon.

Tarragon is best propagated by carefully dividing the

Artemisia dracunculus, French tarragon

roots in spring and transplanting one-inch sections of root tips with a bud. The roots should be carefully teased apart before replanting. First-year plants will expend their energy establishing themselves. Second-year plants exhibit the most lush growth. The roots of third-year plants begin to twine around themselves and become crowded. These plants can be divided the following spring. Tarragon can also be propagated by summer cuttings, which take about eight weeks to root. The cutting should be about two inches in length and the leaves should be cleared off the lower inch. Those interested in commercial propagation of French tarragon through cuttings should see the paper by J. Quinn (1987) for exact details. French tarragon, the flavorful clone cherished by herb gardeners, must be propagated asexually. If you buy tarragon seed, you are getting Russian tarragon. Seeds germinate in about twenty days. Give plants one-to-two-foot spacings.

A moderately rich, well-drained soil with a pH range from 6.2 to 7.8 is suitable for tarragon. Optimum pH range

should fall between 6.2 and 6.5. Plant under full sun. It's a relatively hardy plant if soil drainage is good, but if the roots sit in water, plants will invariably winter-kill. Where temperatures dip below 0° F, mulch well after the ground freezes. Tarragon does best in areas where it has a period of winter dormancy.

Like basil, tarragon leaves bruise easily, and must be handled with care during the harvest and drying process. Harvest should occur in late June.

Tarragon has one of the finer flavors of any culinary herb. It is good with chicken, fish, salad dressings, salads, and all vegetables—especially asparagus. Use the leaves to season chicken livers and roast duck for an unusual treat.

The leaves contain vitamin A, niacin, phosphorus, potassium, calcium, and iron. Medicinal possibilities are very limited. The leaves have been employed to stimulate appetite, settle an upset stomach, promote the menses, and as a diuretic. The root has been chewed to cure toothaches.

Tarragon contains an essential oil with up to 70 percent estragole, plus lesser amounts of capillene, ocimene, nerol, thujone, and phellandrene. It also contains coumarins and the flavonoids rutin and quercetin.

THYMES
Thymus vulgaris L., *T. pseudolanuginosus* Ronn.,
T. x *citriodorus*
(Pers.) Schreb ex Schweiggt and Korte,
T. serpyllum L.
(time-mus vul-gay'-ris; sue-doe-lan-gwin-oh'-sus;
sit-ri-oh'-door-us; ser-i-fil'-lum)
Labiatae (Lamiaceae)—Mint Family
Plate 16 & Plate 17

Like the genus *Mentha, Thymus* is a taxonomic Pandora's box. There are about four hundred species—or a hundred species with four hundred names. They are creeping, woody-based, evergreen perennials concentrated in the Mediterranean region and western Asia. Leaves are small, entire (without teeth), and opposite. Flower heads are usually terminal, compact, whorled bunches of tiny flowers. We will deal only with a handful of species.

If you own *Herbal Bounty,* forget what was said about thyme identification, and let's start all over again. That analysis was based on information in *Hortus Third* (1976). Since that time, Harriet Flannery Phillips (who has also published as Harriet Flannery, and might be known as

Thymus vulgaris, Thyme bed Sabbathday Lake, Maine, Shaker Community

"Dee" Phillips) focused her graduate work at Cornell University on studying the thymes cultivated in the United States. In order to sort out the taxonomic confusion about the identity of these thymes, she grew over 400 different plants representing more than 120 species, cultivars, and named plants found in American horticulture. The American herb community should take time to thank her for her contribution (see H. F. Phillips 1989, 1991).

What she found will be very enlightening for gardeners like you, who try to make some sense out of a very confusing situation. First, in the American markets the name *Thymus serpyllum* is misapplied to plants with a creeping growth habit which are actually *T. praecox* subsp. *arcticus* or *T. pulegioides. T. praecox* subsp. *arcticus* is one of five subspecies of that grown in the United States. The plant is characterized as prostrate, often spreading extensively by creeping sterile shoots (H. F. Phillips 1989). It has hairs only on two opposite sides of the stems, while *T. serpyllum,* which according to Phillips is rarely cultivated in the United States, has hair on all four sides of its quadrangular stem.

T. serpyllum is not only rare in cultivation, but does not even occur in the wild in the United States, contrary to information in many floras and field guides. While no thymes are native to North America, the one that has become naturalized here is *T. pulegioides,* which is apparently the only thyme in America which has hairs only on the angles of the stems. The plant is vigorous, and can be invasive in the garden. It has rather elongate flower heads, and the leaves are somewhat larger than those of *T. praecox* subsp. *arcticus.*

T. vulgaris, common or English thyme, not only has a range of different appearances, but is also highly variable in its chemistry. There are seven known, naturally occurring chemical races or chemotypes. Phillips, using gas chromatography, found that three of the seven are grown in American gardens. The most common one has high amounts of thymol and thus the typical "thyme" fragrance. Phillips suggests that if this was designated *T. vulgaris* 'Narrow-leaf French' in the horticultural trade, thyme plant labeling would be greatly simplified. This is the typical thyme that provides the commercial dried leaf, which is collected and produced in many European countries, including France, Spain, Portugal, and Greece, as well as Israel and the western United States. A chemical race of *T. vulgaris* high in car-vacrol is characterized by a rather acrid, tarlike odor. Chemotypes with essential oil high in alpha-terpineol have a strong bitter-orange, turpentinelike odor, and have been sold under the name *T. vulgaris* 'Orange Balsam.'

T. vulgaris is native to the western Mediterranean region, extending into southeastern Italy. Elsewhere it is widely cultivated. It grows from about six to eighteen inches tall and has linear or elliptical leaves up to five-eighths of an inch long, which do not have ciliate hairs. The leaves are revolute (curving underneath along the margins). The flower tube (corolla) is cylindrical, and varies from white to pale purple. The dense whorls of flowers are terminal or interrupted on upper branches.

T. x *citriodorus,* lemon thyme, is a branching perennial with a distinct lemon fragrance. It grows up to one foot high. Flowers are light lilac, and the leaves are oval. This taxon must be propagated vegetatively rather than grown from seed. The cultivar 'Aureus' has golden yellow leaves; 'Silver Queen' is a silver-leafed cultivar, but is not often seen, though it is certainly welcome in cultivation. Trout Lake

Farm (see mints) grows lemon thyme commercially.

T. pseudolanuginosus, creeping woolly thyme, is a name I'll stick with to designate this plant, since I have no idea what else to call it by looking at the taxonomic literature. It is a low-growing (one-half-inch-tall), hardy perennial, with one-eighth-inch-long, woolly, gray leaves that are elliptical. It produces a few tiny, pale pink flowers in the leaf axils. This plant makes a fabulous ground cover.

T. herba-barona is easy to identify with the average, educated nose. It has an essential oil in which carvone is the predominant chemical component. In other words, it has the distinct fragrance of caraway seed. Hence, it is known as "caraway thyme." The stems are hairy all the way around. The flower heads are somewhat roundish and lax. The bracts beneath the flower heads are similar to the leaves. This endemic of Corsica and Sardinia, where it flourishes on dry, barren slopes, has pale purple flowers.

Thymes are propagated from seeds, cuttings, layering, and root division, although cultivars must be propagated asexually. Give plants six-to-twelve-inch spacings. Six pounds of seed will sow an acre of thyme. Root division is the easiest and fastest means of increasing thyme stock. The roots of the low-growing species reach as deep as two feet. Remove them carefully, retaining as much of the original soil material as possible. Give transplants a generous supply of water.

The soil should be light, warm, rather dry, and well drained, and have a pH of 6 to 8 for good thyme culture. Plants may be killed by frost heaving the crowns or burning the foliage in areas where winter temperatures dip below 10° F. Provide plants with a heavy mulch. Clumps tend to become woody and die out in the center. They should be divided every three or four years. One-half to one ton of dried herb can be expected per acre. Harvest just before it blooms.

Thyme is a well-known culinary herb. It is great in fish chowder, poultry stuffing, egg dishes, meats, cheese, and with vegetables such as broccoli, brussels sprouts, asparagus, and onions. The leaves contain vitamin A, niacin, potassium, phosphorus, calcium, iron, magnesium, and zinc.

Thyme has always been better known as a kitchen herb than a medicinal herb, but its historical and modern place in medicine is worth exploring. Both the fresh and dried herb of common thyme, *T. vulgaris,* have historically been valued as a worm expellant, especially for hookworms; a digestive carminative (relieving gas in the digestive system); an antispasmodic (relieving muscle spasms); mild sedative, an expectorant, and an aid to induce sweating in colds and fevers. It has long been employed in acute bronchitis, laryngitis, whooping cough, gastritis, diarrhea, and lack of appetite. Externally, steeped in baths, it has helped relieve rheumatic pains, as well as aided in the healing of bruises and sprains. Both thyme herb and oil of thyme have been used in medicine. Oil of thyme is a highly concentrated, toxic compound. I know of one person who poured an ounce of oil of thyme into his tub for an "invigorating" bath. The oil of course floated on the surface and clung to his skin. He emerged with irritating chemical burns over his entire body.

In German phytomedicine, practitioners employ a variety of thyme products for the supportive treatment of spasmodic coughs, bronchitis, whooping cough, emphysema, and even asthma. Studies conducted on the mechanism of thyme's action suggest that it has an antispasmodic effect on bronchiolar spasms. If taken internally in minute doses administered by a medical practitioner, oil of thyme, according to Rudolf Fritz Weiss (1988), is largely eliminated through the alveoli of the lung, concentrating the remedy at where its effects are required.

Product forms mentioned by Weiss include dried thyme for teas and infusions, thyme oil, thyme syrup, and a compound syrup of thyme, among others. An inhalation for coughs suggested by Weiss consists of a handful each of chamomile flowers, thyme herb, and marjoram herb placed in a bowl. Boiling water is poured over the herbs to release their volatile oils. The patient sits with a towel wrapped over his or her head, forming a tent over the bowl, to inhale the vapors. While the Europeans seem to be adept at this sort of thing, most Americans would probably rather use Vicks VapoRub for tightness in the chest.

Thyme is a part of a number of proprietary phytomedicines in Germany. The German version of the FDA, the BGA, which publishes monographs on acceptable labeling for herb products, allows thyme to be designated for "symptoms of bronchitis and whooping cough, and catarrhs of the upper airways." One to two grams of the "drug" per cup as an infusion, given several times a day as needed, is the dose. According to the monograph, thyme herb is considered a bronchospasmolytic, expectorant and antibacterial.

It seems that at least in Europe, the employment of the plant in the treatment of lung ailments has stood the test of time. While it was never a major medicinal plant in Europe, oil of thyme and the dried herb have been included in official medical treatises since the sixteenth century. The first mention of the oil is in the *Dispensatorium Noricum* of 1589 (a pharmacopoeia first compiled in 1546 by request of the Nuremberg council, under the direction of Valerius Cordus).

The essential oil, found at a concentration of about 1 percent in the dried leaves, contains thymol, linalool, carvone, cineole, limonene, and dozens of other components. The leaves also have tannins. The oil has antioxidant, antispasmodic, antibacterial, antifungal, expectorant, and carminative properties.

Some commercial species, such as *T. capitatus,* which occurs in Israel, North Africa, and other Mediterranean countries, have high levels of carvacrol (up to 74 percent in their essential oil), thus possessing an "oregano" flavor and a value as an oregano substitute in some areas. Lemon thymes have oils high in citral, which is responsible for the lemon fragrance.

Thymol, a powerful antiseptic, is the chief constituent of oil of thyme. Formerly known as "thyme camphor," thymol was first observed in 1719 by a Berlin apothecary, Caspar Neumann (1683–1737). But it wasn't until 1853 that M. Lallemand purified the compound and gave it the name "thymol." Thymol itself can be highly toxic. It is strongly fungicidal, antibacterial, antioxidant, and toxic to hookworms. Thymol is also obtained from a number of other plants, including two native American species, horsemint (*Monarda punctata*) and common bee balm (*M. didyma*). When European thyme fields were destroyed during the First World War, horsemint was grown commercially in the United States as a source of thymol.

Thymol was official in the *United States Pharmacopeia* (USP) from 1880 through 1947. It is currently an ingredient in over-the-counter lotions, creams, and ointments; feminine hygienic douche powders, and ear drops, and a disinfectant in mouth-care products such as Listerine, or temporary dental fillings. It has also been added as a "dry top note" in lavender products and men's fragrances. For industrial purposes, thymol is an important starting material for the manufacture of synthetic menthol. It has been suggested as an antimold and antimildew agent for papers, and has been used to destroy mold on herbarium sheets, to preserve anatomical specimens, and in embalming fluids.

For more information on thyme identification, cultivation, and culinary applications, see the various articles in *The Herb Companion* (April/May 1991). Portions of the medicinal information in this entry are drawn from "Thyme for Your Medicine" by this author in that publication.

VALERIAN
Valeriana officinalis L.
(val-er-i-ay'-na off-iss-i-nay'-lis)
Valerianaceae—Valerian Family

Valerian is a highly variable, hardy perennial growing to five feet in height. The stems are fairly succulent, hollow, and grooved. The deeply divided leaves are larger at the base, becoming progressively smaller on the flower stalks. Seven to ten pairs of oblong or lance-shaped leaf segments characterize the fernlike leaves. The leaves are entire (without teeth) or toothed. The fragrant, tiny, white, pink, or lavender flowers are borne in flat umbellike clusters. Blooms shoot up in late May, lasting through August.

Valerian occurs in eastern, southeastern and east-central Europe, extending to south Sweden and the southern Alps, and has been locally naturalized to the West. It was brought to North America by colonists at an early date, escaping from cultivation and becoming naturalized from Nova Scotia to Pennsylvania, Ohio to Minnesota, and in Quebec. There are as many as 250 species of valerian found in the northern temperate zone, as well as in South Africa and the Andes. In Europe there are 20 indigenous species. In North America (exclusive of Mexico) there are 16 native or naturalized species, with 5 subspecies and 2 varieties (S. Foster 1987a, 1991j). Valerian is grown commercially in Belgium, Germany, France, the Netherlands, and eastern European countries, and to a limited extent in the United States.

Propagate by seeds or spring and fall root divisions. A vigorous plant will produce six to eight divisions. They root quickly, sending up a rosette of leaves in about two weeks. When planting in autumn, do it early in the season to give the plants a better opportunity to become strongly established. Seeds have a short viability and should be sown when ripe. Plants will self-sow and spread by root runners. They can become weedy. Seeds germinate in about twenty days. Give plants one-foot spacings.

Full sun or partial shade are suitable for valerian. It will grow on a wide range of soils, but does best in a moist, rich loam. A soil pH of 6 to 7 is preferable. Commercial plantings have produced yields of a ton per acre.

Harvest the roots in the fall of the second year, after the vegetative growth begins to yellow and die back to the ground. Harvesting can be facilitated by mowing the tops back to the ground beforehand. The roots can be lifted with a spade or small garden fork, or for larger plantings by shallow plowing. They should be shaken vigorously to remove as much dirt as possible from the intertwining rootlets. Roots three-fourths inch and thicker should be split before drying. Care must be taken to wash off all the dirt. Wash under running water with enough pressure to dislodge adhering particles. Valerian should be dried under shade or low forced heat (below 100° F). Its characteristic odor develops on drying.

Valerian is not often thought of as a culinary herb, but in medieval England its flavor was considered delightful for broths and pottages of the common people. In the first edition of his famous *Herball,* published in 1597, John Gerarde relates that the poorer class of people in the north of England considered valerian an essential flavoring ingredient for broths and soups. According to Leung (1980), valerian is approved as a GRAS (generally recognized as safe) food ingredient in the United States. Extracts and the essential oil are added as flavoring in many processed food items at a maximum level of 0.01 percent.

The first-century Greek physician Dioscorides and his contemporaries wrote about valerian as "Phu," a name which incidentally has the same word root as our colloquial exclamation "phew." And it was rightly named, as there are few roots with such a distinctive odor, at once perfume aromatic, but offensive to the olfactory organs of many. Not to cats, though, for felines are attracted to the aromatic root, some say even more intensely than catnip. It has even been reported that it is so liked by cats that they have tried to scratch labels off apothecary jars to gain access to the herb. A famous eighteenth-century English physician, William Cullen, suggested that the quality of valerian in apothecary shops could be determined by how cats react to it. It is also said to attract rats.

Historically, valerian is considered one of the best of herbal tranquilizers. The value of valerian as an antispasmodic and sleep aid was not well known to the ancients, but evolved out of seventeenth- and eighteenth-century usage. "Its antispasmodic powers in general are very well established: and I trust to many of the reports that have been given of its efficacy," (214) wrote William Cullen (1808). The tea and tincture are good antispasmodics, anodynes, carminatives, hypnotics, and nervines. Valerian also possesses worm-expelling ability. It will help relieve stress, muscle spasms, mental depression and despondency, migraine, insomnia, stomach cramps, fatigue, and nervous conditions in general. The root affects the central nervous system, stimulating it in fatigue and calming it in agitation.

Valerian products were available at local pharmacies until just a few years ago. As recently as the late 1970s, I purchased Eli Lilly's Tincture of Valerian at a drugstore in Maine. At another drugstore in Portland,

Valerian

Maine, I asked the pharmacist for tincture of valerian. He went down into his cellar, then came up with a four-ounce bottle for me. This drugstore (which was no longer in business when I traveled to Maine two years ago) had been in the same location for 150 years. It is likely they had a gallon of old valerian tincture hidden away in a storage room. Whole or cut and sifted valerian root, valerian root powder, valerian tincture, valerian capsules, and standardized extracts are available in health and natural-food markets. Valerian was an official remedy in the *United States Pharmacopeia* from 1820 to 1936, and in the *National Formulary* from 1888 to 1946 (S. Foster 1987a, 1991j).

Over the past twenty or thirty years, well over two hundred scientific studies on the active chemical components and their effects have been published in the scientific literature, especially in Europe. Experimental data indicates a scientific basis for mild sedative, spasm-reducing, and mild pain-relieving qualities, as well as an ability to increase coronary blood flow. Over 120 chemical components have been identified from the root and its essential oil (S. Foster 1987a, 1991j).

Several of these components are involved in the plant's biological activity. Since first isolated in 1966, one group known as "valepotriates" were thought to be primarily responsible for valerian's biological effects, but more recent studies indicate that the plant's sedative qualities are due to several additional components.

In the 1980s, P.D. Leatherwood, F. Chauffard, and other researchers from Switzerland's Nestle Corporation published a number of clinical studies on the effects of valerian extracts on sleep patterns. In one study 128 volunteers reported improvements in their ratings for sleep quality and the time it took to fall asleep, without experiencing a "hangoverlike" effect, which is a common complaint with synthetic sedatives. In the study, those who said that they were habitual poor sleepers, or took a long time to fall asleep, had the best results. The authors conducted several additional studies and concluded that the extracts helped significantly to improve the sleep quality of those suffering from mild insomnia with minimal side effects.

Several authors have noted that one of the most appealing aspects of using valerian as a sedative, besides the lack of hangover, is that it does not interact with alcohol, like barbiturates do. However, some individuals may experience a stimulant effect or develop headaches from the use of the herb. Some of the components of valerian have been found to be toxic to certain types of cells in laboratory experiments, but that data has not been extrapolated to therapeutic doses of whole plant extracts. Any potential negative effects are probably related to large doses taken over a long period of time. Like any other herb or substance, valerian should be used in moderation (S. Foster 1987a, 1991j).

In Germany, a drug monograph (December 1986) allows valerian in sedative and sleep-inducing preparations for states of excitation and difficulty in falling asleep due to nervousness. The European Scientific Cooperative for Phytomedicine (ESCOP) produced a monograph on valerian root in 1990, defining it as the rhizome, roots, and stolons of *V. officinalis* that have been carefully dried at a temperature below 40° C (about 104° F). It should contain at least 0.5 percent essential oil. Indications include nervous tension, excitability, restlessness and sleep disturbances, and traditionally, stress and anxiety states. No side effects, special warnings, contraindications or drug interactions are noted.

Valerian contains the valepotriates valtrate and didrovaltrate, tannins, choline, alkaloids, and an essential oil composed mainly of bornyl acetate and isovalerate. Other constituents with sedative action include valerenic acid and valerenone. Hazelhoff and coworkers (1979) suggest that there is an interaction between these constituents. Valerian, valerenic acid, and the esters of eugenyl and isoeugenyl are spasmolytic (Hendriks and coworkers 1981). Whether the pharmacological and therapeutic activity of botanical preparations results from a single chemical component, or a complex interaction of compounds, is a question that constantly arises. The sedative effect of valerian appears, at least for the present, to result from a combination of direct relaxation of the smooth muscle and a depression of some centers in the central nervous system (S. Foster 1987a, 1991j).

The German physician Rudolf Fritz Weiss (1988) puts the conflicting information into proper context: "Considerable difficulties arise when plant chemistry and pharmacology are applied to a medicinal plant on the one hand, and to the use and value of such a plant in practice on the other. These difficulties often seem insurmountable, particularly with a plant such as valerian where the actions are mainly in the mental sphere, so that animal experiments yield no convincing evidence, or at least none that will easily transfer to man. The valerian issue is therefore still very much under discussion." (283)

WILD GERANIUM, CRANESBILL

Geranium maculatum L.
(jer-ayn'-ee-um mak-yew-lay'-tim)
Geraniaceae—Geranium Family

A denizen of open woods and field edges from Maine to Manitoba, south to Georgia, and west to Oklahoma, this indigenous American plant is a showy addition to herb gardens. It is an erect, hardy perennial standing a foot to a foot and a half tall. Long-stemmed leaves arise from the roots, while short-stemmed to sessile-opposite leaves grow on the main stem. They are divided into three to seven lobes with sharp teeth at each lobe's end. The leaves are somewhat hairy and mottled with whitish-green splotches—hence the specific name *maculatum* (spotted). The attractive rose-purple flowers, one to one-and-a-half inches in diameter, are borne on terminal panicles. Wild geranium blooms from April to June, generally for about a three-week period. One form, *Geranium maculatum* f. *albiflorum,* has white flowers. The roots are horizontal, about one-half inch in diameter, contorted, knobby, and pinkish gray on the interior.

Wild geranium grows from seed collected in late summer and sown in fall or the following spring. The seeds need a period of cold stratification, so fall planting is best. Sometimes they may take as much as two years to germinate. Seedlings should be at least six weeks old before attempting to plant them. Roots may also be divided in the fall. The horizontal rhizomes, usually about four to six inches long, have several leaf clusters arising from them. In autumn, the rhizomes can be cut into several sections, each with a bud. Replant at about a one-inch depth. Established plants self-sow freely. Give plants six-inch spacings.

This plant is particularly attractive when grown in colonies of six or more. It needs partial shade and good drainage, and will grow in a variety of soils, tolerating a pH range of 4.5 to 7. It thrives in a moisture-retentive, humus-rich soil. The plant has a tendency to spread, so it may be necessary to keep it in check so that it doesn't crowd out ginseng, goldenseal, or other woodland plants that are grown in the shaded garden.

The root gathered in autumn is the part used. It contains tannins and gallic acid. It has a relatively low moisture content and is easily dried under low, even heat in the shade. Too rapid drying can harden outer cell layers, causing spoilage. Wild geranium root was a well-known remedy among Native Americans and early settlers. The Cherokees employed the root as an astringent and styptic for open wounds, and as a wash for the treatment of canker sores. Decocted with fox grapes, it made a mouthwash for thrush in children. The Meskwakis of the upper Midwest found the root beneficial for sore gums, pyorrhea, toothache, and hemorrhoids. The decocted root was a wash for burns. The Iroquois chose the root to treat sore throat, mouth sores, canker sores, gonorrhea, and in combination with other herbs (*Cornus alternifolia* and *Sambucus canadensis*), to treat the navel of a baby when it does not heal. "It is said that the western Indians consider the geranium as the most effectual remedy they have for the venereal disease," wrote John Eberle (1834, 1: 384).

Caucasian settlers to the continent adopted similar uses

Wild Geranium

for the root from native peoples. Boiled in milk, it was a popular remedy for intestinal ailments of children. Diarrhea, dysentery, leucorrhea, gonorrhea, and syphilis have all reportedly responded to treatment with the root. Basically, it is helpful wherever a styptic or astringent is called for. I have made a gargle from the powdered root to relieve canker sores. The common name for *G. maculatum,* alumroot, reflects this traditional use.

Nineteenth-century physicians who relied heavily on astringent herbs for these conditions depended on wild geranium. It was official in the *United States Pharmacopoeia* from 1820 to 1990. Throughout the nineteenth century, it remained well known as a treatment to stop bleeding, both internal and external. Its advantages included that it created no adverse reactions and had a pleasant taste. It was not considered irritating to the stomach, and thus was suitable for treating children or patients with weak digestion. It was given to children decocted in sweetened milk. To treat diarrhea or dysentery in children, Dr. Charles Lee (1859) made a decoction of one ounce of the root by boiling it for fifteen minutes in milk, then straining it, sweetening it with sugar, and adding cinnamon or nutmeg for flavor. In addition to the crude dried root used for teas or decoctions, commercial products included solid and fluid extracts and tinctures. John Eberle (1834, 1: 383) assessed that "this root is the most agreeable astringent we possess. Its astringency is not associated with bitterness or any other unpleasant taste. In the disease of children, where astringents are indicated, a decoction of it in milk, is a very convenient and efficacious remedy. . . . From considerable experience with this medicine, as well as from the testimony of many other physicians, I am entirely satisfied that it is one of the most useful vegetable astringents we possess." (1: 383)

Wild Ginger

Asarum canadense L.(ass-ar'-um can-a-den'-see)
Aristolochiaceae—Birthwort Family

Wild ginger is a perennial denizen of the eastern deciduous forest from New Brunswick to North Carolina, west to Arkansas and Kansas. The three-to-seven-inch-wide, hairy, heart-shaped leaves have stems up to one foot long. The peculiar reddish-brown, fleshy, urn-shaped flowers have three corollalike sepals but no petals. Flowers appear in forks between the leaf stems and are often hidden by leaves that fell the previous autumn. Blooming is from April to June. The

root is a creeping rhizome.

Propagate by seeds or root division. The seeds, which mature about six weeks after the flowers appear, are hidden underneath the leaf mold or closely hug the ground. They can be sown soon after ripening in a well-prepared seedbed and kept moist for germination the following spring. The seeds require a period of cold, moist afterripening before germination. This is best achieved by wintering the seeds over outdoors in the seedbed. The easiest method of propagation is simply dividing the rhizomes in fall or spring. Root cuttings can be started in a medium suitable for stem cuttings. Give plants six-inch spacings.

Wild ginger likes a moist, rich soil with lots of humus provided by leaf mold. A pH range of 4.5 to 6.0 is suitable for *Asarum.* About 75 percent shade should be provided. Plant ginger among goldenseal and ginseng beds.

The rhizomes which creep on the surface of the ground just below the leaf mold can be harvested in the autumn as the leaves wither. It is possible to slice a section of rhizome between two established plants, effectively harvesting the beneficial part of the plant without reducing its numbers.

In the nineteenth century, the root was a substitute for true ginger, because of its aromatic, somewhat gingerlike fragrance. The similarities end there. The fresh roots are fun to nibble while hiking through the forest. Candy the roots as you would calamus or angelica roots.

The plant was widely utilized by American Indian groups in its range. The Rappahannocks infused the root for typhoid fever. Mixed with red cedar berries (*Juniperus virginiana*), wild ginger was a treatment for asthma. Spikenard (*Aralia racemosa*) and wild ginger were combined as a wash by the Ojibwa for fractured limbs. The Montagnais found the plant to be a general tonic. Sore throats, earache, and stomach cramps were treated with wild ginger by the Meskwakis. Along with many other tribes, they also cooked the root with spoiled meat to prevent ptomaine poisoning, and with other foods to render them palatable. It was cooked with catfish to improve the flavor. Fishermen chewed the root and then spit on their bait, using wild ginger's aroma to attract fish. The Menominees employed the fresh or dried root as a mild stomachic for patients with weak stomachs. The Iroquois valued the root to prevent bad dreams, to treat headaches, and first and foremost for the treatment of fevers. Four pieces of two-inch-long roots were infused for five minutes in two cups of hot water; then the patient drank a half cup of the warm tea before meals. Afterward the patient lay down and was covered with blankets to promote sweating. The process was repeated two to three times a day to allay fever. The Iroquois also found the root beneficial for coughs, measles, a spring tonic for the elderly, urinary disorders, and boils. Wild ginger possesses stimulant, carminative, tonic, diuretic, and diaphoretic properties. Stomach ailments, kidney problems, and delayed menstruation were treated with ginger root by early settlers.

Wild ginger has yet to reach its full potential as a fragrance, culinary, or medicinal herb for the American herb market. The fresh and dried roots are highly aromatic. The essential oil of this and other *Asarum* species from Europe and Asia are sometimes added as a fragrance ingredient in perfumes. The roots were formerly candied or pickled on a limited commercial scale in the United States.

Wild ginger's essential oil contains pinenes, delta-linalool, borneol, terpineol, geraniol, eugenol, methyleugenol, asarene, and azulene. The oil is antibacterial, especially against Gram-positive and pus-forming bacteria. The root also has aristolochic acid, a compound that has been developed medicinally in both Europe and Asia. Experiments with aristolochic acid have shown it reduces recurrence of herpes lesions. Aristolochic acid also competes with toxic chemicals to inhibit lymphocytic surface receptors, thus protecting against the effects of several toxic compounds. A tablet of aristolochic acid has been used clinically in China to treat wounds and promote healing of ulcers, burns, and scalds. It has also been combined with antibiotics to treat bronchitis and tonsillitis. Aristolochic acid enhances phagocytosis of leucocytes and macrophages, and thus is considered an immunostimulant. Preparations of wild ginger's European relative, *A. europeaum,* are used as immunostimulants in Europe (Wagner and Proksch 1985; Wren 1988). Aristolochic acid, itself, is known to be carcinogenic and mutagenic. Plants containing the compound should be used with caution.

This is a plant with a long history of use in the United States that parallels the tradition of closely related species in both Europe and Asia, which has been supported by modern research. Wild ginger is another American medicinal and aromatic plant that remains underexplored and undeveloped.

WITCH HAZEL

Hamamelis virginiana L., *H. vernalis* Sarg.
(ham-am'-e-lis vir-gin-i-ay'-na; ver-nay'-lis)
Hamamelidaceae—Witch Hazel Family
Plate 15

This genus has about six species of small trees and shrubs native to temperate regions of eastern North America and eastern Asia. *Hamamelis virginiana,* common witch hazel, is a shrub growing to fifteen feet tall, found from New England south to Georgia, and west to Minnesota. The straight-veined, scallop-edged leaves are oval. Branches are long, angled, and curve upward. The bark is light brown to gray, and marked by light-colored circular spots and scales. The round, slender twigs are covered with rough brown hairs. Crimson and yellow hues of autumn foliage are particularly striking. September through November, as the leaves drop, the flowers unfold in clusters or heads tightly hugging the stems. The four yellow, long, narrow petals give the flowers a spiderlike appearance. Each seed capsule contains two shiny black seeds, with oily, white, edible interiors. When

Wild Ginger

mature, the capsules burst with a pop, projecting seeds several feet from the shrub.

H. vernalis, vernal witch hazel, is native to the Ozark plateau from southern Missouri, Arkansas, and Oklahoma, to Louisiana and Alabama. Here in the Ozarks, the orange-red blossoms emerge in the last week of December after the last flowers of common witch hazel have withered. These two species ensure that at least one plant is blooming year-round in the Ozarks, surviving the bitterness of -5° F temperatures. In the North, plantings of vernal witch hazel will bloom in early spring.

Witch hazel is not the easiest plant in the world to propagate, but it can

be increased by seeds, cuttings, or layering. Ripe untreated seeds can be sown in late fall and may germinate the following spring or take two years to emerge. Cold stratification at 41° F for ninety days will help break the seed's dormancy. Sow stratified seeds in spring in a moist, humus-rich soil under shade. Plant seeds at eight-to-twelve-inch spacings. Cuttings can be made of green twigs, pencil size or smaller, and rooted in moist sand. Roots develop in about ten weeks. Young suckers from an established plant can be layered to increase stock.

Common witch hazel grows naturally in a wide range of soils, from poor, rocky, high-mountain ones, to rich stream banks with silty loam. Vernal witch hazel prefers a rich, moist soil with a pH between 6 and 7. Tolerant of air pollution, this shrub will grow in cities. Full sun or partial shade is acceptable, though young seedlings should be protected from the sun.

The easiest and surest way to get witch hazel started in your yard is to buy plants. Both of the American species, plus the Japanese species, *H. japonica,* and the Chinese, *H. mollis,* are commonly sold by nurseries. A number of hybrids and cultivars are also available. Witch hazels are greatly overlooked as landscape plants. They are easy to grow, and depending upon the species, cultivar, or region, will provide flowers in late autumn, winter, or early spring.

For over two hundred years, witch hazel has been a popular plant-derived domestic remedy in North America. Even today over a million gallons of witch hazel "extract" are sold each year in the United States. Bottled witch hazel water, one of the few commercial medicines prepared from a wild American plant, is available in virtually every pharmacy. Witch hazel is an over-the-counter drug approved as an astringent to relieve external pain and protect the skin. An external anorectal, it is primarily employed for the relief of hemorrhoids.

Today's bottled witch hazel is actually distilled witch hazel water, made from the dried leaves, twigs, and partially dried dormant branches. The recently cut twigs are soaked in twice their weight of warm water for about twenty-four hours. This infusion is then

Witch Hazel

distilled and sufficient alcohol (22 percent) is added to preserve the distillate (S. Foster 1989g).

The practical applications of witch hazel, as is the case with most American medicinal plants, are products of Native American ingenuity. The Potawatomi employed witch hazel to relieve sore muscles. The twigs were infused in water, then hot stones were added to create steam. A poultice of the bark soothed eye inflammations. The Iroquois made a beverage tea from the leaves, sweetened with maple sugar. Some tribes rubbed a decoction of the bark on the legs of game participants to keep muscles limber.

In the 1840s, Theron T. Pond of Utica established an association with the Oneida Indians of central New York. He learned from the medicine man that they held a shrub in high esteem for all types of burns, boils, and wounds. It was witch hazel. Pond learned as much as he could about the extract, and finally after several years, in 1848, Pond and the medicine man decided to market it under the trade name "Golden Treasure." After several moves and sales of the company, a manufacturing facility was established in Connecticut, and the name of the witch hazel preparation was changed to "Pond's Extract." The witch hazel industry is still centered in Connecticut with the E. E. Dickinson Co., the T. N. Dickinson Co., and the American Distilling and Manufacturing Co. producing most of the witch hazel extract sold on the American market (J. U. Lloyd and J. T. Lloyd 1935).

The leaves and bark are astringent, hemostatic, slightly sedative, and anodyne. A poultice of bark will relieve pain and swelling. Poultices, tinctures, or infusions are beneficial for bruises and insect bites. I use a homemade tincture of witch hazel on poison ivy. It dries up the discharge and relieves itching. Gather five or six three-foot-long dormant winter branches, scrape off the bark, and add it to twice its weight of vodka. Soak for two weeks, shaking occasionally. Commercial witch hazel products are available at every corner drugstore. They include hemorrhoid suppositories, ointments, lotions, and cloth wipes. These products relieve itching, irritations, and minor pains. Witch hazel water has

also been valued for the treatment of sprains and bruises, spots and blemishes, and as an astringent in eye drops, aftershave lotions, and other cosmetics.

In Europe, fluid extracts of witch hazel have been proven vasoconstrictive and are treatments for varicose veins. Witch hazel ointments and suppositories are considered one of the best treatments for hemorrhoids, and in most cases provide relief equal to corticoid ointments. Witch hazel ointment is also helpful in the treatment of wounds, ulcerations, and skin problems, especially in children (Weiss 1988).

The leaves contain about 10 percent crude protein, phosphorus, calcium, and tannins. The bark has hamamelitannin, saponins, a wax, a fixed oil, an essential oil, and resin. Steam-distilled witch hazel products are tannin-free. Extracts of the leaves, bark, and stem contain gallic acid and hamamelitannin, as well as proanthocyanidins. The leaves and stems have two to three times more proanthocyanidins and gallic acid than the bark. The bark has thirty-one times more hamamelitannin than the leaf, and eighty-seven times more than the stem (Vennat et al. 1988).

WOODRUFF
Galium odoratum (L.) Scop.
(*Asperula odorata* L.)
(gay'-lee-um oh-dor-ay'-tum)
Rubiaceae—Madder Family

There are about four hundred species recognized in the

Galium odoratum, Woodruff

Artemisia pontica, Roman Wormwood

linen closets. May wine is a refreshing beverage prepared by soaking the fresh or dried leaves for a couple of hours in a slightly sweet white wine.

Woodruff possesses diaphoretic, diuretic, sedative, antispasmodic, and cholagogic qualities. It has primarily been brewed as a tea to relieve migraines, insomnia, liver infections, jaundice, bladder stones, and nervous tension in children and the elderly. The bruised herb makes a soothing poultice for fresh wounds and cuts. In Europe, sweet woodruff preparations are used to treat varicose veins and thrombophlebitis.

Woodruff contains coumarin in a bound glycoside form that is activated by wilting or drying. Asperuloside, monotropein, tannin, bitter principles, and a trace of nicotinic acid are found in the leaves. Asperuloside, as well as extracts of sweet woodruff, have proven antiinflammatory benefits.

genus *Galium. G. odoratum* is an erect or spreading perennial from six to twelve inches high, native to Europe, North Africa, and parts of Asia. It is common in alkaline soils of deciduous woods, particularly beech forests throughout most of Europe, though it is rare in the Mediterranean region. Whorls of six to eight lance-shaped leaves, up to an inch and a half long, with rough, bristle-tipped margins, characterize this plant. The white, four-part, star-shaped corollas bloom on loose, branching, terminal heads from May to June. The flowers are about one-fourth inch long. The fruits have small, hooked hairs which catch on the fur of passing animals, thus dispersing the seed. The creeping rhizomes produce lush carpets in deciduous forests, and favor a beech canopy.

Woodruff is best propagated by dividing the creeping rhizomes in spring. It may also be propagated from cuttings or seeds planted soon after ripening. Fresh seeds are essential. Space plants at one-foot intervals.

This is an excellent ground cover or edging for shaded areas. It tends to be a rapid spreader in rich, moist soils. To make a poor soil suitable for woodruff, fork in a generous supply of leaf mold. Soil pH should hover between 6 and 8.3.

Harvest the herb just before flowering. Odorless when fresh, the plant develops a distinctive new-mown hay scent upon drying or wilting.

The dried leaves make a wonderfully fragrant sachet for

Wormwood, Southernwood, Roman Wormwood

Artemisia absinthium L., *A. abrotanum* L., *A. pontica* L.
(are-te-miz'-i-a ab-sin'-thi-um; ab-roh-tay'-num; pon'-tic-ca)
Compositae (Asteraceae)—Aster Family
Plate 15

Artemisia absinthium, common wormwood, is a coarse, sprawling perennial, native to most of Europe and naturalized in the northeastern and central United States. This bitter-tasting herb reaches a height of four feet and has finely divided gray leaves with rounded oblong segments. The nodding, one-eighth-inch-wide, yellow flowers are difficult to imagine as members of the same family to which sunflowers belong. They bloom in late summer. The essential oil is variable, and several chemotypes have been recognized in Europe.

A. abrotanum, southernwood, is a shrubby perennial, usually about three feet tall. The finely divided leaves are smooth and green, with narrow linear leaf segments. The tiny, yellowish-white flowers are seldom seen in the herb garden.

A. pontica, Roman wormwood, is one of the most delicate-appearing artemisias. It is a short (two-foot) shrubby perennial native to central and eastern Europe, and naturalized locally elsewhere. The leaves are finely divided and densely covered with tiny gray hairs on both surfaces. The one-eighth-inch-wide pale yellow flowers are borne on loose panicles.

These plants are easily propagated by root division with the exception of southernwood, which is best propagated from cuttings. Root divisions can be made in the spring or fall. The wormwoods can be grown from seed, but the seed is tiny and difficult to handle. In commercial plantings, the seed of wormwood is broadcast or drilled in autumn, often following a grain crop. The seeds can also be sown in seedbeds in spring. Transplanting is best accomplished in cool, overcast weather. Sow on the soil's surface, as the plant needs light to germinate. Germination takes place in about three weeks. Give plants eighteen-inch spacings.

Wormwoods will do well in an average garden soil, though they prefer somewhat dry, well-drained, ones. They seem to do equally well in rich garden soils. Partial shade or full sun is tolerable. A neutral to slightly alkaline soil is best. Both mugwort and Roman wormwood spread by root runners and must be given room or be kept under control. Wormwoods are winter hardy. Commercial perennial plantings are maintained for up to ten years, though production peaks during the second or third year. For essential-oil production, the herb is harvested two times a year when in flower. Commercial plantings may produce one to two tons of dried herb per harvest during peak growth cycles. Traditionally, the dried leaves are stripped by hand from the main stems after drying. The leaves should be carefully dried under shade. Commercial use of the plant is very limited.

The leaves of wormwood secrete a bitter principle which inhibits the growth of other plants. Give wormwood at least a three-foot buffer between it and adjacent plants. Once I let an herb garden go wild just to see what would happen. Mints and oregano growing within three feet of wormwood were only about six inches high, where as plants outside the perimeter were two feet tall and lush. A 1943 study by Funke confirmed that wormwood has an inhibitory effect on the

development of plants grown within about a yard of it. All eighteen species included in the experiment, grown in different locations over two summers, were adversely affected. Lovage was actually killed by close proximity to wormwood. In another experiment, when the fresh leaves of *A. absinthium* were dug into the soil, they reduced the percentage of seeds of the plant species tested which germinated and hindered the development of seedlings. Korean researchers soaked the fresh leaves of wormwood in a quart of water for twenty hours and found that the infusion significantly reduced germination of a number of weed seeds, and completely stopped the germination of plantain. Perhaps a wormwood tea could serve as a home-made garden herbicide.

The leaves of wormwood and southernwood can be placed in drawers to deter moths and beetles. Replenish the supply every six months. There is scientific evidence that the essential oil or extracts of *A. absinthium* and *A. abrotanum* have limited insecticidal or repellent effects.

Wormwood and Roman wormwood are used to flavor vermouth. Wormwood was the main ingredient in the now outlawed alcoholic beverage absinthe. In the mid-nineteenth century, the consumption of absinthe was so popular in France that it threatened to become as serious a social problem as the smoking of opium in China. The hour between five and six in the afternoon was known to Parisians as the "absinthe hour." Effects included auditory and visual hallucinations and excitation. Not only did absinthe contain wormwood as a primary ingredient, but copper sulphate was added to tint the beverage green, while antimony chloride gave it its milky opalescence. With its social and toxic effects becoming more widely known, absinthe was banned in much of Europe by the turn of the century, and finally outlawed in France in 1915. The French consumed two-thirds of the world's supply of the psychoactive beverage. Absinthe continued to be available in Germany into the 1920s. Studies have suggested that absinthe's effects may be similar to marijuana, as they may both interact with the same central nervous system receptors (Chandler 1987, Tyler 1987).

Wormwood works as a bitter tonic to stimulate appetite and aid digestion. Weiss (1988) believes that wormwood is one of the best drugs for the treatment of dyspepsia because it acts on the stomach and gallbladder, especially in conditions involving atony of these organs. It lessens symptoms of atonic and achytlic states of the stomach, assisting digestion and helping to relieve the sensation of fullness and accumulation of gases in the digestive system. It has also been used for liver disorders. All of the artemisias discussed possess emmenagogic, vermifuge, diuretic, and antiseptic qualities. Wormwood essential oil (too toxic for human consumption) has antibacterial and antifungal effects. It is employed externally in some parts of the world for the relief of rheumatic pain. A tincture (10 to 30 drops in water) or a teaspoonful in a glass of hot water is a typical dose recommended by European phytopractitioners, though the herb should be taken for only a short period of time (no more than three weeks).

Typically, *A. absinthium* contains thujone as the major component of its essential oil, along with beta-caryophyllene, pinene, sabinene, phellandrene, and azulenes. However, various European chemotypes have different predominant constituents in their essential oils. The oil, found at levels of 0.2 to 3.1 percent, may contain thujone and thujyl alcohol as primary components, or myrcene and sabinene, myrcene and isothujyl alcohol, cadinene, cadinene and s-guajazulene, proartemazulene, or other azulenes (Tétényi 1970). The sesquiterpene lactones, responsible for the intensely bitter flavor of wormwood, include absinthin, anabsinthin, artabsin, matricin, and others (Chandler 1987). In large doses, thujone causes convulsions. Thujone-free wormwood extracts serve as flavoring ingredients in some commercial food products.

Southernwood, which has been a part of medicinal preparations in Europe, has been taken internally for the treatment of chilblains, and liver, spleen, and stomach problems, and applied externally for wens, whitlows, and tumors. The primary constituent of its essential oil is absinthol. Abrotanin is a bitter principle found in the leaves. They also contain adenine, adenosine, choline, scopoletin, tannins, and other components (Duke 1985).

YARROW
Achillea millefolium L.
(ak-i-lee'-a mil-e-foh'-li-um) Compositae
(Asteraceae)—Aster Family

About eighty-five species are found in the genus *Achillea,* with over fifty occurring in Europe. *A. millefolium* grows throughout temperate and boreal regions of the Northern Hemisphere and to some extent in the Southern Hemisphere. It is a hardy, highly variable, aromatic perennial growing to three feet tall. The finely divided feathery leaves

are about two to eight inches long, becoming progressively smaller toward the top of the plant. The white (or sometimes pink) flower heads are in terminal flat clusters. Each flower head is about one-fourth inch across. The entire cluster is three to four inches in diameter. It blooms from June to September. There are numerous cultivars, including the flaming pink 'Rubra' and the light pink 'Rosea.' Reports on use of yarrow in North America may involve *A. millefolium,* or the widespread and common *A. lanulosa,* which is native to eastern North America and nearly identical in appearance. Reports of yarrow use in western North America (California

Yarrow

to Alaska) may feature *A. borealis*.

Yarrow (*A. millefolium*) is a highly complex species group. It occurs throughout Europe in grasslands and waste places, but is rare in the Mediterranean region. Plants once described as varieties of subspecies of *A. millefolium* have now been separated into nine separate species in Europe. Hybridization with other species in the genus is common so identification is difficult. For the professional botanist, the only reliable way to separate one genetic entity from another in the *A. millefolium* complex is by determining the number of chromosomes. Genetic differences are also associated with chemical variations in the essential oils (Chandler 1989; Chandler and coworkers 1982).

Propagate yarrow by seeds or root divisions in spring and fall. Plants should be given eight-to-twelve-inch spacings. Clumps should be divided every three to four years to stimulate growth. The tiny seeds can be tamped on the surface of a well-prepared seedbed. They germinate in ten to fourteen days.

Yarrow likes almost any soil, but prefers an acidic situation (pH 4.5 to 7). It requires little care, is drought resistant, and should have full sun. Plants become weak and leggy under shade. Keep it well-weeded.

Harvest plants as they come into bloom, as the essential-oil content is maximized at the beginning of flowering. Yarrow dries quickly and easily. It can be expected to produce twelve hundred to fifteen hundred pounds of dried herb per acre.

The flowers have stronger medicinal qualities than the leaves. Yarrow has been valued to stop bleeding and heal wounds by cultures from the ancient Greeks to North American Indians. Wild yarrow grew around the perimeters of the Shaker herb gardens at Sabbathday Lake. Whenever herb harvesters cut themselves, we went to the garden's edge, crushed yarrow flowers or leaves in the palm of our hands, washed the wound, then applied the yarrow directly to the cut. Without any additional aid, the bleeding stopped and even deep cuts healed without infection within a few days— often to the amazement of the wounded. It is important to clean the cut before applying yarrow; otherwise the poultice will close the dirt within the wound.

American Indians treated sprains, bruises, swollen tissue, rashes, itching, nosebleeds, fevers, colds, headache, delayed menstruation, and a host of other ailments with yarrow. Hemostatic, expectorant, analgesic, carminative, diaphoretic, emmenagogic, antiinflammatory, antipyretic, antiseptic, and stomachic properties are locked in a tincture of yarrow. Yarrow has been most universal in the treatment of rheumatism, colds, catarrh, fevers, hypertension, and amenorrhea (Wren 1988). Cultures throughout the regions of the world where it occurs employ it for parallel purposes. I feel it is one of the more beneficial of home remedies.

Over 120 compounds have been found in yarrow. A complex and variable essential oil contains prochamazulene, pinenes, caryophyllene, eugenol, borneol, cineole, camphor, and other compounds. At least fourteen different chemical races have been identified in Europe. In addition to genetic variation, the habitat, climate, and geology in which the plant occurs can also effect the quality of the chemical content. One study found that the frequency of proazuelene-containing yarrows correlated with increased concentrations of plant-available phosphate, magnesium, and manganese in the soil—a possible direction to pursue for potential growers (Preitschopf and Arnold 1989). Sesquiterpene lactones may be responsible for yarrow's antiinflammatory qualities. The alkaloid achilleine is an active hemostatic agent. Flavonoids may account for the antispasmodic activity.

Yarrow also contains tannins and coumarins. The root of yarrow is reported to yield a volatile oil with the odor of valerian, though this characteristic has not been commercially exploited. Unfortunately, in many cases voucher specimens have not been retained by chemical researchers doing work on yarrow, therefore it is often impossible to tell exactly what species was involved. As a commercial food-flavoring ingredient for beverages, yarrow or its oil is allowed to be used if free from thujone. Yarrow is generally considered nontoxic, though it may produce dermatitis in some individuals.

YERBA BUENA
Satureja douglasii (Benth.) Briq.
(sat-you-ree'-a dug-las'-ee-i)
Labiatae (Lamiaceae)—Mint Family

The good herb—yerba buena—was also the original name of the city of San Francisco. Too bad they changed it. This plant is an evergreen perennial with trailing, often rooting, stems up to two feet long. The opposite leaves are oval or rounded, about an inch and a half long and one inch wide, smooth, and scalloped at the edges. Solitary flowers emerge from the leaf axils on one-half to five-eighths-inch-long pedicels (flower stems) from April to September.

Flowers are about three-eighths of an inch long and white or purple in color. Yerba buena is native to the shaded coniferous woods of western North America from British Columbia south to Los Angeles County, California. Under the shade of trees, it has a more sprawling habit with wider-spaced leaves and a less pungent scent than plants grown under full sun. Spanish-speaking peoples give the name "yerba buena" to spearmint as well.

Plant breeder remarkable Luther Burbank took notice of this plant and its potential diversity:

> The *yerba buena* is a common little trailing plant in the red wood forests, sometimes growing also among shrubs and along the edge of fields. It has sweet-scented, round leaves, and small, pale, insignificant, purplish flowers.
>
> This plant is fairly constant in any given locality, but specimens from different regions vary a good deal, some being rather packed growers, while others sun out to great lengths, with long, runner-like branches. (1914, 7:161).

Yerba buena is easily propagated from stem cuttings and layerings. Offshoots that have become rooted on their own may be cut from the parent plant and transplanted in the spring or fall.

At Taylor's Herb Gardens, a patch of yerba buena receiving full sun during most of the day has a tight, compact growth and a strong camphor fragrance. In southern regions with hot summer sun, yerba buena will need shade. In other regions, it will take full sun. It is most prolific in slightly acid, rich, moist, sandy loam. If this plant was indigenous to the Mediterranean region rather than a West Coast American native, it would probably have found its way into European herb gardens, subsequently becoming a favorite plant of American.

The leaves can be harvested anytime during the growing season. They dry quickly and easily. California Indian groups collected the vines, and rolled them up to dry.

The dried or fresh leaves make an excellent tea. Yerba buena was highly esteemed by California Indians as a carminative for colic, a blood purifier, a febrifuge, a reliever of arthritic symptoms, and a general tonic and panacea. The leaf tea was a remedy for upset stomach.

The Costanoan Indians made a strong decoction of the herb for pinworms, or held the leaves in their mouths to treat toothache. The warm leaves were also poulticed on the outside of the jaw to treat toothache (Bocek 1982). To disguise their human odor, deer hunters would rub the leaves on their bodies.

Yerba Buena

BIBLIOGRAPHY

Abdullah, T. H., O. Kandil, A. Elkadi, and J. Carter. 1988. Garlic Revisited: Therapeutic for the Major Diseases of Our Time? *J. of the National Medical Assn.* 80 (4):439–45.

Abdullah, T. H., D. V. Kirkpatrick, and J. Carter. 1989. Enhancement of Natural Killer Cell Activity in AIDS with Garlic. *Deutsch Zeishrift für Oncology* 21:52–53.

Adams, J. 1987. *Landscaping with Herbs.* Portland, Oreg: Timber Press.

Adler, P. R., J. E. Simon, and G. E. Wilcox. 1989. Nitrogen Form Alters Sweet Basil Growth and Essential Oil Content and Composition. *HortScience* 24 (5):789–90.

Akerele, O. 1988. Medicinal Plants and Primary Health Care: An Agenda for Action. *Fitoterapia* 59 (5):355–63.

_____. 1992. WHO Guidelines for the Assessment of Herbal Medicines. *Fitoterapia* 63 (2):99–110.

Akerele, O., V. Heywood, and H. Synge, eds. 1991. *Conservation of Medicinal Plants (Proceedings of the Chiang Mai Consultation).* Cambridge: Cambridge Univ. Press.

Akhtar, M. S., A. H. Akhtar, and M. A. Khan. 1992. Antiulcerogenic Effects of *Ocimum basilicum* Extracts, Volatile Oils and Flavonoid Glycosides in Albino Rats. *Int. J. of Pharmacognosy* 30 (2):97–104.

Al-Naghdy, S. A., M. O. Abdel-Rahman, and H. I. Heiba. 1988. Evidence for Some Prostaglandins in *Allium sativum* Extracts. *Phytotherapy Research* 2 (4):196–97.

Alstat, E., ed. 1989. *Eclectic Dispensatory of Botanical Therapeutics.* Portland, Oreg.: Eclectic Medical Publications.

American Herbal Products Association. 1992. Herbs of Commerce. Austin, Tex.: American Herbal Products Assn.

Anderson, E. 1952. *Plants, Man and Life.* Berkeley: Univ. of California Press.

Anderson, J. E., W. W. Ma, D. L. Smith, C. J. Chang, and J. L. McLaughlin. 1992. Biologically Active g-Lactones and Methyletoalkenes from *Lindera benzoin. J. of Natural Products* 55 (1):71–73.

Attelmann, H., K. Bends, H. Hellenkemper, J. Reichert, and H.-J. Warkalla. 1972. Agnolyt® in the Treatment of Gynecological Complaints. *Zeitschrift für Präklinische Geriatrie* 2:239.

Awang, D. V. C. 1987a. Comfrey. *Canadian Pharmaceutical J.* 120:100–104.

_____. 1987b. Feverfew (*Tanacetum parthenium*). *The Pharmaceutical J.* 239:487.

_____. 1989a. Feverfew. *Canadian Pharmaceutical J.* 122 (5):266–70.

_____. 1989b. Chemotaxonomy and the Regulation of Commercial Plant Products—Identity and Standardization. Presentation to the 57 Congrès de l'Association Canadienne Francaise pour l'Advancment des Sciences, Montréal, 15–19 May.

_____. 1990a. Feverfew Feedback. Letter. *HerbalGram* 22: 2, 34, 42.

_____. 1990b. Borage. *Canadian Pharmaceutical J.* 123: 121–26.

_____. 1991a. Comfrey Update. *HerbalGram* 25:20–23.

_____. 1991b. St. John's Wort. *Canadian Pharmaceutical J.* 124:33–35.

_____. 1993. Feverfew Fever—A Headache for the Consumer. *HerbalGram* 29 (in press).

Awang, D. V. C., B. A. Dawson, and D. G. Kindack. 1991. Parthenolide Content of Feverfew (*Tanacetum parthenium*) Assessed by HPLC and ¹H-NMR Spectroscopy. *J. of Natural Products* 54 (6):1516–21.

Bach, N., S. N. Thung, and F. Schaffner. 1989. Comfrey Herb Tea-Induced Hepatic Veno-Occlusive Disease. *American J. of Medicine* 87:97–99.

Barkley, T. M., ed. 1986. Flora of the Great *Plains.* Lawrence: Univ. Press of Kansas.

Barton, B. S. [1798 and 1804] 1900. *Collections for An Essay towards a Materia Medica of the United States.* Reprint. Bulletin of the Lloyd Library, no. 1, Reproduction Series no. 1. Cincinnati: Lloyd Library.

Bastien, J. W. 1987. Heal*ers of the Andes: Kallaway Herbalists and Their Medicinal Plants.* Salt Lake City: Univ. of Utah Press.

Bauer, K., D. Garbe, and H. Surburg. 1990. *Common Fragrance and Flavor Materials.* 2d. ed. New York: VCH Publishers.

Bauer, R., and S. Foster. 1989. HPLC Analysis of *Echinacea simulata* and *E. paradoxa* Roots. *Planta Medica* 55:637.

———. 1991. Analysis of Alkamides and Caffeic Acid Derivatives from *Echinacea simulata* and *E. paradoxa* Roots. *Planta Medica* 57:447–49.

Bauer, R., and H. Wagner. 1991. *Echinacea* Species as Potential Immunostimulatory Drugs. In vol. 5 of *Economic and Medicinal Plant Research*, ed. H. Wagner and N. R. Farnsworth, 253–322. New York: Academic Press.

Beattie, J. H. 1937a. *Production of Garlic.* USDA Leaflet, no. 138. Washington, D.C.: U. S. Government Printing Office.

———. 1937b. *Production of Parsley.* USDA Leaflet, no. 136. Washington, D.C.: U. S. Government Printing Office.

———. n.d. *Production and Preparation of Horseradish.* USDA Leaflet, no. 129. Washington, D.C.: U. S. Government Printing Office.

Beaubaire, N. A, and J. E. Simon. 1987. Production Potential of *Borago officinalis* L. *Acta Horticulturae* 208:101–13.

Belaiche, P., and O. Lievoux. 1991. Clinical Studies on the Palliative Treatment of Prostatic Adenoma with Extract of *Urtica* Root. *Phytotherapy Research* 5:267–69.

Bennett, B. C., C. R. Bell, R. T. Boulware. 1990. Geographic Variation in Alkaloid Content of *Sanguinaria canadensis* (Papaveraceae). *Rhodora* 92 (870):57–69.

BGA (Bundesgesundheitsamt). 1985. Monographie: Passiflorae herba. *Bundesanzeiger*, no. 223 (30 November).

———. 1989. Monographie: Echinaceae purpureae herba. *Bundesanzeiger*, no. 43 (2 March).

———. 1992a. Monographie: Echinaceae purpureae Radix. *Bundesanzeiger*, vol. 44, no. 162 (29 August).

———. 1992b. Monographie: Echinaceae pallidae Radix. *Bundesanzeiger*, vol. 44, no. 162 (29 August).

———. 1992c. Monographie: Echinaceae angustifoliae/ pallidae Herba and Echinaceae angustifoliae Radix. *Bundesanzeiger*, vol. 44, no. 162 (29 August).

Bigelow, J. 1817–1820. *American Medical Botany.* 3 vols. Boston: Cummings and Hilliard.

———. 1822. A *Treatise on the Materia Medica Intended as a Sequel to the Pharmacopeia of the United States.* Boston: Charles Ewer.

Blumenthal, M. 1989. Antidepressant Properties of St. John's Wort. *Medical Nutrition,* Summer: 49.

Bocek, B. 1982. Ethnobotany of Costanoan Indians, California, Based on Collections by John P. Harrington. *Economic Botany* 38 (2):240–55.

Bomme, U., J. Hölzl, C. Hessler, and T. Stahn. 1992. Wie Beeinfulßt die Sorte Wirkstoffgehalt und Ertrag von *Echinacea purpurea* (L.) Moench im Hinblick auf die Pharmazeutische Nutzung? Parts 1, 2. *Landwirtschaftliches Jahrbuch* 69 (2, 3): 149–64, 324–42.

Bordia, A. 1981. Effect of Garlic on Blood Lipids in Patients with Coronary Heart Disease. American J. *of Clinical Nutrition* 34:2100–2103.

Braly, B. 1987. *Supplement to the Ginseng Research Institute's Indexed Bibliography.* Wausau, Wis.: Ginseng Research Institute.

Brann, J. W., J. A. McClintock, J. Rosenbaum, and H. H. Wheztel. 1916. *Ginseng Diseases and Their Control.* USDA Farmers Bulletin no. 736. Washington, D. C.: U. S. Government Printing Office.

Briggs, C. J. 1986. Evening Primrose: La Belle de Nuit, the King's Cureall. *Canadian Pharmaceutical J.* 119 (5):249–54.

Bring, M., and J. Wayemburgh. 1981. *Japanese Gardens: Design and Meaning.* New York: McGraw-Hill.

Brown, O. P. 1878. *The Complete Herbalist.* Jersey City, N.J.: O. Phelps Brown.

Browne, D. J. 1832. *Sylva Americana.* Boston: William Hyde and Co.

Buist, R. 1832. *The Family Kitchen Gardener.* New York: C. M. Saxton.

Burbank, L. 1914. *Luther Burbank: His Methods and Discoveries and Their Practical Applications.* 12 vols. New York: Luther Burbank Press.

Burkill, I. H. 1966. *A Dictionary of the Economic Products of the Malay Peninsula.* 2 vols. Kuala Lumpur: Ministry of Agriculture & Cooperatives.

Bushland, R. C. 1939. Volatile Oils as Ovicides for the Screwworm, *Cochliomyia americana* C & P. *J. of Economic Entomology* 32 (3):430–31.

Bye, R. A. 1986. Uses of Plants by Hispano Americans in the Valley of San Luis in South-Central Colorado. *J. of Ethnobiology* 6 (2):289–306.

Chandler, R. F. 1987. Wormwood. *Canadian Pharmaceutical J.* 120 (10):602–4.

_____. 1989. Yarrow. *Canadian Pharmaceutical J.* 122 (1):41–43.

Chandler, R. F., S. N. Hooper, and M. J. Harvey. 1982. Ethnobotany and Phytochemistry of Yarrow, *Achillea millefolium,* Compositae. *Economic Botany* 36 (2):203–23.

Charles, D. J., and J. E. Simon. 1990. Comparison of Extraction Methods for the Rapid Determination of Essential Oil Content and Composition of Basil. *J. of the American Society of Horticultural Science* 115 (3):458–62.

_____. 1992. A New Geraniol Chemotype of *Ocimum gratissimum* L. *J. of Essential Oil Research* 4:231–34.

Charles, D. J., J. E. Simon, and M. P. Widrlechner. 1991. Characterization of Essential Oil of *Agastache* Species. *J. of Agricultural and Food Chemistry* 39:1946–49.

Charles, D. J., J. E. Simon, and K. V. Wood. 1990. Essential Oil Constituents of *Ocimum micranthum* Willd. *J. of Agricultural and Food Chemistry* 38:120–22.

Chaytor, D. A. 1937. A Taxonomic Study of the Genus *Lavandula. J. of the Linnaean Society, Botany* 51:170–71.

Clark, G. 1939. *The Man Who Talks with Flowers: The Life Story of Dr. George Washington Carver.* St. Paul, Minn.: Macalester Park Publishing Co.

Cobbett, W. 1821. *The American Gardener.* London: C. Clement.

Combie, J., T. E. Nugent, and T. Tobin. 1982. Inability of Goldenseal to Interfere with the Detection of Morphine in Urine. *Equine Veterinary Science,* Jan./Feb.: 16–21.

Council of Scientific and Industrial Research. 1948–1985. *The Wealth of India.* 11 vols. New Delhi: Publications and Information Directorate, Council of Scientific and Industrial Research.

Courter, J. W., and A. M. Rhodes. 1969. Historical Notes on Horseradish. *Economic Botany* 23 (2):156–64.

Craker, L. E. 1987. Agronomic Practices for Dill Production. In *Proceedings of the Second National Herb Growing and Marketing Conference,* ed. J. E. Simon and L. Grant, 58–61. West Lafayette, Ind.: Purdue Research Foundation.

Crellin, J. K., and J. Philpott. 1989. *Herbal Medicine Past and Present.* 2 vols. Durham, N.C.: Duke Univ. Press.

Crompton, C. W., I. V. Hall, K. I. N. Jensen, and P. D. Hildebrand. 1988. The Biology of Canadian Weeds. *Hypericum perforatum* L. *Canadian J. of Plant Science* 68:149–62.

Cronquist, A. 1968. *The Evolution and Classification of Flowering Plants.* Boston: Houghton Mifflin Co.

Crooks, D. M., and A. F. Sievers. 1941. *Medicinal Plants.* Washington, D.C.: USDA Bureau of Plant Industry.

_____. 1942. *Condiment Plants.* Washington, D.C.: USDA Bureau of Plant Industry.

Culbreth, D. M. R. 1906. *Materia Medica and Pharmacology.* Philadelphia: Lea Brothers and Co.

Cullen, W. 1808. *A Treatise of the Materia Medica.* 2 vols. Philadelphia: Mathew Carey.

Culpepper, N. 1787. *The English Physician Enlarged.* Dublin: H. Colbert.

Cuthbertson, T. 1978. *Alan Chadwick's Enchanted Garden.* New York: E. P. Dutton.

Darrah, H. H. 1974. Investigation of the Cultivars of the Basils (*Ocimum*). *Economic Botany* 28:63–67.

_____. 1980. *The Cultivated Basils.* Independence, Mo.: Buckeye Printing Co.

DeBaggio, T. 1988. Growing Rosemary. *Fine Gardening,* July/Aug.:51–55.

_____. 1989. Hardy Lavenders. The Herb *Companion,* Apr./May:10–15.

de Gingins-Lassaraz, B. F. [1826] 1976. *Natural History of the Lavenders.* Reprint. Boston: New England Unit of the Herb Society of America.

Denny, E. F. K. 1981. The History of Lavender Oil: Disturbing Inferences for the Future of Essential Oils. *Perfumer and Flavorist* 6:23–25.

Densmore, F. [1928] 1974. *How Indians Use Wild Plants for Food, Medicine and Crafts.* Reprint. New York: Dover Publications .

Der Marderosian, A., and L. Liberti. 1988. *Natural Product Medicine: A Scientific Guide to Foods, Drugs, Cosmetics.* Philadelphia: George F. Stickley Co.

De Vincenzi, M., and M. R. Dessi. 1991. Botanical Flavouring Substances Used in Foods: Proposal of Classification. *Fitoterapia* 62 (1):39–63.

DeWolf, G. P. 1956. The Mints. *The Herb Grower* 10:46–54.

Dirr, M. A., and C. W. Heuser, Jr. 1987. *The Reference Manual of Wood Plant Propagation: From Seed to Tissue Culture.* Athens, Ga.: Varsity Press, Inc.

Dixon, W. H. 1867. *New America.* 3d ed. Philadelphia: J. B. Lippincott.

Dremmond, C. 1980. *The Basils.* Redwood City, Calif.: Redwood City Seed Co.

Duke, J. A. 1977. Vegetarian Vitachart. *Quarterly J. of Crude Drug Research* 15:45–66.

_____. 1978. Making a Mint with Herbs Is Not All That Difficult. In *USDA Yearbook*, 218–23. Washington, D. C.: U. S. Government Printing Office.

_____. 1981. *Handbook of Legumes of Worldwide Economic Importance.* New York: Plenum Press.

_____. 1982. Ecosystematic Data on Medicinal Plants. In *Cultivation and Utilization of Medicinal Plants,* ed. C. K. Atal and B. M. Kapur, 13–23. Jammu-Tawi, India: Regional Research Laboratory, Council of Scientific and Industrial Research.

_____. 1985. *CRC Handbook of Medicinal Herbs.* Boca Raton, Fla.: CRC Press.

_____. 1988. Evening Primrose—The Morning After. *Let's Live* 56 (7):56–57.

_____. 1989. *Ginseng: A Concise Handbook.* Algonac, Mich.: Reference Publications, Inc.

_____. 1990a. Mountain Dittany. *Dittany: Annual J. of the New Zealand Herb Societies* 11:49–51.

_____. 1990b. Monardas: The Red, White, and Blue. *The Herb Companion,* Aug./Sept.: 35–39.

_____. 1992. *Handbook of Edible Weeds.* Boca Raton, Fla.: CRC Press.

Duke, J. A., and S. J. Hurst. 1975. Ecological Amplitudes of Herbs, Spices, and Medicinal Plants. *Lloydia* 38:404–10.

Duke, J. A., and E. E. Terrell. 1974. Crop Diversification Matrix: Introduction. *Taxon* 23:759–99.

Duke, J. A., S. J. Hurst, and J. L. Kluve. n.d. *Botanicals as Environmental Indicators.* Beltsville, Md.: USDA.

Duke, J. A., S. J. Hurst, and E. E. Terrell. 1975. Economic Plants and Their Ecological Distribution. *Informacion al Dia Alerta. IICA-Tropicos, Agronomia* 1:1–32.

Düker, E. M., L. Kopanski, H. Jarry, and W. Wuttke. 1991. Effects of Extracts from *Cimicifuga racemosa* on Gonadotropin Release in Menopausal Women and Ovariectomized Rats. *Planta Medica* 57:420–24.

Duncan, A. 1789. *The Edinburgh New Dispensatory.* 2d ed. Edinburgh: C. Elliot and T. Kay.

Dunmire, J. R., ed. 1979. *New Western Garden Book.* Menlo Park, Calif.: Lane Publishing Co.

Duthie, H. L. 1981. The Effect of Peppermint Oil on Colonic Motility in Man. *British J. of Surgery* 68:820.

Dymock, W., C. J. H. Warden, and D. Hooper. [1890–1893] 1972. *Pharmacographia Indica.* 3 vols. in 1. Reprint. Karachi, Pakistan: The Institute of Health and Tibbi Research.

Eastman, L. M. 1976. *Sassafras Trees in Maine.* Augusta, Maine: Critical Areas Program.

Eberle, J. 1834. *A Treatise of the Materia Medica and Therapeutics.* 2 vols. Philadelphia: Grigg and Elliot.

Eichenberger, M. D., and G. R. Parker. 1976. Goldenseal (*Hydrastis canadensis* L.): Distribution, Phenology and Biomass in an Oak-Hickory Forest. *Ohio J. of Science* 76 (5):204–10.

Ellingwood, F. 1902. *Materia Medica and Therapeutics.* Chicago: Chicago Medical Press Co.

Emboden, W. 1979. *Narcotic Plants.* New York: Macmillan Co.

Emerson, G. B. 1875. *A Report on the Trees and Shrubs Growing Naturally in the Forests of Massachusetts.* 2d ed. 2 vols. Boston: Little, Brown and Co.

Engeland, R. L. 1991. *Growing Great Garlic: The Definitive Guide for Organic Gardeners and Small Farmers.* Okanogan, Wash.: Filaree Productions.

Epling, C., and C. D. Jativa. 1962. A New Species of *Salvia* from Mexico. *Botanical Museum Leaflets* 20 (3):75–76.

Erichsen-Brown, C. 1989. *Medicinal and Other Uses of North American Plants.* New York: Dover Publications.

Ernst, E. 1987. Cardiovascular Effects of Garlic (*Allium sativum*): A Review. *Pharmatherapeutica* 5 (2):83–89.

European Scientific Cooperative for Phytotherapy (ESCOP). 1992. Vol. 3 of *Proposal for European Monographs on the Medicinal Use of : 1). Calendulae Flos/Flos Cum Herba; 2). Menthae Piperitae Aetheroleum; 3). Taraxaci Folium; 4). Taraxacum Radix; 5). Uvae Ursi Folium.* Bevrijdingslaan, Netherlands: European Scientific Cooperative for Phytotherapy.

Farnsworth, N. R. 1969. Vol. 6 of *The Lynn Index: A Bibliography of Phytochemistry.* Pittsburgh: Norman R. Farnsworth.

_____. 1974. Vol. 8 of *The Lynn Index: A Bibliography of Phytochemistry*. Chicago: Norman R. Farnsworth.

Farnsworth, N. R., R. N. Blomster, M. W. Quimby, and J. W. Schermerhorn. 1971. Vol. 7 of *The Lynn Index: A Bibliography of Phytochemistry*. Chicago: Norman R. Farnsworth.

Felter, H. W., and J. U. Lloyd. [1906] 1983. *King's American Dispensatory*. 18th ed. 2 vols. Reprint. Portland, Oreg.: Eclectic Medical Publications.

Fenton, W. N. 1941. Contacts between Iroquois Herbalism and Colonial Medicine. In *Annual Report of the Smithsonian Institution*, 503–56. Washington, D.C.: U.S. Government Printing Office.

Ferguson, J. M., W. W. Weeks, and W. T. Fike. 1988. Catnip Production in North Carolina. *The Herb, Spice, and Medicinal Plant Digest* 6 (4):1–4.

Fernald, M. L. 1970. *Gray's Manual of Botany*. 8th ed., corrected. New York: D. Van Nostrand Co.

Fernald, M. L., A. C. Kinsey, and R. C. Rollins. 1958. *Edible Wild Plants of Eastern North America*. New York and Evanston: Harper and Row.

Flannery, H. B., and R. G. Mower. 1979. *Gardening with Herbs*. Ithaca: New York State College of Agricultural Life Sciences, Cornell Univ.

Flückiger, F. A., and D. Hanbury. 1879. *Pharmacographia. A History of the Principal Drugs of Vegetable Origin Met with in Great Britain and British India*. 2d. ed. London: Macmillan and Co.

Foster, G. B. 1966. *Herbs for Every Garden*. New York: E. P. Dutton.

Foster, G. B., and R. F. Louden. 1980. *Park's Success with Herbs*. Greenwood, S.C.: George W. Park Seed Co., Inc.

Foster, S. 1978. A Taste of Sarsaparilla—Medicinal Uses of Maine Plants. *Maine Audubon Quarterly*, Summer: 14–15.

_____. 1979a. Ginseng: Are You Confused? *Well-Being* 46:43–50.

_____. 1979b. Spiderwort—Nature's Geiger Counter. *Well-Being* 50:39–41.

_____. 1980. The Historical Battle over Lobelia. *Well-Being* 56:32–34.

_____. 1984. *Herbal Bounty: The Gentle Art of Herb Culture*. Layton, Utah: Gibbs M. Smith, Inc.

_____. 1985a. Echinaceas—The Purple Coneflowers. *American Horticulturist* 64 (8):14–18.

_____. 1985b. Bountiful Basil. *Business of Herbs* 3 (2): 4–7.

_____. 1985c. The Alluring Lavenders *Business of Herbs*. 3 (4):4–5, 13.

_____. 1986. *East West Botanicals: Comparisons of Medicinal Plants Disjunct between Eastern Asia and Eastern North America*. Brixey, Mo.: Ozark Beneficial Plant Project.

_____. 1987a. Valerian. *Business of Herbs* 4 (6):4–5, 14.

_____. 1987b. French Tarragon. *Business of Herbs* 5(2):4–5.

_____. 1987c. Goldenseal—A Future Crop? *Business of Herbs* 5 (6):4–5, 24–26.

_____. 1988a. Motherwort—An Ancient Link to the Future. *Business of Herbs* 6 (4):12–14.

_____. 1988b. Medicinal Ornamentals. *Fine Gardening* 3:28–30.

_____. 1988c. Lovage—Not to Be Neglected. *Business of Herbs* 6 (3):14–16.

_____. 1989a. *Growers Fact Sheet on Dandelion, Taraxacum officinalis*. Helena, Mont.: Great Northern Botanical Assn.

_____. 1989b. *Growers Fact Sheet on Dill, Anethum graveolens*. Helena, Mont.: Great Northern Botanical Assn.

_____. 1989c. *Growers Fact Sheet on Borage, Borago officinalis*. Helena, Mont.: Great Northern Botanical Assn.

_____. 1989d. *Growers Fact Sheet on Comfrey, Symphytum officinalis*. Helena, Mont.: Great Northern Botanical Assn.

_____. 1989e. *Growers Fact Sheet on Purple Coneflowers, Echinacea*. Helena, Mont.: Great Northern Botanical Assn.

_____. 1989f. Phytogeographic and Botanical Considerations of Medicinal Plants Disjunct in Eastern Asia and Eastern North America. In Vol. 4 of *Herbs, Spices, and Medicinal Plants: Recent Advances in Botany, Horticulture, and Pharmacology*, ed. L. E. Craker and J. E. Simon, 115–44. Phoenix, Ariz.: Oryx Press.

_____. 1989g. The Wiley Witch Hazel. *The Herb Companion*, Jan.: 34–36.

_____. 1989h. Goldenseal—Masking of Drug Tests from Fiction to Fallacy: An Historical Anomal. *HerbalGram* 21:7, 35

_____. 1989i. The Chaste Tree. *Business of Herbs* 7 (4):16–20.

_____. 1989j. Garden Pharmacy. *Harrowsmith* 9 (6):77–83.

_____. 1989k. Yarrow—Unexplored Potential. *Business of Herbs* 6 (6):8–11.

_____. 1990. Echinacea: Beauty and Medicine for Your Garden. *The Herb Companion,* Oct./Nov.: 33–38.

_____. 1991a. Passionflower. *The Herb Companion* Aug./Sept.: 18–23.

_____. 1991b. Echinacea—The Purple Coneflowers. Botanical Series, no. 301. Austin, Tex.: American Botanical Council.

_____. 1991c. *Milk Thistle, Silybum marianum.* Botanical Series, no. 305. Austin, Tex.: American Botanical Council.

_____. 1991d. *Peppermint, Mentha* x *piperita.* Botanical Series, no. 306. Austin, Tex.: American Botanical Council.

_____. 1991e. *Chamomile, Matricaria recutita* and *Chamaemelum nobile.* Botanical Series, no. 307. Austin, Tex.: American Botanical Council.

_____. 1991f. *American Ginseng, Panax quinquefolius.* Botanical Series, no. 308. Austin, Tex.: American Botanical Council.

_____. 1991g. *Goldenseal, Hydrastis canadensis.* Botanical Series, no. 309. Austin, Tex.: American Botanical Council.

_____. 1991h. *Feverfew, Tanacetum parthenium.* Botanical Series, no. 310. Austin, Tex.: American Botanical Council.

_____. 1991i. *Garlic, Allium sativum.* Botanical Series, no. 311. Austin, Tex.: American Botanical Council.

_____. 1991j. *Valerian, Valeriana officinalis.* Botanical Series, no. 312. Austin, Tex.: American Botanical Council.

_____. 1991k. Thyme for Your Medicine. *The Herb Companion,* Apr./May: 38

_____. 1991l. *Echinacea: Nature's Immune Enhancer.* Rochester, Vt.: Healing Arts Press.

_____. 1991m. Herbs for Health. *American Horticulturist (News Edition)* 70 (11):2–5.

_____. 1991n. The Milk Thistle. *Business of Herbs* 8 (6):14–16.

_____. 1992a. Garlic: The Past Meets the Future. *Health Foods Business,* Feb.: 33–34.

_____. 1992b. Comfrey: A Fading Romance. *The Herb Companion,* Feb./Mar.: 50–55.

_____. 1993. Chamomile. *The Herb Companion,* Dec./Jan.: 64–68.

Foster, S., and J. A. Duke. 1990. *A Field Guide to Medicinal Plants: Eastern and Central North America.* Peterson Field Guide Series, no. 40. Boston: Houghton Mifflin Co.

Foster, S., and B. Liebert. 1987. *Lobelia—History, Cultivation and Uses.* Growers Information Series, no. 1. Brixey, Mo.: Ozark Beneficial Plant Project.

Foster, S., and C. X. Yue. 1992. *Herbal Emissaries: Bringing Chinese Herbs to the West.* Rochester, Vt.: Healing Arts Press.

Foster, S., and C. H. Yueh. 1991. Disjunct Occurrence and Folk Uses of Medicinal Plants in the Ozarks and in China. *Missouri Folklore Society J.* 10 (1988):27–36.

Fulder, S. 1988. Scorn Not Garlicke. *Pharmacy Update,* Oct.: 327–29.

_____. 1989. Garlic and the Prevention of Cardio-vascular Disease. *Cardiology in Practice* 30:34–35.

Fulder, S., and J. Blackwood. 1991. *Garlic—Nature's Original Remedy.* Rochester, Vt.: Healing Arts Press.

Funke, G. L. 1943. The Influence of *Artemisia absinthium* on Neighboring Plants. *Blumea* 5 (2):281–93.

Gail, P. 1989. *On the Trail of the Yellow-Flowered Earth Nail: A Dandelion Sampler.* Cleveland Heights, Ohio: Goosefoot Acres Press.

Galambosi, B., and Z. Szebeni-Galambosi. 1992. The Effect of Nitrogen Fertilization and Leaf-Harvest of the Root and Leaf Yield of Lovage. *J. of Herbs, Spices, and Medicinal Plants* 1 (1/2):3–13.

Garrabrants, N. L., and L. E. Craker. 1987. Optimizing Field Production of Dill. *Acta Horticulturae* 208:69–72.

Geiger, C., and H. Rimpler. 1990. Ellagitannins from Toermentillae Rhizoma and Alchemillae Herba. Poster presented at Biology and Chemistry of Active Natural Substances, Bonn, 17–22 July.

Genest, K., and D. W. Hughes. 1969. Part 4 of Natural Products in Canadian Pharmaceuticals: *Hydrastis Canadensis. Canadian J. of Pharmaceutical Science* 4: 41–45.

Gerarde, J. [1633] 1975. *The Herball* or *Generall Historie of Plantes.* Reprint, rev. and enl. by Thomas Johnson. New York: Dover Publications.

Gibbs, W. M. 1909. Spices *and How to Know Them.* Dunkirk, N.Y.: W. M. Gibbs.

Gildemeister, E., and F. R. Hoffman. 1900. *The Volatile Oils.* Trans. from the German by E. Kremers. Milwaukee: Pharmaceutical Review Publishing Co.

Gill, J. D., and W. M. Healy. 1973. *Shrubs and Vines for Northeastern Wildlife.* Upper Darby, Pa.: Northeastern Forest Experiment Station, U. S. Forest Service, USDA.

Gilmore, M. R. [1919] 1977. Uses of Plants by Indians of the Missouri River Region. In *Thirty-Third Annual Report of the Bureau of American Ethnology,* 43–124. Washington, D.C.: Smithsonian Institution. Reprint. Lincoln: Univ. of Nebraska Press.

Glasby, J. S. 1991. *Dictionary of Plants Containing Secondary Metabolites.* New York: Taylor and Francis.

Gleason, H. A. 1952. *Illustrated Flora of the Northeastern United States and Adjacent Canada.* 3 vols. New York: New York Botanical Garden.

Gleason, H. A., and A. Cronquist. 1991. *Manual of Vascular Plants.* 2d. ed. New York: New York Botanical Garden.

Goethe, J. W. [1790] 1974. T*he Metamorphosis of Plants.* Reprint, with introduction by Rudolf Steiner. Wyoming, R.I.: Bio-Dynamic Farming and Gardening Assn., Inc.

Goldstein, B. 1975. Ginseng: Its History, Dispersion, and Folk Tradition. *American J. of Chinese Medicine* 3 (3): 223–34.

Good, P. P. 1845. *Vol. 1 of Good's Family Flora.* New York: J. K. Wellman.

Gossel, T. A. 1990. Capsaicin in Painful Neuralgias. *U.S. Pharmacist,* Dec.: 27–30.

Graustein, J. E. 1967. *Thomas Nuttall Naturalist— Explorations in America 1808–1841.* Cambridge, Mass.: Harvard Univ. Press.

Gremillion, K. J. 1989. The Development of a Mutualistic Relationship between Humans and Maypops (*Passiflora incarnata* L.) in the Southeastern United States. *J. of Ethnobiology* 9 (2):135–58.

Grieve, M. [1931] 1971. *A Modern Herbal.* 2 vols. Reprint. New York: Dover Publications.

Griffith, R. E. 1847. *Medical Botany.* Philadelphia: Lea and Blanchard.

Guenther, E. [1948] 1982. *The Essential Oils.* 6 vols. Reprint. Huntington, N.Y.: Robert E. Kieger Publishing Co.

Gunther, E. 1973. *Ethnobotany of Western Washington.* Seattle: Univ. of Washington Press.

Gunther, R. T. [1934] 1968. *The Greek Herbal of Dioscorides.* Reprint. New York: Hafner Publishing Co.

Hahn, G. 1992. *Hypericum perforatum* (St. John's Wort)—A Medicinal Herb Used in Antiquity and Still of Interest Today. *J. of Naturopathic Medicine* 3 (1):94–96.

Haines, J. D. 1991. Sassafras Tea and Diaphoresis. *Postgraduate Medicine* 90 (4):75–76.

Hale, E. M. 1864. *New Homeopathic Provings.* Detroit: E. A. Lodge, Homeopathic Pharmacy.

Hälvä, S. 1990. Angelica—Plant from the North. *The Herb, Spice, and Medicinal Plant Digest* 8 (1):1–4.

Hälvä, S., L. E. Craker, J. E. Simon, and D. J. Charles. 1992. Light Levels, Growth and Essential Oil in Dill. *J. of Herbs, Spices, and Medicinal Plants* 1 (1/2):47–58.

Hamel, P. B., and M. U. Chiltoskey. 1975. *Cherokee Plants, Their Uses—A 400 Year History.* Sylva, N.C.: Herald Publishing Co.

Harrington, S. 1978. *Sassafras.* Santa Cruz, Calif.: Herb Trade Assn.

Hartman, H. T., D. E. Kester, and F. T. Davies, Jr. 1990. *Plant Propagation: Principles and Practices.* 5th ed. Englewood Cliffs, N.J.: Prentice-Hall, Inc.

Hassan, I. 1967. Some Folk Uses of *Peganum harmala* in India and Pakistan. *Economic Botany* 21:284.

Hausen, B. M. 1979. Test Results and Cross-Reactions in Compositae-Sensitive Patients. Part 3 of The Sensitizing Capacity of Compositae Plants. *Dermatologica* 159:1–11.

Hausen, B. M., E. Busker, and R. Carle. 1984. Experimental Investigations with Extracts and Compounds of *Chamomilla recutita* (L.) Rauschert and *Anthemis cotula* L. Part 7 of The Sensitizing Capacity of Compositae Plants. *Planta Medica* 50:229–34.

Hazelhoff, B., B. Weert, R. Denee, and T. M. Malingre. 1979. Isolation and Analytical aspects of *Valeriana* Compounds. *Pharaceutisch Weekblad Scientific Edition* 1 (4):956–64.

Hedrick, U.P., ed. 1919. *Sturtevant's Notes on Edible Plants.* Twenty–Seventh Annual Report, vol. 2, part 2. Albany, N. Y.: State of New York, Dept. of Agriculture.

Henderson, P. 1889. *Henderson's Handbook of Plants and General Horticulture.* New York: Peter Henderson and Co.

Hendriks, H, and R. Bos. 1990. The Presence of Parthenolide in Dutch Tansy. Poster presented at Biology and Chemistry of Active Natural Substances, Bonn, 17–22 July.

Henkel, A., and G. F. Klugh. 1908. *The Cultivation and Handling of Goldenseal.* USDA circular no. 6. Washington, D.C.: USDA Bureau of Plant Industry.

Heptinsall, S., D. V. C. Awang, B. A. Dawson, D. Kindack, D. W. Knight, and J. May. 1991. Parthenolide Content and Bioactivity of Feverfew (*Tanacetum parthenium*): Estimation of Commercial and Authenticated Feverfew Products. *J. of Pharmaceutical Pharmacology* 44:391–95.

Herrick, J. W. 1977. Iroquois Medical Botany. Ph.D. diss., State Univ. of New York at Albany.

Hikino, H., and Y. Kiso. 1988. Natural Products for Liver Disease. In vol. 2 of *Economic and Medicinal Plant Research,* ed. H. Wagner, H. Hikino, and N. R. Farnsworth, 39–72. New York: Academic Press.

Hill, A. F. 1948. Chamomile. *The Herbarist,* no. 8:8–16.

Hill, J. 1812. *The Family Herbal.* Bungay, England: C. Brightly.

Hill, M., and G. Barclay. 1987. *Southern Herb Growing.* Fredericksburg, Tex.: Shearer Publishing.

Hills, L. D. 1976. *Comfrey: Fodder, Food, and Remedy.* New York: Universe Books.

Hirono, I., H. Mori, and M. Haga. 1978. Carcinogenic Activity of *Symphytum officinale. J. of the National Cancer Institute* 61 (5):865–68.

Hitchcock, C. L., and A. Cronquist. 1973. *Flora of the Pacific Northwest.* Seattle: Univ. of Washington Press.

Hobbs, C. 1988–1989. St. John's Wort. *HerbalGram* 18/19:24–33.

_____. 1989a. *The Echinacea Handbook.* Portland, Oreg.: Eclectic Medical Publications.

_____. 1989b. *Taraxacum officinale:* A Monograph and Literature Review. In vol. 1 of *Eclectic Dispensatory of Botanical Therapeutics,* ed. E. Alstat, 6.156–6.205. Portland, Oreg.: Eclectic Medical Publications.

_____. 1989c. Feverfew, Tana*cetum parthenium:* A Review. *HerbalGram* 20 (Spring): 26–35.

Hocking, G. M. 1965. *Echinacea angustifolia* as a Crude Drug. *Quarterly J. of Crude Drug Research* 5:679–82

_____. 1966. *Peganum harmala. Quarterly J. of Crude Drug Research* 6:913–15.

Hoffer, A., and H. Osmond. 1967. *The Hallucinogens.* New York: Academic Press.

Hood, S. C. 1916. *Commercial Production of Thymol from Horsemint* (*Monarda punctata*). USDA Farmers Bulletin no. 372. Washington, D.C.: U. S. Government Printing Office.

Hruby, H. 1984. Silibinin in the Treatment of Deathcap Fungus Poisoning. *Forum* 6:23–26.

Hsu, P. 1979. Why Chinese Prefer American Ginseng and How They Use It. In *Proceedings of the First National Ginseng Conference,* ed. D. L. Hensley, S. Alexander, and C. R. Roberts, 104–6. Lexington, Ky.: Governor's Council on Agriculture.

Hu, S. Y. 1976. The Genus *Panax* (Ginseng) in Chinese Medicine. *Economic Botany* 30:11–28.

_____. 1977. A Contribution to Our Knowledge of Ginseng. *American J. of Chinese Medicine* 5:1–23.

Huizing, H. J., T. W. J. Gadella, and E. Kliphuis. 1982. Chemotaxonomical Investigations of the *Symphytum officinale* Polyploid Complex and *S. asperum* (Boraginaceae): The Pyrrolizidine Alkaloids. *Plant Systematics and Evolution* 140:279–92.

Husain, A., O. P. Virmani, A. Sharma, A. Kumar, and L. N. Misra. 1988. *Major Essential Oil-Bearing Plants of India.* Lucknow, India: Central Institute of Medicinal and Aromatic Plants. '

Huxtable, R. J. 1992. The Myth of Beneficent Nature: The Risks of Herbal Preparations. *Annals of Internal Medicine* 117 (2):165–66.

Huxtable, R. J., J. Lüthy, and U. Zweifel. 1986. Toxicity of Comfrey-Pepsin Preparations. *New England J. of Medicine* 315 (17):1095.

Ichikawa, S. 1978. The Spiderwort Strategy. *Bio-Dynamics* 127:35–43.

Jacobson, M., R. E. Redfern, and G. D. Mills, Jr. 1975. Screening of Insect and Plant Extracts as Insect Juvenile Hormone Mimics. Part 2 of Naturally Occurring Insect Growth Regulators. *Lloydia* 38:455–72.

Janick, J., J. E. Simon, J. Quinn, and N. Beaubaire. 1989. Borage: A Source of Gamma Linolenic Acid. In vol. 4 of *Herbs, Spices, and Medicinal Plants: Recent Advances in Botany, Horticulture, and Pharmacology,* ed. L. E. Craker and J. E. Simon, 145–86. Phoenix, Ariz.: Oryx Press.

Janick, J., J. E. Simon, and A. Whipkey. 1987. In Vitro Propagation of Borage. *HortScience* 22 (3):493–95.

Jartoux, P. 1714. The Description of a Tartarian Plant called Ginseng. *Philosophical Transactions of the Royal Society of London* 28:237–47.

Jeavons, J. 1979. *How to Grow More Vegetables.* Berkeley, Calif.: Ten Speed Press.

Jeavons, J., M. Griffin, and R. Leler. 1983. *The Backyard Homestead, Minifarm, and Garden Log Book.* Berkeley, Calif.: Ten Speed Press.

Jerry, H., and G. Harnischfeger. 1985. Influence on the Serum Concentration of Pituitary Hormones in Ovariectomized Rats. Part 1 of Studies on the Endocrine Effects of the Contents of *Cimicifuga racemosa. Planta Medica* 51:46.

Jerry, H., G. Harnischfeger, and E. Düker. 1985. In Vitro Binding of Compounds to Estrogen Receptors. Part 2 of Studies on the Endocrine Effects of the Contents of *Cimicifuga racemosa. Planta Medica* 51:316–18.

Johnson, E. S., N. P. Kadam, D. M. Hylands, and P. J. Hylands. 1985. Efficacy of Feverfew as a Prophylactic Treatment of Migraine. *British Medical J.* 291:569–73.

Johnson, L. 1884. *A Manual of the Medical Botany of North America.* New York: William Wood and Co.

Johnston, A. 1970. Blackfoot Indian Utilization of the Flora of the Northwest Great Plains. *Economic Botany* 24:301–24.

Karlowsky, J. A. 1991. Bloodroot: *Sanguinaria canadensis* L. *Canadian Pharmaceutical J.* 124 (5):260–67.

Keville, K. 1992. *The Illustrated Herb Encyclopedia.* New York: Mallard Press.

Khemani, S. P. 1954. Coriander as a Crop. *The Herb Grower* 8:96–110.

Kindscher, K. 1987. *Edible Wild Plants of the Prairie.* Lawrence: Univ. Press of Kansas.

———. 1989. Ethnobotany of Purple Coneflower (*Echinacea angustifolia,* Asteraceae). *Economic Botany* 43 (4):498–507.

———. 1992. *Medicinal Wild Plants of the Prairie.* Lawrence: Univ. Press of Kansas.

King, J. 1887. *Echinacea angustifolia. Eclectic Medical J.* 42:209–10.

King, J., and R. S. Newton. 1852. *The Eclectic Dispensatory of the United States of America.* Cincinnati: H. W. Derby.

Kleijnen, J., P. Knipschild, and G. Terriet. 1989. Garlic, Onions and Cardiovascular Risk Factors: A Review of the Evidence from Human Experiments with Emphasis on Commercially Available Preparations. *British J. of Clinical Pharamacology* 28:535–44.

Koepf, H. H., B. D. Pettersson, and W. Schaumann. 1976. *Bio-Dynamic Agriculture.* Spring Valley, N. Y.: Anthroposophic Press.

Kong, Y. C., C. P. Lau, K. H. Wat, K. H. Ng, P. P. H. But, K. F. Cheng, and P. G. Waterman. 1989. Antifertility Principle of *Ruta graveolens. Planta Medica* 55:176–78.

Krochmal, A. n.d. *The Taming of Lobelia.* Upper Darby, Pa.: Northeastern Forest Experiment Station, U. S. Forest Service, USDA.

Krochmal, A., L. Wilken, and M. Chien. 1972. Plant and Lobeline Harvest of *Lobelia inflata* L. *Economic Botany* 26 (3):216–20.

Lamaison, J. L., C. Petitjean-Freytet, F. Duband, and A. P. Carnat. 1991. Rosmarinic Acid Content and Antioxidant Activity in French Lamiaceae. *Fitoterapia* 62 (2):166–71.

Landing, J. E. 1969. *American Essence: A History of the Peppermint and Spearmint Industry in the United States.* Kalamazoo: Kalamazoo Public Museum.

Larrey, D., T. Vial, A. Pauwles, A. Castot, M. Biour, M. David, and H. Michel. 1992. Hepatitis after Germander (*Teucrium chamaedrys*) Administrations: Another Instance of Herbal Medicine Hepatotoxicity. *Annals of Internal Medicine* 117 (2):129–32.

Lau, B. 1988. *Garlic for Health.* Wilmot, Wis.: Lotus Light Publications.

Lawrence, G. H. M. 1951. *Taxonomy of Vascular Plants.* New York: Macmillan Co.

Lee, C. A. 1859. Remarks on *Rhus glabra, Geranium maculatum,* and *Hamamelis virginica. J. of Materia Medica and Pharmaceutic Formulary,* July: 193–202.

Leicester, R. J., and R. H. Hunt. 1982. Peppermint Oil to Reduce Colonic Spasm during Endoscopy. *The Lancet,* Oct. 20, 989.

Leung, A. Y. 1980. *Encyclopedia of Common Natural Ingredients Used in Food, Drugs, and Cosmetics.* New York: John Wiley and Sons. [Second edition by A. Y. Leung and S. Foster in progress, 1994.]

Lewis, W. H. 1986. Ginseng: A Medical Enigma. In *Plants in Indigenous Medicine and Diet: Biobehavioral Approaches,* ed. N. L. Etkin, 290–305. Bedford Hills, N.Y.: Redgrave Publishing Co.

Lewis, W. H., and V. E. Zenger. 1982. Population Dynamics of the American Ginseng, *Panax quinquefolium* (Araliaceae). *American J. of Botany* 69 (9):1483–1490.

L. H. Bailey Hortorium, Staff of the. 1976. Hortus Third. New York: Macmillan Co.

Liu, J. H-C., and E. J. Staba. 1980. The Ginsenosides of Various Ginseng Plants and Selected Products. *J. of Natural Products* 43 (3):340–46.

Lloyd, J. U. 1900. *Stringtown on the Pike.* New York: Dodd Mead.

_____. 1921a. *Origin and History of all the Pharmacopeial Vegetable Drugs, Chemicals, and Preparations, with Bibliography.* Cincinnati: Caxton Press.

_____. 1921b. *A Treatise on Echinacea.* Drug Treatise no. 30. Cincinnati: Lloyd Brothers Pharmacists, Inc.

Lloyd, J. U., and C. G. Lloyd. 1884–1885. *Ranunculaceae.* Vol. 1 of *Drugs and Medicines of North America.* Cincinnati: J. U. and C. G. Lloyd.

_____. [1886–1887] 1931. Vol. 2 of *Drugs and Medicines of North America.* Reprint. Bulletin of the Lloyd Library, no. 31, Reproduction Series no. 9. Cincinnati: Lloyd Library.

Lloyd, J. U., and J. T. Lloyd. 1935. History of Hamamelis (Witch Hazel), Extract and Distillate. *J. of the American Pharmaceutical Assn.* 24 (3):220–24.

Locock, R. A. 1987. *Acorus Calamus. Canadian Pharmaceutical J.* 120 (5):341–44.

Loewenfeld, C. 1965. *Herb Gardening.* Newton, Mass.: Charles T. Bradford Co.

Lowman, M. S. 1946. *Savory Herbs: Culture and Use.* USDA Farmers Bulletin no. 1977. Washington, D.C.: U. S. Government Printing Office.

Lutomski, J., and B. Malek. 1974. New Method of Chromatographic Separation and Flurometric-Planimetric Determination of Alkaloids and Flavonoids in Harmane Raw Materials. Part 1 of Pharmacological Investigations on Raw Materials of the Genus *Passiflora* (in German). *Planta Medica* 26:311–17.

Mabberly, D. J. 1987. *The Plant Book: A Portable Dictionary of the Higher Plants.* New York: Cambridge Univ. Press.

Mahran, G. H., H. A. Kadry, Z. G. Isaacs, and C. K. Thabet. 1991. Investigation of Diuretic Drugs in Plants. *Phytotherapy Research* 5:169–72.

Mann, C., and E. J. Staba. 1986. The Chemistry, Pharmacology, and Commercial Formulations of Chamomile. In vol. 1 of *Herbs, Spices, and Medicinal Plants: Recent Advances in Botany, Horticulture, and Pharmacology,* ed. L. E. Craker and J. E. Simon, 235–80. Phoenix, Ariz.: Oryx Press.

Marhan, G. H., H. A. Kadry, C. K. Thabet, M. M. El-Olemy, M. M. Al-Azizi, P. L. Schiff, Jr., L. K. Wong, and N. Liv. 1992. GC/MS Analysis of Volatile Oil of Fruits of *Anethum graveolens. Int. J. of Pharmacognosy* 30 (2):139–44.

Martis, G., A. Rao, and K. S. Karanth. 1991. Neuropharmacological Activity of *Acorus calamus. Fitoterapia* 62 (4):331–37.

Maruzzella, J. C., and J. Balter. 1959. The Action of Essential Oils on Phytopathogenic Fungi. *Plant Disease Reporter* 43 (11):1143–47.

Maruzzella, J.C., D. A. Scrandis, J. B. Scrandis, and G. Grabon. 1960. The Action of Odoriferous Organic Chemicals and Essential Oils on Wood-Destroying Fungi. *Plant Disease Reporter* 44 (10):789–92.

Máthé, A. 1988. An Ecological Approach to Medicinal Plant Introduction. In vol. 3 of *Herbs, Spices, and Medicinal Plants: Recent Advances in Botany, Horticulture, and Pharmacology,* ed. L. E. Craker and J. E. Simon, 175—205. Phoenix, Ariz.: Oryx Press.

Máthé, A., I. Máthé, and J. Svab. 1989. Chamomile Production in Hungary. In *Herbs '89 Proceedings,* ed. J. E. Simon, A. Kestner, and M. A. Buehrle, 85–88. Mundelien Ill.: International Herb Growers and Marketers Assn.

Mattocks, A. R. 1980. Toxic Pyrrolizidine Alkaloids in Comfrey. *The Lancet,* Nov. 22, 1136–37.

_____. 1986. Toxicity of Pyrrolizidine Alkaloids. *Nature* 217:724.

McCourt, R. 1991. Some Like It Hot. *Discover,* Aug., 48–52.

McGregor, R. L. 1968. The Taxonomy of the Genus E*chinacea. Univ. of Kansas Science Bulletin* 68:113–42.

Meehan, T. 1880. *The Native Flowers and Ferns of the United States.* Series 2. 2 vols. Boston: L. Prang and Co.

Millspaugh, C. F. 1887.*American Medicinal Plants.* 2 vols. Philadelphia: Boericke and Tafel.

Ministry of Agriculture, Fisheries, and Food. 1960. *Culinary and Medicinal Herbs.* London: Her Majesty's Stationery Office.

Mitchell, B., and J. Wayembergh. 1981. *Japanese Gardens: Design and Meaning.* New York: McGraw-Hill.

Mittman, P. 1990. Randomized, Double-Blind Study of Freeze-Dried *Urtica dioica* in the Treatment of Allergic Rhinitis. *Planta Medica* 56:44–46.

Moerman, D. E. 1986. *Medicinal Plants of Native America.* 2 vols. Technical Reports, no. 19, Research Reports in Ethnobotany, contribution 2. Ann Arbor: Univ. of Michigan Museum of Anthropology.

Moore, M. 1979. *Medicinal Plants of the Mountain West.* Santa Fe: Museum of New Mexico Press.

_____. 1989. *Medicinal Plants of the Desert and Canyon West.* Santa Fe: Museum of New Mexico Press.

_____. 1990. *Los Remedios de la Gente.* Santa Fe: Red Crane Books.

Morales, M., D. Charles, and J. Simon. 1991. Cultivation of Finnochio Fennel. *The Herb, Spice, and Medicinal Plant Digest* 9 (1):1–4.

Morelli, J. 1980. Angelica. Unpublished manuscript.

Morton, J. F. 1977. *Major Medicinal Plants —Botany, Culture, and Uses.* Springfield, Ill.: Charles C. Thomas.

_____. 1991. Food, Medicinal and Industrial Uses of Perilla, and its Ornamental and Toxic Aspects. In *Progress on Terrestrial and Marine Natural Products of Medicinal and Biological Interest,* ed. J. Pezzuto, A. D. Kinghorn, H. S. Fong, and G. A. Cordell, 34–38. Austin, Tex.: American Botanical Council.

Mostesa-Kara, N., A. Pauwels, E. Pines, M. Biour, and V. G. Levy. 1992. Fatal Hepatitis after Herbal Tea. *The Lancet* 340:764.

Muenscher, W. C., and M. A. Rice. [1955] 1978. *Garden Spice and Wild Pot Herbs.* Reprint. Ithaca: Comstock Publishing Associates, Cornell Univ. Press.

Munz, P. A. 1968. A *California Flora and Supplement.* Berkeley: Univ. of California Press.

Murphy, J., S. Heptinstall and J. R. A. Mitchell. 1988. Randomized Double-Blind Placebo-Controlled Trail of Feverfew in Migraine Prevention. *The Lancet,* July 23, 189–192.

Murray, M. J., D. E. Lincoln, and P. M. Marble. 1972. Oil Composition of *Mentha aquatica* X *M. spicata* F₁ Hybrids in Relation to the Origin of *M. x piperita. Canadian J. of Genetic Cytology* 14:13–29.

Murray, M. T. 1987. Eneric [s:c] Coated Peppermint Oil for the Irritable Bowel Syndrome. *Phyto-Pharmica,* Fall: 6.

National Institute of Medical Herbalists. 1979. Comfrey as Medicine. Leicestershire, England. Press release.

Ng, T. B., and H. W. Yeung. 1986. Scientific Basis of the Therapeutic Effects of Ginseng. In Folk Medicine: The *Art and the Science,* ed. R. P. Steiner, 139–51. Washington, D.C.: American Chemical Society.

Nicholson, G. 1886–1905. *Dictionary of Gardening.* 8 vols. London: L. Upcott Gill.

Nishizawa, A., G. Honda, Y. Kobayashi, and M. Tabata. 1992. Genetic Control of Peltate Glandular Trichome Formation in *Perilla frutescens. Planta Medica* 58:188–91.

Nonnecke, I. L. 1988. Development of *Oenothera biennis.* Evening Primrose as a Commercial Crop. In *Proceedings of the Third National Herb Growing and Marketing Conference,* ed. J. E. Simon and L. Z. Clavio, 73–77. West Lafayette, Ind.: Purdue Research Foundation

Nykänen, I, Y. Holm, and R. Hiltunen. 1989. Composition of the Essential Oil of *Agastache foeniculum. Planta Medica* 55:314–15.

Olin, B. R., ed. 1990. Bloodroot. *Lawrence Review of Natural Products,* Nov.

_____. 1992a. *Podophyllum. Lawrence Review of Natural Products,* Jan.

_____. 1992b. Rosemary. *Lawrence Review of Natural Products,* Feb.

Öztürk, Y., and S. Aydm. 1992. Hepatoprotective Activity of *Hypericum perforatum* L. Alcoholic Extracts in Rodents. *Phytotherapy Research* 6:44–46.

Pfeiffer, E. 1938. *Bio-Dynamic Farming and Gardening.* New York: Anthroposophic Press.

Philbrick, H., and R. B. Gregg. 1966. *Companion Plants.* Old Greenwich, Conn.: Devin-Adair.

Phillips, H. Flannery. 1989. What Thyme Is It: A Guide to the Thyme Taxa Cultivated in the United States. In *Proceedings of the Fourth National Herb Growing and Marketing Conference,* ed. J. E. Simon, 44–50. Silver Spring, Penn.: International Herb Growers and Marketers Assn.

_____. 1991. The Best of Thymes. *The Herb Companion,* Apr./May: 22–29.

Phillips, H. R. 1985. *Growing and Propagating Wild-flowers.* Chapel Hill: Univ. of North Carolina Press.

Pickering, C. 1879. *Chronological History of Plants.* 2 vols. Boston: Little, Brown and Co.

Pontius, J. C. 1987. The Process Budget: A Tool for Analyzing Your Production System and Potential Returns. *The Herb, Spice, and Medicinal Plant Digest* 5 (3):1–2, 12–13.

Porcher, F. P. 1849. Report on the Indigenous Medical Plants of South Carolina. *Transactions of the American Medical Assn.* 2:677–862.

Prakash, V. 1990. *Leafy Spices.* Boca Raton, Fla.: CRC Press.

Precheur, R., and N. Garrabrants. 1984. Weed Control in Dill. *The Herb, Spice, and Medicinal Plant Digest* 2 (1):5–6.

Preitschopf, B. M., and C.-G. Arnold. 1989. *Achillea millefolium:* Occurrence, Ploidal Level and Proazulene Variation. *Planta Medica* 55:596.

Primack, R. B. 1985. Sex Ration and Sexual Constancy in Spicebush (*Lindera benzoin*). *Rhodora* 87 (851):305–8.

Protech Products, Inc. 1979. Spiderwort: The People's Radiation and Pollution Monitor. Santa Barbara, Calif. Press release.

Pursh, F. 1814. *Flora Americae Septentrionalis.* London: White, Cochrane, and Co.

Quinn, J. 1987. Propagation of French Tarragon. In *Proceedings of the Second National Herb Growing and Marketing Conference,* ed. J. E. Simon and L. Grant , 88–90. West Lafayette, Ind.: Purdue Research Foundation,

Quinn, J., J. E. Simon, and J. Janick. 1989a. Recovery of Gamma-Linolenic Acid from Somatic Embryos of Borage. *J. of the American Society of Horticultural Science* 114 (3):511–15.

_____. 1989b. Histology of Zygotic and Somatic Embryogenesis in Borage. *J. of the American Society of Horticultural Science* 114 (3):516–20.

Quinn, J., A. Whipkey, J. E. Simon, and J. Janick. 1987. Embryo Development of *Borago officinalis* L. *Acta Horticulturae* 208:243–49.

Rabin, J. 1987. Parsley Production for Fresh Market. In *Proceedings of the Second National Herb Growing and Marketing Conference,* ed. J. E. Simon and L. Grant, 43–47. West Lafayette, Ind.: Purdue Research Foundation.

Rabin, J., and G. A. Berkowitz. 1986. Successful Parsley Production Programs in New Jersey. *The Herb, Spice, and Medicinal Plant Digest.* 4(1)1–6.

Rafinesque, C. S. 1828, 1830. *Medical Flora* or *Manual of the Medical Botany of the United States of North America.* 2 vols. Philadelphia: Samuel C. Atkinson.

Randhawa, G. S., A. Singh, and R. K. Mahey. 1987. Optimizing Agronomic Requirements and Seed Yield and Quality of Dill Oil. *Acta Horticulturae* 208:61–68.

Rees, W. D. W., B. K. Evans, and J. Rhodes. 1979. Treating Irritable Bowel Syndrome with Peppermint Oil. *British Medical J.* 6:835–36.

Riddle, J. M. 1985. *Dioscorides on Pharmacy and Medicine.* Austin: Univ. of Texas Press.

Riddle, J. M., and J. W. Estes. 1992. Oral Contraceptives in Ancient and Medieval Times. *American Scientist* 80:226–33.

Ridker, P. M., S. Ohkuma, W. V. McDermott, C. Trey, and R. J. Huxtable. 1985. Hepatic Venocclusive Disease Associated with the Consumption of Pyrrolizidine-Containing Dietary Supplements. *Gastroenterology* 88:1050–54.

Riedlinger, R. J., ed. 1990. *The Sacred Mushroom Seeker —Essays for R. Gordon Wasson.* Portland, Oreg.: Dioscorides Press.

Robinson, W. 1883. *The English Flower Garden.* London: John Murray.

Rollins, E. D., and A. O. Tucker. 1992. The Other *Origanums. The Herb Companion,* Feb./Mar.: 23–27.

Roulet, M., R. Laurini, L. Rivier, and A. Calame. 1988. Hepatic Veno-Occlusive Disease in Newborn Infant of a Woman Drinking Herbal Tea. *J. of Pediatrics* 112 (3):433–36.

Russell, G. A. 1921. *Drying Crude Drugs.* USDA Farmers Bulletin no. 1231. Washington, D. C.: U. S. Government Printing Office.

Ruttle, M. L. 1938. Some Common Mints and Their Hybrids. *The Herbarist* , no. 4:17–29.

Salamon, I. 1992a. Chamomile: A Medicinal Plant. *The Herb, Spice, and Medicinal Plant Digest* 10 (1):1–4.

_____. 1992b. Chamomile Production in Czecho-Slovakia. *Focus on Herbs* 10:1–8.

_____. 1992c. Production of Chamomile, *Chamomilla recutita* (L.) Rauschert, in Slovakia. *J. of Herbs, Spices, and Medicinal Plants* 1 (1/2):37–46.

Scarborough, J. 1989. Contraception in Antiquity: The Case of Pennyroyal. *Wisconsin Academy Review* 35 (2):19–25.

Schauenberg, P., and F. Paris. 1977. *Guide to Medical Plants.* New Canaan, Conn.: Keats Publishing, Inc.

Schenck, P. A. 1857. *The Gardener's Text Book.* New York: A. O. Moore.

Schermerhorn, J. W., and M. W. Quimby. 1957–1962. *The Lynn Index: A Bibliography of Phytochemistry.* 5 vols. Boston: Massachusetts College of Pharmacy.

Schöpf, J. D. [1787] 1903. *Materia Medica Americana Potissimum Regni Vegetabilis.* Erlangen, Germany. Reprint. Bulletin of the Lloyd Library, no. 6, Reproduction Series no. 3. Cincinnati: Lloyd Library.

Schopmeyer, C. S. 1974. *Seeds of Woody Plants in the United States.* Washington, D.C.: U. S. Forest Service, USDA.

Schultes, R. E., and N. R. Farnsworth. 1980. Ethnobotanical, Botanical, and Phytochemical Aspects of Natural Hallucinogens. *Botanical Museum Leaflets* 28:123–214.

Schultes, R. E., and A. Hofmann. 1973. *The Botany and Chemistry of Hallucinogens.* Springfield, Ill.: Charles C. Thomas.

Segelman, A. B., et al. 1976. Sassafras and Herb Teas— Potential Health Hazards. J. of the American Medical Ass*n.* 236:477–78.

Shibata, S., O. Tanaka, J. Shoji, and H. Saito. 1985. Chemistry and Pharmacology of *Panax.* In vol. 1 of *Economic and Medicinal Plant Research*, ed. H. Wagner, H. Hikino, and N. R. Farnsworth, 218–84. Orlando, Fla.: Academic Press.

Shideman, F. E. 1950. A Review of the Pharmacology and Therapeutics of Hydrast*is* and its Alkaloids, Hydrastine, Berberine and Canadine. *Commission on the National Formulary Bulletin* 18 (102):3–19.

Sievers, A. F. [1919] 1949. *Goldenseal under Cultivation.* Rev. Walter Van Fleet. USDA Farmers Bulletin no. 613. Washington, D.C.: U. S. Government Printing Office.

_____. 1929. *Peppermint and Spearmint as Farm Crops.* USDA Farmers Bulletin no. 1555. Washington, D. C.: U. S. Government Printing Office.

_____. 1948. *Production of Drug and Condiment Plants.* USDA Farmers Bulletin no. 1999. Washington, D.C.: U. S. Government Printing Office.

Sigmond, C. J., and E. F. MacNally. 1969. The Action of a Carminative on the Lower Oesophageal Sphincter. *Gastroenterology* 56:13–18.

Simon, J. E. 1987. *Sweet Basil: A Production Guide.* Publication no. HO–189. West Lafayette, Ind.: Purdue Univ. Cooperative Extension Service.

_____. 1990. Essential Oils and Culinary Herbs. In *Advances in New Crops*, ed. J. Janick and J. E. Simon, 472–83. Portland, Oreg.: Timber Press.

Simon, J. E., and M. L. Overley. 1986. A Comparative Evaluation of Parsley Cultivars. *The Herb, Spice, and Medicinal Plant Digest* 4 (1):2–4, 7.

Simon, J. E., and D. Reiss-Bubenheim. 1992. Water Stress-Induced Alterations in Essential Oil Content and Composition of Sweet Basil. *J. of Essential Oil Research* 4:71–75.

Simon, J. E., A. F. Chadwick, and L. E. Craker. 1984. *Herbs : An Indexed Bibliography 1971–1980.* Hamden, Conn.: Archon Books.

Simon, J. E., J. Quinn, and R. G. Murray. 1990. Basil: A Source of Essential Oils. In *Advances in New Crops*, ed. J. Janick and J. E. Simon, 484–89. Portland, Oreg.: Timber Press.

Simon, J. E., J. Rabin, and L. Clavio. 1990. *Parsley: A Production Guide.* Publication no. HO–202. West Lafayette, Ind.: Purdue Univ. Cooperative Extension Service.

Simons, C. M. 1972. *John Uri Lloyd: His Life and Works.* Cincinnati, Ohio. Privately printed by the author.

Smith, E. B. 1988. *An Atlas and Annotated List of the Vascular Plants of Arkansas.* 2d ed. Fayetteville, Ark.: E. B. Smith.

Smith, H. H. 1923. Ethnobotany of the Menominee Indians. *Bulletin of the Public Museum of the City of Milwaukee* 4 (1):1–174.

_____. 1928. Ethnobotany of the Meskwaki Indians. *Bulletin of the Public Museum of the City of Milwaukee* 4 (2):175–326.

_____. 1932. Ethnobotany of the Ojibwe Indians. *Bulletin of the Public Museum of the City of Milwaukee* 4 (3):327–525.

_____. 1933. Ethnobotany of the Forest Potawatomi Indians. *Bulletin of the Public Museum of the City of Milwaukee* 7 (1):1–230.

Smith, L. W., and C. C. J. Culvenor. 1981. The Alkaloids of *Symphytum* x *uplandicum* (Russian Comfrey). *J. of Natural Products* 44:129–52.

Smith, P. [1813] 1901. *The Indian Doctor's Dispensatory, Being Father Smith's Advice Respecting Diseases and Their Cure.* Reprint. Bulletin of the Lloyd Library, no. 2, Reproduction Series no. 2. Cincinnati: Lloyd Library.

Soldati, F., and O. Tanaka. 1984. *Panax ginseng:* Relation between Age of Plant and Content of Ginsenosides. *Planta Medica* 50:351–52.

Somerville, K. W., C. R. Richmond, and G. D. Bell. 1984. Delayed Release of Peppermint Oil Capsules (Colpermin) for the Spastic Colon Syndrome: A Pharmacokinetic Study. *British J. of Clinical Pharmacology* 18:638–40.

Speck, F. G. 1917. Medicine Practices of the Northeastern Algonquins. *Proceedings of the Int. Congress of Americanists* 19:303-321.

Staba, E. J. 1985. The Case of Ginseng—Part 2. *The Lancet*, Dec. 7.

Staba, E. J., and S. E. Chen. 1979. An Overview of Ginseng Chemistry, Pharmacology, and Anti-Tumor Effects. In *Proceedings of the First National Ginseng Conference*, ed. D. L. Hensley, S. Alexander, and C. R. Roberts, 91–100. Lexington, Ky.: Governor's Council on Agriculture.

Stannard, J. 1982. The Multiple Uses of Dill in Medieval Medicine. *Gelerter de Arzenie, Ouch Apoteker* 70:411–24.

Steiner, R. 1958. *Agriculture.* London: Bio-Dynamic Agricultural Assn.

Steinhoff, B. 1992. Worldwide Aspects of Phytotherapy. *European Phytotelegram* 4:5–8.

Steinmetz, E. F. 1957. *Codex Vegetabilis.* Amsterdam: E. F. Steinmetz.

Steuart, G. 1987. Growing Alkaloid-Free Comfrey. *The Herb, Spice, and Medicinal Plant Digest* 5 (4):9.

Steyermark, J. A. 1977. *Flora of Missouri.* Ames: Iowa State Univ. Press.

Stille, A., and J. M. Maisch. 1880. *The National Dispensatory.* Philadelphia: Henry C. Lea's Son and Co.

Stockberger, W. W. 1928. G*inseng Culture.* USDA Farmers Bulletin no. 1184. Washington, D.C.: U. S. Government Printing Office.

_____. 1935. *Drug Plants under Cultivation.* USDA Farmers Bulletin no. 663. Washington, D.C.: U. S. Government Printing Office.

Stuart, M., ed. 1979. *The Encyclopedia of Herbs and Herbalism.* New York: Crescent Books.

Suzuki, O., Y. Katsumata, M. Oya, S. Bladt, and H. Wagner. 1984. Inhibition of Monoamine Oxidase by Hypericin. *Planta Medica* 50:272–74.

Tantaquidgeon, G. 1942. *A Study of Delaware Indian Medicine Practice and Folk Beliefs.* Harrisburg: Pennsylvania Historical Commission.

Tatum, B. J. 1976. *Billy Joe Tatum's Wildfoods Cookbook and Field Guide.* New York: Workman Publishing.

Taylor, B. D., D. K. Luscombe, and H. L. Duthie. 1983. Inhibitory Effect of Peppermint Oil on Gastrointestinal Smooth Muscle. *Gut* 24:992.

Tétényi, P. 1970. *Infraspecific Chemical Taxa of Medicinal Plants.* Budapest: Akadémiai Kiadó.

Thatcher, J. 1813. *The American New Dispensatory.* 2d rev. ed. Boston: Thomas B. Wait and Co., and C. Williams.

Thomas, J. 1961. Liquidambar. *Arnoldia* 21:59–64.

Thompson, G. A. 1987. Botanical Characteristics of Ginseng. In vol. 2 of *Herbs, Spices, and Medicinal Plants: Recent Advances in Botany, Horticulture, and Pharmacology.* ed. L. E. Craker and J. E. Simon, 111–36. Phoenix, Ariz.: Oryx Press.

Thomson, S. 1835. *New Guide to Health.* Boston: J. Q. Adams.

Thorton, R. J. 1814. *A Family Herbal.* London: B.&B. Crosby and Co.

Tucker, A. O. 1974. Botanical Aspects of Oregano Reconsidered. *The Herbarist* , no. 40:11–13.

_____. 1981. The Correct Name of Lavandin and its Cultivars (Labiatae). *Baileya* 21 (3):131–33.

_____. 1985. Lavender, Spike, and Lavandin. *The Herbarist,* no. 51:44–50.

_____. 1986. Botanical Nomenclature of Culinary Herbs and Potherbs. In vol. 1 of *Herbs, Spices, and Medicinal Plants: Recent Advances in Botany, Horticulture, and Pharmacology,* ed. L. E. Craker and J. E. Simon, 33-80. Phoenix, Ariz.: Oryx Press.

_____. 1989. A Summer's Passion. *Fine Gardening* 7 (May/June): 41–45.

_____. 1992. Will the Real Oregano Please Stand Up? *The Herb Companion*, Feb./Mar.: 20–22.

Tucker, A. O., and T. DeBaggio. 1984. 'Irene Doyle' Lavender. *HortScience* 19 (4):595.

Tucker, A. O., and K. J. W. Hensen. 1985. The Cultivars of Lavender and Lavandin (Labiatae). *Baileya* 22 (4):168–77.

Tucker, A. O., and B. M. Lawrence. 1987. Botanical Nomenclature of Commercial Sources of Essential Oils, Concretes, and Absolutes. In vol. 2 of *Herbs, Spices, and Medicinal Plants: Recent Advances in Botany, Horticulture, and Pharmacology,* ed. L. E. Craker and J. E. Simon, 183–220. Phoenix, Ariz.: Oryx Press.

Tucker, A. O., and E. D. Rollins. 1989. The Species, Hybrids, and Cultivars of *Origanum* (Lamiaceae) Cultivated in the United States. *Baileya* 23 (1):14–27.

Tucker, A. O., and S. S. Tucker. 1988. Catnip and the Catnip Response. *Economic Botany* 42 (2):214–31.

Tucker, A. O., J. A. Duke, and S. Foster. 1989. Botanical Nomenclature of Medicinal Plants. In vol. 4 of *Herbs, Spices, and Medicinal Plants: Recent Advances in Botany, Horticulture, and Pharmacology,* ed. L. E. Craker and J. E. Simon, 169–242. Phoenix, Ariz.: Oryx Press.

Tucker, A. O., R. M. Harley, and D. E. Fairbrothers. 1980. The Linnaean Types of *Mentha* (Lamiaceae). *Taxon* 29 (2/3):233–55.

Tucker, A. O., M. J. Maciarello, and J. T. Howell. 1980. Botanical Aspects of Commercial Sage. *Economic Botany* 34 (1):16–19.

Tyler, V. E. 1986. Plant Drugs in the Twenty-First Century. *Economic Botany* 40 (3):279–88.

——. 1987. *The New Honest Herbal.* 2d ed. Philadelphia: George. F. Stickley.

——. 1992. Phytomedicines in Western Europe: Their Potential Impact on Herbal Medicine in the United States. Lecture delivered at annual meeting of the American Chemical Society, San Francisco, April.

Tyler, V.E., L.R. Brady, and J.E. Robbers. 1988. *Pharmacognosy.* 9th ed. Philadelphia: Lea and Febiger.

Underbrink, A. G., L. A. Schairer, and A. H. Sparrow. 1973. *Tradescantia* Stamen Hairs: A Radiobiological Test System Applicable to Chemical Mutagens. In *Chemical Mutagens: Principles and Methods for Their Detection,* ed. A. Hollaender. New York: Plenum Press.

United States Consular Reports. 1885. *The Licorice Plant.* Washington, D. C.: U. S. Government Printing Office.

The United States Homeopathic Pharmacopeia. 1878. Chicago: Duncan Brothers.

Uphof, J. C. 1968. *Dictionary of Economic Plants.* Lehre, Germany: J. Cramer.

Valdés, L. J. III, G. M. Hatfield, M. Koreeda, and A. G. Paul. 1987. Studies of *Salvia divinorum* (Lamiaceae), an Hallucinogenic Mint from the Sierra Mazateca in Oaxaca, Central Mexico. *Economic Botany* 41 (2):283–91.

Vanderplank, J. 1991. *Passion Flowers.* Cambridge, Mass.: MIT Press.

Van Fleet, W. 1911–1912. The Cultivation of *American Ginseng.* USDA Farmers Bulletin 551. Washington, D.C.: U. S. Government Printing Office.

Van Hevelingen, A. 1990. French Tarragon. *Fine Gardening,* Jan./Feb.: 25–27.

Vennat, B., H. Pourrat, M. P. Pouget, D. Gross, and A. Pourrat. 1988. Tannins from *Hamamelis virginiana*: Identification of Proanthocyanidins and Hamamelitannins Quantification in Leaf, Bark, and Stem Extracts. *Planta Medica* 54:454–57.

Verlet, N. 1988. History, Production and Marketing of Lavender in France. In *Proceedings of the Third National Herb Growing and Marketing Conference,* ed. J. E. Simon and L. Z. Clavio, 146–54. West Lafayette, Ind.: Purdue Research Foundation.

Vestal, P. A., and R. E. Schultes. 1939. *The Economic Botany of the Kiowa Indians.* Cambridge: Harvard Univ. Botanical Museum.

Vogel, V. 1970. *American Indian Medicine.* Norman: Univ. of Oklahoma Press.

Vokou, D., S. Kokkini, and J-M. Bessière. 1988. *Origanum onites* (Lamiaceae) in Greece: Distribution, Volatile Oil Yield, and Composition. *Economic Botany* 42 (3):407–12.

Wacker, A., and W. Hilbig. 1978. Virus Inhibition by *Echinacea purpurea. Planta Medica* 33:89–102.

Wagner, H., and A. Proksch. 1985. Immunostimulatory Drugs of Fungi and Higher Plants. In vol. 1 of *Economic and Medicinal Plant Research,* ed. H. Wagner, H. Hikino, and N. R. Farnsworth, 113–55. Orlando, Fla.: Academic Press.

Wall, D. A., and G. H. Friesen. 1986. The Effect of Herbicides and Weeds on the Yield and Composition of Dill Oil. Crop Protection 5:137–42.

Wasson, R. G. 1962. A New Mexican Psychotropic Drug from the Mint Family. *Botanical Museum Leaflets* 20 (3):77–84.

Webster, H. N. 1939. *Herbs: How to Grow Them and How to Use Them.* Boston: Charles T. Bradford Co.

Weiss, R. F. 1988. *Herbal Medicine.* Trans. from the German by A.R. Meuss. Beaconsfield, England: Beaconsfield Publishers Ltd.

Weston, C. F. M., B. T. Cooper, et al. 1987. Veno-Occlusive Disease of the Liver Secondary to Ingestion of Comfrey. *British Medical J.* 295:183.

Whallon, D. C. 1974–1975. Oregano—Botanical and Culinary. *The Herb Grower* 4:94–96.

Whipkey, A., J. E. Simon, and J. Janick. 1988. In Vivo and In Vitro Lipid Accumulations in *Borago officinalis* L. *J. of American Oil Chemists Society* 65 (6):979–84.

Williams, L. O. 1957. Ginseng. *Economic Botany* 11 (4):344–48.

_____. 1960. *Drug and Condiment Plants.* Agricultural Handbook no. 172. Washington, D.C.: USDA, Agricultural Research Service.

Williams, L. O., and J. A. Duke. 1973. *Growing Ginseng.* USDA Farmers Bulletin no. 2201. Washington, D.C.: U. S. Government Printing Office.

Wood, G. B., and F. Bache. 1849. *The United States Dispensatory.* 8th rev. ed. Philadelphia: P. Blakiston's Son and Co.

Wren, R. C. 1988. P*otter's New Cyclopedia of Botanical Drugs and Preparations.* Rev. E. M. Williamson and F. J. Evans. 8th ed. Essex, England: C. W. Daniel Co.

Yanovsky, E. 1936. *Food Plants of the North American Indians.* USDA Miscellaneous Publication no. 237. Washington, D.C.: U. S. Government Printing Office.

Yatskievych, G., and J. Turner. 1990. *Catalogue of the Flora of Missouri.* St. Louis: Missouri Botanical Garden.

Zalkow, L. H., M. M. Gordon, and N. Lanir. 1979. Antifeedants from Rayless Goldenrod and Oil of Pennyroyal: Toxic Effects of the Fall Armyworm. *J. of Economic Entomology* 72:812–15.

Zheng, G. Q., P. M. Kenney, and K. K. T. Lam. 1992. Anethofuran, Carvone, and Limonene: Potential Cancer Chemopreventative Agents from Dill Weed Oil and Caraway Oil. *Planta Medica* 58:338–41.

APPENDICES

PLANT AND SEED SOURCE

Please note: Many of these businesses charge for their catalog, and the price may change from year to year. Send a self-addressed stamped envelope to inquire on price and availability of catalog.

Abundant Life Seed Foundation
P.O. Box 772
Port Townsend, WA 98368

Edible Landscaping
Rt. 2, Box 77
Afton, VA 22920

Elixir Farm Botanicals
General Delivery
Brixey, MO 65618

Forest Farm
990 Tetherow Rd.
Williams, OR 97544

J. L. Hudson, Seedsman
P.O. Box 1058
Redwood City, CA 94064

Keift Bloemzaden B.V.
P.O. Box 1000
1695 ZG Blokker
Holland

Logee's Greenhouses
55 North St.
Danielson, CT 06239

Missouri Wildflowers Nursery
Rt. 2, Box 373
Jefferson City, MO 65109

Native Gardens
Rt. 1, Box 494
Greenback, TN 37742

Natural Gardens
4804 Shell Ln.
Knoxville, TN 37918

Nature's Catherdral
R.R. 1, Box 120
Blairstown, IA 52209

Prairie Nursery
P.O. Box 365
Westfield, WI 53964

Prairie Moon Nursery
Rt. 3, Box 163
Winona, MN 55987

Prairie Ridge Nursery
RR 2, 9738 Oberland Rd.
Mt. Horeb, WI 53572-2832

Otto Richter & Sons
Goodwood
Ontario
Canada LOC 1A0

Sunlight Gardens
Rt. 1, Box 600-A
Hillvale Rd.
Andersonville, TN 37705

Taylor's Herb Gardens, Inc.
1535 Lone Oak Rd.
Visa, CA 92083

Thompson & Morgan
P.O. Box 1308
Jackson, NJ 08527

We-Du Nurseries
Rt. 5, Box 724
Marion, NC 28752

Woodlanders
1128 Colleton Ave.
Aiken, SC 29801

INFORMATION RESOURCES

ORGANIZATIONS

The American Botanical Council
P.O. Box 201660
Austin, TX 78720-1660

Publishes *HerbalGram*. Also publishes booklets on specific herbs, reprints of important papers from the scientific literature, note cards and other publications.

American Herb Association
P.O. Box 1673
Nevada City, CA 95959

Publishes quarterly newsletter and resources lists. AHA publishes a descriptive listing of herbs schools and correspondence courses.

American Herbalist Guild
P.O. Box 1683
Soquel, CA 95073

GUILD FOR PROFESSIONAL MEDICAL HERBALISTS

The Herb Research Foundation
1007 Pearl St., Suite 200
Boulder, CO 80302

Memberships begin at $35.00 per year, co-publisher of *HerbalGram*.

International Herb Growers and Marketers Association (IHGMA)
1202 Allanson Rd.
Mundelein, IL 60060

Trade association. Memberships start at $80.00 per year, sponsors major herb conference. Publishes newsletter, conference proceedings. *Back issues available.*

PERIODICALS

American Herb Association Newsletter
Kathi Keville, Editor.
P.O. Box 1673
Nevada City, CA 95959

Newsletter serving professional herbalists. $20.00 per year.

Botanical & Herb Reviews
Steven Foster, Editor
P.O. Box 106
Eureka Springs, AR 72632

Quarterly book reviews, $10.00 per year. Other publications, photography and consulting services.

Business of Herbs
David & Paula Oliver, Editors
RR 2, Box 246
Shevlin, MN 56676-9535

Bimonthly periodical, with resource and development information for herb businesses. $20.00 per year.

Garden Literature: An Index to Periodical Articles & Book Reviews
Sally Williams, Editor
Garden Literature Press
398 Columbus Ave., Suite 181
Boston, MA 02116-6008.

Quarterly index of garden literature. Excellent resource. Annual subscription rate $50 for individuals and $75 for institutions.

Health Foods Business
Gina Geslewitz, Editor
Howmark Publishing, Co.
567 Morris Ave.
Elizabeth, NJ 07208

Monthly trade magazine. Subscription: $33 per year.

The Herb Companion
Linda Ligon, Editor
201 E. Fourth St.
Loveland, CO 80537

Bimonthly, popular four-color herb magazine for consumers, emphasis on gardening, decorative and culinary use. $21.00 per year.

The Herb Quarterly
Linda Sparrowe, Editor
P.O. Box 689
San Anselmo, CA 94960

America's oldest quarterly consumer herb periodical. $24.00 per year.

The Herb Spice and Medicinal Plant Digest
Lyle E. Craker, Editor.
Department of Plant and Soil Sciences
University of Massachusetts
Amherst, MA 01003.

Quarterly newsletter. Subscriptions: $10 per year.

HerbalGram
Mark Blumenthal, Editor
P.O. Box 201660
Austin, TX 78720-1660

Quarterly, peer-reviewed four-color journal. Four issues: $25.00.

Journal of Herbs, Spices, and Medicinal Plants
Lyle E. Craker, Editor
Haworth Press
10 Alice St.
Binghamton, NY 13904-1580

Quarterly scientific journal, for professionals in herbs and herb production. $24 per year for individuals.

Medical Herbalism
Paul Bergner, Editor
P.O. Box 33080
Portland, OR 99723

Quarterly newsletter for medical herbalists.

Natural Foods Merchandiser
Frank Lampe, Editor
New Hope Publications
1301 Spruce St.
Boulder, CO 80302

Monthly trade magazine. Subscription: $40 per year.

DIRECTORIES OF SOURCES OF HERBS, PLANTS, SEEDS & OTHER RESOURCES

Anderson Horticultural Library's Source List of Plants and Seeds
Compiled by Richard T. Isaacson

Computerized listing of thousands of plants in American horticulture. 1989. 214 pp. $29.95. Available from:

The Andersen Horticultural Library
Minnesota Landscape Arboretum
3675 Arboretum Dr., P.O. Box 39,
Chanhassen, MN 55317

Cornucopia: A Source Book of Edible Plants
by Stephen Facciola

An incredible resource on seeds and planting stock of useful plants. 1990. 677 pp. $37.75 postpaid. Available from:

Kampong Publications
1870 Sunrise Dr.
Vista, CA 92084.

The Herb Companion Wishbook and Resource Guide
Compiled by Bobbi A. McRae.

Listing and addresses of more than one thousand herb suppliers and resources . 1992. 301 pp. $16.95. Available from:

Interweave Press
201 E. Fourth St.
Loveland, CO 80537

Northwind Farm's Herb Resource Directory: 1992-1993 Edition.
By Paula Oliver.

Names and addresses of over eleven hundred sources are included. 1992. 97 pp. Paper. $12.95 plus $2.50 postage and handling. Available from:

Northwind Farm Publications
RR 2, Box 246
Shevlin, MN 56676-9535

This represents only a sampling of major organizations, seed and plant sources, periodicals and other resources available to those interested in herbs. The directories listed above will lead you to thousands of additional sources.

GLOSSARY

Abortifacient: Abortion-producing agent.

Acuminate: Leaf tip tapered to an acute tip (generally a tip with concave sides).

Adaptogenic: Non-toxic drug having a positive general effect on the body irrespective of disease condition, especially under stress. Example: ginseng.

Alkaloid: Large varied group of complex nitrogen-containing compounds, usually alkaline, and which usually react with acids to form soluble salts, many with physiological action in humans. Includes nicotine, cocaine, caffeine, etc.

Alterative: Generally obsolete drug term referring to drugs that produce a favorable change in the function of the body or metabolism.

Amenorrhea: Absence of, or abnormal ending of, the menses.

Analgesic: Pain-relieving substance.

Anaphrodisiac: Agent that diminishes sexual drive.

Annual: Plant that completes its life cycle in one year or season.

Anodyne: Pain-relieving substance.

Anorectal: Pertaining to both the anus and rectum.

Anthelmintic: Agent that expels intestinal parasites.

Anther: Pollen-bearing portion of the stamen.

Anti-infective: Infection-inhibiting agent.

Anti-retroviral: Agent that inhibits retroviruses (such as HIV).

Antibilious: Agent useful against biliousness, or minor health disturbances related to mild liver dysfunction.

Anticarcinogenic: Agent with a positive influence against cancers.

Anticonvulsant: Agent used to allay muscle spasms.

Antidepressive: Agent useful against depression.

Antidiarrheal: Agent useful against diarrhea.

Antifeedant: Agent that deters insect feeding.

Antifertility: Agent aiding in the prevention of fertility.

Antifungal: Agent that inhibits fungal infestations.

Antigingivitis: Agent used against gum inflammation.

Antihistaminic: Agent tending to neutralize the action of or inhibit the production of histamine in the body; used for symptomatic relief of allergies.

Antiinflammatory: Agent that inhibits inflammation.

Antimicrobial: Agent used against microorganisms.

Antimigraine: Agent used to allay the symptoms of migraine.

Antinauseant: Agent that allays nausea.

Antioxidant: A preservative which prevents oxidation.

Antiperiodic: Agent which prevents regularly occurring symptoms, such as those of malaria.

Antiphlogistic: Agent preventing or reducing inflammation.

Antiplaque: Agent used to inhibit the formation of plaque.

Antipyretic: Fever-reducing or -preventing agent.

Antirheumatic: Agent used for the symptomatic treatment of rheumatism.

Antispasmodic: Spasm-relieving agent.

Antithermic: Agent having the potential to reduce heat from fever or inflammation.

Antitussive: Cough-preventing or inhibiting agent.

Antiviral: Agent used against viral infections.

Anxiolytic: Anxiety-relieving agent.

Aphrodisiac: Substance which increases sexual appetite or sensitivity.

Astringent: Agent that connects tissue.

Autosomal: Pertaining to chromosomes (other than those of a sex cell) normally occurring in pairs.

Axil: Point at which a leaf stalk or flower stalk meets the stem.

Bechic: Cough-soothing agent.

Biennial: Plant completing its life cycle in two years.

Biomass: Net amount of plant material harvested, fresh or dried, from a given point, before or after processing.

Bract: Leaf-like structure at the base of flower stalks.

Bracteole: Secondary bract or bractlet.

Bronchospasmolytic: Agent having a spasmodic effect on the bronchi.

Bulblet: Above-ground small bulb, perhaps produced instead of flowers.

Calmative: Agent having a mild sedative effect.

Calyx: Sepals; located below the corolla and enveloping the flower bud.

Carcinogenicity: Of or pertaining to cancer-causing substances.

Carcinogenisis: Production or origin of cancer.

Cardiotonic: Substance that increases heart tone.

Carminative: Agent that relieves flatulence.

Cataplasm: Wet poultice, usually applied warm or hot to the skin.

Cathartic: Agent clearing the bowels; a laxative.

Chemopreventative: Agent that prevents development of cancer.

Chemotaxa: Pertaining to plant taxa of related or differing chemical profiles.

Chemotype: Pertaining to plant taxa with specific chemical markers.

Cholagogic: Agent stimulating bile flow from the gallbladder.

Ciliate: Fringed hairs along a margin.

Concoction: Preparation; a mixture of ingredients.

Cordate: Heart-shaped, as at the base of a leaf.

Corolla: A flower's collective petals .

Corymb: Flowers arranged in a comb-like cluster.

Coumarins: Group of pleasantly fragrant neutral compounds obtained from plants, often developing sweet fragrance upon drying. Example: Sweet woodruff

Cruciferous: Pertaining to members of the mustard family (Cruciferae are also known as the Brassicaceae).

Cultigen: Plant or plant group known only under cultivation, and unknown in the wild. Example: Garlic.

Cultivar: Plant variety produced under cultivation which retains its characteristics when asexually or sexually propagated.

Decoction: Preparation made by boiling plant parts (usually root or barks) in water for fifteen to twenty minutes.

Decumbent: As in a plant stem with a tendency toward drooping, or lying down, but the apex of the plant is ascending.

Demulcent: Soothing agent for irritated membranes, especially mucous membranes.

Deobstruent: Agent removing obstructions.

Depurative: General purifying or cleansing agent; blood purifier.

Detoxicant: Agent with the potential to eliminate or reduce reactions after ingestion of a toxin.

Diaphoretic: Perspiration-producing agent .

Diuretic: Agent producing or promoting urination.

Dysmenorrhea: Difficult or painful menstruation.

Embrocation: Application of a liniment.

Emetic: Agent which produces vomiting.

Emmenagogue: Agent that produces or regulates menstruation.

Emollient: Agent that soothes and softens irritated membranes.

Endemic: Pertaining to native plant with distribution restricted to a limited area or region.

Entire: In leaves, edges that are not serrated.

Estrogenic: Agent having the action of female hormones.

Ethnomycology: Study of traditional uses of mushrooms by humans.

Expectorant: Agent that helps expel pulmonary secretions.

Febrifuge: Agent that reduces or eliminates fever.

Fibrinolytic: Agent that causes the destruction of fibrin in clotted blood (causing it to become fluid).

Filiform: Long, slender thread-like leaf.

Flavonoid: Carotenoid water soluble plant pigments occurring free or as glycosides.

Fungicidal: Agent that kills fungi.

Fungistatic: Fungi-inhibiting agent.

Galactogogue: Lactation-promoting agent .

Germplasm: Genetic material from which off-spring generates.

Glabrous: Without hairs.

Glaucous: Covered with a fine white, often waxy, film which rubs off.

Herbaceous: Non-woody.

Hemostatic: Stops bleeding.

Hepatotoxicity: Having a toxic effect on the liver.

Hypermenorrhea: Profuse or prolonged menses.

Hypertensive: Having high arterial blood pressure or hypertension.

Hypnotic: Sleep-producing agent.

Hypotensive: Characterized by low blood pressure or a loss of blood pressure.

Immunostimulant: Agent stimulating the immune system.

Inflorescence: All the flowers growing on a single plant.

Infraspecific: Below the rank of species.

Infusion: Boiling water poured over herbs in a tightly closed vessel.

Insecticidal: Insect-killing agent.

Internode: Axis or line between two nodes.

Interpecific: Between or among species.

Lactogogue: Lactation-promoting agent

Lanceolate: Lance-shaped, in reference to leaves.

Larvicidal: Larvae-killing agent.

Leucorrhea: White or yellowish viscid vaginal discharge.

Ligulate: Strap-shaped flower or leaf.

Mastodynia: Breast pain.

Menstruum: Fluid (solvent) containing another substance in solution.

Mericarp: One half of a dry fruit that splits away as if separate, such as a single "seed" of caraway.

Mutagen: Substance or force causing mutation.

Naturalized: Alien or introduced plant that has established itself without cultivation.

Nematicidal: Nematode-killing agent.

Nervine: Agent that soothes and quiets the nerves.

Obovate: Referring to leaf shape—oval, but broader toward apex.

Ovate: Oval, but broader toward base.

Panicle: Branching flower group, the branches usually racemes.

Palae: Chaffy bracts, such as the spiny protrusions on an *Echinacea* seed head.

Palmate: Having three or more leaflet divisions originating from the same point.

Panicle: An inflorescence consisting of several racemes.

Pappus: Modified flower part expressed as the scales, bristles or hairs attached to the fruits, especially in members of the aster family. Example: the "parachute" of a dandelion seed.

Pedicel: Flower stalk.

Perennial: Plant that lives more than two years.

Petiole: Leaf stalk.

Pharyngitis: Inflammation of the mucous membrane and pharynx.

Pheromone: Substances secreted by one individual that attract another individual resulting in a specific behavioral reaction.

Photodermatitis: Skin eruptions resulting from ingestion of a substance that subsequently reacts from exposure to sun light.

Photosensitization: Sensitivity to sunlight following ingestion of a plant.

Phototoxin: Substances capable of causing photosensitization resulting in photodermatitis.

Phytomedicine: Usually well defined, whole plant preparation with a predictable level of active constituents.

Phytotherapy: Treatment involving phytomedicines.

Polymenorrhea: Unusually short menstrual cycles.

Polyploidism: Cases in which an individual organism has one or more sets of chromosomes, exceeding the normal of two sets in diploid organisms.

Pruritus: Itching.

Psychopharmaceuticals: Pharmaceutical drugs that affect the psyche, or mood.

Psychotomimetic: Effect of hallucinogen-producing phantasms.

Psychotropic: Drugs that effect the psyche; hallucinogens.

Pubescens: Hairy or pertaining to hairs.

Raceme: Elongated simple inflorescence with pedicelled flowers.

Reflexed: Abruptly bent downwards or backwards.

Resolvent: Agent that eliminates or reduces inflammations.

Revolute: Rolled backwards toward the underside, as in leaf margins.

Rhizome: Creeping underground stem.

Rubefacient: Externally applied agent which reddens the skin.

Saponin: Glycoside principle common in plants, which when shaken with water, has a foaming action.

Scape: Flower stem arising from the ground among radical leaves (leaves emerging from the root).

Sepal: Leaf of a calyx.

Sesquiterpene: Hydrocarbon component of many volatile oils containing 15 carbon atoms and 24 hydrogen atoms.

Sessile: Without a leaf stalk.

Shrublet: Small shrub.

Soporific: Sleep-producing agent.

Spadix: Inflorescence with a thickened spike.

Spasmolytic: Checking spasms or cramps.

Spicule: Small needle or spine.

Spike: Elongated inflorescence with stalkless flowers.

Stamen: Flower's male reproduction parts, consisting of anther and filament.

Stimulant: Agent which increases activity of a specific organ or general organism.

Stipule: Leaf-like appendage arising from the base of a leaf or petiole.

Stolon: Underground stem from which new plants arise.

Stomachic: Agent which stimulates the stomach's action.

Strobile: Conelike structures loosely arranged along a central axis, such as the fruiting bodies of hops.

Subshrub: Woody-stemmed plant, which is generally not persistent.

Subspecific: Taxonomic rank below species (between species and variety).

Taxa: Plural of taxon.

Taxon: General term used to refer to a taxonomic grouping.

Tincture: Diluted alcohol solution extracting a plant's medicinal virtues.

Tetraploid: Polyploid with a value of $4n$.

Tomentose: Having dense, often matted, woolly hairs.

Tonic: Agent increasing strength and tone.

Trichome: Hair or bristle.

Triploid: Polyploid with value of $3n$.

Umbel: Flat-topped inflorescence from which a number of nearly equal flower stalks radiate from the top of a single axis.

Urethritis: Inflammation of the urethra.

Vasoconstrictive: Causing narrowing of the blood vessels.

Vasodilation: Dilation of the blood vessels.

Vermifuge: Worm expellant.

Verticillasters: Whorl-like opposite pairs of cymes, appearing to surround stem, like the flowerheads of many mint family members.

Vitiligo: White patches on the skin, or eruptions of various etiology.

Vittae: Oil tubes, especially those of the fruits of parsley family members.

Vulnerary: Agent used to treat wounds.

Whorled: Three or more leaves or flowers encircling a central axis.

INDEX